Alcohol and Nationhood in Nineteenth-Century Mexico

D1453618

THE MEXICAN EXPERIENCE

William H. Beezley, series editor

DEBORAH TONER

ALCOHOL and NATIONHOOD in NINETEENTH-CENTURY MEXICO

University of Nebraska Press | Lincoln and London

Acknowledgments for the use of copyrighted
material appear on page viii, which
constitutes an extension of the copyright page.

Library of Congress Cataloging-in-Publication Data

Toner, Deborah, author.
Alcohol and nationhood in nineteenth-century
Mexico / Deborah Toner.
pages   cm—(The Mexican experience)
Includes bibliographical references and index.
ISBN 978-0-8032-6974-3 (cloth: alk. paper)
ISBN 978-0-8032-7432-7 (pbk.: alk. paper)
ISBN 978-0-8032-7437-2 (epub)
ISBN 978-0-8032-7438-9 (mobi)
ISBN 978-0-8032-7439-6 (pdf)
1. Mexican literature—Political aspects—History—
19th century. 2. Drinking customs—Political
aspects—Mexico—19th century. 3. Alcohol—
Political aspects—Mexico—19th century. I. Title. II.
Series: Mexican experience.
PQ7111.T66 2015
860.9'972—dc23
2015001126

Set in Scala OT by M. Scheer.

CONTENTS

ILLUSTRATIONS

ACKNOWLEDGMENTS

In the course of writing this book, I have been able to indulge a love of tequila, melodramatic novels, and travel through one of the most fascinating countries in the world. I have also incurred many debts of gratitude to both institutions and individuals. The generous financial support of several research councils, libraries, and universities made this research possible: the Economic and Social Research Council, the History Department and Institute of Advanced Study at the University of Warwick, the Royal Historical Society, the Institute of Latin American Studies (formerly Institute for the Study of the Americas) at the University of London, and the College of Arts, Humanities, and Law at the University of Leicester all contributed enormously to the research that went into this book.

The expertise and time of numerous staff members at the various libraries and archives in which I have conducted this research were also invaluable, including the Bodleian Library in Oxford, the British Library, and the Wellcome Library in London, the Instituto Mora, Biblioteca Nacional, Archivo Histórico del Distrito Federal, and the Archivo General de la Nación in Mexico City. I gratefully acknowledge the assistance of Linda Arnold, who generously offered me her time and help in gaining access to several collections of documents in Mexico City that I never would have found on my own. I would also like to thank the Getty Research Institute, Los Angeles; the Instituto Nacional de Antropología e Historia, Mexico City; the Museo Andrés Blaisten, Mexico City; the Universidad Autónoma de Nuevo León, and paperofrecord.com for their assistance in selecting images for the book. The expertise, enthusiasm, and professionalism of many people, especially Kristen Elias Rowley, have also made it a pleasure to worth with the University of Nebraska Press.

A very big thank you goes to Rebecca Earle, who was nothing short of inspirational as a doctoral supervisor. She has given enormous support and encouragement to the development of this book since I first had a half-baked idea about it as an undergraduate student. Many other colleagues and scholars have also commented critically and thoughtfully on various parts of the manuscript and ideas within it: in particular, Guy Thomson, Will Fowler, John King, Francisco Eissa, Andrea Cadelo, Helen Cowie, Mark Hailwood, Angela McShane, Erica Segre, Beat Kümin, and James Kneale. The detailed comments of the reviewers were also enormously helpful in refining and clarifying various aspects of this book. Earlier versions of parts of chapters 1 and 2 were published respectively in *Social History of Alcohol and Drugs* and the *Bulletin of Hispanic Studies*. Many thanks to the editors of both journals for giving their permission to develop these publications further in this book.

Special thanks are owed to the Eissa Barroso family, who welcomed me into their home in Mexico City and made many a Mexico-related dream come true (especially those involving food), and to their son Francisco, who has been an endless source of useful information and a wonderful friend. Catherine Armstrong, Mark Hailwood, Katherine Foxhall, Lydia Plath, Laura Sangha, Matthew Hill, Karla Kerr, Mairead McKendry, and Sinead Latta have all provided friendship, support, and academic acumen at exactly the right times. My new colleagues at the University of Leicester, especially George Lewis and

Clare Anderson, have also helped me to acclimate to a new job and new city rapidly during the final stages of completing this book. The encouragement, support, and generosity of my parents, Patrick and Kathleen Toner, over many years have been so invaluable that thanks seem hardly enough.

Finally, I would like to dedicate this book to Paul Whitehouse, who first came into my life when I had little more than an unfeasible idea for a doctoral thesis, and who became my husband as I was making the final changes to the book manuscript. He never fails to remind me of the joys of studying literature and history, his kindness and support are truly cherished, and he always, always makes me laugh.

INTRODUCTION

Alcohol, Literature, and Nation-Building

Rather than borrowing foreign phrases such as "nectar of the liquor goddess" use the term pulque; and, in your stories . . . do [not shy away] from . . . placing jugs of pulque next to champagne bottles. . . . And instead of intoning the "Marseillaise" or "God Save the Queen," have your characters in your stories singing our own patriotic songs. . . . It is shameful that our government has not yet been able to forge a nation.

—GUILLERMO PRIETO

It is what stupefies the masses, mires the destitute in rags, robs all intelligence, terrorizes the family, murders whole generations, and awakens pain and suffering; and it is the dementia that goes out from the mouth of this century to cast the songs of our marvelous progress into disarray. [It is] the threat that extinguishes our dreams of prosperity, gnaws away at and eventually devours our great hopes for peace, and undermines the future of our industry and our sciences. . . . It is alcoholism, sirs, the only work of man that has dared to create the very antithesis of God, for if God said "Let there be light," alcohol has said "Let there be chaos."

—TRINIDAD SÁNCHEZ SANTOS

The contrasting statements of Guillermo Prieto and Trinidad Sánchez Santos suggest that Mexican intellectuals could proffer very different answers to the question posed by the protagonist of an 1893 Mexican novel, who asked, "What's wrong with a little drinking?"[1] Prieto, a prominent costumbrista poet, prose writer, journalist, educator, and politician writing in 1845, suggests that the drinking customs of the Mexican people were suitable material for inclusion in the work of contemporary writers, that identifying the specifically Mexican aspects of such customs would be a crucial element in the creation of a patriotic, national literature, and that Mexico could not yet call itself a nation, partly because such a national literature did not then exist. Sánchez Santos, meanwhile, a prominent Catholic journalist and vocal opponent of the government of Porfirio Díaz at the end of the nineteenth century, pointed to an array of social problems caused by alcohol consumption, which together undermined the "marvelous progress" that Mexico had thus far made as a nation and placed in serious jeopardy the future prosperity and development of the Mexican nation. Despite Prieto's belief that the depiction of Mexican drinking customs, such as the consumption of pulque (a traditional, fermented alcoholic beverage dating back to preconquest times), could add local color and cultural specificity to works of national literature, Sánchez Santos clearly believed that there was rather a lot "wrong" with drinking, as alcoholism threatened to unleash chaos on society and destroy the Mexican nation.

Together, the comments of Prieto and Sánchez Santos allude to the set of issues with which this book is concerned. How did nineteenth-century fiction contribute to nation-building processes? What opportunities and problems did the drinking customs of the Mexican population create for fiction writers trying to celebrate Mexican culture and nationhood? How did alcohol feature in novels that sought to promote a patriotic spirit, a model of liberal citizenship, or a more scientific understanding of society? What was "wrong" or, indeed, "right" with drinking?

Examining the historical importance of drinking, as both an important feature of Mexican social life and a persistent source of concern for Mexican intellectuals and politicians, offers a range of insights into how the nation was discursively constructed and deconstructed in the nineteenth century. The apparent predominance of excessive alcohol consumption among the indigenous population had concerned government and church authorities throughout Mexico's colonial history and, with increasing urbanization and social unrest in the decades before independence, the drinking habits of the lower classes as a whole became increasingly subject to scrutiny. In the aftermath of the Wars of Independence (1810–21), hampered by political factionalism, foreign invasions, and civil wars, Mexican intellectuals and public officials sought to create a cohesive sense of national identity and to educate the general population on how to behave as productive, patriotic, and civilized citizens. Drinking habits were a specific target of such educative endeavors but drinking also acted as a metaphor for different problems and as a pivot around which other social ills revolved, making alcohol a revealing theme to explore the ways in which nineteenth-century intellectuals interpreted their country and their fellow countrymen.

Overall, the book has two central aims. First, it is a literary history that aims to expand the ways in which scholars understand nineteenth-century Mexican literature, and that of nineteenth-century Latin America more generally, in terms of the relationship between literature and the construction of national identity in the postindependence period. Secondly, the book is a cultural history of alcohol's roles, both positive and negative, in nation-building discourses in the nineteenth century. By examining how alcohol as a general category, different alcoholic beverages, different drinking places, and the social, moral, and physical effects of alcohol consumption were discussed and represented in newspapers, judicial records, medical texts, and novels, I aim to demonstrate the connections between ideas about drinking and numerous issues that were central to the nation-building project, including class politics, crime, insanity, citizenship, patriotism, cultural authenticity, gender, sexuality, race, and ethnicity.

The book does not, however, intend to be a comprehensive social history of drinking in nineteenth-century Mexico. The predominant focus is on the ideas about drinking, drinkers, drunkenness, and alcoholism that shaped debates about the nation as they were articulated by the political and lettered classes. The views analyzed here are predominantly those of the intellectual, political, and economic elite, who often exaggerated the negative aspects of popular drinking culture, failed to appreciate the complexities of popular culture, and overestimated their own importance as spokespeople for the nation-building project. Moreover, while regional locations feature quite regularly in the novels I discuss, the perspectives these depictions reveal are decidedly urban, with Mexico City clearly positioned as the modern, central hub of the nation (although not always in a positive sense), and rural, provincial areas depicted variously as bastions of unsophisticated backwardness, idealized embodiments of cultural authenticity, or unruly peripheries obstructing national harmony.

Nevertheless, each chapter grounds these elite perspectives about alcohol within a wider social context, utilizing a range of sources that provide insights into how ordinary Mexicans might have understood, accepted, challenged, or completely ignored intellectual, government, and medical ideas about drinking and nationhood. While the book primarily examines how members of the elite interpreted and represented the drinking practices of ordinary Mexicans, I also aim to highlight productive ways of investigating the importance of alcohol to everyday life, the contestation of ideas and practices surrounding alcohol at different levels of society, and the articulation of alternative understandings of alcohol and national identity.

Literature and Nationhood

Mexican novels contributed to nation-building processes and discourses in a much more diverse and complex manner than has previously been suggested by scholars such as Benedict Anderson and Doris Sommer. Anderson has argued that the predominant contribution of novels to nation-building is in the articulation of national commonalities, the commemoration of shared historical experiences, and the mobilization of languages centered on love, duty, and family.[2] Sommer, meanwhile, has drawn on Anderson's model to argue that the fundamental means through which Latin American authors "imagined" their emergent nations in the nineteenth century was through a narrative device of allegorical romance, in which fictional lovers divided by class, ethnicity, civil conflict, and other obstacles represented the tensions within their national community and, through the success or failure of their relationship, the path towards national unity or collapse.[3] This book, by situating fictional explorations of Mexican drinking practices in the context of wider sociocultural, legal, political, and medical debates about alcohol consumption, reveals the more ambiguous and ambivalent ways in which novels helped to imagine Mexican nationhood: destabilizing imagined social boundaries, figuratively linking internal and external "enemies" of the nation, and demonstrating both desire for and fear of modernization.

In his seminal work *Imagined Communities* (1983), Benedict Anderson argued that novels and newspapers "provided the technical means for 're-presenting' the kind of imagined community that is the nation." The novel and the newspaper were important to the development of nationalisms around the world because, as forms, they mirrored the structure of the nation as a community of individuals linked together by imaginary bonds and thus enabled their readers to imagine such a community and to imagine themselves as part of it. The different characters moving through a novel, like citizens of a nation, may never meet or even hear of one another, but they are linked because they are embedded in an imagined society and in the mind of the omniscient reader. Newspapers, meanwhile, consist of the arbitrary inclusion and juxtaposition of varied events, held together only because they occurred at the same time and are categorized according to their occurrence in definitely bounded spaces, whether local, provincial, national, or foreign.[4]

Timothy Brennan agrees with Anderson that the novel in particular, "as a composite but clearly bordered work of art," has been crucial in the creation of national identities.[5] The novel identifies the simultaneously individual and general character of national life and also imitates the structure of the nation as a mixture or conglomerate of languages, voices, and styles within definable borders. Although Anderson has been roundly criticized for his application of this theory to the Spanish American case, as he confused creole patriotism with nationalism proper and overestimated its importance in causing the independence movement, his insight into the potential of fictional discourse to participate in the creation of nations is a useful starting point for further investigation into the specificities of Spanish American nationalisms and nation-building discourses.[6] Indeed, despite their shortcomings, Anderson's ideas have been put to excellent use in scholarly analyses of literature's role in nation-building in nineteenth and twentieth-century Spanish America.

Doris Sommer's *Foundational Fictions* (1991) has probably been the most influential study in this regard, as she highlighted the central importance in imagining the nation of allegorical romance within the canonical historical novels of nineteenth-century Spanish America. By treating historical settings, nineteenth-century writers sought to "establish the legitimacy of the emerging nation[s]" within the larger historical trajectory of their pasts, while their love stories commonly acted as allegories for the ways in which conflicts, divisions, and tensions within the contemporary nation ought to be resolved in order to guarantee a happy future. Typically, the obstacles that the fictional lovers face represent the problems that the nation itself has yet to overcome, such as racial difference, social prejudice, slavery, or political polemicism; and the means through which the lovers surmount these obstacles represent a potential course of action to facilitate national progress.[7]

Many scholars continue to employ Sommer's broad framework of interpretation, expanding their analysis beyond the canonical works on which she focused. Nina Gerassi-Navarro, for instance, has examined the figure of the pirate in nineteenth-century Spanish American literature to highlight the profound difficulties many intellectuals encountered in their literary explorations of nationhood in the face of so many sociopolitical and cultural differences within their own borders. Expanding Sommer's analytical perspective beyond those romance novels subsequently institutionalized as "foundational fictions," Gerassi-Navarro chooses lesser-known works that include a liminal pirate figure, not subject to spatial boundaries and "free to imagine his own place," as a means of investigating the various ways in which Spanish American elites conceptualized themselves and their national spaces through fiction.[8]

Amy Wright's 2006 thesis on the serial historical novel in Mexico and Spain, meanwhile, argues that the serial novel, printed in installments in newspapers before being published in book form, was a particularly privileged medium for the dissemination of models of behavior, citizenship, and individualism in the nineteenth century, as it tended to reach a much larger audience than more expensive books and captivated that audience with melodramatic love stories. Wright perceptively analyzes four Mexican novels by Justo Sierra, Juan Díaz Covarrubias, and Vicente Riva Palacio to present an overall argument that supports Sommer's original thesis in *Foundational Fictions*. In these four novels, Wright observes as the central theme "allegorical romances that involved the struggle of a virtuous pair against evil forces representative of the obstacles to the modernization and progress in the country under question. The background to most of these romances are historical or current events of great import to the country's identity, a fact that further imbued the story with ideological messages to the readers, as the romances and the history were often interconnected, thus cementing their foundational nature."[9] Wright and Gerassi-Navarro both confirm, therefore, that allegorical romance was a very important trope, not only in the canonized works of fiction that Sommer analyzed, but in other nineteenth-century novels that have been less institutionalized within the national literatures of Spanish America and have received less attention from scholars of literature and history.

In contrast, this study gives very little attention to the trope of allegorical romance in order to highlight a range of other paradigms through which we can interpret the rich body of fiction written in nineteenth-century Latin America. By examining a wide range of novels, across a long time period and across genre boundaries, within a single national context, that of Mexico, I highlight the varied ways in which nineteenth-century authors constructed ideals of nationhood and ways of belonging to, and participating in, the nation. This broader interrogation of a range of literature also exposes more of the ambiguities and paradoxes contained within various writers' imagined visions of the nation, to show that, at times, nineteenth-century Mexican novels were far from "foundational."

It is clear that most Mexican writers sought to portray positive and patriotic images of the Mexican nation, to explore solutions to divisive issues and social problems, and to mold their readers into productive citizens capable of contributing to the nation's progress. Many nineteenth-century novelists were prominent public figures, working as politicians, government officials, journalists, or military officers in the various civil and international wars that Mexico fought in the nineteenth century. They thus took an active role in the consolidation of Mexican nationhood, in territorial, political, and economic terms, as well as in terms of cultural identity and social cohesion through their literary work.[10] Indeed, Mexican novelists often stated explicitly that they wanted their literature to foster national pride, heal divisions, encourage social reform, and create a truly national identity among a population that was made up of many different regional, ethnic, and social groups. Ireneo Paz, for instance, grandfather of the much more famous twentieth-century poet Octavio Paz, stated in the 1880s that the purpose of his contribution to Mexican literature, a compilation of Mexican legends and historical tales, *Leyendas históricas* (1885–1902), was "to give merited exaltation to the heroic deeds of our forefathers, to engrave on the hearts of the people the magnificent events of that terrible epoch, to make known . . . the character and the feelings of the men who figured in it and to contribute in so far as we can to the diffusion of this kind of knowledge which not only serves to invigorate the soul with patriotic memories, but also comprises the experience of nations."[11]

Paz was not unusual among nineteenth-century Mexican writers in explicitly stating his intention to consolidate or even create a sense of national identity among his fellow countrymen through his fiction. In the prologue to his 1858 novel

Gil Gómez el Insurgente, Juan Díaz Covarrubias hoped that he would have enough literary talent to do justice to "the glories . . . and the customs of my patria." A journalist writing in 1872, meanwhile, attributed a potentially vital conciliatory role to literature in uniting previously bitter enemies: "Political passions are palpitating in the heart of this society, egotism is debilitating it, civil war is destroying it; and still, literature endeavors to become the only thing that can save the current situation from being shipwrecked in a sea of blood."[12]

To inscribe within a corpus of literature the common history, both magnificent and terrible, of the Mexican populace was thought to provide some common ground for that hugely diverse and divided people to come together as an imagined community. Such a corpus of literature could also act as proof that Mexico should be counted on the international stage of nations, with a culturally autonomous and unique identity, rather than languishing in the status of a mere adjunct to European metropoles. Furthermore, many authors thought this literature could be circulated within national borders to educate the masses on how to behave as loyal, productive, and patriotic citizens. Ignacio Manuel Altamirano—often considered the greatest of Mexico's nineteenth-century writers—declared the novel to be "a way of initiating the people into the mysteries of modern civilization and of gradually educating for the priesthood of the future."[13]

Despite such clearly defined authorial intentions, this patriotic and didactic literary process was neither uncontested nor wholly successful. Literary theorists, such as Homi K. Bhabha, Timothy Brennan, and Simon During, have highlighted the ambivalence involved in the experience of nationhood and in the languages used to describe it in literature. Both experience and language, they argue, carry the potential for diffusion, division, and domination as well as for creation, production, and guidance, regardless of any single authorial intention. Literature, often unintentionally, draws attention to the ambivalence and ambiguity in attitudes, meanings, and experiences regarding the nation, since the nation only exists, not as a touchable, discrete object, but as a shifting complex of narratives or discourses.[14] Amaryll Chanady recognizes the importance of Bhabha's theory for an analysis of Latin American literature: "At the same time that the nation is constructed, it is deconstructed by the successive, and always complementary and substitutive, interpretations whose incompleteness and constant succession and mutual contradictions demonstrate the inexistence of any originary center."[15] While it is still necessary to identify the different ways in which nineteenth-century intellectuals imaginatively constructed the nation in their fiction, it is also necessary to unpick the contradictions, paradoxes, and ambiguities within their textual constructions of the nation to gain a full understanding of the extent, and the limitations, of their contribution to nation-building discourse.

It should be noted here that many of these theoretical works about the relationship between literature and the nation are focused on how novels help to imagine nations into being, creating a national community in the minds of their readers and contributing to the expression and inculcation of nationalist sentiment and national identity. This study discusses a more specific area, given that the community of readers of nineteenth-century novels was largely limited to a small social sector, namely the creole (of Hispanic descent, born in the Americas) middle and upper classes. Most novels were also written by men of a similar middle- to upper-class creole background. The impact of these literary works in terms of creating nationalist sentiment and identity among the wider Mexican populace was therefore minimal during the nineteenth century. Nevertheless, the social group involved in the reading and writing of these works saw themselves as builders of the Mexican nation, and they were actively involved in developing the political, economic, social, and cultural institutions and ideas that would become fundamental to more properly "nationalist" discourses in the twentieth century. Consequently, throughout this book I refer to the role of literary explorations of alcohol in nation-building discourse, or in relation to ideas about the nation and nationhood, rather than in terms of nationalism or national identity.

Why Alcohol?

Debates surrounding the consumption of alcohol offer profound insights into the ways in which a society understands its cultural sense of self, diagnoses its problems and celebrates its achievements, and constructs both internal and external "others" against which its own identity can be defined. Social drinking practices also play an important role in the discursive construction of a wide range of identity formations, including those organized around race, ethnicity, social class, gender, sexuality, occupation, generation, community, and region. As testified to by a growing and diverse body of work on drinking studies, examining the literary, political, legal, and medical discourses about drinking in specific national contexts can provide new and unexpected insights into the mechanics of nation-building.[16]

Drinking and drunkenness had been prominent parts of both Mexican popular culture and elite concerns with regard to that culture throughout the colonial era, and even during preconquest times, as the research of William Taylor, Juan Pedro Viquiera Albán, Raúl Guerrero Guerrero, and Tim Mitchell has shown. In the preconquest era, much attention has been given to the apparently stringent rules that the Aztecs imposed regarding the social control of drunkenness. According to Aztec law, only the highest military, religious, and political figures were allowed to become drunk in public, except during particular religious festivals in which communal consumption of pulque was permitted. Pregnant women, lactating women, and the elderly were also allowed to drink pulque, for its associations with fertility, purification, and renewal, but the quantities they could legally consume were restricted and consumption was often sanctioned by a particular ritual context. Moreover, several sources, including the Codex Mendoza and the Florentine Codex, indicate that there were very strict penalties—up to and including the death penalty—for any commoners found guilty of excessive consumption or public drunkenness.[17]

These rules were in place because drunkenness was a form of intoxication that established connections and facilitated communications between humans and various gods, which only the elite in Aztec society were normally deemed important enough to experience.[18] But these strict rules may not have been widely enforced and applied in the fifteenth century. There is little evidence of their implementation beyond the Valley of Mexico, since the ruling Aztec elite had little administrative involvement in many city-states further afield within the empire or, indeed, control over the drinking practices of those indigenous societies outside the empire. Moreover, most of the information we have about the strictness and rigid enforcement of these laws comes from indigenous nobles remembering or recounting the preconquest era several generations after the Spanish Conquest of the sixteenth century. Their picture of preconquest society is often skewed toward an elite perspective, overemphasizing the power, authority, and brutality of the Aztec leadership and overly idealizing the preconquest period as a time of order, stability, and rigid social hierarchy. Nor should the Aztec experience be construed as representative of preconquest indigenous norms in Mexico and Mesoamerica, as archaeological and iconographic evidence across chronological and geographical areas suggests that beliefs, practices, and rituals involving alcohol were in fact quite diverse.[19]

FIG. I. Section of *Mural de los bebedores* (Mural of the drinkers), Museo Nacional de Antropología, Mexico City. Photograph by the author. The original mural was created at Cholula, Mexico, around AD 200, and shows seated men and women engaged in a drinking ceremony, probably involving the consumption of pulque. Courtesy of the Instituto Nacional de Antropología e Historia.

But the fact that such rules were written down, even if they were less rigidly and effectively enforced than has been suggested, is significant, as they reveal that for the elite political, religious, and military leaders of the Aztecs, drunkenness was considered a privilege afforded to the most accomplished, brave, and important members of society so that they might assist the gods in their struggle to maintain the universe against impending collapse. It is worth noting that this is the same fight for which the Aztecs offered many human lives in their infamous bloody sacrifices. The fact that it was *public* drunkenness that was at issue, meanwhile, suggests that for the Aztec leadership, the elite monopoly on drunken comportment was as much about displaying and performing the power that leaders held over the ordinary population, as it was about communing with the gods. Additionally, drunkenness was conceived as a state of instability, one that affected the transcendence of the mutable boundaries between divine, human, and natural forces, but one that could easily violate or offend such boundaries and protocols in the wrong hands. Not only were commoners not important enough to engage in public, ritualized displays of drunkenness but the laws forbidding it asserted that they were also incapable of controlling and channeling the unstable state for appropriate purposes, again asserting the Aztec leaders' political legitimacy.[20]

During the colonial period, drunkenness became a stigma attached to the indigenous identity, along with sinfulness, barbarism, idolatry, and other failings discursively associated with indigeneity. Spanish chronicles and other accounts written during the sixteenth and seventeenth centuries contain many alarmed descriptions of indigenous communities engaging in mass drunkenness, particularly during religious festivals. Opinion was divided among Spanish conquistadors, colonial officials, and missionaries over the reasons behind this phenomenon. Some thought that the social dislocation caused by the fall of the Aztec empire, or the relaxation of its supposedly strict rules about alcohol consumption (or a combination of the two), had caused Indian communities to engage in excessive drinking. This explanation, however, is based on the problematic assumption that the extremely strict legislation recorded for the preconquest era had been widely applied.[21]

Other colonial accounts argued that the Indians' extreme drunkenness derived from their religious customs, which many early colonial missionaries believed showed satanic influence. Because missionaries often failed to understand the significance of intoxication as an altered state of being that facilitated indigenous spiritual experiences of divine communication, and which could be induced by numerous substances and experiences besides the consumption of alcohol, they structured their teachings so as to encourage total abstinence among the Indians. In doing so, the Spanish missionaries defined drunkenness as a form of sin and associated it with a range of other "sinful" practices that they believed indigenous people to be inherently drawn toward, such as idolatry, sexual deviancy, and violence.[22]

Many colonial accounts are also inflected with general assumptions about indigenous inferiority and difference as compared to Spanish and European conceptions of civility, morality, and advancement, partly as a means of rationalizing and justifying Spanish colonialism. As such, textual accusations of widespread indigenous drunkenness must be read with caution. Several observers cited the supposedly innate indigenous propensity for drunkenness as the main cause of Indian mortality in the sixteenth century (thus absolving Spanish exploitation), while others claimed that drunkenness was responsible for the escalating rebelliousness of Indian peasants during the eighteenth century (again, absolving any inequalities in the colonial system).[23] Much other evidence suggests that, quite to the contrary, alcohol featured in indigenous social and spiritual practices that emphasized community solidarity: as a neighborly offering of hospitality, as an offering to a local patron saint, as a gift in exchange for the services of village officials, or as a symbolic sign of community membership during village celebrations.[24]

During the eighteenth century, alcohol consumption became increasingly associated with popular urban culture, taking shape in the street festivals, pulquerías, and public games of Mexico City. With an increasing proportion of Indian inhabitants among the impoverished urban population, the evolving, drink-orientated popular culture helped to reinforce the ethnic stereotype of the "drunken Indian" that grew out of earlier religious and political discourse. During the eighteenth century, elite ideas about the drunkenness and incivility of Mexico's lower-class population as a whole melded with, and to some extent changed, existing ideas about the drunkenness, sinfulness, and inferiority of Mexico's indigenous population.[25] But as Steve Stern has demonstrated, for those of lower social status—men in particular—urban drinking houses represented a crucial social space for congregating; exchanging information; organizing economic transactions; meeting friends; and releasing tensions through games, music, and dancing. The companionship of other men of a similar social and ethnic level—with an inbuilt means for competing with one another through displays of drinking prowess, sociability, and bravado should a dispute arise—helped to create "cultural spaces to affirm their valor and competence."[26]

By the beginning of the nineteenth century, therefore, there had already been a long, contested history regarding the social consumption of alcohol in Mexico. Debates about drinking were connected to issues of colonial power, social class, race and ethnicity, religious practice, cultural identity, and gender. In the postindependence era, drinking continued to be an important feature of Mexican social life, and alcohol-related problems consistently featured in Mexican intellectuals' concerns about Mexico's prospects as a nation and in programs for reform. Within nineteenth-century literary discourse, moreover, socially constitutive and socially destructive images of alcohol consumption came together in representations that reveal the wide range of ways that the intellectual and political elite imagined Mexican nationhood.

Alcohol-related discourses reveal some long-term continuities across periods of Mexican history with respect to the subordination of the indigenous population through evolving ideas about "drunken Indians." Although the terms of these discourses changed from the sixteenth to the nineteenth century—explaining indigenous drunkenness in terms of religious deviancy, cultural inferiority, irrationality, or biological predisposition—alcohol consumption has been consistently involved in colonial and postcolonial discourses that rationalized Indian subordination. Only during the late eighteenth and earlier nineteenth century, as I argue in chapter 3, did architects of elite discourse partially disengage from ideas about "drunken Indians," focusing attention instead on the state's responsibility for social problems connected to alcohol consumption among the lower classes as a whole.

In addition to shedding light on how cultural stereotypes regarding alcohol consumption contributed to the maintenance of unequal power relations, focusing on debates surrounding alcohol can also reveal the more contested aspects of nation-building discourse. While Mexican government officials and intellectuals typically viewed popular drinking practices with contempt and suspicion, some writers acknowledged the positive roles alcohol could play in imaginative constructions of nationhood. For instance, the representation of "authentic" cultural spaces such as pulquerías (drinking establishments serving the traditional alcoholic beverage pulque) was enthusiastically encouraged by Guillermo Prieto, in 1845, and other writers would mobilize particular styles of drinking in the fictional construction of heroic masculine figures. These competing visions of the cultural significance of alcohol consumption help to reveal how the importance of drinking as a sociocultural practice among the population influenced the ways that Mexican intellectuals interpreted the history, culture, and identity of their society and their countrymen in their explorations of Mexican nationhood.

Organization

The question posed in the opening paragraph of this introduction—What's wrong with a little drinking?—frames the book as a whole. Politicians and other public figures exhibited a wide array of concerns about the Mexican population's drinking habits in terms of the potential threat to the control of public space and to the maintenance of family values; the crimes committed by drunken revelers; the feared inability of ordinary Mexicans to become rational, productive citizens; and even the mental and physiological deterioration of the entire populace. At the same time, literary works hoping to become part of a national literature through the celebration of Mexican history and culture also produced gloomy portraits of the future of Mexican nationhood and the Mexican people, through their representations of alcohol consumption.

This book is organized into two major parts, each of which is further divided into two chapters. Part 1 explores how images of drinking and drunkenness contributed to the formation of ideas about the Mexican nation and cultural identity, focusing on how different drinking places were involved in the delineation of bounded social and cultural spaces, and how different drinking patterns were connected to idealized models of Mexican masculinity in both social and literary discourse. Part 2 turns to the evolution of the understanding of drinking and drunkenness over the course of the nineteenth century and establishes how these changing perspectives intersected with wider discourses about the nation. In the early to mid-nineteenth century, drunkenness was predominantly understood as one among a long list of immoral vices that resulted from the body's natural desires, which could be overcome through the application of reason, but the later stages of the nineteenth century saw a progressive medicalization of thought regarding alcohol consumption, which was connected to physiological disorders, mental illness, crime, and racial degeneration.

Chapter 1, "Everything in Its Right Place? Social Drinking Spaces, Popular Culture, and Nationhood," examines how different drinking places were involved in the demarcation of social boundaries in Mexico City in the nineteenth century and in the construction and negotiation of conceptual boundaries of class within the imagined Mexican nation. Newspaper reports, advertisements, licensing applications, and judicial records are used to explore the ways in which Mexico City's pulquerías, vinaterías (taverns primarily selling distilled spirits), and cafés (establishments for the sale and consumption of liqueurs, wines, nonalcoholic beverages, and food) figured in this process. Literary representations of drinking places, meanwhile, are shown to reveal changing perceptions of popular culture among elite intellectuals, for whom the belief that the indigenous and mestizo (or mixed race) masses could be integrated into the national community through liberal education and reform gradually eroded during the course of the nineteenth century. The fictional work of José Joaquín Fernández de Lizardi, Ignacio Manuel Altamirano, and Ángel de Campo reveals this gradual change over time. At the same time, however, there was also a significant and related continuity in nineteenth-century literary depictions of drinking places, centered on the elite desire for the maintenance of a hierarchical social structure as a necessary component of national harmony, as evidenced by the short stories of José Tomás de Cuéllar and the two preeminent novels of Manuel Payno.

Chapter 2, "Patriotic Heroes and Consummate Drunks: Alcohol, Masculinity, and Nationhood," explores the relationship between drinking, masculinity, and nationhood in literary and social discourse. Through an analysis of judicial records and newspaper reports, this chapter establishes that drinking practices played a significant role in the negotiation and performance of masculine identities in nineteenth-century Mexico, particularly regarding the expected contribution of artisans and soldiers to the national community of citizens. The examination of literary representations of drinking and masculinity outlines two broad arguments. The first relates to the novels of Ignacio Manuel Altamirano and Manuel Payno, whose male characters were divided very sharply into heroes and villains, partially through the assignment of very different relationships to alcohol of the male characters. The second explores more ambiguous representations of the relationship between drinking and masculinity, in the creation of masculinized female drinkers in the work of Ángel de Campo and in the portrait of a simultaneously heroic and antiheroic, masculine and emasculated, alcoholic male character in Heriberto Frías's *Tomóchic*.

Chapter 3, "Yankees, Toffs, and Miss Quixote: Drunken Bodies, Citizenship, and the Hope of Moral Reform," examines how conceptualizations of drunkenness featured in the interconnected discourses about morality, citizenship, and patriotism in nineteenth-century Mexico. Mexican politicians and intellectuals debated Enlightenment and Cartesian philosophies that regarded the human body as fundamentally inclined toward irrational, passionate impulses and vices and recommended the application of reason to overcome drunkenness and improve public order. In the literary sphere, Lizardi, Payno, Nicolás Pizarro Suárez, and Juan Díaz Covarrubias all portrayed enemies of the Mexican nation in their fiction as irrational, vice-ridden bodies in order to denounce the obstacles preventing Mexico from becoming a rational, enlightened, and modern nation. The fictional work of Lizardi and Pizarro Suárez also suggested that certain vices, such as drunkenness, gambling, and indolence, were more prominent in Mexico among the lower-class, mixed-race, and indigenous populations as a result of government failures to provide these social and ethnic groups with the access to the education and good moral example needed for the development of strong reasoning faculties.

Chapter 4, "Medicine, Madness, and Modernity in Porfirian

Mexico: Alcoholism as the National Disease," discusses the institutionalization of the medical concept of alcoholism and its manifestation in literary discourse during the late nineteenth and early twentieth century. Many Mexican writers of the time portrayed alcoholism as a potent threat to national development and also used the condition as a metaphor for national decay in the context of Porfirian modernity. This literary examination of alcoholism was intimately related to contemporary medical and political discourses surrounding alcohol consumption and society, as the Porfirian administration, under the influence of a variety of positivist ideas, sought to analyze and control social phenomena through pseudoscientific methods. The fictional work of Federico Gamboa, Ángel de Campo, Pedro Castera, and Amado Nervo reveals an increasingly pessimistic and deterministic prognosis regarding Mexico's harmful drinking practices. These writers mobilized an increasingly medicalized language, associating alcoholism with criminality, mental illness, and racial degeneration, to foreground concerns about Mexico's experience of modernity in the Porfirian period.

Literary and broader sociopolitical discourses about alcohol reveal numerous elite concerns about Mexico's social structure, class divisions, and gender relations; its historical roots and image on the international stage of nations; the racial and ethnic differences of the population; the development of its political systems; and its level of economic progress. Rather than providing detailed insights into the actual customs, values, and practices of the ordinary Mexican population in the nineteenth century, what these alcohol-related discourses help to reveal most clearly are the core issues that troubled Mexico's nineteenth-century nation-builders, the ways in which some of their proposed solutions structured social policy and political debates, and how they created enduring images of Mexican nationhood.

Alcohol and Nationhood in Nineteenth-Century Mexico

Part 1

Imagining the Nation
through Alcohol,
Class, and Gender

ONE

Everything in Its Right Place?

Social Drinking Spaces, Popular Culture, and Nationhood

[This pulquería] is America personified, and should be recognized as the queen of all these singular taverns where the liquor discovered by the beautiful Xóchitl is dispensed.

—MANUEL PAYNO

Manuel Payno's rather nostalgic and romantic description of a pulquería in Puente de la Leña, a bustling Mexico City barrio, stands in stark contrast to the vulgarity and violence that drinking frequently produces elsewhere in the same novel, *Los bandidos de Río Frío* (1888–91). Although the author notes that pulquerías (taverns primarily selling pulque, a traditional fermented alcoholic beverage) represent a "very dangerous temptation," his description of a rustic, open air venue and reference to the abstract ideals of both "America" and "Xóchitl"—the mythical discoverer of pulque—combine to create for the reader an image of an "authentic" Mexican cultural space.[1] Payno also notes in this passage that his musings on popular customs would have a most interesting "ancient novelty value" not only for foreigners but "even for those *enlightened and Parisian* Mexicans who live in the city center."[2] The italicization of these words emphasizes the distance the author felt to exist between elite and popular culture in Mexican society, while the passage as a whole suggests that popular culture could have the potential to become the basis of an authentic and unique Mexican identity. Payno's positive portrayal of the pulquería is striking because alcohol consumption, especially when practiced by the lower orders of society, often has highly negative consequences in his fiction. This incongruity between the representation of a rustic, relatively harmless drinking place and the condemnation of drunken, depraved, destructive behavior emanating from similar places is indicative of a persistent tension that nineteenth-century intellectuals felt between identifying a unique and authentic Mexican identity and relating it to the reality they experienced as part of the political and social elite.

This chapter examines the involvement of drinking places in social and literary discourses about class, cultural identity, and nationhood. Newspaper reports, advertisements, licensing applications, and judicial records are used to explore how Mexico City's pulquerías, vinaterías, and cafés figured in the delineation of social boundaries that were being drawn in Mexico City's urban space during the long nineteenth century, as authorities sought to impose greater standards of order, civility, and control over the expanding city and its population.

Across the nineteenth century there was a marked solidification of social divisions across the urban geography of Mexico City that the regulation of elite and popular drinking places helped to create. While popular drinking places, such as pulquerías and vinaterías, were repeatedly targeted with successive waves of regulation in an effort to control their patrons' behavior and to restrict their location to the poorer areas and peripheries of Mexico City, cafés became increasingly important as drinking places and social spaces for the elite sectors of society. The social background of their clientele became more exclusive from the mid-nineteenth century onward, when cafés marketed themselves as the purveyors of luxury foods and drinks, and they proliferated in the more prestigious and central areas of Mexico City. We will consider the ways in which various social actors, including proprietors and customers of popular drinking places, reacted to and negotiated with the increasing regulation of Mexico City's social space in the nineteenth century.

This chapter will also analyze literary portrayals of drinking places and their transformation into literary spaces for intellectual constructions of Mexicanness. Representations of drinking places in the work of José Joaquín Fernández de Lizardi, Ignacio Altamirano, and Ángel de Campo reveal a gradual erosion of confidence in the ability of liberal reforms and education to sanitize popular culture and integrate the indigenous and mestizo masses into the national community. This erosion was linked to a persistent fear about the potential disruption to social hierarchies that liberal policies might generate. Despite their clear support for liberal policies of education, reform, and equality before the law for all citizens, many of these intellectuals retained a strong desire to preserve a stable, static, and largely hierarchical social structure as a necessary component of national harmony and unification. Although popular culture remained alluring as a potential space for the location of authenticity in elite depictions of Mexican nationhood, many Mexican intellectuals imagined the cultural practices of elite and non-elite social groups as spatially distant, helping to destabilize their attempts to imagine Mexican nationhood into being.

Mexico City and Its Spaces of Drink: From Colony to Nation, 1520–1845

Drinking places featured prominently in the social life of colonial Mexico City and became a persistent focus of governing officials' concerns about social disorder. Attempts to regulate drinking places often focused on their location within the city's urban landscape, which colonial authorities had tried to order according to social and racial hierarchies since its establishment in the early sixteenth century. Mexico City was constructed atop the ruins of Tenochtitlan, which had been the center of power of the Aztec empire, and the geographical layout of the city was to mirror the new political structure that colonialism demanded, making the city center the preserve of the Spaniards, and limiting the indigenous population to the outskirts of the city. Many of the major political, economic, and cultural institutions of New Spain were established in the center of Mexico City, around the central square known as the Plaza Mayor or Zócalo, including the Audencia (High Court), the viceregal palace, the offices of royally appointed merchants, and the metropolitan cathedral.

Although the spatial division of the city, into a Spanish center and an indigenous periphery, had never been fully observed in practice, by the end of the colonial period these spatial boundaries were under increasing pressure due to an influx of impoverished migrants to the city from surrounding rural areas.[3] As a succession of agricultural crises, disease epidemics, and land seizures by wealthy landowners hammered the rural population, the population of Mexico City increased during the final decades of the eighteenth century, from approximately 98,000 in 1742 to 104,760 in 1790, and perhaps to as many as 138,000 inhabitants by 1803.[4] This development resulted in the growing presence of indigenous people in the urban milieu, together with a growing mestizo and casta (mixed-race) population, a substantial creole population (people of Hispanic descent born in the Americas), and a cosmopolitan mix of permanently resident and traveling Europeans.

Spanish colonists established Mexico City's first commercial tavern, a vinatería, on December 1, 1525. Before the conquest, pulque, a fermented alcoholic drink made from the maguey species of the agave plant, was sold in Tlatelolco market, the Aztecs' main commercial center, but there were no commercial taverns. Pulque was sold in the market for household consumption, religious festivals, and community celebrations, and, although the limitations of the available sources make it difficult to establish the exact degree of regulation, most historians concur that there were tight controls over how much pulque could be sold, to whom, when, and for what purpose. When the first commercial tavern, a vinatería, appeared in Mexico City in 1525, vinaterías were primarily wine-selling taverns for the exclusive patronage of Spaniards, whereas, by the eighteenth century, the vinaterías predominantly sold aguardiente (a distilled liquor, usually made from sugar cane), and their clientele was ethnically and socially mixed.[5]

Pulquerías similarly developed from an early stage of the colonial period. Twelve mobile pulque-selling stands had been licensed in Mexico City by the 1530s; by the 1550s, there were twelve more and some had been granted permission to establish a fixed location with rudimentary premises. Their number continued to grow throughout the colonial period; William Taylor estimates that there were approximately 250 unlicensed, illegal pulquerías in Mexico City by 1639, while Áurea Toxqui has identified the existence of 212 legally licensed pulquerías in 1650. As with the exclusivity of vinaterías—with their initial remit as a drinking venue for the exclusive patronage of Spaniards—pulquerías were initially intended solely to serve the needs of indigenous drinkers, and they were all located in the peripheral indigenous neighborhoods of Mexico City. However, by the seventeenth century, as these neighborhoods also became home to a wide ethnic mix of poor creoles, mestizos, and castas, the clientele of pulquerías diversified and pulquerías also spread to the central part of the city that was officially reserved for Spaniards.[6]

Historians concur that urban drinking places were an important index of how social hierarchies operated in Mexico City. By the end of the colonial period, Mexican society was characterized by a complex system of racial, ethnic, and class stratification, in which the predominantly Spanish and creole upper- and middle-class elite dominated positions of economic and political power, while the popular classes were made up of indigenous and mixed-race peoples, as well as poor creoles. Class and racial categorizations, however, were fluid and interactive, with social and cultural practices having a significant impact on the status of individuals. In colonial society, although a person's identity and status were usually recorded in official documentation in racial terms such as Indian, mestizo, or Spaniard, the determination of such a status included considerations of color, occupation, wealth, purity of blood, honor, integrity, place of birth, and social comportment.[7] Together, all these characteristics helped to form Mexico City society into two broad categories, each of which had a complex internal hierarchy of its own: the elite, or the *gente decente* (decent people) were well-educated, at least reasonably wealthy, dressed in European-style fashions, and socialized in private residences as well as more respectable public places; the popular classes, or *el pueblo* (the people), tended to have modest or low levels of income, lacked education, and socialized in popular drinking places like pulquerías and vinaterías, as well as *pulperías* (stores selling alcoholic drinks and groceries), markets, theaters, *fondas* (small restaurants), plazas, and parks. Of course, the *gente decente* did visit many public spaces for social purposes as well, but if the setting and its clientele were known as disorderly or morally suspect, frequenting such a place too often could damage their social reputation as *gente decente*.[8]

Drinking places provided a vital arena for the conduct of social recreation, communication, and business transaction among their customers, but colonial administrators consistently viewed these social spaces with suspicion and considered them threatening to public order. A viceregal ordinance of 1671 stipulated that pulquerías had to be located in city squares and that they could only have one wall and a roof, leaving three sides open so that they could be viewed more easily by patrols. Vinaterías, meanwhile, were more often allowed to be fully equipped with tables, benches, and storage facilities, but they were ordered to keep their doors open and to situate the bar adjacent to the entrance. Furthermore, the sale of food, playing music, and loitering were prohibited in an attempt to discourage the raucous social atmosphere that had developed in these popular social spaces. However, the repeated reiterations of these laws in subsequent decades suggest that such attempts to control the social activities of pulquería and vinatería patrons were largely unsuccessful. An investigation of 1784, for instance, revealed that of the forty-five legal pulquerías in Mexico City, only seven complied with all the regulations laid out by colonial administrators.[9]

During the colonial period, the most notorious episode in the ongoing struggle for control over urban space between popular drinking places and Mexico City authorities was the temporary prohibition of pulque following a popular riot in 1692. On June 8, 1692, a large crowd, comprised of Mexico City's ethnically mixed urban poor, attacked the central institutions of Spanish colonial authority in the city, setting fire to the doors of the Viceregal Palace, the *ayuntamiento* (city council), and the large merchant houses. Douglas Cope's detailed study of the riot indicates that this outburst of popular violence grew out of a crisis in food supply, which was then exacerbated by a lack of communication between colonial officials and the protesters.[10] However, colonial officials and other members of the urban elite did not understand the 1692 riot as the result of their failure to engage with the legitimate grievances of protestors. Instead, the riot was largely interpreted as a consequence of the degenerating character of the city's lower class, and especially indigenous, population. Indians, already widely thought to be more susceptible to habitual and excessive drunkenness than other ethnic groups, were now also exposed to an ethnically mixed, plebeian atmosphere of sociability in Mexico City's pulquerías, which many elite commentators believed to be extremely deleterious for the indigenous population's moral development and for social order in general.[11]

Carlos Sigüenza y Góngora, a leading public intellectual and priest in late seventeenth-century Mexico, argued that the riot was a malicious outburst of a drunken urban mob that carried alarming racial connotations. He claimed that Indians were protesting the rising maize prices so vociferously out of self-interested greed and that they only had themselves to blame for their poverty and hardship: "The Indians would spend all their profits on pulque," Sigüenza y Góngora claimed, "and, considering how abundant this drink was in the city at this time, they often got drunk," and conspired with other societal dregs in the pulquerías to attack colonial officials and institutions.[12] To elite observers, therefore, the interethnic social milieu provided by popular drinking places like pulquerías seemed extremely dangerous.

In the wake of the 1692 violence, the production and sale of pulque were temporarily banned in an attempt to diffuse the social danger posed by drunken gatherings of the lower orders. The large-scale revenue that taxes on pulque provided for the Royal Treasury ensured that the ban was short-lived: pure, unmixed pulque was legalized less than two months after the riot occurred, while *pulque mezclado* (mixed pulque) and pulquerías were legalized again in 1697.[13] However, the conviction that popular drinking places represented a significant danger to the preservation of social order and sociopolitical hierarchies remained potent throughout the colonial period and returned to particular prominence during the final decades of the eighteenth century, when Mexico City underwent considerable changes in its social geography.

From 1782, royal officials undertook a major spatial reorganization of Mexico City, creating eight major districts, which were divided further into thirty-two minor districts. Magistrates were made responsible for the registration of all streets, houses, and places of business in each district, as well as the maintenance of cleanliness and order in public spaces. This reorganization was designed to facilitate greater control and surveillance of public space in both the central part of the city and the poorer, outlying neighborhoods. Viceroy Martín de Mayorga (1779–83) highlighted the problems posed by Mexico City's urban space, particularly in terms of the potential disorder it could produce among the popular classes: "The vast expanse of this city, the irregular arrangement of its neighborhoods and suburbs, and the way the dwellings in these are situated . . . makes it impossible to keep a register of them . . . and their enormous populations, especially among the masses."[14] Colonial authorities intended to rationalize the city's space, "to make it functional and beautiful, promote economic growth, and cleanse it in every sense," and in the process improve the civility, morality, and social behavior of all the city's residents, especially the lower orders.[15]

In 1784 a report recommending reform of the city's drinking places added to this program of spatial reorganization. The report focused predominantly on Mexico City's forty-five legal pulquerías, since these were much larger than vinaterías and so offered a greater space for disorderly social gatherings to develop. Situated in the plazas of outer districts, pulquerías were also more difficult to supervise than vinaterías, which were mostly located in or near the city center. Among the measures proposed were the removal of seats and benches to discourage drinkers from lingering in the pulquerías, a reduction in the size of pulquerías so that fewer people could gather therein, and the assignment of specific pulquerías to specific police officials to ensure more intensive supervision. As a result of a series of bureaucratic delays, these recommendations were not translated into legislation but, in the 1790s, Viceroy Revillagigedo did launch a serious crackdown on pulquerías to enforce the removal of seats and benches, as well as the previous regulations that forbade the sale of pulque after sunset, the sale of food in or near the establishments, and the performance of music, dancing, and gambling.[16]

The focus on pulquerías, however, allowed other popular drinking places to flourish and city authorities soon felt the need to broaden their regulatory agenda. Reports submitted in 1805 by the district magistrates of the minor districts twenty-nine, thirty, thirty-one, and thirty-two—the outer suburbs of Mexico City—complained that the growing number of large and small vinaterías in these areas was causing an escalation of petty violence, robbery, indecent behavior, murder, and the frequent appearance of "drunken wretches lying in the street as if they were dead." In the same year, a group of priests from various Mexico City parishes wrote to the municipal authorities requesting that vinaterías, as well as pulquerías, should be obliged to keep their premises more open, that small vinaterías—known as *zangarros*—should be prohibited, that the overall number of vinaterías should be reduced, and that the remaining establishments be kept at a distance of at least two hundred yards apart. These concerns about the clustering of drinking places together in small spaces outside the reach of proper supervision were reiterated in 1807 by several magistrates who complained that "there is a prodigious number [of *zangarros*] mainly in the outlying neighborhoods and suburbs."[17]

Indeed, the number of popular drinking places did proliferate as Mexico City and its population grew larger in the early decades of the nineteenth century. According to Michael Scardaville, by the beginning of the nineteenth century, Mexico City had some 1,600 drinking places, including 593 vinaterías, 45 pulquerías and 120 aguardiente-selling stores— variously known as *tiendas, pulperías*, and *cafeterías*—which were all legally recognized establishments. There were also approximately 850 illegal *casas de pulque* (pulque houses), and *tepacherías* (illegal bars selling tepache, a drink made from soured pulque, brown sugar, and citrus fruits). In addition, an unknown number of itinerant pulque vendors traded from stalls in the city's various markets.[18] During the early decades of the nineteenth century, the official cap on pulquería numbers was gradually lifted, partly because the municipal and national governments were desperate for revenue and partly because they recognized that forty-five pulquerías could not meet public demand, which therefore turned toward illegal channels. In 1825 the number of licensed pulquerías stood at 80, by 1831 there were 250, and by 1864, this figure had more than doubled to 513.[19]

Despite recognizing that licensed trade was better than unlicensed trade, pulquerías and other popular drinking places continued to generate concern and alarm among the political elite in the early republican period, as they were routinely blamed for public disorder and immorality. In June 1821 the city's magistrates identified "the excessive number of vinaterías and pulquerías" as the source of "evils of incalculable consequence." In order to deal with "this political cancer that so corrodes moral standards, and to remove from public sight such abominations," they announced a redoubling of efforts to enforce previous regulations relating to both vendors and customers, including those of June 1810 that specified strict opening hours for alcohol-selling premises, the prohibition of pulque sales from informal dispensaries, and the arrest of any men and women found drunk in the streets.[20] A September 1823 law further stipulated that pulque stalls had to be removed from all public squares, except for a limited number of licensed vendors in the Plaza del Volador in the city center and four other selected squares further outside the center, in order to "avoid clandestine and dangerous gatherings," and to maintain "the beauty and cleanliness of the capital."[21]

Such regulations, however, were routinely ignored. In 1831 the senior magistrate, Francisco Fagoaga, lamented the lack of observation of previous laws and the continuing disorder produced by the "multitude of pulquerías that exist in the city and its barrios." He reiterated a series of regulations that had been issued in 1825, which prohibited pulquerías from having adjoining private rooms, seats, or spaces for patrons to socialize. The counter had to be fixed at the entrance, and proprietors were obliged to prevent customers from going behind it. Like many previous regulations, those issued by Fagoaga were principally concerned with preventing pulquerías from becoming spaces of popular sociability.[22]

There were some clear continuities between late colonial and early republican regulations, particularly regarding the goal of limiting sociability within popular drinking places and reforming both central and peripheral venues. However, there were also some interesting changes to the principles informing these regulatory decisions. In the background to Fagoaga's 1831 orders, the city council engaged in prolonged discussions about how to balance a program for the reduction and spatial restriction of pulquerías with the "principles of liberty." While it was necessary to avoid the "monopolization of pulque," commerce in pulque had to be restricted to some degree to prevent the multiplication of "scandals and abuses."[23] This tension between the liberty of commerce and the preservation of order continued to trouble municipal authorities during the 1830s. In announcing a new range of closures

FIG. 2. José Agustín Arrieta, *Tertulia de pulquería* (Gathering in a pulquería), 1851. Oil on canvas, 95 x 115 cm. Museo Andrés Blaisten, Mexico City. Arrieta was a costumbrista artist, whose work was intended to depict local customs and everyday culture in Mexico. Like many real-life pulquerías, Arrieta's imagined pulquerías would have broken numerous legal restrictions, including the prohibitions against fixed furniture, gatherings of customers, and the sale of food. A vibrant political discussion appears to be taking place in the scene, where several men are holding pamphlets. Mexico City authorities were consistently worried about the possibility of such popular sociability leading to social unrest, crimes, and deviant behavior. Courtesy of Museo Andrés Blaisten.

and restrictions on pulquerías in December 1833, Governor José María Tornel explained that new pulquerías and other taverns could no longer be allowed to open at will because this "had produced an increase in drunkards, uncleanliness, brawls, and other disorders, so that they are even within the reach of our Capital's honorable residents." Future license decisions would, he said, be based purely on "considerations of the public good." Although these regulations were swiftly revoked, due to strong protests from pulque traders, this episode shows how the principles informing policy decisions were starting to change.[24]

Moreover, by the 1830s, the government's understanding of the underlying origins of alcohol-related social disorder had begun to shift, although only partially, away from the late colonial era's emphasis on the disordered urban environment. Republican-era authorities also began to indicate that they thought of alcohol-related disorder as a national problem, even as they focused their principal attention on urban taverns in the capital city. In his preamble to the 1833 regulations, Tornel made reference to Mexico's historical development in explaining the problem of public drunkenness: "The corruption of the people [*pueblo*], called 'low' by the Spaniards, was one of the saddest methods they used to establish their odious dominion. Since this has happily been destroyed, it has been the foremost priority and endeavor of the Mexican authorities to correct those vices that degrade and debase our humanity. Drunkenness being the most shameful of these vices, expedient measures have been announced to tackle it since 1821, in an effort to improve public morality."[25]

Such measures had repeatedly tried to make drinking places purely functional spaces for the dispensation of economically and gastronomically essential beverages. However, patrons of popular taverns continued to use them as spaces of sociability in defiance, or perhaps disregard, of the law. In 1802 a vinatería owner named José Antonio Merino was fined for permitting a large group of people to gather and play music in his establishment; among the revelers were a soldier, a cigarette factory worker, and two indigenous men. Felipe Galan was similarly prosecuted in 1804 for allowing large groups of patrons to gather together, playing music and dancing in his pulquería near the main park in the parish of Santa Cruz, just south of the city center. Vinaterías and pulquerías were regularly patronized by an interethnic clientele and groups of young men, who sometimes got into trouble after drinking too much and fighting. Sociability especially thrived in popular drinking places during festival days. On one such occasion in May 1821, three of José Ysita's pulquerías were caught accommodating large groups of drinkers, as well as providing customers with hot food and places to sit.[26]

In addition to patrons and proprietors being caught in contravention of the regulations about music, food, gambling, and loitering within popular drinking places, court proceedings also suggest that owners and managers were sometimes deliberately obstructive to attempts at law enforcement. Proprietors of drinking places were usually called to testify in cases where regulations had been broken and in cases where a disturbance or crime had been committed on their premises. It was not unusual for owners of drinking places to plead ignorance regarding such incidents. In March 1858 Antonio Mendez, a pulquería owner in the San Juan neighborhood, claimed to have been away on business when a soldier had been arrested in his pulquería for being publicly drunk, fraternizing with an army deserter, and engaging in "scandalous" behavior with two naked women. Despite being unable to provide evidence of his business transactions, the court upheld Mendez's testimony and the charges against the soldier were dropped for lack of reliable evidence. The soldier's own dubious story, that he (while shirtless) stumbled upon the deserter engaging in illicit relations with the two naked women and then intervened, trying to stop him, was apparently accepted as the best available explanation.[27]

In other cases, proprietors themselves came up with unlikely cover stories. Pulquería owner Felipe Galan admitted that a large group of musicians and their acquaintances, none of whom he had previously met, had been drinking pulque in his establishment for several hours. But, he claimed, the loud music that a patrolling officer noticed did not emanate from this large group of drunken musicians, but was played by a poor blind man seeking charity from the pulquería patrons. Hence, Galan claimed, good-natured pity, and not a disregard for the law, led him to relax his normally "great efforts . . . to contain" such activities. The judicial officials involved in Galan's case were rather less trusting than those who released the drunken soldier caught in flagrante in Antonio Mendez's pulquería, and Galan was duly fined a considerable sum.[28]

While there is, therefore, evidence to suggest that patrons and proprietors were prepared to flout legal regulations that tried to eliminate social activities from popular drinking places—such as singing, dancing, gambling, and staying longer than the time allotted for consuming a drink—many other proprietors demonstrated a greater degree of willingness to engage with the regulatory directives of municipal authorities, as a means of protecting their livelihoods. License applications and appeals made during the first half of the nineteenth century reveal that proprietors of drinking establishments were acutely aware of the authorities' concerns about social and spatial disorder. They took care to highlight their knowledge of the different laws and legal requirements, emphasizing their acceptance of the principles that underpinned the regulation of drinking places, including the need to control urban social space and improve public morality.[29]

Pedro José del Valle successfully objected to the forced relocation of his licensed pulquería in the Plaza del Volador to a site further from the local church. He argued that "a tavern, clean and managed with order and the necessary precautions to prevent the wickedness that comes with drunkenness" posed no threat to the dignity of a church. He emphasized that his establishment only sold high-quality, unadulterated pulque that did not smell, that no food was available to customers,

and that there were no seats that might encourage drunkenness or inappropriate relations between men and women. By
demonstrating that he not only observed the regulations but
understood and agreed with their purpose, del Valle was able
to renegotiate the terms of his license agreement.[30] Similarly,
Manuel Alfaro was able to secure an exemption from an 1825
order to close all pulque stalls not located in the four plazas
of del Volador, Jesus, Santa Catalina, and Factor, by demonstrating that his establishment in the Plazuela de la Paja was
just as orderly and easy to supervise as the others. He drew
particular attention to his understanding of the government's
plan to limit disorder by restricting pulquerías to locations
that were open to inspection: "[My pulquería] is situated on
the corner of a much frequented and very public street, so
that it is impossible for even the slightest disorder or misde-
meanor to occur there without the authorities being able to
see and put a stop to it."[31]

Proprietors' attempts to defend their interests in this way,
however, did not always work. The government's conflicting
priorities of simultaneously improving the public image of the
city, especially in the center, and of increasing standards of
surveillance citywide at times led to proprietors' appeals falling on deaf ears. In 1806 Manuel Cerrano applied to renew
his license for a pulquería at the entrance to Chapultepec forest and to open a further pulque stall at the bridge leading
into the nearby Romita neighborhood. Like other applicants,
Cerrano emphasized that his proposal would help to eliminate
contraband trading of pulque and tepache in the area around
Chapultepec forest and that his previous record as a pulque
vendor testified to his respect for legislative restrictions regarding social activities inside drinking places. He also offered to
move his existing pulquería closer to the residential area of
Chapultepec to facilitate better police supervision. While the
municipal authorities agreed that Cerrano's proposal would

serve an existing demand in a busy area, reduce contraband, and facilitate greater supervision, they concluded that positioning a stall at the Romita bridge would lower the tone of a respectable area and that his existing pulquería should also remain at the entrance to Chapultepec forest, just outside the boundaries of the city center.[32] Rather than debasing the more central areas on which Cerrano proposed to encroach, therefore, they denied his request, even though this meant that contraband trade could continue and that his existing pulquería would often go unsupervised, due to the difficulties involved in stretching police resources to the outer limits of the city.[33]

This emphasis on maintaining order, morality, cleanliness, and propriety in the central parts of the city became the top priority between the middle and the end of the nineteenth century, not only for the government but for the political, economic, and intellectual elite more broadly. One of Mexico City's most important daily newspapers, *El Siglo XIX*, complained in the 1840s that there was a "multitude of taverns known as pulquerías, vinaterías and others, in some of which gather the common people, and in the rest gather people of different social classes. . . . In them, a certain number of idle vagabonds gather daily, acting as examples of demoralization; and this happens in all parts, from the most prominent street, even in the streets next to the building where the patrol itself resides, to the most miserable suburb."[34] The journalist clearly links his concerns about popular drinking places to both the clientele that frequented them and the spatial arrangement of these places around the city. The boundaries between the center and the peripheries of the city were being crossed as the social space of the various taverns seemed to infiltrate the whole urban landscape. Preventing the crossing of these social and spatial boundaries became the dominant goal of public policy toward popular drinking places for much of the next half century.

Urban Modernization and Social Space, 1845–1910

Limiting the use of drinking places as centers of popular sociability remained a key concern of the government throughout the nineteenth century, but, beginning in the 1840s, the desire to protect the image and respectability of central and well-to-do parts of the city began to supersede the goal of monitoring and controlling popular behavior throughout the city as a whole. By the end of the nineteenth century, this impulse had produced an increasing segregation of elite and popular public spaces into the wealthy and poor districts of the city. Moreover, in contrast to earlier regulations that called for pulquerías to be as open as possible to facilitate surveillance, at the turn of the twentieth century, the Porfirian government enacted a series of measures to hide the activities of pulquería interiors from public view. These were intended to prevent pulquerías from offending the sensibilities of the upper and middle classes and damaging the modern image of the city as the urban embodiment of the government's mantra "Order and Progress." Many scholars highlight the elevated levels of migration to the capital city in search of work, and in response to changing conditions of land ownership, as the driving force behind the Porfirian government's renewed determination to contain popular social spaces and to establish firmer boundaries between elite and popular spaces.[35] However, it is important to recognize that this was also the outcome of longer-term debates about the best means of containing the threat to social order posed by popular drinking places.

Debates that had emerged in the early nineteenth century, about the tension between allowing liberty of commerce and maintaining public order, continued throughout the middle and late nineteenth century. However, liberal principles shaped regulation in new ways from the 1850s to the late

1870s, as various regulatory codes placed legal obligations on customers, as well as proprietors, to observe standards of conduct in drinking places. Using the law to make individual drinkers responsible for improving public order and morality was, however, only a temporary approach, as regulatory directives returned to making proprietors responsible for what happened in their premises from 1878 onward. The return to proprietors' responsibilities in maintaining orderly drinking places, and the increasing concentration of popular drinking places in poorer regions of the city, was accompanied by a consolidation of pulque commerce into more elite economic hands, with major pulque producers controlling an increasing number of retail outlets. This consolidation of the pulque business also allowed proprietors to develop more organized lobbying campaigns against unfavorable regulation, and in doing this they adopted the language of social and spatial order even more thoroughly than previous generations of proprietors had done.

Drinking places continued to be a major target of official concern regarding the spatial organization of Mexico City in the mid- to late nineteenth century, but the emphasis was increasingly on the harm that popular drinking places could cause to elite sectors of society and more elite spaces within the city. In 1845 the city council formed a special commission to recommend action to reduce the problem of drunks appearing daily on the street "causing scandals and offence to morality." Leandro Pinál, an expert in political economy and member of the Council for Commercial Development, argued that action was needed urgently "to contain the reprehensible abuse of alcoholic drinks, since this is not just endangering the wretched classes who give themselves over to drink with such abandon, but it also endangers the whole population through the scandalous behavior this vice engenders, and the consequent discomfort inflicted on residents in even

the most central streets of the city." He went on to emphasize that the best way of avoiding the contamination of more
respectable people and spaces within the city was to restrict
the location of popular drinking places to open squares outside the city center. Greater vigilance could be maintained
in the open squares, but it was crucial to expel them from
the city center so that "the main streets will be free from the
dangers and irritations that these places bring with them."[36]

The regulations issued in 1845 did not contain the spatial
restrictions envisaged by Pinál, focusing instead on limiting
the use of pulquerías as spaces of sociability. Like many previous edicts, this one prohibited music, dancing, food, seats,
and games from pulquerías and stipulated that the premises
should be easy to monitor and must not have adjoining rooms
where drinkers could seclude themselves. However, the 1845
rules introduced some new elements to the requirements that
indicated priorities were starting to change. In applying for
licenses, pulquería managers had to produce testimony from
three witnesses who could vouch for their "good behavior" and
accept responsibility for preventing drinkers from befouling,
passing out, or otherwise causing an obstruction in the surrounding area of the pulquería.[37] And while the 1845 regulations stopped short of creating a pulquería-free zone in the
city center, the idea of doing so remained on the agenda and
was enacted eleven years later.

Complaints from prominent citizens and newspaper commentators helped to keep concerns about the impact of popular drinking places on the respectable parts of society fresh in
government minds. In 1845 approximately thirty residents of
the Calle del Refugio, which they described as "one of the most
central and important streets in the capital," claimed that the
neighborhood had been defiled, both physically and morally,
by the presence of numerous pulquerías. It would be far better to keep these establishments in the suburbs, they argued,

so that young men and women would not be corrupted by the sight of "semi-naked men . . . habitual drunkards profaning even the most sacred of things . . . [and] foul-mouthed, brutish, dirty women" spilling out of the local pulquerías. It was unacceptable, they said, that such immorality and vice should be allowed to prosper in "the heart of the city."[38] A letter published in *El Siglo XIX* several months later highlighted the government's inaction in response to the petition and reiterated the importance of protecting the center of the city from pulquerías, which were "a disgrace to the city's beauty and harmful to public morality."[39]

By 1854 the city authorities were convinced of the need to prioritize the order, propriety, and image of the central district of the city, admitting that it was "shameful that the Capital of the Republic, residence of the Supreme Authority and of the Excellencies, Ambassadors of foreign nations, presents at every step in even its most frequented, most important streets, these pulquerías, which are constantly dirty in spite of the best efforts of the police and serve the most idle reprobates in society. They are an insult to beauty and decency; they are the epitome of obscenity and a proving-ground for vice."[40] Consequently, in 1856, an exclusionary zone, extending eighty-five blocks north and south of the Zócalo, was established to prevent any more pulquerías opening therein and to make the closure of existing pulquerías within the zone easier. In a useful dissertation that includes maps of this zone, and its subsequent extensions and alterations in 1873, 1878, 1884, and 1901, María Áurea Toxqui Garay has argued that this policy highlighted the internal "contradictions" of Mexican liberalism in the nineteenth century. While the principle of freedom of commerce ought to have led to the abolition of such restrictions, the liberal desire to transform Mexico City and its population into a more modern, "civilized," sober, and productive society led to continued attempts to regulate the population's social behavior and to protect orderly public spaces from being infiltrated by the disorder associated with popular drinking places, especially pulquerías.[41]

This contradiction did not go unnoticed at the time, as pulque vendors highlighted constitutional guarantees to contest the policy of exclusion. A group of major players in the pulque trade, including Ignacio Torres Adalid and Javier Torres Adalid, petitioned the government in April 1861 to complain about the 1856 decree. They were careful to emphasize their understanding of the reasons underpinning the exclusionary zone, including the concern that "the indecent acts of drunkards would be more powerfully contagious and damaging" when witnessed by more "moderate and decent people" in the city center and would convey "a sad impression of the civilization of our country" to visiting or resident foreigners. Despite these good intentions, however, the protesters opined that licenses had in fact been granted to Francisco Espinosa as a political favor, in total contravention of both the 1856 law and the 1857 constitutional guarantee to abolish privileges and monopolies. Espinosa and the proprietors of older establishments within the zone that had been given leave to remain were, the complainants argued, effectively in possession of a commercial monopoly. The pulque traders proposed an alternative system of regulation in which there would be no restrictive zones, but they would transform pulquerías into more respectable establishments, "like the cafés of Mexico City," with comfortable furnishings, newspaper subscriptions, clean exteriors, and managers who could prove their good moral standing and credentials.[42]

The plan was not adopted; however, there were some attempts to reconcile the conflict between freedom of commerce and principles of public order, particularly with recourse to improving the public appearance of pulquerías and in making customers responsible for their own conduct. In 1862, for instance, a short-lived decree declared the commerce in pulque free, but maintained a smaller restricted zone in which no new pulquerías could be established. New licensees would have to ensure that their establishments were "clean and smart, without grotesque, indecent, or immoral paintings," with sufficient seats to accommodate customers, and no access to secluded interior spaces. While the decree made proprietors responsible for preventing music, dancing, games, and obstructions in the street, maintaining strict opening hours, and promptly reporting any disturbances, customers were subject to the same fines and penalties for breaking any of these rules. It was also an offence to drink to excess or be drunk, even if the customer was not engaged in other disorderly activity.[43] As Toxqui has demonstrated, laws stipulating the obligations of customers appeared regularly between 1856 and 1878, in an attempt to shape individuals into more responsible, sober, and virtuous citizens.[44]

Further experimentation in striking the balance between public order and freedom of commerce occurred in the 1870s, when legislation was implemented that created two different types of pulquerías: interior-sale and exterior-sale pulquerías. The former would be more like cantinas and *fondas*, providing customers with seats, tables, food, and longer opening hours, while the latter would operate like off-licenses, selling pulque to be taken away and consumed elsewhere. However, having legally allowed in some pulquerías the development of convivial social atmospheres that had been the target of punitive action for several hundred years, liberal officials quickly concluded that this measure actually exacerbated the problem of social disorder—indeed, many felt they had inadvertently sanctioned it—and the dual-licensing law was also revoked in 1873.[45]

As the apparent contradiction in policies regarding the principle of freedom of commerce and the regulation of popular drinking places continued, some liberal writers tried to reconcile the conflict by emphasizing the constitutionality of limiting freedom of commerce when it threatened the social good. In 1872 *El Siglo XIX* argued for the inapplicability of the principle of freedom of commerce in the case of pulquerías:

> This reason is next to worthless because, according to an article of the constitution, one of the restrictions placed upon the right to freedom of property is that, in dealing with it, no harm must be done to society. Consequently, any embarrassing, unhealthy, and dangerous establishments are necessarily subject to certain restrictions by the constitution. No-one could question that pulquerías are, at the very least, embarrassing establishments, and therefore that the authorities are perfectly justified in prohibiting them from being established in selected places in the city.[46]

The author's dissatisfaction is clearly focused on the negative impact pulquerías had on the image, as well as the reality, of Mexico City society. Despite the liberal principle of freedom of commerce, therefore, many liberals believed that in order to construct an orderly, modern, and productive society, popular drinking places would have to be strictly controlled in terms of their location and operational conditions. These regulations and restrictions constituted an integral part of a larger process through which the social organization of Mexico City itself was geared toward the creation and preservation of orderly, modern, and elite social spaces that could be kept separate from the disorder associated with popular drinking places.

The increasing desire to marginalize popular drinking places to more peripheral and impoverished areas of Mexico City over the latter half of the nineteenth century was accompanied by the emergence and proliferation of expensive and socially exclusive elite drinking places, especially cafés. While cafés had not featured significantly in colonial Mexico City, they flourished in the first decade of the nineteenth century, serving, as they did in many European cities in the eighteenth and nineteenth centuries, as meeting places for the more educated sectors of society to discuss politics, read newspapers, and hold literary debates, while having refreshments such as coffee, hot chocolate, and pastries. European café culture of this era is often viewed as a sober social space for middle- and upper-class sociability, but Mexico City's cafés were generally alcoholized social spaces, although their clientele had not always been limited to the elite sectors of society.[47]

Clementina Díaz y de Ovando has shown that, up to the mid-nineteenth century, cafés acted as quite inclusive social spaces for the gathering, communication, and recreation of a range of clientele, including the idle poor, as well as clerics, soldiers, writers, and fashionable ladies. From the middle of the nineteenth century onward, however, many cafés became more cosmopolitan and expensive, often serving imported high-end wines, liqueurs, and cuisine. Consequently they catered more exclusively for the elite sector of society: successful businessmen, hacendados, high-ranking military officers, wealthy foreigners, and prominent public figures. The most renowned and respected of these establishments, including La Gran Sociedad, Café del Bazar, Café del Progreso, Café de la Concordia, and El Tívoli del Eliseo, were all located in either the downtown central area of the city or in the prestigious District Eight to the southwest. Their spatial location within the city reflected the higher degree of respectability and esteem they commanded as social spaces, in comparison to popular drinking places that were located on the impoverished east side and in the other peripheries of the city.[48]

In contrast to the denigration and suspicion that pulquerías and vinaterías received in the Mexican press, cafés were frequently extolled for their finery, excellent produce, and convivial atmospheres in articles and opinion pieces, as well as in advertisements. In 1849 *El Monitor Republicano* described the newly established Café del Bazar with admiration, noting that it was "decorated with the most exquisite taste" and served the "highest quality of coffee, chocolate, liqueurs, etc, etc."[49] The "magnificence" and "luxury" of La Gran Sociedad's decor was extolled by *El Siglo XIX* in 1872, which also detailed its impressive array of wines and edible delicacies imported from France, Germany, England, Holland, and Spain.[50] Advertisements for certain elite drinking places also began to emphasize their special family areas, indicating a desire to portray these establishments as respectable, safe, and orderly social spaces. In February 1872, for instance, the Restaurante del Hotel Iturbide hosted a masquerade ball, serving its usual array of fine wines and French cuisine and reserving "suites and private rooms for families." Providing a more regular service, the Café de la Bella Unión announced the availability of their new "beautiful private rooms" to cater for families, and the Café del Refugio also emphasized its newly expanded area for entertaining families: "In order to provide greater comfort to the families that honor us with their custom, the PRIVATE SUITES and ROOMS in the upper levels of the establishment have been augmented."[51]

Cafés and the grand social occasions they catered for were also credited with providing a social space that fostered harmony between national political rivals. In 1849 *El Monitor Republicano* reported that the Tívoli had been host to "a splendid banquet" for the third and fifth battalions of the National Guard, noting that although they had a history of bitter disputes, "the gathering of all of them in the same place will have given them a mutual satisfaction, and the conviction that the two sides would like to conserve at all costs the greatest harmony between them." Similarly, in 1872, *El Siglo XIX* praised a New Year's banquet held at the elegant Tívoli de San Cosme for its atmosphere of "frank and expansive happiness [and] . . .

sincere and cordial friendship," despite its eighty guests hailing from a range of different political positions. Several other functions at the Tívoli del Eliseo, the Café de la Concordia, and the Tívoli de Petit Versailles also exuded "the greatest harmony and a boundless cordiality," despite the attendance of renowned political opponents. In contrast to the disorder that was frequently associated with popular spaces of sociability, journalists frequently emphasized the harmonizing potential of more elite social spaces to heal political divisions among the middle and upper classes of Mexican society.[52]

This difference between elite and popular social spaces, as spaces of harmony and disorder, was, however, more imagined than real. In 1850 *El Monitor Republicano* reported on a violent disturbance that had occurred in the Café de la Bella Unión when several drunken military sergeants instigated a brawl that resulted in serious injuries to themselves and to the café's staff. Tellingly, the journalist's commentary on this disturbance reveals a social expectation that cafés should be immune to such disorder: "Excesses of this kind are intolerable among the same class of people destined to conserve order, especially in these public establishments where decent people gather, and where one should be able to find shelter from such unforeseen occurrences."[53] The officers' fight was condemned because it besmirched the reputation of a public space that was supposed to offer decent people (the journalist used the term *gente* rather than *pueblo*) a refuge from coming into contact with antisocial behavior, as they might, by implication, expect to find in popular spaces such as pulquerías and vinaterías.[54]

Disruptive incidents continued to occur in more elite social spaces, including cafés and restaurants, in the late nineteenth and early twentieth centuries, but they were not subject to the same alarm and regulatory obsession as more popular social spaces like pulquerías. Café and restaurant proprietors were regularly fined for after-hours sales of alcohol and admittance of customers, despite having much longer opening hours than pulquerías.[55] In August 1912, a ball held at the Salón Reforma on the Calle de Bucareli had to be cut short by the authorities, due to the "drunkenness of many people" and the "great disorder" they were causing, making clear that lower-class pulque drinkers were not the only members of the public to disrupt public decency.[56] There was also something of a double standard in judging café and restaurant proprietors. Even after a café on the Avenida de la Paz had been written up for after-hours sales six times in the space of three months, and reported for harboring prostitutes twice in the same time period, the inspector sent to investigate the establishment refused to order its closure. Recommending instead that the café's license for late opening and music be temporarily withdrawn, he stated that "it has the appearance of a small, modest restaurant, not one of these *fondas* that sells pulque." Again, the implication that the sort of immoral, illegal activity described in these reports was to be expected of pulque-selling venues, but not cafés, is indicative of a significant disparity between the perception and treatment of popular and more elite spaces of sociability.[57]

By the turn of the twentieth century, the liberal authorities had not eliminated the use of popular drinking places as spaces of sociability, but they had largely succeeded in enforcing the spatial boundaries between elite drinking places in the center and southwest of the city and popular drinking places in the city's peripheries. Eastern, southeastern, and northeastern parts of the city, particularly district one around the edges of Lake Texcoco, were neglected, with crowded tenements and irregular neighborhoods providing the living space for the urban poor. The downtown center of the city, which had previously been characterized by a "mixture of wealthy and poor residents," as well as commercial offices and trading

FIG. 3. Charles Burlingame Waite, *Calle des Artes & Paseo de la Reforma, Mexico*, ca. 1904. The photograph shows the wide avenues, historical monuments, and elegant buildings that characterized the Paseo de la Reforma, and the central and southwestern districts of the city in the late nineteenth and early twentieth century. Courtesy of the Getty Research Institute, Los Angeles.

activities, became the hub for large-scale commercial enterprise and finance, while its residential function all but disappeared. With poorer residents clustered on the underdeveloped east side, the elite moved to "more exclusive residential divisions called colonias" to the west of the city. The most exclusive *colonias* developed in the southwestern District Eight, encompassing the Paseo de la Reforma, Chapultepec Castle, and Avenida Juárez, which attracted much investment and was comprised of modern, elite residences, hotels, restaurants, and businesses.[58]

These transformations had a significant effect on the spatial regulation of drinking places in the city. Pulquerías were, again, particularly targeted for marginalization even as their number had grown: in 1901 there were 946 licensed pulquerías and approximately 365 illegal ones. Restrictive laws against pulquerías were passed in 1901–2, echoing previous concerns regarding their contamination of elite social spaces. A new licensing regime banished pulquerías from the areas surrounding the Alameda, Mexico City's central park, where tourists and the city's elite gathered to socialize, and from the southwestern areas of the city that were developing into elite neighborhoods, with elegant residences, fashionable restaurants, and shopping complexes. Although pulquerías did remain in all of the city's eight districts, they were heavily concentrated in districts one and two, in the eastern, poorer areas. They were also required to be located at least sixty meters apart from one another, their opening hours were restricted from 6:00 a.m. to 6:30 p.m., and food, music, games, and seats were prohibited, in a familiar attempt to obstruct their role as spaces for popular social interaction. Additional measures were taken to assist enforcement on this occasion, such as a 1904 municipal law prohibiting the sale of food "in doorways and entrances and especially outside of pulquerías and taverns." Moreover, the city's police force had additional resources at its disposal in the enforcement of these regulations, including "422 mounted police, 1,872 gendarmes on foot, and a corps of secret police" by the beginning of the twentieth century, and these resources were especially concentrated in the central districts of the city.[59]

Also striking about the new waves of regulations against pulquerías at the turn of the twentieth century was their emphasis on hygiene and image. The law passed in 1901 stipulated that all pulquerías were required to install porcelain urinals with running water, which would be subject to regular inspection by the Superior Council of Sanitation. In guidance to police officials issued shortly after the law, the maintenance of hygienic conditions was among several articles singled out for particular attention, since the "dangers of poor sanitation . . . abound in these establishments, not only due to the quality of their goods, but also due to the social class of their patrons."[60] Much of the bureaucratic documentation about pulquerías in the early years of the twentieth century dealt with the new hygiene regulations; in particular, numerous establishments were subject to closure due to the inadequate provision of urinals and general lack of cleanliness that was deemed harmful to public space.[61]

Discussions about the possibility of further extending the exclusionary zone for pulquerías reveal the importance of cleanliness and image, now entwined with older concerns about morality and vice, in driving the segregation of urban space into popular and elite areas. The city council informed the Superior Council for Sanitation in 1907 that the *colonias* of Juárez, Roma, Condesa, San Rafael and Santa María de la Ribera" should be added to the list of areas where new pulquerías could not be established. This measure should be taken "because these areas are inhabited almost exclusively by the civilized [*culta*] classes of Mexican society and foreign families; the elegance of the buildings, both existing and under construction, make these neighborhoods unsuitable for this class of taverns, which are generally frequented by the worst kind of people, with their vice-ridden customs and their lack of cleanliness. Pulquerías are unbecoming for such neighborhoods, in addition to being a serious obstacle to their progress, and to the well-being and safety of their residents."[62] Accordingly, a significant extension to cover most of these neighborhoods in the prestigious southwest of the city was made to the exclusionary zone in 1909.[63]

In contrast to much earlier legislation that required pulquería interiors to be as visible as possible to facilitate surveillance, the 1901 laws required pulquerías within particular areas of the city to be fitted with "blinds that close automatically, similar to those that are used in cantinas," in a deliberate attempt to render pulquerías less offensive to upper- and middle-class sensibilities. Tellingly, both of these new regulations, which were emphasized so heavily for pulquerías within the city, were much less strictly applied to establishments in the federal districts outside the city limits, indicating that the government had fully prioritized the creation of a modern urban image, at the expense of comprehensive surveillance of popular spaces of sociability.[64]

Campaigns to regulate Mexico City's social spaces, targeting popular drinking places in particular, were common to the colonial, early national, and Porfirian periods. Although there were significant continuities across the nineteenth century in regulating popular drinking places, particularly regarding the need to limit their use as spaces of popular sociability, government priorities changed in several ways. In the late colonial period, laws about pulquerías and vinaterías concentrated on balancing the need for surveillance with a desire to rationalize, beautify, and order public space throughout the city, as a means of improving the moral character of all its inhabitants. This tension, between surveillance and urban beautification was complicated in the early republican period by increasingly vocal debates about liberty of commerce, since the practice of restricting pulquería sales to selected public plazas clearly inhibited commercial freedoms. While this debate continued to surround regulatory practices in the mid-nineteenth century, there was an increasing willingness to exclude pulquerías from central and well-to-do districts of the city, with the first restrictive zone being established in 1856, accompanied by the first experiments in making individual customers as equally liable for their behavior in taverns as proprietors. As the Porfirian government sought to make Mexico City an emblem of national modernization and progress, popular drinking places were affected by a more rigidly segregated spatial organization. While increasingly upmarket cafés, restaurants, and social clubs were populating the increasingly fashionable, modernizing, and exclusive central and southwestern areas of the city in the late nineteenth century, pulquerías and other popular drinking places were restricted to the poorer districts and peripheral neighborhoods and were required to adapt their image and condition to the modernizing urban environment with new sanitation and decoration regulations.

The geographical exclusion of popular drinking places from the city center and wealthier neighborhoods was also compounded by their conceptual exclusion from the social space of modern, urban, respectable Mexicans. Despite the diverse ethnic and social makeup of the clientele of late colonial and early republican drinking places, including pulquerías, vinaterías, *and* cafés, the prevailing attitudes regarding their various levels of respectability as social spaces became more rigidly separated as the nineteenth century progressed, mirroring the geographical entrenchment of social divisions into the urban landscape into an elite, respectable, orderly center and southwest and an impoverished, disorderly, and unsanitary east. Yet these boundaries were perhaps less rigid in practice than they were often imagined to be in elite discourse. Despite municipal authorities' and prominent social commentators' desires for the popular and elite classes to each "know their place," cafés were not always the bastions of harmony and order they were hoped to be, nor had the social exchanges and convivial atmospheres long associated with the disorderly social spaces of pulquerías and vinaterías been stamped out.

Drinking Places and Literary Spaces

Nineteenth-century literary representations of Mexico's different drinking places similarly reflect on the social and spatial boundaries that marked out Mexico's elite and popular groups. Mexican costumbrista writers, in particular, endeavored to promote national sociocultural integration through their fictionalized accounts of popular customs, which were designed to render such customs more intelligible to the middle- and upper-class readership of nineteenth-century novels.[65] Costumbrista fictions cannot be taken as historical evidence of the sociocultural practices they often depict—in other words, how ordinary Mexicans actually experienced and practiced everyday activities like visiting a pulquería—but they do provide valuable insights into *elite understandings* of popular culture and how they mobilized popular culture in constructing an imagined nation.

The inclusion of the pulquería and other drinking places in Mexican novels illustrates the desire of Mexican intellectuals to formulate images of nationhood around certain elements of popular culture, while maintaining their own cultural difference from such aspects of popular life. This paradoxical representation exposes many of these intellectuals' anxieties regarding Mexico's potential for national integration in the nineteenth century. Since the writers' own cultural practices and those of the elite population in general were similar to those of the well-to-do in European society, Mexican intellectuals sought alternative, more local sources and features of Mexican culture from which to construct an image of authenticity within their discourse of nationhood. However, the unqualified positioning of popular culture as the foundation of national identity would be problematic, as this would have effectively alienated those intellectuals, and their mainly creole readership, from the very identity that they were trying to create.[66] With such an important public intellectual as Manuel Payno describing the common pulquería in his fiction as one of the most interesting spaces for "those *enlightened and Parisian* Mexicans" to observe the "ancient novelty value" of popular customs, it seems that an investigation of the ways in which various intellectuals portrayed drinking places in their fiction could shed considerable light on the spatial conflict between elite and popular culture in constructions of Mexican nationhood.

From Ordinary Rogues to the Hopeless Masses:
Drinking Places, Social Spaces, and Liberal Reforms

During the course of the nineteenth century, literary representations of drinking places reveal a gradual erosion of elites' faith in the capacity of liberal reforms and education to integrate non-elite groups into a national community as loyal, productive, and responsible citizens. At the beginning of the nineteenth century, José Joaquín Fernández de Lizardi's fiction was filled with proselytizing advice on how to rectify Mexico's social problems through liberal education and the implementation of various reforms in the legal, economic, political, medical, religious, and social realms. His depictions of drinking places portray popular customs as problems to be overcome for the promotion of productivity and social harmony among the population and also indicate the need for creole elites to lead the lower orders in this regard, by example and by instruction. Ignacio Manuel Altamirano's novels of the 1860s and 1870s, by contrast, propose a more accommodating relationship between liberalism and popular culture, drawing on the latter to portray the "authentic" and unique origins of Mexican identity within the "civilizing" context offered by the former. At the end of the century, meanwhile, Ángel de Campo's fiction expresses a growing pessimism regarding the ability of liberal policies to improve the condition of the masses or to ever achieve a "civilized" and inclusive national identity, as drinking places are portrayed as a false source of refuge that helps to keep Mexico City's urban lower classes in a vicious circle of impoverishment.

Mexico's first novelist of the nineteenth century, José Joaquín Fernández de Lizardi (1776–1827), imbued his fiction with the Enlightenment texts and ideas that had permeated the late colonial administration's program of social, economic, and political reforms. Lizardi, also known as El Pensador Mexicano (the Mexican Thinker), was born to a middle-class creole family in Mexico City and became a government administrator in Taxco during his late twenties, supplementing his income from writing. Following a complicated political situation when Taxco was occupied by proindependence rebels during the first stages of the independence wars, which broke out in 1810, Lizardi was briefly imprisoned and lost his government job. Back in Mexico City, Lizardi became actively involved in the burgeoning free press, establishing *El Pensador Mexicano*, one of the city's first nongovernmental periodical publications in 1812. The political commentary and satire produced in the pages of this and other publications earned Lizardi several short stays in prison over the following years, and his fictional writing is often referred to as a strategy for evading censorship and persecution. Fiction also afforded him greater license in exploring alternative visions for society and greater possibilities for engaging a wide readership through entertainment as well as erudition and debate.[67] Drinking and drunkenness featured prominently among the social problems and vices that Lizardi addressed in his work. In an 1825 pamphlet, he argued that habitual drunkenness was one criterion for which a citizen's rights in the new republic should be suspended, and he proposed sentences of up to ten years in public work projects for those appearing drunk and disorderly in public places.[68]

Lizardi's most famous novel, *El Periquillo Sarniento* (The Mangy Parrot), published in 1816, narrates the life story of Pedro, a creole youth from a respectable, moderately wealthy family, who systematically refuses repeated attempts to endow him with a useful education and productive occupation. The novel is a picaresque narrative, with the protagonist being subject to a series of scrapes and adventures as he moves—as idly as possibly—through various social circles, professions, and geographical locations. Often amusing and farcical, the novel is also extremely didactic: Pedro is the foil through which readers are supposed to learn lessons, which are explained, sometimes at great length, by various characters who try to educate Pedro about the ways of the world, social and political injustices, moral improvement, intellectual engagement, reason and rationality, and many other ideals.

The values of work and utility are at the center of the narrative, which also suggests that these values needed to be instilled in Mexico's population through a suitable program of education to facilitate the country's progress. Early in the narrative, Pedro delineates two types of rogues circulating in Mexican society.

> There are two kinds of roguery: one is the dirty, coarse down-and-out kind, like that of the drunken men in blankets who play hopscotch or jackstones on the corners, who fight with each other in the streets, who spout scandalous obscenities, who bring their barefoot, bedraggled *leperuzcas* [low-class women] with them, and who get drunk publicly in the pulquerías and taverns; and these are known as ordinary rascals and *léperos* [uncouth men].

> The other kind of roguery is decent, performed by genteel but prodigal youths, who, for all their cloaks, jackets, and perfumes, are just so many wasters by nature, in perpetual attendance at all social gatherings, gallants of every coquette that happens along, seducers of as many married women as opportunity offers, gamblers, cheats, and swindlers whenever they see the chance, insolent at dances, the terror of guests, intrusive spongers, shameless, impudent, born fools, schemers, everlasting gossips, dressed-up cheats, scandalous, and harmful to the unhappy society in which they live. Such as

these are the respectable rascals and *léperos*, and this class of rascality, I say, I could have taught professionally.[69]

According to Pedro's description the "ordinary" and "respectable" rogues belong to two very different and separate social spaces, but the language used to describe the different spaces indicates that they might not be so different after all. Parallels in terminology—"roguery" (*tunantismo*), "scandalous," "rascals" (*pillos*), "uncouth men" (*léperos*)—as well as the suggestion that the respectable rogues' clothing acted like a mask covering up the more open roguery of the ordinary rogues, compresses the distance between the two social spaces being presented.

The narrative structure of the novel itself destabilizes the boundaries between these two spaces, as Pedro repeatedly moves back and forth between them, despite his confident conviction that he was only the second type of rogue. After losing a sacristy job for stealing valuables from a corpse, Pedro confesses: "I returned to my usual routine of these misadventured adventures. Gambling dens, the streets, pulquerías, and taverns were my usual sanctuaries, and I had no better friends or comrades than cardsharps, drunkards, layabouts, thieves and all manner of *léperos*, so they usually provided me with some cold morsel to eat, lots of drink, and a vile place to sleep."[70] Pedro's subversion of social and spatial boundaries implies that although middle- and upper-class creole society might usually act within more refined, polite sociocultural spaces, in substance they contributed little more to society than the most impoverished, dissipated, and even criminal groups. As a whole, the novel implores creoles with access to wealth, education, and governmental power to take responsibility for the improvement of Mexico's social problems, among which the popular social spaces that developed in pulquerías and on the streets of Mexico City were considered problematic indeed.

During Pedro's first foray into the seedy world of gambling, the impact of delinquent drinking behavior on the country's economic prosperity is made clear when an artisan explains that his refusal to work on Mondays is a common custom known as San Lunes (Holy Monday):

> "You must know that it's a very old and almost incurable abuse among most artisans not to work on Mondays, because of the havoc that remains after a Sunday devoted to drunkenness, and so they call it San Lunes, not because Mondays are days of observance just for being Mondays, but because the absent workmen abstain from working to cure themselves of their drunkenness.". . . "And how do you cure drunkenness?" I asked. "With another bout."[71]

This illuminating discussion occurs the morning after a difficult night spent (not) sleeping in a squalid gambling den that is inhabited by several down-on-their-luck, drunken, naked vagrants. In this scene, Lizardi creates a claustrophobic and oppressive literary space for the reader through Pedro's disgusted and irritated response to the sight, smell, and sounds of the place and the other people in it:

> As the room was small, and my companions the kind of people who dined on cold, dirty food and drank pulque and *chinguirito* [firewater], they were making an almighty cacophony, whose pestilent echoes, without anywhere else to go, came into my poor nostrils, and within moments I had an unbearable headache, such that my stomach could not withstand the smells any longer and I threw up everything I had eaten hours earlier . . . the two of us slept on the billiard table, and between its hard boards, the headache I had, my fear of these naked wretches whom I charitably judged to be mere thieves, the countless lice in the blanket, the rats that wandered over me, a cockerel that fluttered from time to time,

the snores of the other sleepers, the sneezes that came out of their backsides, and the foul stench they produced, I spent a terrible night.[72]

The clash between the squalor of the material setting and its characters and Pedro's delicate constitution recalls the earlier contrast regarding the different types of roguery and the different social spaces in which they were supposed to operate. This passage and the discussion of San Lunes highlight that Pedro, a chronic sponger with delusions of grandeur, is even less inclined to work than the artisans who wile away their Mondays and is more culpable than they are for his dissipated lifestyle since he has been presented with multiple opportunities to gain an education, a good job, and a productive life, all of which he continues to reject until the novel's end. As a whole, the journey of Pedro's character suggests that until social reforms, instigated by privileged creoles such as Pedro, help to instill values of productivity, responsibility, and order at both the highest and the lowest levels of Mexican society, the program for economic and cultural progress advocated by liberal ideas will not bear fruit. The physical protest of Pedro's body—vomiting—against being in a social space that is so unsuitable to him as a creole emphasizes this point; his misplacement in this lower-class social space effectively demands that creoles should embrace their role at the head of Mexican society—and, following the break from Spain, at the head of Mexican politics—to improve conditions in the new nation as a whole.

In the wake of a succession of conflicts between conservative and liberal political groups in the early nineteenth century, some liberal intellectuals began to rethink the more contentious aspects of the liberal agenda. Reforms intended to curtail the power and influence of the Catholic Church, in particular, had been the source of great conflict in Mexican society, and more moderate liberals began to reformulate their position regarding the church in the interests of promoting national unity. This was intended not only to heal divisions among rival elite factions but also to avoid alienating the overwhelmingly Catholic majority of the population in their literary attempts to construct a vision of Mexican nationhood.[73]

In his 1871 romantic novella *La Navidad en las montañas* (Christmas in the mountains), Ignacio Manuel Altamirano (1834–93) outlined a model of liberal integration with the Catholic Church, locating popular rural religion at the center of an authentic Mexican identity that could undergo selected modernizing liberal reforms without losing its unique sense of self. Altamirano was born in the village of Tixtla, Guerrero, to a Nahua Indian family. As his father was the mayor of Tixtla, Altamirano received an unusually comprehensive education for an indigenous child and, after his weak health forced him to withdraw from a blacksmith's apprenticeship, he won a scholarship to study at the Literary Institute of Toluca in 1849, where he also worked as a librarian. From an early age he was a committed liberal activist, leaving his place at the College of San Juan de Letran in Mexico City to participate in the 1854 Revolution of Ayutla, the Reform War, and the liberal campaign against the French in the 1860s. As well as being one of the most successful Mexican novelists of the nineteenth century, Altamirano also wrote much literary criticism, giving support to emerging literary talents, establishing several influential periodicals, including *El Renacimiento*, in 1869, and encouraging the development of a national literature. In addition to his illustrious literary career, Altamirano taught at several Mexico City schools and took up a range of political posts, in the Mexican Congress, in the Supreme Court, in the Ministry of Public Works, and in the diplomatic service.[74]

Recognizing that a staunchly antireligious stance was alienating for the vast majority of the non-elite population, and that the liberal policy of redistributing corporate property was very disruptive to Indian communities in the countryside, Altamirano's literary work postulates a harmonization between the goals of the Catholic Church and those of the liberal state: the village priest acts as the bearer of modernization in his novella. In fact, since the traditions of Mexican Catholicism lay outside a modernizing agenda modeled on European patterns of economic development, Altamirano indicates that popular religious culture could form the basis of an "authentic" national identity, provided, of course, that it was allied to the liberal reform movement. As Edward Wright-Rios notes, *La Navidad* portrays an idealized rural religion as "a sanctified liberalism that unites the book's characters in worship, civic morality, and progress."[75]

In this novella, Altamirano contrasts two situations involving the use of alcohol to delineate an ideally civilized and modern, yet rural and religious, Mexican space and a stereotypically irrational, superstitious, and backward rural village space. The novella describes the transformation of a traditional mountain village into a modestly productive, educated, and polite community, instigated by the enlightened priest who founds schools, introduces technological training, improves agriculture, and eliminates superstitious religious practices without having to resort to the radical reform-era liberal changes.[76] This exemplary community welcomes the narrator, an exiled, liberal army captain, into their midst to celebrate Christmas Eve with a relatively temperate banquet at which alcohol features in gestures of community and hospitality: "Some wine was shared out; the shepherds raised a glass of aguardiente to the health of the magistrate and the curate, and to me they presented a bottle of dry sherry, which is very common in those parts."[77]

Amidst the feast's pleasant, refined, and civilized atmosphere, the newly appointed village schoolteacher discusses his previous experiences in a neighboring village: when he had objected to the local priest's encouragement of idolatry, irrationality, and intolerance, "the townsfolk, drunk and wound up by the curate's sermon, came to my house, took me from it, and brought me to a ravine near here intending to kill me."[78] *La Navidad* thereby demarcates two spaces in which distinct patterns of alcohol use are operating—and, correspondingly, where religious occasions have different content and consequences—which helps to establish his model for liberal progress and to verify its efficacy even in remote, traditional villages. The as-yet-untreated village is volatile, irrational, idolatrous, aggressive, and inclined toward drunkenness, both in physical terms and metaphorically, since the misleading words of their fanatical priest have intoxicated the villagers perhaps as much as any alcohol. By way of contrast, the reformed village has taken in the modernizing knowledge of their priest to create a harmonious, productive, hard-working, hospitable, virtuous community where a more refined, modest style of alcohol use prevails alongside a decorously conducted religious ceremony.

Significantly, Altamirano notes the differentiation between drinks at the latter's banquet, with the humble shepherds drinking aguardiente as they present the respected guest, an army official, with a more sophisticated sherry, but no details are included as to what the angry mob from the neighboring village had inebriated themselves with before attacking the teacher.[79] The hierarchical ordering of drinks according to social status in the exemplar village suggests that for rural popular culture to be afforded a legitimate space within the imagined national identity as the locus of authenticity, it would have to be retained within a stable, recognized, and accepted social order. Meanwhile, in the village given over to superstition and intolerance, the faceless mob is simply drunk, hostile, and destructive, embodying precisely the characteristics that were to be eliminated from the national community for modernization and liberal progress to prosper. Altamirano does not condemn the backward village to oblivion but shows both the continued existence of disordered spaces within the nation in need of taming—through the display of drunken, violent behavior emanating from one such disordered space—and the means to achieve their integration through the model represented in the ideal community, whose members drink harmoniously in their socially ordered space.

In contrast to Altamirano's ideal of harmonious social differentiation integrated within a unified national community, some realist writers at the end of the nineteenth century had all but given up on the prospect of achieving such integration in Mexico. Turning away from the highly stylized and idealized romantic fiction of the earlier nineteenth century, Mexican realists broadly sought to depict their society more objectively through an examination of seemingly banal, everyday occurrences and ordinary, unspectacular characters. Stylistically, this meant more detailed, stark, graphic prose in place of the sentimentalist language, mythological overtones, and idyllic landscapes of historical romantic novels. Thematically, realists frequently focused on social problems, describing the squalor and desperation of everyday life among the lower classes, while also speculating on the causes and possible solutions to these social problems, in the process revealing that their representations were no more "objective" than other literary texts.[80]

Concluding that uncompromised liberal ideals were perhaps impossible to achieve, and questioning the validity of those ideals amid the relative prosperity of the Porfiriato, realist authors such as Ángel de Campo (1868–1908) depicted sharp class distinctions, social injustices, and popular customs with a pronounced air of pessimism. This pessimism was partly a reaction to the curtailment of liberal democratic politics under the strong centralizing government of Porfirio Díaz, as well as an expression of skepticism about the transformative power of policies based on the scientific observation, investigation, and experience of Mexican society, which positivist intellectuals were formulating as a means of encouraging economic development, political unity, and social regeneration.[81]

De Campo communicates his skepticism and pessimism through his portrait of a downtrodden, impoverished, urban, lower class in his collection of short tales, *Ocios y apuntes* (Pastimes and sketches; 1890), and his novella, *La Rumba* (La Rumba; 1890–91).[82] De Campo was born to a middle-class family in Mexico City and worked as a journalist and literature teacher in the National Preparatory School for many years; his minute attention to detail in much of his prose writing earned him the nickname Micros.[83] The drinking places he depicts, providing relief, escapism, or simply a space in which to wallow, are emblematic of his representation of the condition of Mexico's popular classes: unchanging, squalid, and downtrodden.

By the end of the nineteenth century, Mexico City had about one thousand pulquerías and many of them bore romanticized names like Fountain of Love, the Remedy of Heartache, and the Brave, evoking the sense of a space for the popular classes to seek some relief from the hardship of their everyday lives.[84] In the opening passages of *La Rumba*, which describe the neighborhood as a space of poverty, menace, loneliness, monotony, disheveled clothing, and mangy animals, de Campo follows this pattern, naming the local pulquería the Dreams of Armando.[85] Although this pulquería does not feature in the subsequent plot, the inclusion of the name in the initial description of the story's spatial setting foreshadows de Campo's overall depiction of drinking places as spaces of ephemeral but necessary refuge for the miserable popular classes of Mexico City.

De Campo dwells on the inescapability of the lower-class condition through, among other techniques, the portrayal of drinking places as a damaging but ingrained part of popular culture. In "Idilio y elegia" (Romance and elegy), a caretaker called Severiano drinks himself to death after discovering that the woman he loves, the chambermaid Micaela, is having an affair with their employer's son. De Campo declares that Severiano is the "embodiment of the masses" and emphasizes both his character's typicality and doomed nature by describing the object of his affections, Micaela, as "capable of turning the head of a professor of morality. Tall and brown-skinned, a pure-blood Malintzin."[86] Here de Campo echoes a current of intellectual thought in which Malintzin (also known as Malinche or Doña Marina) was decried as a libidinous traitor of the conquest period who betrayed the Mexican people and brought about their downfall through her affair with Hernán Cortés in the sixteenth century.[87]

Having established a correlation between Severiano's own demise and that of the preconquest indigenous population of Mexico, de Campo subsequently portrays habitual drunkenness as part of lower-class sociocultural space, along with poverty, perpetual toil, sickness, and anonymity: "Assisting in the bricklayer's worksite, in the blacksmith's, in the carpenter's workshop; carrying out the orders of an elderly lady, and later being in the spotlight of the bullfights or drunk in the pulquerías. And after crawling through a miserable life, fleeing from education, that mother who opens her arms, to get sick, to die in hospital, to be cut up in the morgue and then on to a common grave. Such are the masses."[88] Severiano's fate imbues a sense of inevitability, predictability, and futility into this literary space so that the reader can imagine a nameless figure from the nameless masses trudging through the prescribed set of places and sociocultural spaces accessible to him. The drinking places are listed as one of the stock spaces of popular culture, usually intended to provide refuge—however temporary, destructive, and futile that refuge might be—from the general misery of working-class life. The pessimistic tone with which de Campo portrays this monotonous and gloomy lifestyle suggests scant possibility of change or improvement. In de Campo's vision, the urban popular classes inevitably turn to the illusory solace afforded them in drinking places, bullfights, and other spaces of popular culture precisely because they are trapped in their social space at the bottom of society, where, he suggests with some dismay, perhaps they belong.

La Rumba reiterates this image of hopelessness regarding the popular classes of Mexico City, through the portrayal of the drinking place as a dangerous and negative, but necessary, part of the sociocultural space in which they live. The "neighborhood cantina" is filled with the "miserable collections of nauseating concoctions, the cheap poisons of the masses," implying its typicality as a lower-class social space. A more extensive description, detailing the sights, sounds, and smells within the cantina, reinforces the sinister, depressing impression: "A thick cloud of cigarette smoke floated in its atmosphere saturated by alcohol. Artisans were bruising each other in the corner; the cobbler carrying his cuttings of soles, the carpenter his brace, the porter his mule, and they asked, they asked with fury and in high voice, for drink after drink, measure after measure."[89] Reminiscent of Lizardi's seedy gambling hall, de Campo's smoke- and alcohol-filled room has an overbearing atmosphere that seems to contribute to the frenzied demands for alcohol of the workers inside.

Yet the stock descriptions of each worker, characterized only by the tools he needs to do that work, give the impression that these typified drinkers are such cantina regulars that they equally shape the nature of the space they frequent. In contrast to Lizardi's scene, in which Pedro is so out of place in the lower-class social space that his body physically rejects it, in de Campo's portrait, drinker and cantina become a symbiotic whole, each giving rise to the other, just as the impoverished condition of the working classes and the undesirable elements of popular culture were thought to reproduce one another. Whereas El Pensador Mexicano used Pedro's social boundary-crossing behavior to highlight the potential of reforming and improving ordinary Mexicans, de Campo's depiction of the drinker and cantina in a symbiotic relationship reflects a more pessimistic outlook, according to which government programs for education and positivist reform were incapable of effecting real social change or national integration.

Instead, the conclusion to *La Rumba* suggests that the lower classes would be better off left to their own devices, living lives that are suited to their condition, without the temptations of greater wealth, education, and high society. Dissatisfied with her life in the neighborhood as the daughter of a drunken blacksmith, the heroine, Remedios, defies her father's wish for her to marry the local cantina owner, to elope with a well-to-do Spaniard, Napoleón Cornichón. If Mauricio's cantina is an emblem of lower-class sociocultural space in general, and of the lower classes' confinement within that space, then Remedios's rejection of Mauricio can be read as her rejection of sociospatial boundaries. Life with Cornichón, however, proves even worse for Remedios, as he fails to support her financially and becomes an increasingly violent alcoholic. Remedios is left destitute at the end of the novel, after being prosecuted for Cornichón's murder, and realizes the value of her previous simple life with her family, having lost it forever.

Twice in the novella, Remedios's boundary-defying behavior is attributed to her education. The local priest chastises

her mother, rather significantly named Porfiria, for allowing Remedios to study such things as physics, arithmetic,
and geometry, and he identifies this as the source of her
rebelliousness. Again, in the prosecutor's damning statement at the end of Remedios's trial, her education beyond
the realm of domestic skills and responsibilities is portrayed
as a contributing factor to her supposedly cold-blooded murder of Cornichón.[90] Although the latter's death had actually been an accident in the midst of his drunken attack
against Remedios, and so no causal link between her education and homicidal tendencies is definitively portrayed,
de Campo does reiterate that by encouraging her to try to
climb up the social ladder and cross sociospatial boundaries, Remedios's education had contributed to her downfall,
a conclusion that could hardly contrast more with Lizardi's
ardent faith in the socially transformative power of education, especially for women.[91]

Remedios herself acknowledges that she should have recognized the value of her prior humble existence as a poor
blacksmith's daughter betrothed to a poor shopkeeper and
bound within a prescribed sociocultural space. This, together
with the emphasis on the detrimental effects of her education, implies that not only for their own benefit, but for
the greater good of society, the lower classes should remain
precisely that—low. Although de Campo differed from his
predecessors like Lizardi and Altamirano in his abnegation
of education as a potential source of social improvement
and national integration, the anxiety expressed about the
consequences of the lower orders trying to improve their
social station and move beyond popular sociocultural spaces
became an increasingly consistent feature of nineteenth-
century Mexican literature.

Everything in Its Right Place? Finding a Space for
Popular Culture in Mexico's Imagined Nationhood

The careful differentiation of drinks according to social status in Altamirano's exemplar village suggested that for rural popular culture to be afforded a legitimate space within national identity as the locus of authenticity, it would have to be retained within a stable, recognized, and accepted social order. Although Altamirano undoubtedly supported the program of liberal reforms designed to raise levels of education, productivity, and integration among the urban and rural lower classes, his fictional portrait of an ideal community that had a carefully delineated and accepted social hierarchy reveals a latent anxiety that such reforms could seriously destabilize Mexico's social structure. Both José Tomás de Cuéllar and Manuel Payno dealt with this same dilemma by granting popular drinking cultures a space signifying authenticity within their fictional visions of national identity. Like Altamirano, they also granted this space on the condition that it was confined to the lower end of the social ladder, at a considerable distance from elite sociocultural space, which in turn—for them—signified the dignity and legitimacy of the Mexican nation on the international stage.

José Tomás de Cuéllar (1830–94), also known by the pseudonym Facundo, was a satirical novelist, journalist, and dramatist famous for his series of short novels called La linterna mágica (The magic lantern). These are often described as photographic snapshots of Mexican society, but ones which had a sharply critical framing, particularly when examining the emergent middle class. De Cuéllar actually studied photography and painting for a time, after serving as a military cadet in the 1847 defense of Chapultepec Castle when the North American army occupied Mexico City, and later held several posts in the Mexican diplomatic service.[92] The magic

lantern series, published between 1871 and 1892, highlights
the need for Mexican literature to address popular culture as
a means of defining the features that constituted Mexicanness: "This is the magic lantern: it brings neither customs
nor patents from abroad; everything is Mexican, everything is
ours, important to us alone; and leaving aside Russian prin-
cesses, dandies, and the kings of Europe, we shall be enter-
tained by the woman in traditional dress, the street bum, the
fashionable young lady, the actress, the Indian, the liberal
soldier, the shopkeeper, and all that is here." The author also
notes that the Magic Lantern was the name of "a pulquería
in a small town" that he saw in passing, indicating that the
drinking place would be a pertinent window of observation
in his fiction and that the demarcation of particular sociocultural spaces for different social groups would be a feature of
his vision for society.[93]

In "Baile y cochino" (Dancing and piggery), de Cuéllar satir-
ically ridicules the vain attempts of a nouveau-riche family to
situate themselves within elite sociocultural space by throwing a lavish, luxurious ball in their newly acquired, stately
home. The head of this family orders expensive champagnes
and liqueurs, delectable foods, lavish decorations, music, and
outfits, all constituting the extravagant accoutrements that
such occasions typically featured. Despite the high-end provisions, the ball quickly descends into a chaotic mêlée involving
extreme drunkenness, indecent dancing, and violence.[94] Chapter 8, entitled "How the Heat from Candles, Combined with a
Fine Cognac and Other Evils, Usually Creates Pandemonium
at a Ball," is told through a comic, mock-operatic tone and
structure, in which the tension builds during Perico's swirl-
ing, passionate dance with the attractive Gumesinda before the
room erupts into panic when he collapses. At this point, the
rest of the guests break into violent hysterics thinking Perico
is dead, when he is merely drunk, having rapidly consumed

large quantities of a very expensive cognac. Saldaña, the family friend who had orchestrated all the arrangements for the ball on behalf of his patron Don Bartolo, and who had tried to hide this expensive cognac for himself, attempts to wrest the situation back under control, before eventually giving up, hiding in a cupboard, and—naturally enough—falling asleep.

De Cuéllar sets Saldaña up for this humiliating fall, portraying him as a social hypocrite, who tries to simultaneously occupy elite and popular sociocultural spaces. Mocking Don Bartolo's lack of taste and refinement, Saldaña conspires with the wine merchant Don Quintin Gutiérrez to overcharge his patron:

> "Is he a connoisseur?" Don Quintin asked him. "Get out of here! A connoisseur indeed! Do you remember the Chateau Larouse we tasted the other day?" "Yes." "He thought it was horrible. He is one of these people who get rich overnight and thinks that's enough to know all about these things. That's right, he pretends to be very elegant and refined and he loves anything that's expensive." "Well then, in that case we'll draw up a special bill for him."[95]

It quickly becomes evident, however, that Saldaña is guilty of pretensions himself. Not long after visiting the wine merchant, Saldaña visits Lupe, the mother of his children, with a range of foods typical of the Mexican popular classes, including enchiladas, tortillas, beans, and a pail of pulque.[96] This common mestiza is the most sympathetically portrayed character in the piece as she remains true to her humble Mexican identity. Lupe feels out of place at the luxurious, pretentious ball and de Cuéllar makes it clear that she ought to; as a poor mestiza, her proper place is in her simple home in the barrios, eating beans and tortillas, and drinking pulque. By characterizing Lupe as an ordinary, lower-class woman who has no aspirations to a higher social position and is more comfortable in humble, modest, and down-to-earth surroundings, de Cuéllar establishes an appropriate space in which popular culture—here represented by common foods and pulque—should reside. Moreover, Lupe's acceptance and embrace of her own, lower social position is contrasted with the socially aspiring Saldaña and the pretensions of the middle classes who try to adopt the trappings of elite sociocultural spaces.

Lupe conducts herself honestly according to her sociospatial position, as a Mexican mestiza should, while Saldaña has to confront the consequences of his and his employers' farcical attempts to emulate elite, French-influenced cultural practices. Upon waking in the cupboard where he had been hiding from the chaotic, drunken violence, Saldaña faces a "scene of debauchery that had only recently been abandoned by human beasts."[97] De Cuéllar describes the transformation of the previously glamorous, luxurious ballroom into a filthy, abhorrent space filled with noxious, repellent sights, smells, and sounds that have been created by the expensive delicacies that were misused by the out-of-place, socially aspiring guests:

> A kind of alcoholic vapor went out through the doors of the dining room and ballroom; it was a human vapor but so heavy that it almost dragged along the ground, as if it did not want to clash with the clean, diaphanous atmosphere of the dawning day. . . . The carpet was impregnated with wine and sewn with shards of glass; there was gruyere cheese on the armchairs, under the table, inside the glasses, and on the hats. . . . The table bore all the carnage of a battlefield, because there were more glasses and bottles knocked over and broken than there were remained standing.[98]

By forsaking more typically Mexican forms of entertainment in an attempt to portray themselves as sophisticated, refined, and wealthy elites, most of the hosts and guests at the ball expose their more base tendencies and origins. This does not simply suggest that middle- and lower-class Mexicans per se were incapable of conducting themselves with decorum; Lupe's manners and comportment are impeccable even as she remains uncomfortable and awkward in the ballroom. The drunken denouement to the ball instead conveys both the need to locate a source of unique and authentic Mexican cultural identity and the dangers to that identity posed by the transgression of sociospatial boundaries.[99] By adopting the trappings of elite cultural spaces—the expensive cognac, champagne, French furnishings, fashions and dances—middle- and lower-class mestizos not only debased those cultural spaces for "real" elites but also threatened to devalue the potential that popular cultural spaces—inhabited by pulque, beans, tortillas, and figures such as the humble Lupe—had for the expression of a unique and authentic national identity.

This double-edged proposition is further exemplified in the narrative's treatment of another mestiza, Leonor Machuca, who differs markedly from the humble Lupe. The Machucas are another recently moneyed family, having profited from connections forged during Porfirio Díaz's rise to political power in his 1876 military coup. Leonor and her two sisters "had the appearance of belonging to the Caucasian race, as long as they wore gloves, but when they took them off, the hands of La Malinche appeared on the marble bust of Ninon de Lenclos. As long as they didn't speak, they appeared quite refined; but their tongues, in the basest of treacheries, would always betray them."[100] Again, the figure of Malinche is invoked to foreground the issue of betrayal. In this case, the Machuca sisters have betrayed their true identities, having abandoned their sociocultural space as humble mestizas.

The futility of Leonor's attempt to hide her social origins is eventually exposed through her drinking habits and behavior at the ball. Leonor's suitor, Enrique Pérez Soto, is a cultured and wealthy Mexican elite who has traveled widely and been educated in Germany. Although his friends warn him that "she drinks like a fish," Enrique at first remains reluctant to believe that such an elegantly dressed woman could have "such a repugnant flaw as drunkenness." His illusions are completely dispelled, however, as she admits to drinking six cognacs and a lot of champagne at the ball, an event and social space that should, in the appropriately upper-class context, be a space for refinement, connoisseurship, and polite courtship. Leonor's elegant façade crumbles as she becomes drunk and Enrique fully appreciates her common voice, vulgarity, stupidity, proclivity for gambling, and, of course, her habitual drunkenness. Enrique concludes, "She has evaporated; she doesn't exist, she never existed. Therefore, I am a free man, and shall return to Europe."[101]

This rather dramatic statement—negating Leonor's very existence—in the midst of a largely comic narrative, constitutes de Cuéllar's warning for Mexican society. Having rejected her humble mestiza roots, Leonor has been corrupted by her desire to become accepted in a social space in which, like the humble Lupe, she does not belong. In trying to emulate elite culture, an endeavor that she lacks the social breeding to pull off, Leonor only manages to humiliate herself and to drive away the educated, elite man with whom she ought never to have been involved. More ominously for Mexican nationhood, her effective nonexistence foreshadows the fate that could await distinctively Mexican elements of national culture and identity, if those who should embody them cease to do so. De Cuéllar's approving portrayal of Lupe as a docile, humble mestiza enjoying her pulque in the barrios of Mexico City suggests that, in its proper social space, popular culture could be a central feature of imagined national identity, since it offered a uniquely Mexican, "authentic" character. If non-elites like Leonor abandoned this popular culture in favor of elite cultural norms, which they would inevitably debase, the authentic aspect of national culture and identity would be lost in the midst of a botched version of elite, European-inspired cultural practices.

Manuel Payno's major novels, *El fistol del Diablo* (The Devil's scarf pin; 1845–46) and *Los bandidos de Río Frío* (The bandits of Río Frío; 1888–91) also exhibit pronounced anxieties about the permeation and permeability of sociospatial boundaries, while simultaneously recognizing the need to afford popular culture a space in Mexico's national identity as the locus of its authenticity.[102] These novels combine political commentary on contemporary events, realist costumbrista sketches of Mexican middle- and lower-class cultural habits, and romantic melodrama in complex, suspense-driven plots involving several different interweaving stories. Payno was a prominent public figure throughout the second half of the nineteenth century, holding administrative, advisory, and ambassadorial offices within successive governments. Of a moderate political persuasion, Payno examined a rich mosaic of Mexican cultural customs, as well as the causes of Mexico's social problems and inequalities, in his fiction and in his many contributions to periodical publications such as *El Monitor Republicano, El Siglo XIX,* and *El Federalista.*[103] As alluded to in the quotation with which this chapter begins, the double-edged tension between the need to provide a space for popular culture within constructions of Mexican identity while maintaining a degree of spatial distance between popular and elite culture is most prominent in Payno's treatment of drinking places, particularly the pulquería.[104]

In addition to the figurative associations between the pulquería of the "beautiful Xóchitl" with American and preconquest identities, Payno elsewhere links pulque drinking, as a characteristic feature of popular cultural spaces, to a more contemporary, concrete idea of what it meant to be an archetypal Mexican. From the very beginning of *Los bandidos*, the honest, hard-working, modest, rural family of the mestiza, Doña Pascuala, her Indian husband, Espiridión, and their son, Moctezuma III, enact the typical values associated with popular rural cultural spaces, including the consumption of indigenous food and drinks like tortillas, tamales, atole, and tlachique, a sweetened low-grade pulque.[105] During his courtship of Cecilia, a Mexico City market trader, the wealthy official Lamparilla is treated to a traditional Mexican meal of tortillas, eggs, and chili when he remarks "This dish, which a Frenchman would call the disgusting concoction of savages, is among the best that one could ask for, and if you had some flavored pulque, I could wish for nothing more."[106] Tortillas and pulque, then, although typical features of popular social spaces, ought to be appreciated even by the sophisticated French and, by implication, those "enlightened and Parisian" Mexican elites who showed disdain for popular culture in general. The suggestion here is perhaps that Mexican elites had become too spatially distant from the features of popular culture that were traditionally, authentically, and uniquely Mexican.

In *El fistol del Diablo*, Payno narrates an incident in which mourners at the funeral of Pablo Argentón, a reckless businessman and gambler, represent themselves as more or less Mexican in the food and drinks they choose: "Some ate lunch at ten, dinner at four, had chocolate or something sweet during prayers, and had supper at eleven; some, after the French manner, had lunch at noon and dinner at seven in the evening, not forgetting their Bordeaux or sherry; the ones who called themselves Mexicans above all, were not without pulque, *molito de pecho* [a rustic kind of stew], and refried beans for their supper."[107] The phrase "the ones who called themselves Mexicans," however, suggests that the consumption of traditionally Mexican fare was a *performance* of authentic

Mexican identity that could be rendered unstable if the wrong people—that is, those who were acting outside of their appropriate social space—took part in such a performance.

Indeed, Payno alludes to the ephemeral and often hypocritical nature of such self-representations by exploring the transgression of sociospatial boundaries and the potential for societal chaos when the ideally distant spaces of elite and popular culture intersect. In the midst of a popular festival in the Belén barrio of Mexico City, a group of almost cartoonlike caricature villains, with names such as Culebrita (Little Snake), Diablo (Devil), Muerte (Death), and Zorro (Fox), gather in a run-down house located in the "gloomy alleyways" of Belén. The place as a whole is scattered with dirty, worn-out furniture, and the peeling walls are covered with images of saints and soldiers, making it a popular yet sinister space that carries none of the romantic, rustic beauty or figurative associations with the preconquest culture of the pulquería in Puente de la Leña. The criminals are seated around a dirty, uncovered wooden table bearing a container of *sangre de conejo*.[108] They are plotting the robbery of a wealthy, corrupt official, Don Pedro, who is the major villain in the novel, masterminding an elaborate network of treachery and embezzlement. During the robbery itself, the thieves raid Pedro's larder and indulge in his luxurious champagne, wines from Burgundy, and imported cheeses, a trio of products generally associated with elite sociocultural spaces. Amused by his protests and feeling mischievous after drinking his expensive liquors, they then force him to humiliate himself by dancing a vulgar popular dance: "As the champagne had produced some effect, the thieves were adamant they wanted to see him dance the jorobante."[109]

Pedro had abused his position as a member of the social elite, a status that is signified through his sophisticated tastes in food and drinks; Payno then transfers these signifiers of elite culture to the normally pulque-drinking ruffians to inflict a traumatic social inversion on Pedro as poetic justice for his crimes against society, commenting wryly that "everything is compensated for in this world."[110] Payno is not, however, sympathetic to the bandits, and this incident does not advocate the exclusion of elite culture from Mexican society. Indeed, that the bandits are first encountered in a sinister and disheveled place, drinking *sangre de conejo*, a beverage that Payno seems to preserve for his descriptions of particularly aberrant behavior, suggests that we are not really meant to approve of their actions, even though their crime inflicts a just comeuppance upon Pedro.[111] It is Pedro's deviant behavior that warrants his humiliation by common criminals. The uncomfortable portrait of social inversion is meant to highlight that Pedro is, in reality, no better than the thieves who attack him. His own corruption and criminality mean that he is no longer entitled to partake of elite cultural consumption and to move through elite social spaces.

Los bandidos also raises concerns about the denigration of uniquely Mexican popular culture, as we see the transformation of a quaint and charming pulquería into a squalid den of crime and violence, through the combined influence of unscrupulous bandits at the lowest end of the social scale and a wealthy, corrupt, military official who ought to be leading his country from the top in a time of national crisis. Relumbrón, a fictional incarnation of a senior military official of the Santa Anna era (Colonel Juan Yañez), assumes control of an elaborate system of organized crime, of which the bandits are a fundamental component.[112] His fraudulent credentials are underscored by his predilection for luxurious European fashions, furnishings, wines, and delicacies, which cultivate a respectable image that masks his gambling addiction, loveless marriage, and illegal activities. As in the case of Pedro in *El fistol del Diablo*, the characteristics of elite cultural space are used to foreground the hypocrisy and self-serving behavior of certain members of the elite social class who betray their responsibilities, as elites, to work for the good of the nation.

To serve as the base for Relumbrón's criminal activities, the bandits take over a once-famed pulquería in Mexico City, renowned for its friendly, traditional atmosphere, decor, and merchandise: "a large pulquería that captured one's attention, due to the images of Xóchitl and Netzahualcóyotl painted in vibrant colors on the wall's white façade . . . with good will, the owner offered the services of his wife to cater for their every wish, as he was accustomed to do for all his customers, to prove the famous pulquería de Xóchitl's worth, selling the finest pulques from the plains of Apam."[113] Again drawing on Xóchitl, as well as Netzahualcóyotl, the Texcocan philosopher-king, to highlight the traditional, uniquely Mexican nature of the pulquería, Payno constructs a hospitable, positive image of a popular cultural space.

Under Relumbrón's direction, however, this pulquería becomes an iniquitous recruiting ground for bandits. Despite the accoutrements associated with elite sociocultural space that Relumbrón introduces, including elegant white tables, porcelain crockery, "fine wines and the delicious Gambrinus beer," the renovated pulquería becomes the frequent scene of drunken brawls, licentious behavior, gambling, and, of course, criminal conspiracies.[114] The damage Relumbrón does to Mexican culture in the defamation of the once highly regarded pulquería mirrors the much more serious damage to Mexican society inflicted by his ring of organized crime. As the bandits begin to target ordinary, relatively poor victims instead of wealthy landowners and become increasingly violent, Relumbrón loses control of the gang's activities. He is eventually caught and publicly executed. Upon witnessing this, Relumbrón's estranged mother is so disturbed that she is committed to a mental hospital.

FIG. 4. José Guadalupe Posada, *Expendio de pulque de la Hda. de Sn. Nicolás El Grande* (Pulquería of the hacienda of Nicolás the Great), no date. Woodcut, 22.5 x 33.5 cm. Fondo Francisco Díaz de León, Museo Andrés Blaisten, Mexico City. Posada was a prolific illustrator, whose work featured prominently in the Porfirian press. The rustic appearance of this rural pulque outlet, with painted wooden barrels in the background and a cross-section of different Mexican social types, invokes the kind of pulquería that Manuel Payno celebrates in his fiction as a symbol of Mexican culture. Courtesy of Museo Andrés Blaisten.

In interpreting this episode, Adriana Sandoval places greater emphasis on the contrasting models of motherhood that Payno constructs to advocate social mobility and mestizaje as the future of the Mexican nation. Relumbrón's anonymous upper-class mother abandons her son because he was conceived with a lowly male artisan, while the central heroine, Mariana, endures many trials and tribulations to overcome the class divide that separates her from her beloved and their son. Mariana and her family are eventually reunited and live happily ever after, while Relumbrón and his mother meet traumatic ends. The better outcome for the family that actively transgresses traditional social boundaries thus suggests that Payno advocated greater social mobility for Mexico to prosper.[115]

While this is a compelling interpretation, Payno's treatment of drinking places reveals that he also had significant anxieties about social mobility and the potential disorder that could be caused by the transgression of elite and popular sociospatial boundaries. Payno's concern for the erosion of romanticized elements of popular culture echoes José Tomás de Cuéllar's anxieties as evidenced in the projected nonexistence of Leonor Machuca. In Payno's case, it is Relumbrón, a corrupt member of elite society, rather than a socially ambitious mestiza, who is the agent of change bringing about the destruction of Mexico's "authentic" culture. Like Leonor, Relumbrón confuses sociospatial boundaries, descending from his elite social space into a corrupt, criminal underworld, and because he tries to import the accoutrements of elite social space into the popular space of the pulquería, he corrupts that as well. Only after Relumbrón assumes control of the bandits' operations do innocent, ordinary citizens become the victims of robbery, rape, and murder. Relumbrón is responsible for this wave of destruction, which is foreshadowed by his corruption of the renowned pulquería. His violation of sociospatial boundaries and his interference in a space usually reserved for popular culture greatly exacerbates the damage to Mexican society caused by the bandits' activities.

Should we conclude, then, that for Payno, elite rather than popular culture posed the greatest threat to the consolidation of an inclusive, authentic national identity? Although the destruction of the pulquería through Relumbrón's interference suggests a distrust of an elite culture that was increasingly influenced by foreign tastes and practices, Payno's treatment of other drinking places, including other pulquerías, does not fully support this conclusion. Although the "pulquería de los 'Pelos'" is (like the pulquería de Xóchitl) associated with "times before the Conquest" to create a cultural space of authenticity, it is in this place that another villain, Evaristo, drinks himself into a frenzy before murdering his wife.[116] Clearly, therefore, Payno's work does not portray a uniformly positive image of pulquerías as the loci of Mexican history, culture, and identity but also includes negative representations of pulquerías as centers of lower-class drunkenness and violence. The larger concern seems to be a confusion of boundaries between elite and popular sociocultural spaces and the respective roles elite and popular culture could play in the formation of an imagined national identity.

In *El fistol del Diablo*, Payno establishes a clear contrast between the atmosphere, clientele, and behavior of popular and elite drinking places only to later show how unstable such distinctions were. El Sol Mexicano (the Mexican Sun) is portrayed as a very basic *tienda*, or shop, selling aguardiente alongside other general groceries, operating on an informal system of credit, and serving as a gambling venue for its generally lower-class customers. Although it is supposed to close at nine o'clock in the evening, the owners often host lock-ins for their regulars. On one such occasion, Payno shows the dark side of tavern culture, as a raucous card game descends into bloody murder. Culebrita and Juan el Atrevido (the Bold), two of the villains involved in robbing Pedro, become embroiled in a violent dispute over possession of the *fistol*, the precious, mysterious scarf pin of the novel's title, as jealousy, wounded pride, and drunkenness combine to instigate bloodshed. The two men are described as "drunk on anger as well as liquor, with daggers in their hands, ready to kill each other."[117]

Only Juan is fatally injured and, although the shop owner, Mariano, promises not to alert the authorities, El Sol Mexicano is mysteriously burned down within a week, killing most of the family and servants, and leaving the *fistol* shimmering amid the ashes. The involvement of the *fistol* is noteworthy since, for most of the novel, it tends to foreshadow impending doom for the person to whom its possession passes illegally, and so there is an element of inescapability regarding Juan's fate that perhaps reduces the significance of the place in which he met with his sticky end. However, the regularity of drunken violence in popular drinking places such as the shop is emphasized, as Mariano muses in the aftermath of Juan's murder that he wishes he and his adopted family could escape: "We no longer need to have such a rough life, always dealing with drunkards and thieves . . . we could look for a quiet town or a farm where we could make an honest living. . . . But, so help me God, these men have forbidden me to move!"[118] Payno thus establishes the shop as part of a network of urban social spaces inhabited by criminals, which also trapped sectors of the urban poor who had no alternative to an unsavory, unproductive, and dangerous lifestyle.[119]

In stark contrast to the dark and dangerous drinking place of the lower classes, Payno describes a much more elegant and ordered social space that exists in the same city yet seems almost of another world altogether. The Café del Progreso, one of Mexico City's most prestigious real-life cafés, is transposed into Payno's novel as a fashionable place for elite, worldly men to meet, discuss current affairs, conduct their business, and play billiards and dominos. In contrast to Mariano's law-flouting shop, our narrator notes that the café has strictly observed opening hours between six and ten o'clock in the evening and the more sophisticated, and expensive, cognac and hot chocolate are served. Unlike the popular *tienda* and other drinking places in the novel that do not conform to legal requirements, the café plays no major role in the novel's plot and relatively little discussion is devoted to its role as a social space in Mexican society.

To further emphasize the distance between the elite, orderly, social space of the café and that of the shop, the narrator states that the café environment has been adopted from the customs of the "Orientals," which is a striking representation in light of the much more obvious influence of elite French and Western European cultural practices.[120] In combination with the café's minor role in the novel and its orderly observation of the law, the implication that the Café del Progreso derives its sophistication from exotic, Asian cultural influences creates the impression that such sophistication is beyond the reach of the majority of the population; and for those elites who could enjoy it, the café represents an artificial means of distancing themselves from the realities of Mexican society.

The complete opposition set out between the lowly shop and the sophisticated café, and the popular and elite cultural spaces that they represent, is subsequently collapsed through the events that occur in a makeshift cantina set up to serve the largely upper-class *polko* (moderate) battalions of Mexico City's National Guard, as they fight against the rival lower-class *puro* (radical) battalions for control of the capital. The same Mariano who had run the ill-fated *tienda* establishes a pleasant cantina, stocked with wines and assorted liqueurs, where two of the novel's main protagonists, Arturo and Josesito, now enlisted in the *polko* battalions, enjoy a friendly welcome from the other men and a nice evening of eating, drinking, and relaxing. The narrator suggests that this conviviality represents the calm before a storm: "It was like a family, and the war was turned into a party. Such are the Mexicans." Predictably, when the party turns to the swapping of stories among the men, a serious fight breaks out. Amid the chaos, an onlooker comments, "The barracks made up of respectable and well-educated people had turned into a tavern," before Arturo remembers his manners and arranges a duel with his opponent.[121] The cantina's environment of conviviality and camaraderie among the well-to-do clientele becomes not so different from the confrontational, violent scene previously played out in the lower-class *tienda*. The contrast set up between the popular shop and the elite café in their respective drinks and patterns of behavior is broken down in this cantina scene, which combines the more sophisticated wine and liqueurs normally furnishing elite cultural spaces like cafés, with the rough-and-tumble behavior usually associated with popular drinking spaces like the *tienda*, tavern, or pulquería. Set against the context of the *polko-puro* conflict that divided Mexico City's National Guard along class lines in a time of national crisis, this episode allegorizes the danger that such an internal conflict posed to Mexican nationhood.

These episodes, however, do not advocate the dissolution of class divisions per se; on the contrary, they suggest that popular and elite groups should confine themselves to their respective social spaces and behave appropriately, in order to avoid the kind of social conflict that the *polko-puro* struggle epitomized. The outbreak of violence of the kind usually confined to popular social spaces in this more elite space highlights an intellectual anxiety about the confusion of social boundaries. The internal struggles within Arturo's battalion are played out in this hybrid drinking space, which combines an elite clientele and expensive drinks typical of elite drinking places with a lower-class pattern of behavior. This is suggestive of a larger fear that once the different social classes began to challenge the existing social order in open conflict, the integrity of previously coherent social groups could crumble, leaving the Mexican nation vulnerable to attack from external forces and national identity a fantasy. In *El fistol del Diablo*, this threat becomes reality, as the North American army finally manages to defeat the Mexican troops shortly after the resolution of the *polko-puro* conflict. The central characters acknowledge their patriotic duties too late and the novel closes in a night of chaos, with most of the main protagonists dead or near death.

Although Payno follows the standard historical interpretation of Mexico's defeat in the Mexican-American War by emphasizing the weakness created by internal divisions, the association of the *polko-puro* conflict with the cantina that subverted the social boundaries of other drinking places suggests that the novel's denouement amid military defeat also serves as a warning against challenges to the existing social order and against the confusion of social boundaries.[122]

Conclusion

With the new addition of this denouement in the 1887 edition of *El fistol del Diablo*, Manuel Payno shared common concerns with other intellectuals of the later nineteenth century, including Manuel Ignacio Altamirano, José Tomás de Cuéllar, and Ángel de Campo, regarding the consequences of social change for Mexican stability. Although Payno's pulquería de Xóchitl, de Cuéllar's pulque-drinking mestiza Lupe, and Altamirano's rural religious festival sought to locate an authentic and unique Mexican identity in popular drinking places and spaces, the place of popular culture in their imagined vision of nationhood remained problematic. The transformation of the pulquería through Relumbrón's superficial imposition of elite cultural attributes, the negation of the socially ambitious Leonor's existence, the strict differentiation of social groups participating in the religious festival, the vulnerability portrayed in the cantina-tavern hybrid, all betray a deep-seated anxiety about spaces of interaction between elite and popular culture, the confusion and dissolution of sociospatial boundaries, and the ramifications of this for Mexico's nationhood.

Over the course of the nineteenth century, the increasingly stringent regulation of popular drinking places did reflect a partial segregation of popular and elite social spaces in Mexico City. While pulquerías and vinaterías were restricted to poorer and peripheral areas of the city, and their patrons' behaviors were subjected to numerous legal controls, cafés became more socially exclusive in terms of their clientele, more cosmopolitan and expensive in terms of their produce, and more numerous in the prestigious central and southwestern districts of the city. The regulations applied to popular drinking places gradually became more concerned with segregating and hiding from view the activities that went on these places than with putting a stop to them, as pulquerías in particular were excluded from the genteel areas of the city, subjected to sanitary inspections, and ordered to clean up their image. However, the spatial organization of Mexico City's drinking places, into disorderly popular venues like pulquerías and harmonious elite spaces like cafés, was often more imagined than real. What remained consistent were the conceptions held by elite public figures and governing officials that elite social spaces *should* be bastions of order, while they felt it was, however regrettably, to be expected that popular social spaces would remain disorderly and in constant need of restriction, regulation, and surveillance.

This expectation that elite and popular social spaces, and consequently, elite and popular social actors, should be readily distinguishable is equally evident in literary representations of Mexican drinking places concerned with constructing and exploring Mexican nationhood, as it is from government policies and journalists' comments regarding pulquerías and other popular drinking places. Lizardi's fiction, in the early nineteenth century, employed a boundary-crossing figure in *El Periquillo Sarniento,* with Pedro moving between elite social spaces and lower-class drinking places, to advocate liberal education and reform. But this novel did not address the issue of an inclusive sense of nationhood; instead, it dwelt upon the improvement of the creole population in order that they (the creoles) be better equipped to govern the newly independent Mexico and its greater population of mestizos and Indians. As the nineteenth century progressed and liberal reforms began to have an impact on this larger population, and intellectuals were endeavoring to define and portray Mexican nationhood, popular drinking places were depicted as spaces for the enactment of popular culture that could become the locus of authenticity and uniqueness in that vision of nationhood.

Simultaneously, however, these fictional representations of drinking places conveyed the perceived dangers that popular culture posed to society and nationhood if it were not kept in its appropriate social space. Indeed, in de Campo's work, liberal policies of education and reform were decried as not only useless but harmful to the popular classes and to the nation as a whole precisely because they were thought to encourage the popular classes, and the popular culture they were representing, to move beyond their appropriate social space. Although intellectual attitudes varied toward the efficacy of liberal policies in improving the condition of Mexico's population, a striking consolidation in levels of unease at the prospect of significant social change is visible in fictional representations of drinking places in the later stages of the nineteenth century. Popular culture could only be included in elite constructions of national identity if it remained at a safe distance from elite cultural spaces and practices in a social structure that remained hierarchical and ordered. That many of the drinking spaces in nineteenth-century Mexican novels actually facilitate the subversion or inversion of this desired hierarchical social structure, indicates the skepticism, initially latent, of the intellectual elite that a truly inclusive and integrated vision of nationhood could keep popular culture and the popular classes in their place, that is, in their space at the bottom of the social hierarchy.

TWO

Patriotic Heroes and Consummate Drunks

Alcohol, Masculinity, and Nationhood

He drank liquor to give himself courage; but he was not a hardened
drinker; he was impudent, violent, and daring, but a coward at heart.

—MANUEL PAYNO

Manuel Payno so describes Evaristo, the antihero of
his epic novel *Los bandidos de Río Frío* (1888–91),
identifying his dependence on alcohol as the chief
means the character uses to create an illusion of masculine
prowess and to cope with his inadequacies as a man. Contrasting patterns and styles of drinking behavior featured prominently in nineteenth-century literary explorations of Mexican
masculinity, in novels that sought to articulate or critique gendered ideals of the nation. This chapter explores how drinking practices contributed to the gendering of social relations
in Mexico City, and how literary ideals of nationhood were
built upon gendered models partly defined through particular drinking behaviors.

The opening sections establish that drinking in both all-
male and mixed-gender settings played an important role in
the social performance of masculinities, the consolidation of
group identity among particular groups of men, the competition for status within these groups, and in the articulation
and practice of social and gender hierarchies. In addition,

newspaper articles, police reports, and judicial records suggest that the drinking habits of two classes of men in particular—artisans and soldiers—were subject to intense scrutiny in the nineteenth-century, as their roles within the national community were considered particularly important. The central role of masculinity in the literary imagination of Mexican nationhood is explored, giving particular attention to the debate between Doris Sommer and Robert McKee Irwin on the relative importance of heterosexual and homosocial relationships in nineteenth-century fictional discourse. The ensuing analysis of literary representations of male drinking practices supports and advances Irwin's argument about the importance of homosocial relationships and the ideals of fraternity and patriotism to nineteenth-century constructions of nationhood.

I examine next the novels of Ignacio Manuel Altamirano and Manuel Payno, whose male characters were divided sharply into heroes and villains, partially through the assignment of contrasting relationships of these male characters to drinking. Altamirano's narratives completely dissociate his heroic male figures (often indigenous) from alcohol consumption, in order to avoid racial stereotypes about the proclivity of the indigenous population toward drunkenness, and included regular drunkenness in the negative qualities assigned to his (usually nonindigenous) villains. To an even greater degree, Payno's work associates villainous characters with pathological patterns of drinking, but it also presents an acceptable, even noble, pattern of masculine drinking: drinking to express or celebrate fraternal bonds, with fellow soldiers and male friends. The final section of the chapter explores more ambiguous representations of the relationship between drinking and masculinity, in the masculinized female drinkers that feature in Ángel de Campo's work and in the simultaneously heroic and antiheroic, masculine and emasculated, alcoholic male character in Heriberto Frías's *Tomóchic*.

It should be noted here that throughout this chapter the female and the feminine receive much less direct attention than the male and the masculine. There is considerable evidence that drinking was a significant part of women's lives in nineteenth-century Mexico, perhaps even comparable to that of men in terms of helping to foster female sociability among the popular classes, and this is a fascinating subject that clearly warrants further investigation. However, this chapter focuses on the male and masculinity, since drinking, in its most positive and negative guises, was overwhelmingly viewed as a masculine activity by nineteenth-century Mexican writers engaged in literary imaginings of the nation.

Drinking in Society: A Masculine Arena?

Many anthropological and sociological studies of drinking and masculinity in Mexico, and the Hispanic world more generally, have centered on the concept of machismo, which suggests the preponderance of heavy drinking, chauvinism, aggression, and violence as extreme, though common, expressions of masculinity in these societies.[1] Other scholars, however, including Matthew Gutmann and Marit Melhuus, have suggested that machismo, as a term classifying an identifiable type of male behavior and identity, is typically used by analysts problematically, in an "offhand, self-evident way" based on the tacit assumption "that we all know what machismo means and what machos do," when in reality the term involves a much broader web of significance.[2]

Matthew Gutmann has argued that in mid-twentieth-century Mexico, attempts to define the national character in literature, film, anthropology, sociology, and official history shaped a stereotypical view of Mexican masculinity as macho in nature. But even in these cinematic and literary explorations of "lo mexicano," machismo came to signify a contradictory set of characteristics that were portrayed as the composite parts of Mexican men: sexual aggression, virility, heavy drinking, gambling, daring behavior, violence, and a defiant attitude toward death, yet also fatherhood, patriotism, honor, loyalty, courage, generosity, hospitality, and stoicism.[3] In many Anglophone societies, including the United Kingdom, Ireland, and North America, the term macho typically carries a narrower meaning, denoting a behavioral pattern of heavy drinking, sexual aggression, bravado, and recklessness, and losing any connotations of paternal strength, patriotism, generosity, or stoicism that it can carry in Mexico and other Hispanic societies. In the Anglophone world, more affirmative valuations attached to macho drinking patterns are commonly associated with a preference for particular drinks deemed "manly" or "hardy," like beer and whisky, and with the ability to "hold one's drink," in other words, to drink large quantities of alcohol without showing the effects.[4]

How these broadly stereotypical codes of machismo actually operate within social relations and in the articulation of gender identities is a far more complex process. With regard to the relationship between drinking and gender, scholarship has overwhelmingly focused on the ways in which particular drinking practices, drinking venues, and drinks are involved in the construction, performance, and competition of multiple masculine identities. In a cross-cultural context, drinking places are commonly associated with the construction of masculine identities due to their separateness from the domestic sphere and their consequent ability to obscure male dependency on female relatives. Henk Driessen, for instance, in a study on drinking practices in southern Spain, states that "men drink to belong, to create and maintain bonds with other men and to mark their identity as true males. Drinking in homosocial settings dramatizes masculinity."[5] Many other studies, exploring societies as different as early modern England, early modern Europe, eighteenth- and nineteenth-century America, and late nineteenth-century Buenos Aires, have demonstrated the different ways that masculinities can be negotiated through drinking and associated practices: drinking contests, participating in rounds, competing with drinking companions in barroom games, telling embellished stories, and gambling.[6]

One must remember, however, that drinking patterns and identity constructions have rarely been so straightforwardly clear-cut. In many societies where the public bar acted as a masculine space, men could also drink in the presence of women and children at family celebrations, women often produced and sold homemade alcoholic drinks, and women could also drink in both private and public contexts, though less conspicuously and less regularly.[7] Even in mixed-gender settings, drinking can be instrumental in constructing masculine identities. Ruth Bunzel's study of two Central American villages in the 1930s, for instance, noted that drinking heavily distinguished older men in positions of authority during market-day celebrations and religious festivals from younger, less established, and less wealthy men, and the drinks themselves were distributed ceremonially according to age, gender, and social standing.[8] Meanwhile, in colonial Mexico, although peasant women produced and consumed alcoholic drinks during community celebrations, they were expected to drink less than men. Their relative sobriety would enable them to look after the men, who were often expected, as part of their roles as community officials, to become drunk or at least to perform the drunkenness socially expected of them.[9]

Several studies of late colonial society have demonstrated that drinking in all-male, or predominantly male, settings became particularly important for the men of Mexico's popular classes. Steve Stern's analysis of gendered politics in the late eighteenth century argued that alternative codes of masculinity—different from elite masculinities—could operate as a "sociocultural resource" for subordinate groups. Unable to compete with elite displays of male honor through public shows of authority, wealth, and social decorum, indigenous and other lower-class men "created cultural spaces to affirm their valor and competence," emphasizing a masculine identity that signified "a fuller sense of empowerment or citizenship as a man among men." Drinking, in conjunction with other competitive activities through which men could prove their masculine prowess, such as gambling, cockfighting, bullfighting, local politics, and community festivals, constituted one such valuable cultural space.[10]

These cross-cultural cases indicate that the social expression of masculinities through drinking can be an integral part of larger social processes: the consolidation of group identity among particular groups of men, the competition for status within these groups of men, and the articulation and practice of social and gender hierarchies. Nineteenth-century judicial records and newspaper reports that provide information about Mexican drinking practices are inevitably charged with negative viewpoints, since they mostly deal with the criminal and destructive aspects of public drunkenness. Nevertheless, these sources do contain evidence that drinking together in all-male groups with a similar social background was an important arena for both the consolidation of group male identity and the competition within these groups for status. Even the situations in which this competition became violent offer an indication of the existence of a nonviolent behavioral pattern, for which most men knew the rules but that could escalate out of control.

Drinking venues, especially pulquerías and vinaterías, acted as an important arena for masculine sociability in the nineteenth century, despite repeated legislative attempts to restrict social activities inside them, including prohibitions against gambling, gathering in groups larger than three, playing music, dancing, and eating food. *El Monitor Republicano*, the liberal newspaper founded by Vicente García Torres in 1844, reported that on the night of October 21, 1849, a police patrol "had to close a *figon* [small restaurant], owned by Don Cristobal Bilchis and situated in the Olla alleyway, dispersing a gathering of men found drinking liquor inside."[11] In December 1864, the *Periódico Oficial del Imperio Mexicano* also reported that several men were arrested "for gathering in a pulquería," including the owner, Juan Reynoso, who had a previous track record of allowing such gatherings to take place.[12] A consortium of people involved in the pulque trade countered accusations that pulquería owners routinely allowed disruptive gatherings to take place on their premises, in their petition calling for pulquerías to remain open over the Easter weekend in 1852, claiming that the artisans who gathered there on Monday mornings only did so while they were waiting for workshops to assign them jobs and that they did so peacefully and convivially.[13]

Contradicting the image created by the pulque vendors' petition of 1852 that groups of artisans used their premises simply as a meeting place to secure work, other records testify to the lively social atmosphere that gathered men enjoyed in such premises, with music, gambling, and games. Felipe Galan, the owner of a pulquería in the Santa Cruz parish of Mexico City, was prosecuted in 1804 when it was reported that his customers "play instruments and dance at all hours of the day."[14] More than a hundred years later, government officials complained about a pulquería in Tacuba that "frequently had musicians inside" to entertain the customers.[15] In its monthly summaries of police reports, *El Monitor Republicano* consistently noted in 1849 a significant number of arrests "for gambling in pulquerías."[16] The same newspaper, in 1849, also denounced a pulquería on the Calle de Ortega as an iniquitous den wherein "many thieves gather daily: regular card games are held in the interior of that establishment."[17] And in the 1848 investigation of a religious chorister accused of living openly with a woman and her children, the defendant's character was further questioned with the accusation that he spent too much time "together with a gang of gamblers, all the men being known thieves, drunkards, and murderers, in the local pulquería."[18]

Just as gambling, music, and dancing continued to enliven the social atmosphere in drinking venues, customers continued to flout the rules about gathering there in groups.[19] Judicial records reveal that this social, group aspect of drinking was indeed significant in the negotiation of masculine identities, both through expressions of solidarity and through processes of competition. The 1845 case of four men arrested for the attempted murder of another man because he owed them money for pulque hardly seems, on the surface, to confirm that bonds of masculine solidarity were created through drinking. That the four defendants shared a profession and that the victim was also significantly younger than them, however, does suggest some interesting elements in the process of articulating masculinity through drinking.[20] Firstly, the four suspects were all butchers by profession and were all married, ranging from twenty-eight to forty years old, thus corroborating the idea that men from similar social backgrounds often drank together to affirm a communal sense of manhood. Secondly, the man they ganged up on was significantly younger (nineteen years old), single, and of a different occupation; in other words, it is unlikely that he belonged to the group as fully as the four older, married butchers.[21] The victim, perhaps already treated with a certain measure of suspicion as a relative outsider to the group of friends, withheld money that he owed to the rest, thereby violating the reciprocal code of each drinker paying their way, which resulted in his attack. It is possible that the older men, who had families and were probably more established in the local community, felt that they were entitled to have the respect of this younger, unmarried man, so they inflicted a severe punishment on him when he failed to honor this entitlement by withholding the money he owed.[22]

Male friends from similar social backgrounds often drank together without causing trouble with men outside their group, indicating that the company of drinking itself could be a sufficient means of solidifying masculine bonds or engaging in masculine competition. In July 1852, two confectioners and a bricklayer, aged between twenty and twenty-eight, were arrested for brawling in the street while drunk. In their statements all three men stressed that they were "friends" having a drink after work, and although they had gotten "a little drunk," they were only "joking around" when the patrol officer came upon them and misread their playful fighting as a violent altercation. Of course, they may have been lying to avoid punishment, but nevertheless, the three men had met up after work to drink pulque together. Whether the fight was real or play, their behavior indicates the importance of physical competition to the social expression of masculinities. The similarity between their separate statements might have been engineered to escape prosecution, but it still indicates a degree of masculine solidarity in facing the judicial process.[23] Fines issued to drinking establishments for after-hours sales of alcohol provide further evidence that it was common for men to drink together in small groups, or pairs. Although most of these records contain minimal information about the customers beyond their names, it is striking that almost none of them refer to alcohol being sold to a solitary person. Instead, the documents commonly note that the vendor was caught selling alcohol to two or three men at once. It is not possible to be certain that these were friends drinking together, but the near absence of cases where only one person was being sold alcohol provides a reasonable indication that they were.[24]

Not all articulations of masculine identity, whether convivial or competitive, however, took place in the absence of women. Indeed, many judicial records attest to the mutual carousing of men and women in public drinking places. José Antonio Merino, the owner of a vinatería on the Calle de Amargura in Mexico City was prosecuted for an altercation with a patrol officer in January 1802, after the latter allegedly found "more than thirty individuals of both sexes, creating a notable disturbance with a guitar," directly outside the vinatería. An official report of 1807 also claimed that "people of all occupations, especially builders, and some women" were gathering to drink in vinaterías from as early as five o'clock in the morning. In 1820 the municipal government received complaints about various drinking places that were playing host to "gatherings of numerous people of both sexes that produced serious improprieties."[25] Neither was it uncommon for men and women to be arrested together for public drunkenness and associated offences such as indecent behavior and fighting.[26]

Newspapers can provide a further, albeit sketchy, indication that the numbers of women being arrested for drunkenness in Mexico City were significantly higher than one might expect. For the twelve months between December 1, 1850, and November 30, 1851, *El Siglo XIX* claimed that of the 18,389 men and 8,729 women sent to prison, 4,670 of the male and 3,039 of the female offenders were accused of public drunkenness, making it the single biggest category of crime committed by both sexes but also accounting for a higher proportion of the female prisoners than the male.[27] Whereas public drunkenness accounted for 25.9 percent of the male prisoners, this offence was charged against 34.8 percent of the female prisoners. Between 1820 and 1850, the total population of Mexico City fluctuated between 160,000 and 205,000, making the percentage of the population arrested for public drunkenness between 3.8 and 4.9 percent, a relatively high proportion.[28] These figures cannot be verified as statistically accurate in terms of male and female patterns of drinking, not least because an earlier issue of *El Siglo XIX* reported the common practice of "arbitrary detention" of innocent citizens on false pretexts, in a city still trying to recover from the social dislocation caused by the North American invasion in the late 1840s. Nevertheless, the comparatively high *proportion* of women accused of public drunkenness is borne out in other newspaper sources.[29]

Between October 7, 1849, and April 10, 1850, *El Monitor Republicano* included summaries of reports made by the city patrols, detailing on an almost daily basis how many men and women were arrested for a range of crimes. Of the 1,307 people arrested for public drunkenness, 794 were men and 513 were women.[30] Here, the overall figures of drunkenness are substantially lower than those reported in *El Siglo XIX* the following year, casting further doubt on the statistical reliability of the latter figures for gauging an accurate measure of the total number of Mexico City drinkers, but the ratio of women to men is similar. According to the figures from *El Siglo XIX*, of the total number of people arrested for public drunkenness, 39.4 percent were women and 60.6 percent were men, and in the figures reported by *El Monitor Republicano*, 39.3 percent of people arrested for this offence were women and 60.7 percent were men. In a smaller sample, the December 1864 issues of *Periódico Oficial del Imperio Mexicano* include police reports stating that of the 133 people arrested for public drunkenness, 64 percent were men and 36 percent were women, while *La Gazeta de Policia* reported that between September 12 and September 18, 1868, of the 118 people apprehended for public drunkenness, 69 per cent were men and 31 per cent were women.[31] Although the latter two examples from the 1860s seem to suggest a decline in the proportion of female drunkenness by this later period, the samples of data, limited by the unavailability of further issues of the two periodicals, are really too small to derive any conclusive observations about such long-term trends.

Therefore, while drinking men consistently outnumbered drinking women, it is apparent that nineteenth-century Mexican women drank in public, often at the same venues as men, and in their company. Does this imply that single-gender social drinking, then, was not a key aspect of the process of masculine identity formation? On the contrary, that so many women also drank socially only serves to highlight the differences in meaning attached to male and female drinking practices. Among social commentators and nation-building elites, male drinking could have both positive, fraternity-enhancing effects and negative, destructive, violent consequences for the national community, while female drinkers were largely condemned as perversions of the childbearing and saintly ideal of femininity. Moreover, although there is evidence to suggest that some men did behave in the aggressive, drink-fueled, reckless manner that macho stereotypes call to mind, judicial records help to reveal that this behavior went against the expectations that family, friends, neighbors, and the authorities held of men to act as responsible, respectable fathers, husbands, and workers. This suggests that, as Matthew Gutmann's ethnographical work showed, masculine identity was formed as much through negotiation with the judgments made and values held by family members, community members, and the authorities regarding drinking practices as through the actual patterns of male and female drinking, which are difficult to glean accurately from the available sources.

Female drinkers were commonly judged to have violated their ascribed social roles as wives and mothers. María Josefa Juárez, an indigenous woman from the village of Acuitlapilco, died in suspicious circumstances in 1804. Her husband, José, was accused of beating her to death but, in his confession that was also corroborated by a (male) neighbor, he pleaded for leniency on the grounds that he hit María several times for being excessively drunk and for drinking in another man's company, and that he had only meant to punish, not kill, her. Although José was sentenced to five years of labor in public works, this was a reduced sentence, as the judge accepted José's argument that he had not meant to kill his wife and that there was just reason for beating her in the first place.[32] In 1808 an indigenous man from Tacubaya sought to have his wife, María Francisca, confined within the women's prison due to her "habitual drunkenness," a propensity for disrespecting him in public, and her neglect of their children. He produced evidence from three senior male residents and the local curate to support his accusations, and their testimonies focused on the "terrible example" her behavior gave to the children, the verbal and physical abuse she gave to her husband, and the "unbearable offence" she caused to the neighborhood as a whole. The supporting witnesses eventually tempered their claims that Maria Francesca quarreled publicly with all the local residents when she successfully demonstrated that her wayward behavior was the result of her husband's own history of drunkenness, adultery, neglect, and abuse. The neighbors' readiness to condemn María Francisca's behavior, without considering that of her husband, indicates the emphasis placed on her failures as a wife and mother as a result of her drinking. In this regard, she seems to have been judged more harshly by the local community than by the municipal authorities, who demonstrated considerable sympathy for her claims that the husband was the real source of the problem.[33]

In another incident, María Andrea was the woman at the center of the scandalous incident in Felipe Galan's pulquería in 1804, as *she* played the guitar to facilitate the dancing of a group of men and women while they shared a bucket of pulque. She was also known as "la macho."[34] Gutmann argues that the terms *macho* and *machismo*, describing a negative type of male behavior, did not have much historical precedent in Mexico prior to the mid-twentieth century but this rare use of the term at the beginning of the nineteenth century to describe a woman "of ill-repute" is highly suggestive.[35] Perhaps the feminization of the masculine noun *macho* indicates that to frequent pulquerías was a hallmark of a macho type of irresponsible behavior. Alternatively, the macho element of her nickname might have alluded to the leadership role she had in the group of revelers as the guitar player. In either case, whether the term macho was intended as an insult or an expression of admiration, the nickname does reveal that some aspect of her persona or behavior was considered *unwomanly*. This figurative masculinization of women caught drinking and misbehaving in public was not common in judicial records; however, it did become a common trope in fictional portraits of drinking women, including the *soldaderas* (camp followers) in Heriberto Frías's *Tomóchic* (1893) and the bandits' women in Altamirano's *El Zarco* (1901). Like "la macho's" behavior, the conduct of these fictional women was portrayed not only as masculine but as a destructive, undesirable model of masculinity.

Some men appear to have followed this same destructive, heavy-drinking, stereotypically violent model of masculinity often described by the term *machismo*. Ignacio Gutiérrez, a forty-year-old, married mestizo, was charged in 1806 "for being a consummate drunkard, a bad-mouthing, shameless person, and for trying to hang his wife."[36] In July 1811 José Guillermo García, a forty-year-old, married builder, faced trial for the murder of another man in the courtyard of a city vinatería. His statement of defense claimed that the two men had been drinking pulque and aguardiente with the vinatería owner when the fight escalated from an exchange of insults instigated by the victim. Although the court investigators were unable to find the vinatería owner as a corroborating witness, García was released in January 1812, when the judges ruled the crime was not premeditated and had been provoked by the victim.[37] José Saganda, a forty-five-year-old, married man, was arrested in 1845 for attacking several drivers in Mexico City's central park with a saber while inebriated.[38] Román Casas, a thirty-year-old widower, was arrested in 1845 for being "drunk and disorderly" and trying to rape a married woman.[39] José Antonio Arroyo, a married cobbler in his late forties, was also arrested in 1845 for drunkenly harassing and insulting a patrol officer, in a typical case of misplaced, ill-judged, drunken bravado.[40] In the first two cases cited, Ignacio Gutiérrez and José Guillermo García were both acquitted: the former on the condition that he would reform his ways, and the latter because the victim had provoked him. Although this might indicate that their violent behavior could at least be tolerated, if not condoned, there are many more examples in which male patterns of drunkenness, aggression, and sexual or physical violence were more strictly condemned.[41]

In 1803 María Arcos took advantage of her forty-two-year-old husband José Manuel Bonilla's arrest, for being found drunk in the street, to launch a series of complaints against him for being a "consummate drunkard," of beating her, of neglecting his financial responsibilities to the family in favor of drinking, and of abandoning his religious devotions. In the course of proceedings, several neighbors, both male and female, corroborated María's story, claiming that they had heard him calling her vile names, that he frequently beat her, and that he was often seen drinking in the local vinatería. Even the couple's son Manuel testified that "his father José Bonilla is a drunk, scandalous, and blasphemes against God," and that he had sold María's clothes to afford more liquor. In his defense, Bonilla claimed that his wife was exaggerating all the charges because she wanted to leave him, but the courts sided with María. After several months in jail, however, Bonilla was released after demonstrating that María had abandoned their children to the care of neighbors, and the couple was ordered to reconcile.[42] Despite the eventual ruling to reinforce Bonilla's patriarchal control over his wife, it is striking that the neighborhood community came out in force to support María's version of events in the initial investigation. It remains unclear as to whether Bonilla had been an irresponsible, drunk, and violent husband, or whether María had indeed fabricated most of the story, but the case demonstrates that such charges were deemed just grounds for their separation, by the courts and even more by the local community in which the couple lived.

Other communities were equally critical of drunken, irresponsible, violent patterns of male behavior. In 1810 in the village of Tlalnepantla, on the outskirts of Mexico City, the local governor, Juan Francisco, was indicted by the leading members of his community in 1810 for being "a consummate drunkard, who is always losing control, and even goes to church in this condition to everyone's outrage. He does not look after the people of the village like a father should, nor does he carry out his duties." Antonio de Torres was a fifty-seven-year-old widower "de calidad Español."[43] He confirmed that Francisco was often seen drunk and disorderly in the streets and that he had acted violently toward various women and indigenous men without provocation on numerous occasions. After several other testimonies similar to that of Torres, Juan Francisco was removed from office and forbidden from holding any future offices.[44]

Alongside the punishment meted out, the terms through which Francisco was criticized provide a telling insight into the socially approved models of masculinity that he had violated. As William Taylor has shown, although community officials in late colonial Mexico were often expected to get drunk (or to perform drunkenness) at community festivals as part of their role, to become a "consummate drunkard" like Juan Francisco was clearly unacceptable.[45] Complaints against him, mostly levied by men of senior age and important social standing in the community, emphasized that Francisco's continual drinking meant that he was not in control of his faculties; that he caused public scandals in, of all places, the church; that he failed to meet his official responsibilities; and that he mistreated the townsfolk when he should have been caring for them "like a father." This list of Francisco's failings indicates, by inversion, the characteristics expected of a man in a position of some authority: to be of sound mind and judgment, to maintain a respectable public reputation, to respect God and the church as greater authorities than he, to conduct his official role with dedication, and to take care of those dependent upon him. Rationality, respectability, humility, hard work, responsibility, and paternalism: these were the characteristics of a model masculinity that the people of Tlalnepantla wanted in positions of authority.

Drinking was not deemed incompatible with these masculine values: local officials were actually expected to get drunk at community festivals. However, the regular, unsanctioned drinking of Juan Francisco and his inability to fulfill his duties when in a state of drunkenness, were cause for dismissal. While drinking was an established element in the expression of social bonds for many individuals, social groups, and occasions in nineteenth-century Mexico, drinking also brought out conflicts and competition within social groups. Drinking together in all-male groups, and mixed male and female groups, offered opportunities for the establishment and performance of masculinities and competition for status. Of course, alcohol-fueled violence was committed by numerous people, but, despite the enduring myth of machismo, cases surrounding the consumption of alcohol reveal that the most highly valued masculine ideals among families, neighbors, and official authorities were responsibility, respectability, integrity, and paternalism, rather than aggression, virility, and recklessness. Not only were women expected to uphold the values of social respectability and family obedience, but men were too, and communities and family members brought these expectations to bear as much as did the judicial authorities. Men in positions of authority, like Juan Francisco, the local governor, were particularly expected to ensure that social activities such as drinking did not prevent them from embodying these gendered ideals.

San Lunes and Dereliction of Duty: Artisans, Soldiers, and Drink

In addition to men in positions of political authority, workers and soldiers, as groups of men occupying crucial roles in the development of national society, were particularly criticized and targeted for failing to live up to the model of masculinity centered on the values of reason, responsibility, guardianship, work, and respectability. In the Mexican press, workers were regularly criticized for their participation in the custom of San Lunes—which we have already seen highlighted as a social problem by José Joaquín Fernández de Lizardi— because this damaged Mexico's economic prospects, as well as affecting social cohesion. With respect to soldiers, not only the press but also civilian and military authorities treated regular drunkenness among officers in a severe fashion, particularly where this was associated with charges of public disorder, insubordination to superior officers, or dereliction of duty.

The custom of San Lunes (Holy Monday), in which artisans often refused to work on Mondays to engage in drinking as a remedy for overindulging on Sundays, was repeatedly identified as a harmful, irresponsible practice by legislators, journalists, social commentators, and novelists.[46] An 1845 decree extended the definition of vagrants, who could be forcibly conscripted into the military and public works scheme, to workers who "without just cause only worked half the days of the week at the most, spending the rest of the days without an honest occupation," thus applying to those workers who took Mondays, as well as Sundays and Saturdays, off work.[47] In 1851 *El Siglo XIX* identified this pattern of drinking as the cause of inflated crime at the beginning of each week:

> Sundays and Mondays, and festival days in general, are the days in which the greatest number of offences are committed, which then decrease as the week goes on. This suggests the necessity of eradicating the custom by which many artisans lose the first days of the week to idleness and dissipation, until they run out of money and need to go back to work. It also suggests that the government should give serious thought to establishing some entertainment events to attract the people on Sundays designated for rest, in order to provide an alternative to vagrancy, gatherings in the taverns, and many other things that are the root cause of the fights and other crimes that are committed on these days.[48]

La Illustration Mexicana in 1852 further complained that the worker who partook in San Lunes was morally corrupt and economically irresponsible, since he was "giving himself over to drunkenness and prostitution, squandering the fruits of his labor, and contracting debts beyond his ability to pay."[49]

The leading article of an 1872 issue dedicated to the subject of drunkenness developed this point to emphasize the repercussions that drinking could have for the ability of artisans to fulfill their social responsibilities as men. The loss of Mondays' potential earnings and the frittering away of existing wages on drinking, it was argued, led to the neglect of wives and children who, becoming impoverished, might turn to robbery or prostitution to support themselves in the absence of a reliable husband or father. Moreover, the "greatest excesses" and neglect of work that drunken men indulged

FIG. 5. *El pulquero* (The pulque seller), in *Los mexicanos pintados por sí mismos*, 12. Not all discussions of San Lunes were explicitly negative. "San Lunes" appears as a caption on a pulque barrel in this image from a multiauthored work first published in 1854 that sought to depict Mexican "types" and typical features of Mexican life. Courtesy of Colección Digital, Universidad Autónoma de Nuevo León. http://cd.dgb.uanl.mx/.

in while "deprived [of] the use of their reason" not only led
to a dishonorable reputation for themselves but also failed to
provide a good moral example for their sons, thus crippling
the development of future generations as respectable, hard-
working citizens for the nation.[50] The problem of San Lunes
persisted into the early twentieth century for governments
trying to mold men into responsible citizens. As late as 1902,
Mexico's city council funded the publication of thousands of
leaflets, with the intention of eliminating "the ancient and
depraved habit of our working class . . . of getting drunk on
Sundays and Mondays of each week."[51]

While it is clear that the consistent campaign against San
Lunes was directed toward increasing Mexico's economic productivity and social stability through the inculcation of labor
discipline, this campaign was often framed in terms of the
expectation that Mexican men should provide for their families, maintain a respectable reputation, and give a good moral
example to contemporaries and future generations. Failure to
do so, as the María Arcos and José Bonilla case showed, could
result in condemnation from not just government authorities
and elite social commentators but also from family and community members. Concerns about drunken soldiers, on the
other hand, and their related violations of the ideal masculine
model of rationality, respectability, humility, work, responsibility, fraternity, and paternalism, came in for the heaviest criticism by military and civilian authorities, as well as in the press.

Arrest lists published by newspapers on a day-to-day basis
generally left the names of the offenders unrecorded, listing
simply the total number of people or the numbers of men
and women arrested for each particular offence. When the
same individual was implicated in a particularly serious crime,
such as murder, or in more than one offence—both drunkenness and fighting, for instance, or for being found drunk and
wounded—he or she was usually named. National guards-

men and soldiers, however, were consistently named in simple cases of public drunkenness, providing evidence that this was an even less acceptable type of behavior for them than it was for ordinary men. Given their role in the defense of the nation, both from external threats and internal disorder, soldiers ought to have been the incarnation of the ideal citizen, working in fraternal cooperation with their fellow men for the good of the nation, and thus providing an example to be followed by men in their roles as citizens. Perhaps sharing a fraternal drink in solidarity with other soldiers would be acceptable, but the loss of self-control, public humiliation, irresponsibility, and vulnerability entailed in being publicly drunk violated the image of both model citizens and model men that soldiers were meant to represent.

Numerous investigations took place during the nineteenth century of soldiers and military officers who exhibited recurrent bouts of drunkenness and thus neglected their duties and responsibilities as soldiers. Corporal Mariano Loranca, based in Tlaxcala, was ordered to spend two years in public works schemes in 1802 after a string of citations for drunkenness, abandoning his post, and having unauthorized absences from the barracks.[52] In 1808 Lieutenant Esteban Hernández was stripped of his rank in the Colima regiment because "he gets drunk almost continually with vice-ridden soldiers and civilians," as well as demonstrating a lack of respect toward his superiors, engaging in illegal card games, and exhibiting general disorderly conduct.[53] Dionisio Jimental, a twenty-seven-year-old grenadier in Campeche, was interred in hospital as a prisoner in August 1827 because he had proven himself "incorrigible and dangerous in the company," as a result of "getting drunk many times" and selling his uniform. Jimental was sentenced to seeing out his term of military service in public works schemes.[54] In 1842 Captain Manuel María Díaz of the Matamoros battalion was suspended indefinitely from his post after being found "collapsed in a public house, completely inebriated," with the tribunal condemning his drunkenness and negligence as a source of dishonor and scandal for his battalion.[55] Sergeant Manuel Flores, based in Tampico on the Gulf Coast, was investigated in 1852 for repeated incidents of drunkenness and abandoning his sentry post.[56] By the late nineteenth and early twentieth century, similar importance had been attached to the public sobriety of municipal police officers.[57]

In 1872 *El Siglo XIX* described as "inexcusable crimes" the behavior of a group of soldiers charged with the transportation of several prisoners, when a serious altercation erupted, leaving one man dead, after they "went into a pulquería, together with the prisoners, where they made repeated libations."[58] Not only had they fallen down on performing their duties as the protectors of law and order, in failing to transport the prisoners safely, but they also showed themselves to be morally lax as men, drinking sociably with the unsavory offenders, making themselves vulnerable to attack and losing control of the situation. Their crime was, therefore, doubly unforgivable: they had forgotten their duty as soldiers to protect social order; and, because as soldiers they ought to behave with exemplary masculine decorum, their excesses in drinking and violence were particularly damaging to the projected masculine ideal centered on the values of responsibility, rationality, self-control, and respectability.

Drunkenness was also frequently cited in cases where officers physically or verbally abused their comrades, indicating that the fraternal ideal of a group of men fighting together for the same (national) cause could be made to look superficial and fragile by the actions of individual soldiers. In 1844 Captain José Olvera was accused of multiple offences, including insulting other officers, impeding their search for a deserter, and being drunk on duty. According to one witness, Olvera's military conduct was ordinarily good "except when he gets drunk" and, on the day in question, Olvera had been drunk, boasting to other officers that "he was the longest-serving captain and was very manly" and calling them "chickens."[59] Accepting that Olvera's military performance was usually good, the tribunal handed out a somewhat lenient sentence of one month in confinement, but two subsequent incidents involving drunken, volatile behavior, fighting with another officer in a cantina, and threatening to kill his lover in a jealous, alcohol-fueled rage, lengthened this punishment. Olvera was still in prison in April 1845 when he was released to participate in a new military campaign.

Corporal Antonio Ayala, stationed in Puebla, was also repeatedly disciplined for his behavior while drunk. Having already been prosecuted for drunkenness while on duty several times, in May 1835 Ayala arrived drunk at his commander's house, late for an important briefing. Despite some supporting statements testifying to his exemplary conduct while sober, the corporal was suspended from his regiment for three months in order to clean up his act.[60] After showing some initial improvement, Ayala was under investigation once more in March 1836 for brazenly insulting superior officers in front of the ordinary troops. While the superior officers in question claimed Ayala had been drunk at the time, other witnesses testified to the contrary, indicating that the superior officers wanted to use Ayala's previous record of drunkenness to portray him as a maverick, irresponsible, disloyal, and arrogant officer, as a means of punishing him for the insults he had thrown at them.[61]

Despite the overwhelmingly negative portrait of drunken soldiers provided by legal records, it is clear that drinking was an important, if not fully sanctioned, part of military life. The cantina to which José Olvera absconded in 1844, for instance, was situated directly beside his company's barracks and was, presumably, located there to take advantage of the substantial business opportunities that soldiers presented.[62] An 1872 article in *El Siglo XIX* also complained that it was unfair on a pulquería owner that his establishment, situated outside an army barracks, was to be closed down as a result of disturbances caused by overexuberant, well-oiled soldiers: "It seems to us that the right course of action would have been to announce measures conducive to stopping the soldiers going to the pulquería instead of causing serious harm to the owner through its closure."[63] That closing the pulquería altogether was, in spite of the newspaper's dissatisfaction, deemed the best means of avoiding such disturbances, suggests that it was considered unlikely that soldiers would stop frequenting such a conveniently located watering hole through normal disciplinary measures. Indeed, the cases cited above, where individual soldiers were disciplined repeatedly for the offence of drunkenness, indicates that only severe punishments—such as indefinite suspension and lengthy imprisonments—were effectual, and these measures were often undesirable when officers were needed in times of war. The case of Olvera is particularly instructive in this regard: his sentence grew to an indefinite length after repeated offences related to drunkenness, but was then commuted upon the commencement of a new military campaign.

The frequency with which fellow officers and soldiers testified in support of accused drunkards, often playing down the frequency and intensity with which the man in question drank, indicates that the military authorities judged drunken soldiers much more harshly than did the men in the offenders' own units. An 1845 investigation into Lieutenant Ramón Robles, for instance, who was accused of being drunk on duty in Mexico City's central park, was abandoned due to the lack of verifiable evidence. The summation closing the report lamented that the only available witnesses, all of whom denied Robles had been drinking at all, were of the same regiment as the accused and were, therefore, likely to be biased in his favor or even to lie outright in his defense.[64] Several testimonies from more junior members in Captain José Olvera's regiment also played down the latter's level of drunken and insulting behavior toward senior officials, claimed that he was not in the habit of getting drunk, and emphasized his good military record, which included two decorations for valor in 1840 and 1843.[65]

Antonio Ayala even tried to defend himself against the accusations that drunkenness had led to his neglect of duties and lack of respect toward his superiors by claiming that he had been obliged to drink in order to fulfill the bonds of fraternity that were supposed to tie him to his fellow soldiers. On his way to a briefing, for which he arrived late and drunk, Ayala claimed he had met two comrades whose father had recently died and "in light of their grief, he was obliged to accept the drink they offered him, which was strong enough to unhinge him."[66] Ayala admitted that he had let down his commanding officers, but his defensive plea reveals that there was a horizontal order within the soldiering community that could be expressed and reinforced through offering and accepting drinks. Although this line of defense was basically ignored and Ayala received a three-month suspension, perhaps he would have been granted more clemency had he arrived at the commander's quarters only slightly late and slightly tipsy, thus corroborating his story that he had consumed a single drink in solidarity with his brothers-in-arms. His case notes, however, record that Ayala arrived in an advanced state of inebriation, indicating that he had been drinking for quite some time. Nevertheless, that the defensive line tried to emphasize Ayala's loyalty to and camaraderie with the men in his regiment suggests that these were considered important traits for a soldier to have and could be legitimately expressed through drinking together, as long as this did not detract from the soldier's responsibilities and obligations to superior officers.

Although drinking among soldiers could be an important element in the expression of fraternal bonds that helped to forge a common identity and purpose, it also brought out conflicts and competition between them, especially notable in the cases where subordinate officers challenged and mocked the authority of higher-ranking officials, who were, in turn, able to articulate the established hierarchy through the prosecution of unruly drinkers. Although the official scrutiny of soldiers' drinking was more intense, given their crucial role in defending the nation, in many ways drinking practices among soldiers mirrored patterns of identity formation, masculine competition, and the articulation of hierarchies that can be observed in the general male population and the reactions of the authorities to them.

The treatment of male and female drinking in the courts and the press indicates the expectations, hopes, and fears that government authorities and intellectuals held about the ability of the Mexican population to contribute constructively to the social, economic, and cultural progress of the nation. While male drinking could both foster the fraternal ideal of citizenship and result in violent confrontations that jeopardized social harmony, female drinkers were portrayed solely as immoral or masculinized figures whose influence on their husbands, brothers, and sons might prove harmful to the nation.

Many nineteenth-century authors, meanwhile, endeavored to construct a heroic, fraternal yet paternalistic model of masculinity and nationhood that employed the language of liberal citizenship, the prioritization of relationships between male characters, and their own interpretations of social practices—including drinking—among the population at large. On the whole, literary portrayals of alcohol consumption in nineteenth-century novels exposed the anxieties intellectuals felt about the ability of Mexico's male population to live up to the ideals of fraternity, patriotism, and civic duty that were so important to their vision of Mexican nationhood.

Gendered Ideals of the Nation

In her seminal work on Spanish American literature, *Foundational Fictions*, Doris Sommer argues that the most common literary expression of a desired unity in national identity took the form of allegorical romance, in which ideal male and female characters "destined to desire one another" represented "reconciliations and amalgamations of national consciousness" across class, racial, political, or regional lines.[67] Other scholars agree that the sentimental romance genre allegorized an individual's or couple's quest for personal happiness within a harmonious nation, although the pervasiveness of unhappy endings in such works calls attention to the artists' anxiety about the elusiveness of social unity.[68] Sommer also argues that the nineteenth-century "foundational fictions" she analyzes created metonymic associations, rather than merely metaphorical parallels, between the love affair and the nation. She explains, "The romantic affair *needs* the nation, and erotic frustrations *are* challenges to national development"; in other words, the union of the fictional couple and the consolidation of the nation are inextricably bound and drive one another forward in a dialectical process. The harmonization of national identity is symbolized if and when the lovers overcome any obstacles hindering their union, and the process through which they achieve happiness with each other represents the process that the author advocated for national unification and progress.[69]

The trope of allegorical romance between idealized male and female characters undoubtedly plays an important role in fictional imaginings of the Mexican nation, but, as Robert McKee Irwin has shown, male friendships and instances of "male homosocial bonding" are even more prominent in nineteenth-century Mexican novels.[70] These male-male relationships often act as a more important arena for the negotiation of national unification and harmonization in nineteenth-century fiction, while the inconsistency of heterosexual love features as a treacherous obstacle and is often described using the language of warfare.[71] Irwin explains the prioritization of relationships between men in fiction as the corollary of the contemporary political discourse wherein national unity was represented as contingent upon fraternal cooperation, across racial and class lines, in political and military activity.[72]

Claudio Lomnitz's compelling dissection of nationalist discourse in Mexico has shown that this ideology of fraternal citizenship, granting theoretical and potential equality to all men, obscured the persistence of hierarchical ties of loyalty in shaping social relationships within the national community.[73] Nineteenth-century novelists participated in the ideological prioritization of the fraternal ideal, since the repertoire of action put forward in their fiction for Mexican men to achieve true manhood centered on the duties of liberal citizenship. A male character's worth is often best observed by his fraternal relationships with other men, his service to the community in general, or his performance on the battlefield—in other words, the ways in which he interacts with and contributes to the public, political, and national arenas, which are constructed as largely masculine spheres of influence.

The ways in which different fictional male characters drank together, or behaved toward one another as a consequence of drinking, were important representational strategies for nineteenth-century novelists to articulate or critique this ideology of fraternal, patriotic citizenship. The fraternal bonding aspect of male drinking was incorporated into the activities of some literary heroes, while excessive drinking featured prominently in the portrayal of destructive, violent, and cowardly male characters who violated the fraternal and paternal ideals of manhood. Moreover, fictional female drinkers were generally masculinized and associated with negative male figures to reinforce the idea that drinking was a specifically masculine activity that could have serious repercussions for social and national harmony.

Alcohol and Male Characters: Unconvincing Heroes and Drunken Villains

A recurrent literary approach to exploring the relationship between alcohol and masculinity was to completely dissociate heroic figures from drinking and to overemphasize the reliance of villainous characters on alcohol, thus delineating good and bad models for male contributions to Mexican nationhood. This is particularly evident in Ignacio Altamirano's 1901 novel *El Zarco*, a highlight of the historical romance genre that explores the persistent problem of banditry. El Zarco, a handsome, blond-haired, blue-eyed rogue, leads the notorious gang of bandits known as the *plateados*, who operated along the Mexico-to-Veracruz highway and in the state of Morelos during the turbulent years of the Reform Wars.[74] The responsible and patriotic hero of the novel is a humble Indian blacksmith named Nicolás, who protects his women, his village and, by extension, his country, from the group of marauding macho-style *plateados*. Dissociating his heroic character from stereotypical images of the "drunken Indian" that had circulated since the early colonial period across Spanish America, Altamirano never mentions alcohol in connection with Nicolás. By contrast, drinking hard liquor is a common activity among the *plateados*, and El Zarco's general disposition is described as having been "accustomed to vice since his youth."[75]

Altamirano continues to use incidents involving alcohol consumption to demonize the bandits. When Manuela rejects

Nicolás to elope with El Zarco, she is brought to the *plateados'* hideout, where her lover introduces her to his "best friends, my comrades, the bosses," a group of men gambling, drinking "bottles of cane liquor," and singing "tavern songs." This homosocial fraternal relationship between El Zarco and his fellow bandits is quickly shown to be false, as these are men without responsibility, without respect for one another, without courage, and without honor. El Zarco permits the other men to insult Manuela by talking openly about her sexuality and to make advances toward her.[76] In stark contrast to Nicolás's staunch defense of his women, his village, and his country, El Zarco leaves Manuela to fend for herself among a gang of predatory men, routinely betrays his brothers-in-arms, and wreaks havoc throughout the countryside, murdering innocent men, women, and even children.

Nicolás's sober virtue is further contrasted with a drunk and corrupt military official, whose failure to tackle the *plateados* is criticized by the upstanding Indian. During an impassioned exchange at the town hall, when the village officials beg the army commandant for protection, the latter, "helping himself to a large glass of cognac," refuses to intervene. Nicolás then asks the commandant for a troop of men to tackle the widespread banditry problem himself. Incensed by this challenge to his authority, the commandant threatens to have Nicolás shot, which only increases our hero's contempt: "Do whatever you want, mister military. You have your troops behind you: I am alone, unarmed, and in front of the authority of my people. You can shoot me, I'm not afraid and I was already expecting it. It's very clear; you have been unable or have not wanted to hunt down and shoot the bandits, as you would have to put yourself in danger to do so, and it's easier for you to murder an honest man who reminds you of your duties." Despite the commandant's subsequent insistence that he can deal with "those who insult me man-to-man," he hurries out of the room and orders a sergeant to arrest the defiant Nicolás instead, thus avoiding a direct, "man-to-man" confrontation.[77]

Both El Zarco and the army officer are linked to a negative model of masculinity through their drinking, carelessness, irresponsibility, and inability to protect others, while the sober Nicolás stands up for what he believes in, demonstrates loyalty and service to his local community, conducts himself with honesty and courage, and is instrumental in defeating the bandits, thereby protecting his village and the woman he loves. Nicolás represents an ideal of masculine identity centered on the duties of responsible citizenship; his respectability, humility, hard work, responsibility, and guardianship are the very qualities that the people of Tlalnepantla valued in a man of authority so much that they campaigned successfully to remove their drunken governor, Juan Francisco, from his position because he lacked them. Moreover, by making his heroic figure Indian, Altamirano sought to demonstrate that inclusion within Mexico's national community and identity should be extended to people of all ethnic groups, but their inclusion depended upon their adherence to the masculine duties of liberal citizenship.[78]

Altamirano's first novel *Clemencia* (1869), another historical romance set during the War of the French Intervention, employs the same technique of contrasted drinking habits to illustrate the difference between a true hero and a cowardly fraud. The two main characters are army officers, whose masculinity and drinking habits were subject to particular social and legal scrutiny during the nineteenth century. Enrique Flores and Fernando Valle, both junior officers in the liberal army fighting the French in 1863, are presented as diametric opposites of one another: the former is virile, flamboyant, and handsome, and the latter is a shifty, pallid, taciturn loner. Moreover, while Valle has an "aversion to the vices of most young army officers"—namely drinking and gambling—his counterpart reveled in them, suggesting that Flores might be the more likely masculine prototype, participating in homosocial, fraternal activities with his fellow officers. Unlike Flores, who "was idolized by his men, much beloved of his fellow officers, and the favorite of his commanding officer," Valle, who "avoided any occasion in which he might have to contribute money to a shared meal or wine with his fellow officers," tended to attract the "enmity" of his colleagues and superiors.[79]

However, it is significant that, in the midst of the initially unappealing description of Valle, an allusion to his gallant, nation-serving credentials, which become more clearly manifest as the novel progresses, is provided by way of his participation in the historic victory at Puebla on May 5, 1862. The heroic highpoint of the Mexican liberals' campaign against the French is thus used to associate patriotism, national unity, and the liberal cause with a masculine ideal of bravery, duty, and guardianship. Moreover, this was the battle in which the National Guard cemented its reputation as a bastion of patriotic liberalism, through which Indian and mestizo peasant men could become useful citizens.[80] Although Flores and Valle are specified to be of the same ethnicity, Valle's skin is nevertheless significantly darker than that of Flores.[81] While Altamirano made a more explicit attempt to dissociate productive male Indians with the "drunken Indian" stereotype through Nicolás in El Zarco, the writer had foreshadowed this idea more figuratively with Fernando Valle in Clemencia. Perhaps this figurative "Indianization" of Fernando is also meant to heighten the reader's identification of the character with Altamirano himself, as Juan Campuzano has noted that Altamirano's novels consistently feature one male character whose love goes unrequited by a woman, an unfortunate circumstance that the author suffered as a young man.[82]

An educated, wise, and noble Doctor L. narrates the story of Clemencia retrospectively and eventually exposes the first impressions of the two male protagonists as utterly false. Flores's charm is revealed as a mask over his self-serving, ambitious, irresponsible character, when he leaves two women broken-hearted and betrays his brothers-in-arms by passing information to the French. While facing death for treason, the veneer of masculine strength that his physical appearance and affinity for the male homosocial drinking arena had engendered dissipates completely: "His heart was close to stopping, like that of a boy or a woman. It did not have the spirit of a man." By contrast, Valle sacrifices himself to help Flores escape, in the hope that the latter could live to make Clemencia happy, and is consequently recognized as the real man, "so brave, so patriotic, and so noble," with his steadfast commitment to the ideals of liberalism, to the defense of the nation, and to the welfare of the woman he loves.[83]

Nevertheless, Altamirano's attempt to promote an ideal of Mexican masculinity struggled to resolve the tensions involved in the inclusion of younger, nonwhite men within the domain of liberal citizenship. Both Nicolás and Valle fulfill key aspects of the model of masculinity centered on responsibility, guardianship, and integrity. However, their nonparticipation in male homosociality through drinking and associated activities typifies their failure in forging the fraternal relationships with other men that were central to the definition of liberal citizenship.[84] Drinking communally was an important social activity for many Mexican men, especially among the non-elite classes and all-male institutions like the army, and was recognized as such by government officials, social commentators, and intellectuals in the nineteenth century. By denying the presence of this form of fraternal interaction in his heroic characters—and, in the case of Valle, specifically referring to his aversion to it—Altamirano misses an opportunity to connect his masculine ideal to the lived experience of Mexican men and fails to establish fraternity as a central feature in the formation of Mexican nationhood. Or perhaps Altamirano was more concerned with highlighting the ongoing injustice of this situation: his nonwhite heroes had proven their worth to the nation on an individual basis but were not yet included fully in the national brotherhood of male liberal citizens as they, and the nonwhite population they metaphorically represented, deserved to be.

Manuel Payno employed a more tempered duality between moderate, occasional drinkers who drank in all-male fraternal settings and heavy-drinking, volatile, and unsociable drinkers to emphasize the differences between heroic, patriotic characters and cowardly, criminal villains in his encyclopedic costumbrista novels, *El fistol del Diablo* (1845–46) and *Los bandidos de Río Frío* (1888–91). In the first novel, the two male protagonists each participate in both homosocial, fraternal instances of drinking and destructive, self-indulgent patterns of drinking. The second novel demarcates good and bad models of drinking and masculinity more sharply into separate characters, with a patriotic hero who drinks in fraternal settings, and a drunken, violent villain who wreaks havoc throughout the novel.

At the beginning of *El fistol del Diablo*, the two main heroes, Arturo and Manuel, are bitter enemies as a result of their attempts to woo the same woman. When both men realize that they no longer desire the woman in question, they cancel their scheduled duel and seal their newly established friendship over a meal and many "exquisite wines" in the Café del Progreso, a prestigious real-life Mexico City café and an important site for fraternal sociability among the middle and upper classes. During the convivial meal, the two men chat happily over their wine, swapping ideas about the best ways to romance women, thus affirming their heterosexuality during this homosocial moment. Manuel insists on paying for the indulgent meal and, on leaving, they are confronted by an old beggar to whom Manuel gives two pesos, the last of his money. The beggar is so overwhelmed by this unusual generosity that he falls to his knees before Manuel, who says "Get up, good man. . . . And don't kneel before anyone other than God."[85] This passing exchange with the beggar reinforces the fraternal atmosphere that had been created between Manuel and Arturo through the shared meal and drink, as Manuel's comment represents the fraternal aspect of the liberal ethos: that all men were equal regardless of social class, or any other distinctions.[86]

Neither Arturo nor Manuel, however, are truly fraternal heroes, since both men repeatedly fail to fulfill their duties to friends, loved ones, and the nation in the course of the 1847 North American invasion of Mexico City, which is narrated in the final stages of the novel. Manuel consistently exhibits a hot-headed, imprudent disposition, losing money through gambling, futilely attacking Rugiero (the devil-in-disguise who appears to cultivate many of the chaotic incidents in the novel), and participating in an ill-fated plot against the municipal authorities, all of which conspire to frustrate his desire to marry his beloved Teresa. Arturo, meanwhile, is consistently indecisive in his choice of women, is easily swayed by the pernicious advice of Rugiero, and exhibits a disturbing lack of faith in his friends.

Both men also suffer as a result of the relationship between their drinking habits and their military service. Believing Teresa to be dead for several years, Manuel, a captain in the regular army, engaged in a dissipated lifestyle of drunkenness, promiscuity, and gambling. Although this period of his life has finished before the novel begins, his former dissolution continues to tarnish his reputation and thwart his plans. Teresa's guardian, the villainous Pedro, conspires to prevent Manuel from marrying Teresa by informing his superior officers that Manuel was "an expert gambler, a cheat, a consummate drunkard," accusations which were taken very seriously by the military authorities in the nineteenth century.[87]

Arturo, meanwhile, falls into a destructive pattern of self-pity and drunkenness after returning from the factional battle between the *polko* and *puro* battalions of the Mexico City National Guard that weakened the city at a crucial point in the defense against the North American invasion; his cycle of binge drinking prevents him from subsequently taking part in that defense, resulting in an American triumph. In stark contrast to the convivial, fraternal, and homosocial drinking in which he had previously participated with Manuel, Arturo's drinking at this stage becomes solitary, broody, and compulsive. He alternately wanders the streets drinking or shuts himself in his room, where he has numerous bottles of aguardiente and cognac hidden in the wardrobe. Arturo claims that his recourse to liquor provides "fantasy, oblivion, rest" from his grief over lost love Aurora, but this is dismissed as a flimsy excuse when Teresa points out to Arturo, and to the reader, that he has never really maintained a steady, lasting interest in one woman.[88]

Despite the initial bonding of the two male protagonists through a fraternal homosocial drink, Manuel's history of dissipation and Arturo's abandonment of military service to wallow in drunken oblivion represent their prioritization of personal issues over the greater, national good. Their dualistic relationship with drinking indicates that Payno considered that the ideal of male fraternity had the potential, but was as yet insufficiently developed and integrated into institutional and social relationships in the 1840s, to effectively unite the nation against external threats. Although both characters reform somewhat and participate more selflessly in the final struggles against the invading army, they are both seriously injured and the novel ends in uncertain chaos, representing the dire consequences of disunity that Payno posits as the central message of his narrative.[89] The characterization of Arturo and Manuel as participants in the military campaigns of the era, whose patterns of alcohol use affected their performances, serves to highlight—as the central issue—their continued inability to put national interests above their own personal desires.

In *Los bandidos de Río Frío*, Payno associates more fully the integrative, fraternal attributes of alcohol consumption with patriotic heroes, while limiting the socially disruptive effects of drinking to villains. Juan Robreño, the handsome, heroic army officer forced into hiding after deserting his military post to protect his secret lover, Mariana, and their newborn child from her tyrannical father, is rarely seen drinking. The one notable occasion when he does affirms his honorable, courageous, and fraternal character. Robreño eventually hands himself in to his superior officers and stoically accepts that they will have to order his execution. Corporal Franco, reluctantly put in charge of arranging the execution, has such respect for the military prowess Robreño had earned during his service on the northern frontier that he feels deep regret and sadness about the sentence he has been entrusted to carry out, and the two men share a drink together in solace. Franco says: "'Let's have a drink, and my Captain will not think badly of me for doing so either . . . because this is hard, but as you know I have to carry out the Coronel's orders.' Juan Robreño took the glass full of liquor, drank a few swigs, and sat down with tranquility."[90]

The remarkable stoicism that Robreño shows in the face of death makes such an impression on Franco that when the firing squad fails to inflict a fatal wound, Franco smuggles Robreño to safety and helps him to assume a new identity. In delightfully melodramatic fashion, the firing squad— unbeknownst to all—includes Robreño's illegitimate son, Juan, who was kidnapped as a baby by a witchdoctor, almost eaten by homeless dogs, rescued, and brought up by an elderly street vendor. Most interpretive analyses of *Los bandidos* focus on the character of Juan junior, as a centrifuge connecting almost all the characters in a very complicated plot, or as a symbol of the coming of age of the Mexican nation. Juan senior, however, is a more interesting figure in terms of masculine characterization as he is the main heroic character who takes an active role in the resolution of the novel's many conflicts. In contrast, for the most part, Juan junior is carried along through the plot by a series of events that merely happen to him.[91] With the character of Juan Robreño, Payno epitomized the patriotic, honorable, fraternal ideal of masculinity in a soldier, whose patterns of drinking and public behavior were particularly scrutinized during the nineteenth century. Payno's emphasis on the fraternal bond established between Robreño and Franco through this shared drink stands out as a template for a model of masculine identity that would serve the Mexican nation well. The experience of sharing a drink had solidified the respect Franco already had for his prisoner into something more binding, more meaningful, and more inspirational: into the kind of relationship patriotic male citizens were supposed to have with each other and with the nation.

Aside from a few episodes where alcoholic drinks are exchanged between various "good" characters as a sign of hospitality and solidarity, Robreño and Franco's fraternal drink together is the only positive portrayal of alcohol use in the novel. Much more frequently and dramatically, Payno associates excessive drinking with destructive, dishonorable, and irresponsible characters that personify what the author believed was wrong in Mexico. The machinist-turned-bandit Evaristo, one of the novel's main villains, is a kind of symbolic compendium of what Payno considered to be Mexico's flaws: "Evaristo, an insalubrious hybrid of the lowly, shrewd Indian and the proud, ambitious Spaniard, had been endowed with the worst qualities of the two races." When the reader is first introduced to Evaristo, habitual drinking, petty violence, and irresponsible behavior have already become central features of his character: "Without being a drunkard, he was increasingly inclined toward drinking, and on four occasions he had been sent to prison for fighting and disorderly behavior." He decides to marry Tules while he is already living with a beautiful and loyal lover, Casilda, but instead of breaking off his relationship with the latter he endeavors to make her leave of her own accord, by abusing her physically and mentally. After a particularly violent beating, Casilda recognizes his weakness and insecurities as a man and defiantly challenges his manhood before escaping: "You're a villain, a killer, a coward. You should die on the gallows. Finish me off if you are a man."[92]

Evaristo's passion for Tules proves equally fickle and, frustrated by his wife's complaints about their lack of money, he turns to male company and drinking to forget about his responsibilities and problems: "Upset by so many arguments, instead of going home he went to a pulquería and had a drink, then he went to a carpenter's workshop that he knew and had another drink with his friends." Evaristo works fewer and fewer hours over the following weeks, leaving his wife and his apprentice (none other than Juan junior) in dire straits. As their complaints grow, he begins to beat them both and borrows money from his fellow artisans but, unfortunately for his dependents, "he squandered almost everything he earned in the vinaterías on Sundays and Mondays."[93]

Evaristo's irresponsible actions escalate into more aggressive and violent behavior, culminating in the brutal murder of Tules. After an extended session drinking *sangre de conejo* and *mistela*, during which Evaristo is humiliated by losing money in card games and losing a fistfight, he relieves his anger, frustration, and feelings of emasculation by exerting his power over Tules, stabbing her repeatedly with a chisel.[94]

Payno's description of the resulting scene accentuates the brutish, depraved, and pathetic aspects of Evaristo's character that the potent mixtures of alcohol and wounded male pride had helped to release: "He fell down next to Tules, vomiting, hurling out through his eyes, mouth, and nose the *sangre de conejo*, the *mistela*, into the blood of his poor wife that he had spilled so wickedly."[95]

It is significant that Evaristo's carousing, his fight with his drinking buddies, and his murder of Tules take place on San Lunes, which Payno refers to scornfully as "this sacred day that the Mexican artisans observe more faithfully than the Muslims observe Ramadan."[96] Despite legislation, press criticism, and leaflet campaigns, authorities were unable to alter this long-standing practice during the nineteenth century, and Payno amalgamates their numerous concerns about the impact of San Lunes on economic and social progress in this scintillating episode. Just as José María Vigil, writing in *El Siglo XIX*, argued in 1872 that families became impoverished as irresponsible artisans wasted existing earnings and lost potential wages due to San Lunes, Tules and Juan junior struggle to pay even for food, while the man who is supposed to provide for them drinks and gambles his money away. Evaristo and his companions also become embroiled in petty violence, which then escalates into the murder of Tules as a result of her husband's humiliation, thus echoing the same newspaper's prediction in 1851 that the drinking en masse of artisans on Mondays would lead to a serious increase in crime.

Both hero and villain of *Los bandidos de Río Frío*, therefore, arise from two categories of men whose drinking habits and contributions to national development were closely scrutinized in the nineteenth century: soldiers and artisans. While Payno constructed his ideal masculine model around the army officer Juan Robreño, he portrays the brutal Evaristo as a typical product of the social and cultural milieu populated by urban workers. The contrast between hero and villain becomes even greater as the novel continues. Evaristo becomes the leader of a group of bandits in the mountains, commits many more brutal offences, including the rape and murder of several domestic servants, and is eventually brought to justice through the combined action of Juan Robreño, Casilda, Juan junior, and several other "good" characters. Facing execution, Evaristo's cowardly reaction could scarcely contrast more with that of the hero, Juan Robreño, earlier in the narrative: "The imminence of death by the garrote filled him with terror and he could do no more than tremble, cry, and wail like a woman and to drink lots of water, because thirst devoured him and burned his insides."[97] The earlier show of stoicism and acceptance by Robreño, our hero, helped by a stiff, shared drink with a brother-in-arms, represents how a real man should behave in service of the nation. Evaristo, the villain, meanwhile, is finally exposed after all his virulent, aggressive deeds as weak, afraid, undignified, effeminate, and tortured by a raging thirst that, in his powerless state, could only be treated with water.

While the self-serving deeds of Arturo and Manuel in *El fistol del Diablo* were highlighted through their self-indulgent patterns of alcohol consumption and criticized for being detrimental to the national good, Evaristo's downfall was more explicitly couched in terms of his emasculation, contrasting his earlier habit of heavy drinking and displays of bravado among male friends to his pathetic, groveling condition while facing death, shaking "like a woman," and only being allowed to drink water. The protagonists in the earlier novel displayed both the positive, fraternal pattern of drinking and the more negative, destructive pattern, suggesting that Payno used these characters to represent the unachieved potential that Mexican men as a whole had for contributing to the consolidation of the nation through responsible, patriotic citizenship. The much sharper delineation of positive and negative drinking patterns into a heroic character on the one hand and a villain on the other in *Los bandidos* indicates a more exclusive, or at least a more critical, view of precisely to which Mexican men the ideal of responsible citizenship could apply. While *El fistol del Diablo* deals almost exclusively with creole sectors of society, Payno makes his villain in *Los bandidos* a mestizo worker, attributing Mexico's social problems to the existence of a rapidly increasing mixed-race and impoverished urban population in Mexico City.

By associating Evaristo so completely with violent crime, Payno exhibited concerns that many of his contemporaries shared in the late nineteenth century about a pathological pattern of male drinking that comprised part of a macho-style model of masculinity revolving around violence, gambling, displays of bravado, and domination over women, thought to be particularly prevalent among the popular classes.[98] He shows this model to be detrimental to the individual, family, and society at large and constructs an alternative ideal of masculinity to which men should aspire based on service, courage, moral strength, and fraternity in the person of Juan Robreño, one of the few characters for whom *Los bandidos* ends happily, reunited at last with his estranged son and finally able to marry his beloved Mariana. By contrasting the two models of masculinity through attitudes toward and the consequences of drinking, the author engaged with the widely debated issue of male drinking practices, and proffered a solution that he hoped Mexico's male citizens would be able to follow, without negating the positive role that drinking could play in the consolidation of fraternal masculinity and nationhood.

Challenging the Fraternal Ideal: *Tomóchic*, Miguel Mercado, and Drunken Women

By the late nineteenth century, several writers were as much concerned about exploring the impact of the nation on the lives of citizens as they were about the impact of unruly citizens on the nation. Although many *modernista* and realist writers would draw on positivist, scientific theories that were prominent in government circles during the Porfiriato in order to rationalize and naturalize the social inequalities in Mexico at the time, some authors actively opposed the Porfirian mantra of "order and progress" in their work. Heriberto Frías (1870–1925) drew on his frontline experience as a low-ranking army officer to compose *Tomóchic*, a novel published in installments in the newspaper *El Demócrata* from early 1893, which narrates the government's ongoing military campaign against the small but determined rebel town of Tomóchic, Chihuahua, an endeavor that earned Frías a prison sentence.[99]

Tomóchic received considerable critical acclaim from writers contemporary to Frías, such as José Juan Tablada, Rubén Campos, and José Ferrel, for its direct, stark prose exposing the realities and chaos of war, and for the complex characterization of the central protagonist, Miguel Mercado, who would also appear in several of Frías's subsequent novels. The character of Mercado exhibited many parallels with Frías's own life: like Mercado, Frías was forced into active military service as a means of providing for his family after the death of his father in 1889, and he also struggled with drinking and drug abuse problems throughout his life.[100] The continual references to alcohol in *Tomóchic* not only identify Mercado with the author, but also provide a substantial insight into Frías's exploration of masculinity and the individual's role within the nation, which challenged the oppositional models of manhood that had been prominent in previous fiction.

Miguel Mercado is a second lieutenant in the federal army's ninth battalion, and he relies on drinking heavily to cope with his problems. Through his portrait of Mercado, Frías critiques the established literary project of constructing Mexican nationhood around a model of heroic masculinity, patriotic duty, and fraternity, which also rejected any weaknesses, problems, or failings from the masculine, national model by concentrating such flaws in villains who were textually excluded from membership in the national community. Instead, Frías's novel plays with the hero-villain conventions of the romantic genre, creating a kind of hybrid in the person of Miguel Mercado and questioning the ideals of manhood that writers such as Altamirano and Payno had promoted through their nation-building fictions. Miguel's turbulent relationship with alcohol consumption is one of the primary ways through which the novel achieves its critique.

Amidst his superior officers' boisterous displays of drunken bravado, Miguel feels out of place and perturbed in the face of such arrogance regarding the campaign in which so many lives, on both sides, were at stake. As a result, he begins to suspect that the idea of the nation as a fraternal brotherhood was little more than a fiction designed to con men into fighting and dying for a cause they knew little about. Mercado also intuits the hypocritical ends to which the fraternal ideal was being put in the Tomóchic campaign, since the rebels themselves, once lauded as bastions of national defense against marauding Apache Indians, had only become excluded from official definitions of the fraternal, national community of citizens after they disagreed with some socioeconomic and political policies of the central government.[101]

After suffering a series of hardships and military setbacks, the troops celebrate raucously following a victory in battle over the rebels and the arrival of badly needed supplies, including barrels of sotol and aguardiente.[102] However, the celebrations, meant to affirm the men's fraternity, masculine prowess, and service to the nation, ring hollow for Mercado: "It was a magnificent spectacle. In that moment they all felt like heroes; everyone was eating, drinking, singing or chatting, happy, and ready for anything. Oh, but in that orgiastic abandon no one remembered the missing, the comrades left behind in the hills, the twisted bodies, horrible and blackened, that lay in the loneliness of the mountains. . . . No, in that moment of furious jubilation, of passionate frenzy, nobody wanted to remember the forgotten victims of Duty."[103] Frías suggests in this passage that such masculine, patriotic, fraternal rites of communal drinking and celebration among soldiers could, or were even intended to, obscure the injustice of the sacrifices endured, and acts of violence performed, on behalf of the nation.

As the campaign gathers momentum and the troops make their preparations for the final march to Tomóchic, Miguel struggles to deal with a hangover, which fuses into his frustration with the duties he is expected, as a soldier and, therefore, an exemplary man, to fulfill for the nation: "He had gotten drunk the night before—as he usually did when not on duty—and again, on awakening from his dark binge, the tumultuous violence of his drunken thoughts disappeared; he felt diminished, apprehensive, ashamed, and infinitely sad. . . . And taking up his sword, he shook his aching head, burning from the previous night's tequila, and arrived steadfast at the command site, prepared, like his comrades, to command and obey. Ready to kill, ready to die." Throughout the novel Miguel experiences feelings of inadequacy, resentment, anxiety, and melancholy and, although he knows that the illusory, temporary nature of alcohol's alluring solution to these insecurities makes it no solution at all, he continues to join in with the other revelers in his encampment, in an attempt to rid himself of these feelings: "Once again the alcohol maddened him, awakening in him bitter memories, after a strange, fleeting happiness. In that moment he became melancholy and tried to be philosophical amidst the Bacchanalian uproar. 'Well, after all,' he said, 'What's wrong with a little drinking . . . if it blots out the pain?'"[104]

Frías questions the abstract masculine and national ideals of patriotism, fraternity, and heroism, embodied in the celebrating soldiers, through Miguel's participation in the communal drinking sessions. Miguel feels the brash displays of fraternity and patriotism that these events elicit are hollow and superficial, yet he continues to engage in them because he wants to block out his moral uncertainties and cynical suspicions about the validity of the campaign against Tomóchic and the general trajectory of Porfirian politics. Miguel also finds it absurd to celebrate the possibility of imminent death and he drinks, not to welcome the opportunity of proving his manhood and patriotism but, rather, to dampen the feeling that he seems to be the only man concerned with his own mortality. In short, Miguel feels like he is the only sane person in a situation full of madmen but, rather than defying the madness, he drinks to participate in it: "The alcohol maddened him." So why does Frías make his protagonist expose the false nature of these fraternal interactions only to then seek comfort in them from his own feelings of inadequacy as a man and as a servant to the nation?

Perhaps the answer can be found in a closer examination of Miguel's gendered representation, which fuses traits from the fraternal masculine ideal with both stereotypically feminine traits and features of the more negative, volatile, macho-style masculinity generally associated with villainous characters in nineteenth-century fiction. Miguel's physique and character, for instance, are set up to contrast sharply with the other men of his corps as well as the rugged rebels. While Miguel is described as extremely thin, pale, nervous, sensitive, and often cowardly, his comrades are "boisterous, intrepid young men" and the men of Tomóchic are described as "heroic, intelligent, gallant . . . invincible, daring, audacious."[105]

These contrasts between Miguel and the other male characters are broken down in the course of the novel. Despite his weaknesses, recurrent fears, and seemingly fragile physique, Miguel actually proves to be one of the few soldiers to maintain his composure while others panic in the confused mêlée of battle. He also serves in the army in order to take responsibility for his impoverished mother, sacrificing his own ambitions of further study to provide for her. His contemplative, compassionate disposition also transforms radically at times. Miguel becomes a hypermasculine, brutish figure in his desperate sexual encounter with Julia, which is tantamount to rape. And in the aftermath of the final defeat at Tomóchic, he experiences a primal satisfaction riding across the decimated town, feeling "deep inside himself, a savage thrill before the desolation wrought by the fire and by death," despite having been moved to tears by the townspeople's plight on previous occasions.[106]

Daniel Chávez interprets the contradictions in Miguel's character, and in several other facets of Frías's narrative, as emblematic of a dialogic process that the novel resolves into a "reaffirmation of the national imaginary."[107] However, the gendering of Miguel's character and the crucial role of alcohol in this gendered portrait suggest that the tensions between nation and individual, civilization and barbarism, the center and the region remain ambivalently and deliberately unresolved. Alcohol plays a key role in Miguel's transitions between the states of emasculated or effeminate weakness, masculine responsibility and service, and hypermasculine virility and violence. Miguel drinks heavily to cope with his lack of courage and interest in military affairs and also to console himself about having to sacrifice his previous bohemian existence as an engineering student to support his mother. Before effectively raping Julia, Miguel had drunk so much that his mood transforms from philosophical melancholy to a "truly manic rage," and, when he feels primal pleasure at Tomóchic's annihilation instead of his previous compassion, he is "delirious on sotol."[108] Rather than simply attributing Miguel's charac-

ter transformations to the effects of alcohol in order to dissociate his essentially heroic figure from his more unpleasant
acts, Frías integrates alcohol use into Miguel's character so
fully that it reveals his heroic and antiheroic natures simultaneously. The passages where Miguel drinks to forget his
problems and dismiss feelings of inadequacy serve to highlight the noble, responsible reasons for his involvement in a
profession that makes him miserable and the highly compe-
tent performances he puts in during the military campaign.
Together with the incidents in which alcohol makes Miguel
more rapacious, these passages also collapse the distance initially established between him and the other male characters,
government soldiers and rebels alike. For if Miguel partici-
pates in the fraternal drinking rituals despite his skepticism
of their meanings, the other soldiers could be sharing his
fears and concerns. Moreover, his transformation into the primal figure who forces himself upon Julia, despite his heart-
felt concern for her plight, and who takes visceral pleasure in
the scene of carnage, despite his obvious sympathy for the
rebels, questions the representation of the Tomóchic people themselves as backward savages, irrational fanatics, and
bloodthirsty maniacs.

Frías's depiction of the multiple aspects of Miguel's per-
sonality through the multifaceted motivations for, and consequences of, his drinking illuminates the meaninglessness
of the fraternal, responsible, respectable masculine ideal that
fictional characters such as Juan Robreño represented. In
Frías's novel, patriotic, fraternal, masculine heroes are shown
to be every bit as constructed and reified as is the official representation of the Tomóchic rebels as barbarous fanatics, and
as far removed from the realities of being a man in the Mexican nation. Whereas Chávez identifies a duality established
between the locals drinking the unrefined, uncivilized sotol
and officers from the national army drinking tequila as an

emblem of the nation and civilization, the significance of Miguel Mercado drinking both sotol and tequila—and that both liquors transform him for the worse—is that Miguel is simultaneously hero and antihero, embodying ambivalence toward the nation.[109] Miguel represents the complexity of masculine identity and nationhood emerging somewhere in the middle of the two extremes, with—most importantly—no fixed, univocal form.

Heriberto Frías's treatment of drunken women reinforces his challenge to established ideals of masculinity. Indeed, many nineteenth-century literary representations of drinking women reflect more on questions of masculinity, and the effects such women had on the ability of men to participate productively in the life of the nation, than on feminine ideals and roles within the nation. Frías depicts the *soldaderas*, who follow their soldier-lovers to the front line in *Tomóchic*, as women without domestic ties and judges them, consequently, as morally questionable: "Their gaunt, blackened faces, their harpies' features and predatory hands tortured and violated him. He had seen them drunk, lewd and wild in the squares and poor neighborhoods of Mexico City, where they swarmed and wallowed in filth, lust, hunger, and *chínguere* and pulque."[110] This highly visceral description of dirty, drunken, seedy, and threatening women mirrors several passages that deal with Miguel's drunken, threatening, and even savage behavior, but there is no significant psychological exploration of the motives behind the *soldaderas*' behavior. Instead, this description is employed to emphasize and reflect on Miguel's own insecurities as a man. That Miguel is so disturbed by these women indicates that he is uncomfortable with their defiance of feminine norms, but he also admires their stamina, selflessness, and duty in service to their men, the very characteristics that he fears he, as a man, cannot fulfill for his nation.

Altamirano's portrait of the female consorts of the bandits in *El Zarco* is also used to accentuate the differing qualities of the male protagonists, as these drinking women are not developed as characters in their own right. The *plateados'* women are described uniformly as "drunken, ragged women," displaced from the security of a domestic setting and led into a lifetime of vice by a gang of equally disheveled and immoral men, of whom the women are mere extensions. This portrait of corrupted women, as reflective mirrors of the corrupt men they love, stands in stark contrast to the more individualized "good and virtuous" character of Pilar, "a strong, brave, and resourceful woman," who marries Nicolás at the novel's conclusion and who, like her husband, is completely dissociated from alcohol consumption.[111]

To reinforce the dissociation further, Altamirano describes the love between Nicolás and Pilar as a bond more chaste and pure than the emotions Nicolás had once felt for Manuela, which "had been intoxicating him for a long time with the deadly aroma of a poisonous flower." The love of Pilar, by contrast, is "the modest flower . . . that could breathe new life into him."[112] The association of Manuela's feminine wiles with the figurative "intoxication" of the otherwise sober Nicolás indicates that her moral strength and corrupting potential are closer to those of the bandits' women than to those of her former friend Pilar. Moreover, it is Manuela's attachment to the bandit leader El Zarco that brings her into this environment, just as the other women are there, living their dissipated lives, in order to be with their men.

Ángel de Campo, a realist writer renowned for his collections of *cuentos*, or vignettes, with an emphasis on the daily life of lower-class Mexicans, also associated female drinking with immorality, poverty, and negative consequences for the nation and its male citizens. In several of his tales, female drinkers are masculinized and associated with a negative model of masculinity based on irresponsibility, sexual profligacy, and heavy drinking, while their male companions are emasculated by their behavior in the narratives. In "El 'Chiquitito,'" the first tale in *Cosas Vistas* (What we see; 1894), a female sparrow, a "consummate drunkard," visits the title character, a lonely male canary, who yearns to fly free and unfettered through the beautiful Mexican landscape beyond the bars of his birdcage.[113] After flirting with El Chiquitito, the female asks for some of his *alpiste*, a word that can be translated both as birdseed and as a colloquial term for alcohol, like "booze." He sends the sparrow away, worrying that he would be tainted with her bad reputation, but then feels the pangs of love. After managing to escape when his owner's servant opens the cage, he flies around in a panic, frightened of a prowling cat and of his owner's attempts to recapture him. On seeing the female sparrow flying with another male bird, he gives in to exhaustion, is recaptured, and dies soon after.

As a representation of the poorer classes of Mexico City, trapped in a cycle of poverty, servile work, and melancholy outlook, El Chiquitito is readily deceived by the female's friendliness and takes reckless action to pursue the ideal of her that he has created for himself. Her illusory nature as a source of happiness is indicated by her habitual drunkenness and her request for some of his *alpiste*, possibly the only reason she wanted to talk with him in the first place. El Chiquitito's death in pursuit of an unattainable ideal reflects de Campo's fatalistic outlook with regard to the potential of Mexico's lower classes to improve their position and become positive contributors to the nation. Rather than excluding the emasculated male figure from the discourse of nationhood, the author positions it firmly at the heart of his vision of the nation, of which the lower classes comprised the majority. That the female character and not the male is the drinker increases the sense of isolation and emasculation that surrounds, and ultimately defeats, El Chiquitito.

In a subsequent collection, *Cartones* (Cartoons; 1897), de Campo reiterates this outlook in a self-referential tale, "El entierro de la 'Chiquita'" (The burial of Miss "Chiquita"), that uses human characters instead of birds. Casimiro Landa attends the burial of his ex-lover, Antonieta, also known as La Chiquita, after she has died from "a simple alcoholic congestion" following a two-day drinking binge in the local bars.[114] Like the female sparrow, Chiquita had earned a bad reputation and, like El Chiquitito, Casimiro has elevated this woman to the level of romantic ideals, symbolic of his happiness, and still loves her despite her infidelity. He had been doing military service, fulfilling his obligation to the nation, when she committed adultery and began drinking habitually in male company, which exacerbates the sense of futility that characterizes Casimiro's attempt to be the kind of noble, patriotic man—in the mold of Payno's Juan Robreño—desired by the nation. The female characters are only experienced by the reader in terms of the hope, disappointment, and dejection they cause in the male characters. Emasculated by the sexual aggression of the female characters and their masculinized drinking behavior, Casimiro and his avian counterpart are portrayed as incapable of making the heroic, productive contribution to national life that liberal ideals of fraternity, masculinity, and nationhood would have prescribed for them.

Calling to mind the raucous behavior in a Mexico City pulquería in 1804 of María Andrea, "la macho," the drinking women in the work of Frías, Altamirano, and de Campo were portrayed not only as masculine but also as related to a destructive, undesirable model of masculinity, and their challenges to traditional models of femininity went largely unexplored by these authors. The main exception to this pattern of describing female drinkers only to reflect more fully on questions of masculine identity and the potential contributions of men to the nation is Federico Gamboa's acclaimed novel *Santa* (1903), in which a female character's descent into alcoholism is treated in great detail.[115] The eponymous Santa is forced into prostitution after she is seduced, impregnated, and abandoned by a soldier, has a miscarriage, and is shunned by her family. She increasingly turns to drunkenness as a measure of solace from her degrading experiences and dies from a combination of alcohol-related diseases and uterine cancer. Her miscarriage, cancer of the womb, and alcoholism all symbolically violate social expectations placed upon women to be devoted, responsible, and respectable wives and mothers to Mexico's men and future generations.[116]

Yet, similar to Frías's *soldaderas* and Altamirano's *plateadas*, Gamboa's Santa is conceded little agency in her violation of social norms of femininity. She is merely the victim of her lover's deception, her family's condemnation, her clients' lust, her boss's avarice, and of modern society in general. Gamboa's novel explores the effects of modernization on Mexican society at the end of the nineteenth century and holds Santa up as an example of the social problems that such modernization could bring. Gamboa does not so much examine the potential role of drinking within feminine identity, as he associates excessive drinking with the negation of feminine ideals of chastity and motherhood in the person of Santa. Toward the end of the novel, Santa's devoted friend Hipólito declares his love for her and cares for her while she is sick. Despite desperately wanting to prove her own love for him through sexual intercourse, the excruciating pain her alcoholism and cancer are inflicting on her body prevent her from fulfilling this desire. At the moment when Hipólito falls on her, she screams out in agony, "I can't, Hipo, I can't . . . It would be better to kill me!"[117] No longer able to perform the act that has defined her as a deviant woman and being tortured by the now-cancerous womb that ought to have defined her as a productive woman, Santa is defeminized by the end of the novel. She is not masculinized through her alcoholism in the same way that Frías's, Altamirano's, and de Campo's drinking women were, but she is progressively stripped of her femininity as her alcoholism advances.

Many nineteenth-century portraits of drunken women also, therefore, contributed to explorations of Mexican masculinity and, to a lesser extent, Mexican femininity. While Gamboa associates the alcoholism of his central character with the gradual loss of her capability to fulfill her reproductive and nurturing roles for the nation, Altamirano mobilized images of drunken women to reinforce his condemnation of the bandit men who induced their women to such a state of immorality. Frías and de Campo also used depictions of drunken women to take their exploration of male characters and masculinity further. The latter included heavy-drinking and promiscuous female characters in his *cuentos* in order to foreground the emasculated state in which he believed the lower-class Mexican male to exist as a result of his poverty, anonymity, and monotonous daily life. Frías, meanwhile, emphasized the disquiet felt by Miguel Mercado regarding the masculine roles he was expected to fulfill on the nation's behalf by describing the mixture of admiration, disgust, and anxiety that the drunken, wanton, heroic, and loyal *soldaderas* inspired in him. Together, the gendered imagery of drunkenness these authors employ points to both the celebration of a heroic, patriotic, and fraternal masculine ideal and the deconstruction of this ideal through ambivalent, alcoholic male characters, drunken female cohorts, and masculinized drunken women.

Conclusion

Representations of male drinking practices in nineteenth-century Mexican fiction offer an illuminating insight into the construction and critique of gendered ideals of the nation. While Altamirano and Payno very clearly identified destructive forces they felt to be threatening Mexican nationhood, through depictions of irresponsible, excessive, and sometimes violent drinking behaviors, they struggled to put forward positive masculine role models who took part in this very masculine activity. Even Juan Robreño, the masculine prototype who embodied the integrative ideal associated with fraternal drinking practices in *Los bandidos de Río Frío*, stands as quite an isolated figure in a sea of more pathological male drinkers in this mammoth novel. Heriberto Frías, meanwhile, began to scrutinize the idealized masculine models like Robreño in relation to the pressures imposed upon individuals by the nation, describing multiple motivations and experiences behind alcohol use and questioning the premise of discovering or creating any single vision of Mexican masculinity and nationhood.

In *Tomóchic*, the troubled Miguel Mercado asks himself and his friends, "What's wrong with a little drinking . . . if it blots out the pain?" [118] The pain Mercado alludes to is essentially the melancholy, self-doubt, and anxiety that might be experienced by men who felt that they could not live up to the high standards set by the fraternal, patriotic, courageous ideal of masculinity. Moreover, in Mercado's case, the pain is also the gnawing suspicion that the nation, and the masculine ideal supposedly at its core, may not be worth fighting, killing, or dying for. Mercado's frequent recourse to drinking as a means of eroding that pain is an ironic inversion of the many instances of celebratory and commemorative drinking in the rest of *Tomóchic*, which glorify both the patriotic, fraternal ideal of masculinity and the nation itself. It is also a pointed critique of other literary portraits of masculine drinking that sharply delineated good and bad models of drinking, and good and bad models of masculinity in their heroes and villains. In this way, Frías highlighted, perhaps more than any other nineteenth-century Mexican novelist, that drinking could foster real bonds between individual men and the nation, at the same time as it could express a man's desire to reject fraternal ideals of masculinity and nationhood.

Part 2

Alcohol, Morality, and
Medicine in the Story
of National Development

THREE

Yankees, Toffs, and Miss Quixote

*Drunken Bodies, Citizenship,
and the Hope of Moral Reform*

Men are fragile beings, spoiled by their corrupt nature, and so it follows that they are always inclined towards evil.

—JOSÉ JOAQUÍN FERNÁNDEZ DE LIZARDI

José Joaquín Fernández de Lizardi's sentiment that human nature is fundamentally inclined toward evil, rather than good, was a common assumption for many literary figures, public intellectuals, and policymakers in Mexico during the first part of the nineteenth century. Elements of Enlightenment philosophy fueled this position, defining civilization, progress, and modernity by the increasing domination of reason and rationality in politics, economics, society, and culture over irrationality, passionate impulses, and indulgence in vices, which were thought to result from the natural bodily desires of individuals. This emphasis on the individual's rationalistic control over bodily urges was formulated in terms of an open/closed dichotomy, in which an open body, with little control over or moderation in what it consumed, excreted, or did, was conceived as dangerous and, at times, grotesque, while closed bodies, subject to reason and moderation, were civilized, ordered, and modern. In postindependence Mexico, the endeavor to keep individual bodies closed and free from vice, especially the vice of drunkenness, featured prominently in nation-building processes and debates, which were trying to define ideals and foster practices of patriotic citizenship among the population.

This chapter examines how literary portrayals of drinking and drunkenness contributed to the interconnected discourses about morality, citizenship, and patriotism in nineteenth-century Mexico. I begin with a brief introduction to evolving ideas about the body in European philosophy and how these ideas influenced public policy and discourse in both Europe and Mexico, with a particular focus on the concepts of closed bodies, rationality, public order, and civilization. The second part of the chapter explores how literary figures mobilized these concepts to denounce national enemies and celebrate patriotic episodes in Mexico's recent history. Novelists including Lizardi, Nicolás Pizarro Suárez, Juan Díaz Covarrubias, and Manuel Payno conveyed patriotism through the depiction of enemies to the nation as open, dangerous bodies, elements to be expunged or defeated in order to make Mexico a rational, enlightened, modern nation. Images of drunkenness comprised a central element in these representations of national enemies, alongside other vices such as gambling, promiscuity, and greed, revealing how drunkenness was conceived primarily as an irrational and corrupting bodily vice that posed a threat to the nation.

Analysis of constitutional texts and selected legal proceedings will then show that ideas about morality, bodily control, vice, and rationality permeated legal and political debates about citizenship and national advancement. Finally, we will examine how literary figures participated in these debates about citizenship, as Lizardi and Pizarro Suárez engaged with selected European philosophical works in their fiction, to show that good citizens could be formed by conquering the human body's susceptibility to passion, vice, and immorality through reason, liberal education, and obedience to the laws of a civilized society. Lizardi's work, in particular, associates the apparent prominence of vices like drunkenness, gambling, and indolence among Mexico's lower-class, mixed-race, and indigenous populations with the exclusion that these socioethnic groups had historically faced from the education and resources that would allow them to exercise reason and thereby overcome their bodily passions and vices.

In the second half of the nineteenth century, these ideas began to be displaced by a more deterministic, medicalized framework, which conceived of social problems as diseases to which lower-class, mixed-race, and indigenous groups were inherently, biologically, and hereditarily, more susceptible. The medicalized outlook of the late nineteenth century also concentrated more exclusively on the problem of excessive alcohol consumption, in contrast to the earlier nineteenth-century discourses that examined drunkenness as one of several irrational and immoral bodily vices, alongside excess in general, sexual promiscuity, idleness, and gambling. Chapter 4 examines this medicalized paradigm in more detail, through an exploration of medical, legal, and literary discussions of alcoholism as a social disease, but the concluding section of this chapter traces a more transitional period, through literary works of the mid- to late nineteenth century that bridge the conceptual divide between the idea of drunkenness as an ultimately redeemable vice and the concept of alcoholism as an inherited disease that was the unfortunate bequest of modernity to certain social and ethnic groups.

Bodies and their Vices: Rationality and Public Discourse in Europe and Mexico

Within many historically oriented studies, the body has been analyzed either as a "signifier" within discourses about the nation, society, and social problems or, as a "site of intervention or inscriptive surface," through which laws, moral values, and material practices are experienced or performed.[1] While Michel Foucault has been perhaps the single most important figure within scholarship of the body, Mikhail Bakhtin's work on the early modern practice of carnival and grotesque imagery in *Rabelais and His World* (1965) gave enormous impetus to the field, in its analysis of the changing conceptualizations of the human body.[2] Bakhtin's analysis of François Rabelais's literary work, and its public reception, suggested that during the Renaissance an important change was taking place in intellectual conceptions of the human body and associated sociocultural practices. While the depiction of bodily orifices and protuberances in a literary mode dubbed "grotesque" by Bakhtin—with a concerted emphasis on the bowels, genitals, nose, mouth, stomach, and breasts—carried both positive and negative associations of life and death until the late medieval period, such images, and the bodily functions with which they were associated, were increasingly viewed as vulgar and distasteful during and after the Renaissance. In the classical mode of representation in art and literature, the body acquired "a private, individual nature, one that was closed off to the world," as the focus of representation shifted from open orifices and appendages to the skin, face, and musculature.[3]

This artistic emphasis on closure, privacy, and individuality was mirrored in the development of social practices in early modern Europe, at least among the upper and middling sectors of society. Norbert Elias's *The Civilizing Process* (1939), another seminal work in the scholarship of the body, traced the evolution of social etiquette placing restrictions on certain bodily functions, eating protocols, and facial expressions that were redefined over time as impolite, uncouth, or inappropriate in so-called civilized society. Sex, urination, and defecation were increasingly confined to private spaces, and sharing food or drink from communal vessels became less common, thereby making these bodily experiences more private and individualized: in other words, more closed. The philosophical closure of the body became more pronounced in the seventeenth century as a consequence of Cartesian dualism—Descartes's theory that the material body and non-material mind, or soul, were separate, but mutually influential entities. Broadly speaking, Descartes advanced the idea, which was further propagated by several Enlightenment philosophes, that the mind was superior to and could control the body but that the body's natural desires, urges, and passions could obfuscate the mind, if the individual lacked sufficient powers of reason and rationality.[4]

For several Enlightenment philosophers, such as Jean-Jacques Rousseau, John Stuart Mill, and Immanuel Kant, the progressive closure of the body, or the progressive domination of rationality and reason over irrationality, passions, and vices, represented the very definition of civilization.[5] These ideas helped to inspire social policy in eighteenth-century Europe, as governments endeavored to regulate public spaces, popular festivals, education, healthcare, and charity, in order to eliminate vices through rationalization. French philosophes denounced the carnival, masquerades, pantomimes, jousts, fireworks, and drinking sessions as "occasions of drunkenness, debauchery, and unrestrained impulses," and recommended instead the celebration of "ceremonies of simple presence, spectacles stripped of the spectacular." At the same time, political figures and medical personnel tried to impose order upon the bodily habits and functions of the lower orders and to eliminate their vices through the promotion of bourgeois moral values that characterized excessive displays of consumption or celebration as aristocratic vice, and overt physicality as plebeian crudeness.[6]

During the eighteenth and nineteenth century in Mexico, intellectuals and government officials were similarly concerned with the prevalence of vices among the population. As Pamela

Voekel has shown, official attitudes to funeral practices and burials changed in the final decades of the colonial period, as Bourbon reformers promoted bourgeois ideals of rationality in ceremonial practices, condemning elaborate funerals, ostentatious sepulchers, and excessive displays of piety as aristocratic vice. Bourbon officials also sought to reform the predominantly plebeian forms of vice—drinking, gambling, and indolence—that they felt were the prominent causes of disorder in Mexico City and issued repeated prohibitions against the sale of food and drinks during religious festivals, in an attempt to curtail raucous behavior.[7]

Repeated petitions against such prohibitions, made by producers, distributers, and vendors of pulque to Mexico City officials, indicate that the extirpation of the vice of drunkenness remained a high priority throughout the nineteenth century. From the 1850s to the 1870s, pulque traders petitioned the Mexico City authorities to cease restrictions on opening hours during public holidays and to lower taxes on the import of pulque to the city, claiming that more efficient policing, broadening the population's access to education, and stimulating employment opportunities would be a more effective means of reducing public drunkenness and removing vice-ridden wastrels from the city's streets during festival days.[8] Wealthier pulque vendors, who managed Mexico City's most established pulquerías, mobilized the language of vice to complain about the effect of increasing competition from smaller vendors on the respectability of their trade. In 1842, about a dozen major traders argued for the reduction of the number of pulquerías so that only proprietors of good moral standing remained. Public disorder, they argued, derived from the pulque trade "falling into the hands of people without honor, morality, and education" who, unlike them, were willing to "harbor vagabonds," indulge gambling, encourage drunkenness, and allow "all manner of public crimes" to take place.[9]

Mexican journalists also campaigned against the levels of vice among the population, using language that depicted closed bodies as healthy, rational, and civilized, and open bodies as dangerous, irrational, and grotesque. An 1842 article in *El Siglo XIX* called for a more comprehensive policing system in Mexico City to control the "the most corrupt people in our population" who "gather together in pulquerías and vinaterías, forgetting about work and dragging down with them the useful artisans, who, at their side, contract the vice of drunkenness and their hatred of work." The article went on to complain about the offensive language and gestures these people frequently inflicted on more respectable passersby, the vulgar comments they made about and to women, and the frequent appearance in "the immediate surroundings of these places . . . [of] some wretched drunks, who, in their nakedness or in their carelessness, leave on show what shame would have them conceal."[10]

The emphasis on the drunkards' offensive words and gestures, their exposed genitalia, and the wretched state of their shameless, vulnerable, open bodies, drew greater attention to the threat such people could pose to otherwise decent workers, who might be corrupted simply by being at their side. In 1872 José María Vigil's leading editorial article "La embriaguez" (Drunkenness) also portrayed drunken bodies as grotesque, irrational, and dangerous. Vigil described drunkenness as "one of the most harmful vices . . . whose horrible physical and moral effects impact as much upon the family and society as they do upon the individual." As drinking deprived "the man [of] the use of his reason," it led him to commit "the greatest excesses" under the sway of "the most brutish passions," and it would reduce him and his family to destitution, in turn leading to prostitution, robbery, and other crimes.[11] Drunkenness, therefore, made a man incapable of exercising his reason and left him at the mercy of his body's most brutish and excessive passions, endangering the well-being of his family and society at large, in the process.

Yanquis Borrachos: The Grotesque Bodies of National Enemies

Mexican novelists, including José Joaquín Fernández de Lizardi, Juan Díaz Covarrubias, Manuel Payno, and Nicolás Pizarro Suárez, used this discourse about drunkenness as an irrational vice and depicted grotesque drunken bodies in their fiction as a means of demonizing dangers to Mexican nationhood. In the early decades of the nineteenth century, Lizardi's work suggested that the creole upper and middle class, who had access to education, wealth, and governmental powers, should take responsibility for the improvement of Mexico's social problems. As part of this representation, the Mexican Thinker exposes the hypocritical protagonist of *El Periquillo Sarniento* to the grotesque bodies that resulted from those social problems, thus highlighting the dangers posed by creole complacency and corruption to the future progress of the newly established Mexican nation. Díaz Covarrubias, Payno, and Pizarro Suárez, meanwhile, writing in the middle of the nineteenth century, set their narratives in recent historical contexts and mobilize the grotesque mode to portray Mexico's foreign enemies as irrational, vice-ridden, and dangerous to national progress. Moreover, Díaz Covarrubias and Pizarro Suárez, as committed liberals, associate these foreign enemies with the forces of conservatism and aristocratic excess. The drunken, grotesque, and irrational bodies are often contrasted with characters representing an enlightened, civilized, and patriotic ideal that will form Mexico's future through an adherence to liberalism and associated forms of citizenship.

In Lizardi's *El Periquillo Sarniento* (1816), the central protagonist, Pedro, is regularly exposed to grotesque, vice-ridden bodies that have been produced by unenlightened colonial institutions and the creole population's preoccupation with aristocratic wealth and privilege. Having squandered the inheritance left to him by his parents in drunken carousing and gambling, Pedro teams up with a petty criminal to finance their continued indulgence in food, wine, and card games through robbery, but they end up in prison. While serving his sentence, Pedro is made to share a cell with a group of "Indians, blacks, *lobos*, mulattoes, and castas," who mock his attempts to make out that he ought not to be in prison, that he was somehow better than them.[12] The prisoners themselves point out that not only was Pedro *not* any better than them, but as a more upper-class creole prisoner, he was likely to have committed substantially worse crimes than they had: "When you and I steal, we steal a *shawl*, a cloak, or something like that; but these guys, when they steal, they steal big."[13]

Creole criminals like Pedro were therefore more reprehensible than their lower-class, indigenous, and mixed-race counterparts; because the latter acted out of some kind of material necessity, their crime could at least be understood, if not condoned. In the ensuing scene, however, Pedro's cellmates are portrayed as grotesque bodies, polluting the room and Pedro himself with their bodily excretions and their verbal insults. Here the grotesque mode does not so much depict lower-class, indigenous, and mixed-race criminals as the enemy to Mexico's future improvement; instead, it exposes *Pedro's* irrationality, openness, and dangerousness in order to critique creole society for failing to tackle the immoral, unproductive, and vulnerable conditions bequeathed to Mexico by the colonial state.

Having already scandalized Pedro with their "countless and horrifying . . . swears, curses, and obscenities," the inmates fling urine-filled containers over him as he tries to fall asleep, leaving him "a piss soup, humiliated, and feeling like hell." His angry reaction is met with a furious onslaught of physical blows until the prisoners tire themselves out and they go to sleep, leaving Pedro to spend the night in pain, in fear, and in sopping wet, urine-stained clothes: "The truth of the matter was that I could sleep no more that night, hounded by fear, the heat, the armies of bedbugs that surrounded me, the out-of-control snores of those rogues, and the damned effluvia that their gross bodies exhaled; not to mention the other things not fit to speak of, for that cellar was drawing room, bedroom, guest room, kitchen, toilet, and dining room all in one. How many times did it remind me of the thankless nights I spent in Januario's *arrastraderito* [den of rogues]!"[14]

This description, with its strong emphasis on bodily fluids and functions, depicts the inmates as open bodies, letting out their urine, effluvia, and "other things not fit to speak of" into the atmosphere of the prison cell. But Pedro's body is open as well: his is the body being penetrated by the others' emanating fluids, smells, noises, and physical abuse. He is soaked in their urine; his ears are beset by their snores, their insults, and their coarse language; his nose is offended by their "damned effluvia"; and his body is afflicted by their blows. Pedro's openness—his susceptibility to the other inmates' openness—further highlights Pedro's self-delusion, already pointed out by one of his fellow inmates, that he was better than the other prisoners.

Although there is no direct mention of drunkenness in this scene, it merges with several closely related, sequential scenes in the novel that form part of the same criminal underworld in which Pedro moves and in which drunkenness is a regular and sinister feature. The prison episode ultimately has the same effect as the scene discussed in chapter 1, where Pedro's body reacts violently against the sights, smells, and sounds of a group of drunken men sleeping in a seedy gambling den: namely, emphasizing how Pedro's roguery is no better, if not worse, than the criminal, lazy, drunken behavior of the lower-class rogues in the novel, since he, as a member

of the creole upper middle class, has had plenty of opportunities to lead a more honest, productive life. Indeed, there are
many parallels between the two scenes, which are separated
by less than five chapters in a novel that comprises more than
fifty: in both, Pedro is offended by many of the same things,
including bugs, a rat running over his body, the snores of
the other men, and the unpleasant "sneezes" that come out
of their backsides. Moreover, in describing the prison scene,
Pedro is reminded of the restless nights he had spent in the
"*arrastraderito*" with Januario, so it is clear that the two scenes
are associated and articulate a similar lesson.

Further incidents, occurring shortly after Pedro's urine-
soaked night, reiterate the association between drunkenness,
vices in general, grotesque bodies, and Pedro's hypocrisy. After
being told that "in prison the only things you can do to pass
the time are drinking and gambling, because there's nothing
else to do here," Pedro befriends the inmates who previously
taunted and disgusted him as a means of gaining access to
their supplies of food and drink, and their gambling sessions.
Drunk on aguardiente and having shared a meal of pig trot-
ters, beef jerky, beans, bread, and tortillas with his newfound
friends, Pedro no longer feels disgusted by them or affected
by the bodily discomforts he experienced previously: "The
toasts came so thick and fast that I, being hardly accustomed
to drinking, was quickly out of it and had no idea what happened next or how I left there. The next thing I knew, when I
came to that night, I was in my bed, not very clean and with
a strong headache; and in this condition, I got undressed and
tried to go back to sleep, which I did not find very difficult."[15]
In contrast to the previous two incidents in which Pedro finds
himself unable to sleep and experiencing considerable bodily
distress—moved to vomit in the first instance and covered in
urine in the second—on this occasion he falls asleep with little trouble, despite being dirty, disoriented, and in pain. The

main difference between this and the previous scenes is that Pedro and his own indulgence in the bodily vice of drunkenness are responsible for his distress, whereas on the other two occasions he had been disturbed by the bodily sounds, smells, and actions of other men.

The associated scenes thereby highlight the similarities between Pedro and the lower-class, criminal characters and reveal Pedro's own corrupt nature, even as Pedro claims rather unconvincingly to be unaccustomed to drinking. Drunkenness and other vices such as gambling, laziness, and bawdiness are embodied in Pedro and the criminals and vagrants with whom he is compared, and condemned through the representation of their vice-ridden characters as grotesque bodies. The grotesque bodies of the prisoners and the drunken men in the gambling den, with their emissions of bodily gases and fluids, progressively penetrate Pedro's own body so that, in the scene where he falls asleep without any trouble, he feels less and less disturbed by being in contact with such men and their bodily effluvia and is much less concerned to even assert his difference from them. In *El Periquillo Sarniento*, then, the grotesque mode helps to illustrate the protagonist's irrationality and openness, his hypocrisy, vulnerability, and self-delusion, which, in turn, serve to criticize any sectors of the upper- and middle-class creole society who were neglecting their duty to act as moral, respectable, and productive citizens.

In the novels of Juan Díaz Covarrubias, Manuel Payno, and Nicolás Pizarro Suárez, meanwhile, the grotesque mode is focused on demonizing foreign enemies of the Mexican nation, as well as the conservative or aristocratic forces with which these foreign enemies are often symbolically associated. Writing in the middle decades of the nineteenth century, these writers set their fiction in recent historical contexts, such as the Wars of Independence, the Mexican-American

War, and the Reform Wars, which had all been important conflicts in the evolution of the Mexican nation and the liberal project. Evil Spaniards attempting to thwart Mexico's heroic struggle for independence, and savage Yankee soldiers violating Mexico's national territory in the Mexican-American War, are given drunken or vice-ridden bodies to accentuate the immorality and irrationality of their actions, and thus, by inversion, to invest the Mexican national cause with morality and rationality.

Juan Díaz Covarrubias (1837–59) is as famous for the tragic end to his short life as he is for his fiction. Born to a relatively poor family in Jalapa, Díaz Covarrubias was educated in Mexico City, initially in the College of San Juan de Letran, and then in the National School of Medicine and the San Andrés Hospital, where he was still training as a doctor at the time of his death. While he was acting as a physician for the liberal forces during the Reform Wars, he was taken prisoner and shot by the conservatives at the Battle of Tacubaya, aged just twenty-two.[16] As a romantic poet and prose writer, he was deeply admired by his contemporaries: Pizarro Suárez even included Díaz Covarrubias as a minor character in the 1861 novel *La coqueta* (The coquette), in which his death at the Battle of Tacubaya is recounted in a poignant footnote.[17] Díaz Covarrubias's highly entertaining novel *Gil Gómez el insurgente* (Gil Gómez, the insurgent; 1858), first published serially in the *Diario de Aviso*, synthesizes a scathing critique of Mexico's foreign enemies, conservatism, and aristocratic vice, which are together depicted as grotesque and obscene.

While this novel was being published, Mexico was sliding into the civil war between liberal and conservative forces that would subsequently claim the author's life, and Mexico had also been invaded twice in the preceding decades. A Spanish force invaded Mexico in July 1829, in response to several months of hostility toward Spaniards living in Mexico and in the midst of a string of *pronunciamientos* (proclamations, or threatened rebellions) by rival political groups in Mexico. The French also launched a short-lived invasion, known as the Pastry War, in December 1838, in response to damage inflicted upon French property in Mexico and the state's default on French loans. Antonio López de Santa Anna, the key player in Mexico's political and military affairs in this period, played a major role in resolving both conflicts, and he famously lost his leg after being wounded in battle against the French, which he later had buried in a full military ceremony in 1842 and which was dug up and dragged through the streets of Mexico City by an angry mob fed up with his rule in 1845.[18]

Written in the wake of these, and amid new, threats to Mexico's national sovereignty and stability, *Gil Gómez el insurgente* evokes a strong patriotic spirit through numerous exuberant descriptions of the Jalapan countryside and even more through its analysis of Mexico's recent history. In an extended passage (in which readers would be forgiven for forgetting they were reading a novel), Díaz Covarrubias vehemently criticizes the portrait of the 1810 Hidalgo uprising made by the conservative historian Lucas Alamán as an unruly mass movement rebelling against a beneficent, civilizing Spanish government. In Díaz Covarrubias's assessment, the Hidalgo uprising reflected a widespread and justified desire to free Mexico, and its indigenous population in particular, from Spanish exploitation.[19] As a whole, the novel elaborates this historical judgment. It is set during the Wars of Independence and uses the grotesque mode focused on bodily vices like drunkenness, lust, and excess to depict the novel's two major villains, highlighting the ongoing dangers to the Mexican nation posed by foreign interlopers and conservative, aristocratic values.

The embittered, predatory, Spanish aristocrat Regina enlists the help of a dissipated, lustful, Spanish courtier Juan de Enríquez to assassinate Miguel Hidalgo as revenge for a personal loss she had experienced at the hands of the independence rebels. Desperate to win Regina's affection, Juan ingratiates himself in the insurgent army, betrays Hidalgo by helping the royalist army to find him, and shoots the novel's young hero, Gil Gómez, who is also a leading figure among the insurgents. Meanwhile, Regina manipulates Francisco, the adopted brother of Gil Gómez and a military officer in the royalist army, into killing Juan. For six months Francisco is consumed by a profound infatuation with Regina that completely obliterates his love for his childhood sweetheart, Clemencia. Regina's attraction is likened to a luxurious, extravagant, Bacchanalian ball in which Francisco indulges his bodily passions, a pursuit that will ultimately prove to have corrosive and damaging effects on his physical and mental well-being: "But after a little while her false caresses shame us, the dance exhausts us, the wine has made us drunk and we leave that sumptuous salon; because we need to breathe in a purer atmosphere." The debauched lifestyle of excess is portrayed as unpatriotic, as the narrator contemptuously comments on a lavish ball thrown at the viceregal court to celebrate a recent victory over the proindependence rebel forces in the Bajío region: "Oh blessed mission of the courtesans, to build orgies upon ruins, to toast the bloodshed of the people!"[20]

The figurative associations between drunkenness, lascivious caresses, wild orgies, dancing, and luxury are further concentrated in the characters of Regina and Juan, who both hail from the Spanish nobility. The courtier Juan is initially described as having aged prematurely, either "through vices or through sorrows," and as we learn more about his character it becomes increasingly evident that vice is responsible. His appearance reveals a "moral ugliness": his sunken eyes are said to give out the suspicious and predatory glances of tigers and hyenas; his widened nose and thin, white lips belie his deceitful character; and "the bulging marks on his head revealed his craftiness and lustfulness."[21] The character's facial features are highlighted in this depiction, which might suggest a classical mode of representation according to the Bakhtinian schema, but the language used in describing these facial features clearly carries elements of the grotesque. Juan's head in general is given an exaggerated form, even bulging out in places as a sign of the large amount of space devoted to immoral thoughts in his brain. His eyes, in contrast, are sunken into his skull and only give out shifty and threatening glances that are likened to those of predatory animals, while his thin, bloodless lips invoke a lizard-like image. These bestial elements of his appearance have been brought about by his dissolute, debauched lifestyle in the Spanish court, regularly overindulging in food and alcohol consumption, as well as illicit sex.

The Spanish aristocrat Regina, meanwhile, possesses an extreme beauty found only in "demons, capable of turning the head of the most rational person . . . with a single look."[22] The description made of her physical features, including her smooth skin, shining eyes, and small, rosy mouth, certainly contain no grotesque elements. However, her beauty is repeatedly described as demonic, supernatural, or unnatural, thus providing allusions to her highly corrupt, grotesque character, as she freely indulges in the vices of the body, including gluttony, alcohol consumption, and sex. Moreover, it is through her mesmerizing and unnatural physical beauty that Regina captures, corrupts, and cajoles men, who then do her evil bidding. Her body, though classically beautiful on the surface, has the rather demonic ability to penetrate the moral defenses of previously virtuous men and to corrupt the already immoral men like Juan still further. In describing her seduction and manipulation of Francisco, Regina is likened to a Bacchanalian orgy. She bombards his senses with the bodily vices of drunkenness, gluttony, and lust and turns his attention away not only from his sweetheart, Clemencia, but also from the hero, Gil Gómez, and the patriotic cause he supports.

Through their immersion in a life of excessive consumption and overindulgence in vices, the grotesque Spanish bodies of Regina and Juan signify the forces of irrationality, immorality, and aristocracy. As their selfish, vengeful actions seriously jeopardize the progress of the Mexican independence movement in the novel, they are therefore associated with the conservative, monarchist factions in Mexico and Spain that opposed independence and continued to oppose the liberal, republican, meritocratic formula for Mexico's future progress during the mid-nineteenth century. Juan and Regina are responsible for the vast majority of the calamitous events that occur in the course of the novel: the execution of Mexico's independence hero, Miguel Hidalgo; the near-fatal injury to the novel's hero, Gil Gómez; and Francisco's romantic neglect of Clemencia, which ultimately results in her death. The novel's portrait of a dissipated, vice-ridden Spanish gentleman and a Bacchanalian Spanish woman in the grotesque (or at least semigrotesque) mode, as the central characters behind all the misfortunes suffered by the good characters and Mexican heroes such as Miguel Hidalgo, is key to its patriotic spirit and its denunciation of conservatism, aristocracy, and foreign interference as the trilogy of forces responsible for Mexico's ongoing national problems.

Gil Gómez el insurgente focused on the Independence Wars as a historical moment crucial to the self-definition of the Mexican nation in order to identify ongoing threats to the integrity of that nation. The novels of Manuel Payno and Nicolás Pizarro Suárez employed more contemporary political settings—the Mexican-American War in particular—to explore similar issues of national sovereignty, national unity, and patriotism. The United States declared war on Mexico in April 1846 in response to political unrest in Mexico that arose after the U.S. annexation of Texas, which had ceded itself as an independent territory from the Mexican republic in 1836. American troops invaded the northern regions of Mexico in 1846, and a second force invaded Veracruz in March 1847, before marching on to take the capital in September 1847. The war came to an end in February 1848 with the Treaty of Guadalupe-Hidalgo, in which Mexico ceded claims to more than half of its national territory, including the modern American states of Texas, New Mexico, Arizona, Nevada, Colorado, and California.[23]

Payno's *El fistol del Diablo* was first published serially in the *Revista Científica y Literaria* between 1845 and 1846 and then significantly expanded in a later edition composed in the 1880s.[24] As a whole, the novel is critical of political and personal opportunism, portrayed as the root cause of Mexico's instability in Mexico in the first half of the nineteenth century.[25] Within this broad canvas, the grotesque mode and images of drunkenness are employed to demonize enemies, both internal and external, of the Mexican nation. *El fistol del Diablo* ends with the North American capture of Mexico City in September 1847, where several key characters contribute to the civic militia's heroic and passionate defense of the city, fighting alongside the general population in street-to-street combat against the invading American army. The American soldiers are described as "bloodied and drunk with liquor and blood," suggesting the brutalized, volatile, and dangerous nature of the Americans' bodies. As the American forces descend upon the country estate of Teresa—the novel's clearest paragon of moral virtue—the soldiers are again described as "drunkards" and likened to the barbarian hordes that sacked Rome. They vandalize Teresa's property, plunder her jewels, deface the holy images in the house, and destroy the military uniform of Teresa's fiancé, Manuel, before gorging themselves on the cold meats, preserves, wines, and liqueurs in her pantry "until they became drunk." Their horses, neglected outside while the troops indulge themselves, were behaving "as if they were also drunk," devouring Teresa's beautiful flower garden, running amok, and clattering into each other, adding to the atmosphere of chaos and to the figurative bestialization of the Americans' bodies. As a new day dawns, the troops recommence their orgiastic consumption and the grotesque aspect of the Americans' bodies is reiterated once more, as "the miasmas of sweat, blood, and the drinking binge" fill the estate.[26] The passage as a whole creates a powerful contrast between the savagery of the American troops, emphasized through the grotesque language that depicts their bodies as drunken, bloodied, and dangerous, and the moral sanctuary that Teresa's country estate had once been.

This scene was added to the novel in the extended edition published in 1887, and José Ricardo Chaves argues that this barbarous portrait of the American troops is a manifestation of the late nineteenth-century *modernista* trope that defined a spiritual Latin culture against a more materialistic, utilitarian, North American mentality, best exemplified in Enrique Rodó's famous essay *Ariel* (1900).[27] Although this was likely an important influence on the inclusion of this scene, it can also be read as an extension and crystallization of the more scattered representations of national enemies in the grotesque mode, in the original version of the 1840s, which was necessarily more improvised as a result of its serialized format. The concluding section set during the 1847 American invasion draws together themes and imagery more latent in the rest of the novel and helps to render Payno's political exploration of the threats to Mexican nationhood more coherent and explicit in the 1887 edition.

On several occasions in the original body of the novel, threats to national development are portrayed in the grotesque mode, focusing on the moral and physical repercussions of bodily vices. For instance, victims of "the fights that frequently occur in the taverns of the barrios" are represented as a disruption of social order and as leaving "bloodied and disfigured corpses." The twisted, unsightly corpses that constitute material evidence of irrationality, vice, and brutality within Mexican society, are visible from the street, as they are dumped in a room attached to the prison of La Acordada, with only a metal grille separating them from full public view. Since the prison is located near some of the most elegant promenades in Mexico City, this meant that ladies and gentlemen passing by the prison in their carriages were routinely confronted with this sight, which is described as an affront "to decency and morality."[28] Not only were these corpses the result of the vice of drunkenness and the irrationality of violence, but they also manifested physical signs of their immorality and irrationality in the bloody and deformed nature of their bodies, and they posed a threat to wider society, by defacing public space in an otherwise respectable and prestigious part of Mexico City. In a separate incident, a group of ne'er-do-wells plot a robbery in the Belén neighborhood, and these characters mostly have animalized or demonized names and disfigured appearances: Culebrita (Little Snake); Diablo (Devil), who sports a deep facial scar; Muerte (Death), who has pallid skin and an oversized mouth; and Zorro (Fox), who is hunchbacked and wears an eye patch, are among the villains. Culebrita and Diablo later murder another man in a bloody barroom brawl, while they are "drunk on liquor and anger."[29]

The concerns mooted in these passages, regarding the connection between excessive drinking and violent crime, were common among literary figures, journalists, and government officials throughout the nineteenth century. In the earlier and middle periods of the nineteenth century, these concerns were often expressed in fiction through the representation of drinking bodies as grotesque, with exaggerated orifices, as in

the case of Muerte, or bodily disfigurements as in Diablo and
Zorro. Payno's disfigured villains are also portrayed as irrational bodies, quick to lash out with violence when drunk and,
therefore, when little exercise of reason over their passions
was possible. In the later edition of the novel, the grotesque
representation of the American soldiers is symbolically associated with the internal threat to social stability represented
by drunken violence and crime, already depicted in the grotesque mode in the original version. This consolidates an overarching interpretive theme presented in the novel, that the
irrational pursuit of individual satisfaction, whether bodily or
otherwise, at the expense of society was responsible for Mexico's national instability and vulnerability to external penetra-
tion in the early to mid-nineteenth century.

Payno's belated addition of drunken, savage American soldiers to the denouement of *El fistol del Diablo* may also have
been shaped by the inclusion of similar depictions, for similar
purposes, in other nineteenth-century fiction, such as Nicolás
Pizarro Suárez's *El monedero* (The coin purse; 1861). Pizarro
Suárez (1830–95) spent most of his life in Mexico City and his
two novels, *El monedero* and *La coqueta* (1861), reveal a fierce
commitment to radical liberalism and the defense of Mexican nationhood. Both novels are written within the romantic
genre and they explicitly deal with political and social themes,
dwelling on the principles of liberalism in the Reform years;
Pizarro Suárez also authored several innovative educational
manuals on grammar and morality. Like many of his contemporaries, Pizarro Suárez studied at the College of San Juan de
Letran and took up important political posts, including positions in the Ministry of War and Foreign Relations, the Ministry for Justice, and the Superior Justice Tribunal.[30]

El monedero is the story of Fernando Henkel, an Indian
mechanic raised and educated by his adoptive German father.
After suffering a romantic rejection at the hands of the beau-

tiful and wealthy Rosita Dávila, accumulating a massive gambling debt, and witnessing the impoverished conditions of indigenous families living on the outskirts of Mexico City, Fernando teams up with an enlightened priest, Luis, to establish a kind of communitarian village for the poor called Nueva Filadelfia. All the inhabitants of the village are guaranteed equal access to church services, education, childcare facilities, employment, and secular recreation centers.[31] The novel ends quite happily in 1858, with no less than two thriving Filadelfias and two happily married couples: Fernando and Rosita are reconciled, and, with a special dispensation from his church, Luis marries an indigenous woman named María.

Despite this romantic fulfillment, all is not as rosy as it seems. The epilogue is presented through the eyes of Benito Juárez and his liberal ministerial cabinet (of which the author himself was actually part), as they pass through Nueva Filadelfia in their flight from the conservative forces during the Reform Wars. Moreover, it is revealed in the novel's conclusion that Fernando had largely financed the utopian community with "counterfeit money." This revelation alludes to the incomplete and precarious condition of the liberal project at this point in Mexican history. Fernando justifies his actions to a critical Luis by identifying the absence of suitable state institutions as the reason why they have had to protect "the people, who provide all the riches for the world that leaves them poor."[32] Earlier in the novel, Luis had explained to Fernando that the primary reason for the Mexican government's hitherto inability to improve the condition of the lower-class and indigenous populations was the country's ongoing state of war since independence, in both civil and foreign conflicts, which deprived the state of the necessary resources.[33] Overall, then, the novel condemns war or, more precisely, it condemns foreign and domestic protagonists of wars that damage the development of a liberal Mexican nation.

This overall theme is forcefully emphasized by depicting warmongering enemies of Mexican liberalism in the grotesque mode. In particular, marauding American soldiers are portrayed as drunken savages, who carry out scandalous sexual violations of Mexican women and transform Mexico City into a filthy cesspool of their bodily excretions. The fourth part of the novel begins with the American troops' seizure of Mexico City in September 1847, where Pizarro Suárez makes a rare but impassioned authorial interjection to lament Mexico's lost heroes and territory and the continued internal divisions that contributed to the national defeat in this war. During the invasion, the Americans storm the Dávila household and almost all the soldiers "appeared to be drunk" and seminaked, while they ransacked the house looking for valuables. In the ensuing chaos, Rosita Dávila is raped, her mother is killed, and her already sick father dies from the shock of witnessing this ordeal.[34]

The danger that these sexually violent, seminaked, drunken American bodies represent is subsequently reiterated in a passage that describes their impact upon Mexico City in general: "The streets presented the saddest sight, transformed into real pigsties by the rotting heaps of rubbish the Yankees dumped there, and because they were constantly scattered with drunkards belonging to the invading army. The frequent and outrageous robberies and murders, perpetrated particularly at night, served to remind the indifferent inhabitants that they were totally at the mercy of this 'soldiery.'"[35] The Americans' threat to the moral and political survival of Mexico is emphasized through the grotesque language that associates their drunken bodies with the filth, violence, and unruly behavior contaminating the streets of Mexico City. The threat is then highlighted further by contrasting these American soldiers to a patriotic Mexican citizen who fights against them.

Mauricio, a carpenter by trade and brother to the Dávila family's domestic servant, battles valiantly against the American invasion of Mexico and comes to Rosita's aid, after her traumatic ordeal. Mauricio's physique and character are described in detail so that we are left with a suitably admirable impression of him:

> Mauricio was slender, of low stature, and fine features; but for the clothes he wore, to look at him you would not believe he was an artisan, and still less would you think that the young lad, who had scarcely begun to shave, was eighteen years old, possessed an untamed heart, and had a strong arm that was quick to punish any insult. Bold but generous, lively, selfless, and devoted to his family, he was truly the typical Mexican artisan, but without being deformed by those qualities that affect many others: the vices of drunkenness and irresponsibility that so degrade our workmen, because, fortunately, his father had given him a good example in this respect and separated him from the bad company that would have perverted him.[36]

Despite being potentially vulnerable to the vices of drunkenness and recklessness that the author asserts are common to his class, Mauricio has managed to avoid falling prey to such vices through the good moral example of his father, and so he is also capable of mastering the more impulsive aspects of his character, in stark contrast to the drunken, slovenly, and wantonly destructive behavior of the American soldiers and their grotesque, uncontrollable bodies, which pollute Mexico City with their waste, violence, and looting.

Ultimately, however, Mauricio's fate foreshadows the novel's deceptively gloomy ending as he is killed after being caught up in a night of violence perpetrated by "some drunken Yankees."[37] The enemies of Mexican liberalism are depicted as the embodiment of the irrational, destructive, uncivilized forces that have hindered the development of the Mexican nation into a more enlightened society. Although the novel shows faith in the liberal project to ultimately overcome these forces, both Mauricio's death at the hands of American soldiers and the conclusion, in which Benito Juárez's government is in flight from the conservative army, warn us that Mexico's liberal, rational future is still in danger.

The fictional work of Pizarro Suárez, Payno, Díaz Covarrubias, and Lizardi all employ the grotesque mode, focusing on bodily parts, functions, and fluids, to depict national enemies as drunken, open, irrational, and dangerous bodies. Lizardi's representation highlights the need for the creole middle and upper classes to conduct themselves with the utmost virtue, reason, and restraint, to learn from El Periquillo Sarniento's mistakes and reject the vice-ridden path that he had taken, and instead to become closed bodies, in full possession of their self-control, rationality, and morality. Payno, Díaz Covarrubias, and Pizarro Suárez, meanwhile, predominantly target foreign bodies for critical representation in the grotesque mode instead of the creole elite, concerned as they were with the Spanish, French, and North American invasions of the first half of the nineteenth century that threatened Mexican sovereignty.

The grotesque and savage bodies of foreign enemies are also often associated with conservative, aristocratic values and vices of excess to highlight the ongoing struggle of Mexican liberals to assert the primacy of their program for transforming Mexico into a rational, civilized, and enlightened nation. In *El fistol del Diablo* and *El monedero* the associations between these dangerous foreign bodies and conservative or aristocratic values are less pronounced and more implicit than they had been in *Gil Gómez el insurgente*. Nevertheless, both Payno and Pizarro Suárez position their good characters, and their more rational, virtuous, closed bodies, firmly on the liberal side of the political divide and show these liberals fighting determinedly against the marauding and grotesque Americans, thus providing evidence of their patriotic credentials as they try to defend the integrity of the nation in the Mexican-American War. In differing contexts, then, all four authors mobilized the grotesque mode to denounce both internal and external threats to the Mexican nation. Within this use of the grotesque, drunkenness featured as one vice among a list that included excessive consumption in general, indolence, sexual promiscuity, or aggression, gambling, and crime, which together produced open, disgusting, irrational, and dangerous bodies that threatened Mexico's future as a nation.

Defining Citizenship: Legal and Political Perspectives

The political and social elite of early to mid-nineteenth-century Mexico—literary figures, statesmen, public officials, judicial authorities, and journalists—all hoped that if rational laws were designed and applied, and if appropriate education was extended throughout society, Mexico's ordinary population could develop the necessary faculties of reason to reject vices like drunkenness, to observe the rule of law, and to contribute to national development as productive citizens.

The discursive construction of the ideal citizen, then, as a rational citizen capable of marshalling his reason in order to master his body's inclination toward vice, is perhaps best observed in official discourse regarding those who did not measure up to the ideal. Silvia Arrom's work on vagrancy laws in the mid-eighteenth to mid-nineteenth century has demonstrated that unemployment and vagrancy were generally conceived of as moral defects, deriving from bodily inclinations toward indolence, self-indulgence, and irresponsibility. In Bourbon and early republican legislation, a vagrant was basically defined as "the person who does not work, despite being capable of working, and who give themselves over to a life of vices, like drunkenness and gambling."[38] This legislation did not simply indicate that the unemployed or vagrant displayed a tendency toward drunkenness and gambling, but was based on the assumption that a person's frequent indulgence in drinking or gambling was *tangible evidence* of their condition of vagrancy: their immoral reluctance or refusal to work in an honest profession.

Even when individuals did have an honest occupation, they could still be classed as vagrants if their corporeal comportment transgressed the parameters of the rational, controlled, civilized, closed body promoted by elements of Enlightenment philosophy and Mexican advocates of reform. An 1845 law, for instance, defined as vagrants "those who provoke scandal in public places with indecent words, gestures, and actions, or who propagate immorality by selling obscene pictures, even when they have an honest means of making a living."[39] José Antonio Serrano Ortega points out that the gradual expansion of the definition of vagrancy, to encompass more and more individuals who displayed moral laxity through indulgence in vices, was intimately related to the increasing need to populate the army and civic militia with recruits and was actively resisted by many officials within the Mexico City Council and the Vagrancy Tribunal in the early decades of the nineteenth century.[40] Despite this opposition, however, the association between unemployment, vagrancy, and immorality, in the shape of bodily vice, was widely held by government officials and public figures in the first part of the nineteenth century.

These associations were clearly under deliberation in Mexico's various constitutional definitions of citizenship in the early nineteenth century. While the 1824 federalist constitution specified no literacy or property qualifications for Mexicans to act as citizens, and provided no details as to the circumstances in which citizenship could be suspended or denied, the more conservative *Leyes Constitucionales* of 1836 reintroduced such qualifications. The *Leyes* also specified, in article 11, that the rights of citizenship would be permanently rescinded "for being a vagrant, a miscreant, or having no occupation or honest means of living." Article 21 of the *Bases Orgánicas de la República Mexicana*, promulgated in June 1843, expanded the criteria for the suspension of citizens' rights to include "for being a habitual drunkard, professional cardsharp, vagrant, or owner of a gambling house," thus focusing negative judgment more closely upon immoral lifestyles and bodily vices. In 1847, the 1824 constitution was restored, reintroducing universal male suffrage, but the 1843 criteria for the suspension of citizenship, scrutinizing bodily vices and immoral practices, was retained in article 3 of this 1847 *Acta Constitutiva*. The liberal constitution of 1857 removed these strictures, however, stating only that citizens must "have an honest means of living," and they would not be reintroduced to the Mexican constitution until 1917.[41] Although not consistently considered to be serious enough criteria for the suspension or permanent loss of citizenship, habitual drunkenness, vagrancy, and involvement in gambling were clearly areas of contestation and debate in early nineteenth-century discussions of citizenship.[42]

During this period, many among the political and social elite believed that liberal education and reform held the power to transform immoral practices among the population, especially the lower-class and indigenous populations, and to mold these groups into good, productive citizens. Estate owners, distributors, and vendors within the pulque trade, for instance, condemned the vice of drunkenness and recommended that the extension of public education to instill better morals and customs in the populace, along with the implementation of more effective police patrols, were more appropriate means of reducing this vice than restricting commerce. In 1852 a group of pulque merchants urged the governor of the Federal District to provide more policing resources in order to arrest and punish the "vagrants whose only occupation is frequenting the taverns and [pulque] stalls," instead of penalizing honest proprietors and honest customers through closing pulquerías and pulque stalls.[43]

A consortium of large landowners engaged in the production of pulque also objected in 1874 to the imposition of a new tax on transporting pulque, rejecting the official rationale behind this tax: namely, that pulque was a leading cause of crime. The landowners argued instead that vagrancy was the biggest cause of crime in Mexico City and that the only solutions to this problem were improved education, to teach men the value of honest citizenship, and "the progress and development of public wealth, obtained through the spread of work and employment, the enemies of drunkenness and of all the other vices that feed on idleness."[44] These pulque magnates and traders clearly had a vested interest in making the argument that taxation and commercial restrictions would be less effective methods of extirpating the vice of drunkenness than education and proper policing, but their mobilization of the language of morality, vice, moderation, and liberal policy to make this point reveals the discursive parameters of the debate that was taking place more generally.

Legal proceedings provide further evidence of the belief that access to liberal education and good moral example were key factors in the fight against irrational bodily vices. In 1827 a lawyer argued that the twenty-seven-year-old grenadier Dionisio Jimental ought to be treated with leniency for his repeated offences relating to drunkenness because "since the beginning of his childhood, his parents, whether due to a lack of resources or to neglect, did not give him the necessary lessons for him to know the difference between right and wrong, to know moderation in vices, and to know how to cope with the workload expected of men . . . all the things that would have made him reject the vice of drunkenness, as he himself says that the lure of drinking was the only means available to him of distracting his passions and forgetting his troubles."[45]

The case file ends with Jimental being given a sentence in a public works project, indicating that the judicial authorities did not accept the rationale that Jimental deserved leniency. Nevertheless, the defense lawyer's mobilization of this argument does suggest that the idea that a better education in the exercise of rationality could improve the morality of a person's behavior was in circulation. Moreover, the lawyer's allusion to the family's social circumstances as a possible explanation for their failure to instill values of moderation, hard work, and decency in their son, raised the suggestion that the state was at least partially responsible for Jimental's lack of morality and work ethic.

Journalists also advanced arguments that the state needed to take action to correct the population's vices through either expanding access to education or tightening police supervision. As Esther Martínez Luna has demonstrated, one of the main priorities of Mexico's first daily periodical, *Diario de México*, established in 1805, was to promote the "civilization" of the masses by reforming their various vices and thus to form educated, virtuous, and productive citizens. This agenda also fueled many other periodicals throughout the nineteenth century.[46] An 1841 article in *El Siglo XIX* called for an increase in policing levels of overcrowded neighborhood tenements to rectify the vice-related problems that resulted from the lower classes' lack of proper education and thus, "to make of them useful and hardworking men . . . those tenements are swarming with vagrants, drunkards, thieves, and above all uneducated children, who sooner or later follow in the disastrous footsteps of their parents, carrying out a string of crimes as a direct consequence of the bad example that they give them."[47]

Another article in 1842 advocated the liberal triad of civil liberty, equality before the law, and public education to rectify the flaws in Mexican customs and to create good citizens, as the sheer experience of these three liberal entitlements was bound to eliminate people's immoral bodily desires for vices like drunkenness, prostitution, and adultery and foster instead rational, spiritual desires like owning property, having a family, and acquiring knowledge.[48] The article also argued that a liberal system, in which property was accumulated through individual effort and talent, would inevitably result in social inequalities, but maintained that the government could enact fiscal legislation and expand education to reduce extremes of inequality, since both extreme opulence and extreme poverty were known causes of vice:

> We complain of the ignorance and perverse education of young people, for which we blame the family, whose disgrace reaches the extreme of inciting their sons to robbery and their daughters to prostitution. We complain of the drunkenness of the fathers and their selfish conniving with respect to the mess their wives find themselves in. We study the causes of these problems and we find them in the difficulties of subsistence. We examine how these vices are introduced and we will be convinced that men are only bad when poverty is their inseparable companion. . . . They give themselves over to drunkenness to bury, among the fumes of wine and intoxication, the acute sensation of their problems.[49]

The recurrent framing of Mexico's social problems in the language of morality, vice, and the necessity of education and liberal reform in journalistic, legal, and political discourse, helped to connect understandings of drunkenness as a bodily condition and immoral vice to important political debates regarding citizenship and national development. Although excessive alcohol consumption was not the only vice discussed in this manner, the inclusion of habitual drunkenness as one criterion for the suspension of citizenship, alongside vagrancy and professional gambling, in the constitutional amendments of the 1840s indicates the prominence of political and social concerns about the population's alcohol consumption. In literary reflections on citizenship and nation-building, too, the vice of drunkenness was prominent among the central social problems to be tackled.

Reforming Mexico's Drunken Bodies: Literary Perspectives

Mexican novelists participated in the wider public discourse that advocated liberal education and reform as the best means of encouraging the ordinary Mexican population to overcome their vices, including drunkenness, through the exercise of reason, in the process becoming good citizens. Lizardi's second major novel, *La Quijotita y su prima* (Miss Quixote and her cousin; 1818), features the retired Colonel Rodrigo Linarte as a model citizen, thoroughly imbued with enlightened precepts of reason, rationality, moderation, and the importance of education. The novel as a whole posits that human nature is fundamentally inclined toward vice but, as Linarte explains to his profligate sister-in-law Eufrosina, this tendency could be overcome by following good moral examples, reason, and the law: "Our nature, corrupted by sin, is always inclined toward satisfying our passions, disregarding the law and reason, and this is why so many people imitate the perverse and the profligate; but . . . we have the necessary aids to avoid transgressing, and one of these aids is the good example of others."[50]

In a subsequent passage, Linarte proposes that impoverished peasants and rural Indians are more likely to have pure souls than the wealthy, who constantly indulge themselves in fine living, as the former would not be blighted by greed or vanity. His young charge, Joaquín, then enquires why, if poor people are naturally less inclined toward these vices, were so many observed to be "mean, brusque, deceitful, superstitious, distrustful . . . drunks and thieves . . . ignorant and given over to the most obscene vices . . . especially [among] the Indians."[51] This description carries echoes of the scenes in *El Periquillo Sarniento*, where the wayward hero is confronted with the drunken, vulnerable, dangerous, and grotesque bodies of some lower-class, nonwhite men in the gambling den and the prison. Linarte goes on to explain in *La Quijotita*, however, that immoral, irrational behavior has developed among the indigenous and lower-class populations of Mexico as a result of their inadequate education, for which the Spanish colonial authorities had been responsible and which Mexico's future liberal governments must rectify:

> The poor farmer, the unhappy Indian, the profligate plebe-
> ian, who is ignorant of the religion he professes, who does not
> know the justice of the law, who is unaware of the gravity of
> the crimes he commits and who, moreover, has been raised
> among a vulgar family, educated with the worst examples of
> ignorant and vice-ridden relatives—what could he be but an
> uncivilized brute and perhaps an eternal addict?
>
> You will ask me: on whom should we call to implement
> the remedy for such things and to watch over the proper edu-
> cation of these people? And I will not hesitate to tell you: the
> government.[52]

Therefore, although Lizardi's novel contains derogatory portraits of lower-class and indigenous drunkenness, and even
depicts them as threatening and irrational bodies similar to
the grotesque bodies that appear elsewhere, the overarching
idea presented in *La Quijotita* is of their possible redemption through proper education fostered by a more liberal and
enlightened government.

Lizardi's fiction also highlights the necessity of good moral
examples to help transform the lower classes and indigenous
population into good citizens. Consequently, the dissipated

rich, who did have access to proper education and financial resources but choose the path of excess regardless, also come in for harsh critical representation in his work. *Don Catrín de la Fachenda*, published posthumously in 1832, is the story of a work-shy, privileged young creole fond of indulging in drunkenness, gambling, and boasting: the very name of the eponymous hero roughly translates as "Master Toff, the Show-Off." Convinced (erroneously) that he is a direct descendent of a noble family of conquistadors, Catrín shuns the opportunity to develop his education with committed study and his father effectively buys a degree for him, thus encouraging the youngster's already potent conviction that he is entitled to prestige, wealth, and power without ever earning it. On hearing of Catrín's intention to enlist in the military, the family priest correctly intuits that "it is not the desire to serve the King or your country that has led you down this path but the love of libertinage," thus connecting Catrín's self-indulgence to the larger fate of Mexico.[53] The implication is that a properly educated, moderate, and moral person would act like a good citizen and serve in the military for the greater good, whereas the reckless, selfish, and profligate Catrín has no regard for such causes and simply seeks to satisfy his bodily passions for drunkenness, gambling, and chasing women.

Most of Catrín's friends demonstrate similarly libertine and unpatriotic attitudes when they get drunk together at a Mexico City café. Tremendo, whose name alludes to both his aggression and wit, encourages Catrín to enroll in the army as he says the advantages of such a career are to get respect without having to give it, to operate outside of the civil legal code, and to have free reign over any women and loot encountered in the course of one's duty. Meanwhile, Taravilla, whose name dubs him a feather-brained chatterbox, becomes very aggressive after consuming much aguardiente, which provokes the chastisement of an unassuming and upstanding young character, suitably called Modesto. The latter moves in a different circle of friends whose monikers simply exude enlightened ideals: Prudencio, Constante, and Moderato.

The confrontation dissolves into a farcical fight that ultimately ends with Taravilla challenging Catrín to a duel, and this gives the author an opportunity to ruminate on the pernicious nature of this aristocratic custom.[54] Modesto tries to dissuade the impassioned pair that "more courage is needed to pardon an insult than to avenge it," citing biblical examples, Cartesian philosophy about reason and self-control, and the rationalized military rules of Sweden's Gustavo Adolfo, in support of his argument.[55] The contrast between the self-indulgent, excessive consumption of Catrín, Taravilla, and Tremendo with their consequent violent, destructive behavior, and the sobriety, rational argumentation, and self-control exhibited by Modesto in this passage, acts as a condemnation of aristocratic forms of vice. Indeed, the portrayal of lower-class vice in *La Quijotita* is much more sympathetic than this attack on the reckless and immoral behavior of the more privileged sectors of society.

The novel ends with Catrín's untimely death as a consequence of his excessive consumption of food and alcohol, which in turn results from his refusal to engage himself in an honest occupation, echoing the emphasis on bodily comportment in contemporary definitions of vagrancy. The narrator refers to the learned opinions of John Owen and Jean-Jacques Rousseau, to show that moderation and dedication to honest work were the crucial values that would create a moral, rational, and productive citizen. Totally lacking in both, Catrín admits that his heavy drinking has gradually destroyed his health, his reputation, and his social standing: "Among the things that were killing me, the greatest without doubt was my excessive drinking. . . . This vice not only endangered my health but also exposed me to a thousand gibes, insults, and quarrels."

However, the novel is not advocating total abstinence. Another character voices the positive benefits of moderate alcohol consumption for the body and mind, indicating that moderation and self-control were the values at stake: "A good drink of wine or aguardiente revives our strength, helps digestion, fortifies the spirit, spreads happiness through our veins, and distracts us from the worries and regrets that surround us, consoling us with a tranquil, beneficial sleep."[56]

Catrín's moral radar and capacity for self-control, however, have been totally destroyed by following the profligate example of his friends, by being given the easy route to success by his parents rather than having to earn it, and by failing to take advantage of the thorough education he had been offered. Mirroring his deplorable moral state, Catrín's physical body is also left ravaged by his indulgent lifestyle: having already had a leg amputated after a fight with one of his lover's husbands, he dies of dropsy, a condition associated with heavy drinking and cirrhosis, leaving the reader to pass judgment on his work-shy and profligate life. The moral lesson seems to be, therefore, that having access to a proper education, following a good moral example, and working in an honest profession were the key means of molding Mexicans, both rich and poor, into good citizens.

In *La Quijotita*, this aristocratic kind of dissipation is also portrayed as a major corrupting influence upon Mexican women, whose role in the emerging national community was designated as the reproduction of good citizens.[57] This definition of women's social role, as the physical and moral producers of upstanding male citizens, was prominent in aspects of Enlightenment philosophy and emerging European bourgeois values, which demanded even greater bodily and moral purity from women than they did from men.[58] Although the Mexican Thinker rejected more extreme philosophical definitions of femininity that designated women completely incapable of reason, his enlightened moral compass in the novel, Colonel Linarte, explicitly states that "according to natural, civil and Divine law, woman, generally speaking, is always inferior to man," and that God made it so in order to keep women out of the realms of government, soldiery, and commerce so that they could devote themselves entirely to procreation and domesticity.[59] The most sustained presentation of this idea is the structuring feature of *La Quijotita y su prima*, which contrasts the upbringing, education, and moral example given to two female cousins, Pudenciana and Pomposa ("La Quijotita," or Miss Quixote, of the title), and the consequently opposite trajectories of their lives.

Pomposa is the arrogant, vain, and decadent daughter of Eufrosina Contreras and Dionisio Langaruto, who ends up dying as an impoverished prostitute after squandering her sizable inheritance on lavish parties and reckless gambling. Pomposa's fate is portrayed as the direct consequence of the bad example and inadequate education offered by her profligate parents, but Dionisio, as the male head of household, is assigned the ultimate blame. As the morally upstanding Linarte notes: "In my experience, women would not be so fatuous, vain or irrational if they always chose husbands that were wise and sensible men who knew how to make them follow the reasonable and just path." Dionisio and Linarte are contrasted sharply in the opening paragraphs of the novel, which focus on their bodily comportment and behavior: the former is described as "totally given over to luxury . . . gambling, balls, social gatherings, fashions, and outings," while the latter is "serious and courtly" and "amused himself without being indulgent . . . in reading appropriate books." Due to the bad example set principally by her father and the inadequate education he provides for her, Pomposa ultimately falls into even more morally reprehensible behavior, "in getting drunk and

involved in all kinds of prostitution," again focusing attention on the destructive, uncontrolled passions of the body.[60]

In a letter to Linarte and his family, Pomposa later confesses

> I prostituted myself with the help of my mother, and while we
> were able to live at first by this wicked and criminal means,
> it quickly became less profitable as I became less attractive
> by the day, and wracked with hunger, we made contacts with
> some public whores, with whom we went to all kinds of broth-
> els, descending the scale to the most wretched places. In one
> of these places, I developed an illicit friendship with a soldier
> from Guanajuato, who deserted a short time ago with a view
> to us fleeing to his land, as he would say; but before this, in
> cahoots with a certain M.R. and others equally as bad as him,
> he carried out a sizeable robbery and my mother and I helped
> to cover up the part he played in it, but as this was not long
> in being discovered, we were arrested and taken to prison.[61]

Pomposa's personal immorality, enacted in her habitual drunkenness and prostitution, stems from the lax moral example
and education provided by her father regarding vice and self-
indulgence, and is thus associated with dangerous, criminal,
antisocial, and even unpatriotic behavior in her liaison with
the AWOL soldier. Pomposa's body, moreover, becoming "less
attractive" as she falls deeper into this immoral world, is now
the locus of the social decay and moral corruption brought
about by the lack of suitable education and moral examples
provided to her as a young woman: her body has become both
an agent enacting her own vices and a receptacle upon which
other people act out their vices.

Linarte's family, meanwhile, represents the epitome of
rationality, self-control, and moderation, mastering inclinations toward bodily vices through the exercise of reason and
embodying the ideal building blocks of a civilized society.
Linarte ensures that his wife and daughter rationally con-

trol their social and moral behavior and that they obey his rule, not out of blind fear or love, but because they have been taught to understand the reason for his rules. Furthermore, the narrative clarifies at a very early stage that such careful treatment of women was not designed to please the fairer sex, but to give them the necessary qualities to nurture, cultivate, and support their men and, thus, society. Linarte opines that it was a woman's role "to be the delight of men, the repository of the wise, the shelter of generals, the throne of kings, the sanctuary of the just and the first altar of the saints; for all this is what makes her the mother, in whose arms and at whose breast wise men, kings, the just, and the saints grow."[62]

La Quijotita thereby posits that the formation of good male citizens would be dependent on the proper education of women like Eufrosina, Pomposa, Pudenciana (Linarte's daughter), and Matilde (Linarte's wife), with respect to rationality, modesty, respect, obedience, and domestic economy, in order to make them better wives and mothers. Pudenciana is presented as the female role model for this process, as she has chaste and moderate habits and proves to be a model mother as well. As Pudenciana had received such a good moral example and education from her parents, she chooses a modest businessman "of moderate habits" as her husband—not altogether subtly named Modesto—and they build an idyllically happy life together, raising two sons and a daughter in their "honest family."[63] As a result of her parents' careful instruction and good moral example, Pudenciana has always been able to exercise reason and keep her body free from immoral vices, and her body can thus become the receptacle for the procreation of future exemplary citizens. In contrast to the positive, productive contribution Pudenciana makes to society, Pomposa, who has always been encouraged to indulge every bodily desire, contributes nothing but further corruption and immorality, when she transforms into a drunken prostitute.

Lizardi's corpus of fiction as a whole, therefore, suggests that for Mexico to become a rational, civilized, and (modestly) prosperous society, its population would have to be weaned away from bodily vices and molded into rational, moral, and productive citizens, primarily through liberal reforms and widened access to education. Vices that arose from bodily desires could be conquered through the development and application of reason and self-control, a process modeled by Linarte, Matilde, Pudenciana, and Modesto. Future liberal governments should take the lead in cultivating these values in "the poor farmer, the unhappy Indian [and] the profligate plebeian," since, for these social types, access to the education and moral example that was needed to overcome their bodies' natural inclinations toward drunkenness and other vices had been historically limited. Overindulgent, profligate Catrines and Quijotitas, meanwhile, were warned against a life of devotion to the bodily vices through an emphasis on the moral and physical decay that drunkenness, lustfulness, and idleness could cause, again positing proper education and good moral example as the best means of dominating one's bodily passions through reason.

Nicolás Pizarro Suárez's 1861 novel *El monedero* dwells on similar themes, suggesting that improved access to education, good moral examples, and the means of making an honest living, would be essential for the transformation of Mexico's nonwhite population into rational, virtuous, and productive citizens. Moreover, it was the government's responsibility to find a way to improve the population's access to such opportunities. In *El monedero* a group of Mexican bandits who grievously injure the hero, Fernando, are initially portrayed in racialized terms as violent drunkards but are eventually redeemed by the idea of the community of Nueva Filadelfia, thus demonstrating that even the most dangerous (lower-class and indigenous) bodies within the nation could be "civilized" through liberal reforms, which would encourage the application of reason over vice.

The bandit leader, El Otomí, is the father of María, the woman who ends up marrying the priest Luis. Initially, however, María falls in love with Fernando, during his brief stay at her family home. Believing that he had taken advantage of his daughter, or had made false promises to her, El Otomí sets off in pursuit of Fernando with his bandit companions, El Gachupín and El Coyote. Due to a suitably melodramatic bout of amnesia, Fernando cannot remember who María is when El Otomí confronts him with the ultimatum to marry her or die, and the bandits consequently force him to drink a lethal poison. In the aftermath of this attack, the bandits feel remorse for their treatment of Fernando, but while El Otomí and El Coyote get drunk and fight one other, El Gachupín helps María to revive Fernando with an antidote and subsequently decides to renounce his life of banditry. El Otomí, meanwhile, dies in the course of his next assault and El Coyote presumably carries on as a bandit, as we are not told otherwise.

At first glance, it seems that the racialized names of these three bandits predetermine their relationship to alcohol, their nature, and their ultimate fate. El Otomí, named for his indigenous ethnic group, recklessly drowns his sorrows in alcohol in accordance with the "drunken Indian" stereotype; El Coyote, whose name was also a racial category, describing a dark-skinned mestizo, becomes abusive when drunk and escalates a petty squabble into a serious altercation, as the working mestizo population of Mexico City were considered particularly wont to do; and El Gachupín, whose name was a common pejorative term for peninsular Spaniards, resists the temptation to get drunk on this occasion, as he fears the potential consequences, and also takes the moral high ground by helping Fernando, thus demonstrating a greater degree of

control over his own bodily passions and vices through reason and morality.

However, it is difficult to reconcile the character of El Otomí
as a simple manifestation of the "drunken Indian" stereotype.
In this passage the narrator specifically notes that El Otomí
"drank aguardiente on the rarest of occasions," and on several
previous occasions he refuses alcoholic drinks.[64] The novel is
peppered with Nahuatl names and words, whose origins and
meanings are fully explained, indicating an interest in, understanding of, and enthusiasm for indigenous culture, rather
than the stereotypical portrait and tone of disapproval that
usually accompanies portraits of "drunken Indians." Moreover, the novel bucks the general trend of nineteenth-century
fiction by investing numerous indigenous characters with
considerable agency and rationality: the hero, Fernando, a positive indigenous role model himself, is recurrently helped by
civic-minded indigenous communities when he finds himself in difficulties.[65] Consequently, a straightforward reading
of the ethnically symbolic alcohol use of these three characters seems too simplistic.

As El Otomí is the only one of the three characters to be
explored in any real depth, and in the context of the social
engineering project that the community of Nueva Filadelfia represents, we might therefore interpret El Coyote and El
Gachupín as alternative trajectories that El Otomí himself could
have followed had he experienced different opportunities in
life. His early years were spent on a hacienda and following a
brief, rather unjust, spell in prison, where he was badly mistreated, El Otomí became a bandit conducting raids against
monopolistic haciendas. During this time, he taught himself
to read and to take advantage of the natural medical remedies
in the surrounding environment. After five years, he extri-
cated himself from banditry in order to establish a family and
returned to the working life in the isolated village of Cacahua-

milpa, built his own house, and raised his own crops, before marrying and conceiving a daughter, María. Unfortunately, El Otomí's wife died and his consequent bitterness led him back to banditry, although on this second occasion he followed a policy of minimal violence against his robbery victims and ferociously punished those in his gang who disobeyed these orders. During Fernando's stay at his family home, El Otomí reads letters about Nueva Filadelfia and yearns to become part of such a community "in which the poor are not humiliated, in which labor is respected and rewarded," in contrast to the exploitation he had experienced that had driven him to a life of banditry, for which he also demonstrates clear remorse.[66]

By the time El Otomí attempts to murder Fernando, we have developed a certain sympathy for and understanding of his character and we know that he carries within him the potential, at least, to act with rationality and morality. In the ensuing scenes, three alternative fates are outlined for the three bandits, representing, by association, three alternative fates for the Mexican nation. El Gachupín, normally "an enthusiastic drinker . . . abstained from taking aguardiente due to the vague fear he felt that 'El Tigre' wanted to poison him." Sober and in control of his physical and moral faculties, El Gachupín rescues Fernando and abandons his dangerous and destructive life of banditry. By contrast, El Otomí, who normally did not drink, felt a similar remorse for his treatment of Fernando and "wanted to drown the disgust by getting drunk," rather than take any action to remedy his misdemeanors, and he is ultimately punished by death in a subsequent raid. El Coyote, for his part, is more concerned that he is not getting more of the booty and, "bolstered by drinking, he told his chief of his many grievances," thereby starting the fight between them, before going off to presumably continue his criminal career more autonomously.[67]

Perhaps this incident points to a need for Mexico to acknowledge its problems and divisions as the first step in exercising greater rational and moral control over society. The three different paths are racialized in the names of the bandits, not to celebrate the Hispanic over the indigenous aspects of Mexican nationality, but rather to emphasize, as the novel does as a whole, that the indigenous people of Mexico tended to have the most limited access to the educational and financial resources that would allow them to conquer their vices and to participate in the national community as rational, moral, and productive citizens. The liberal-socialist utopia of Nueva Filadelfia, encapsulating the author's idea of a Mexican society where the liberal project had been implemented completely, is posited as the means through which the indigenous population could have such access to education, honest occupations, and good moral examples.

Both Lizardi and Pizarro Suárez, then, highlighted the power of liberal education and reform to transform social groups deemed particularly vulnerable to vice—including women and Indians—into good members of society who could exercise rational control over bodily passions. Moreover, rather than attributing the supposed lack of rationality and moral self-control among women and Indians to any inherent weakness in their mental and physical makeup, these works identify the failure of successive Mexican governments to equip women and the nonwhite population with the education, moral examples, and general opportunities needed to dominate their bodily passions as a primary source of the problem. From the middle of the nineteenth century, and increasingly until the beginning of the twentieth century, however, public figures and novelists alike began to lose faith in the ability of liberal education to effect such changes and sought alternative answers in medicine, which singled out drinking from other bodily vices, by defining excessive patterns of alcohol consumption as diseases.

From Morality to Medicine: Losing Faith in Education

During the mid- to late nineteenth century, there was a gradual shift in literary representations of drunkenness, which reflected a broader process of discursive change in discussions of social problems, citizenship, and national development. The concerted faith in the efficacy of education and liberal reform to mold Mexico's lower-class, mixed-race, and indigenous populations into productive and virtuous citizens—evident through literary explorations earlier in the century—became less pervasive. Fernando Orozco y Berra's romantic novel *La guerra de treinta años* (The thirty years' war; 1850), for instance, follows a similar line of argument to Lizardi's fiction, advocating liberal education and reform as the best means of teaching the populace to dominate their inclination toward bodily vices through the application of reason, but concludes on a less confident note regarding the potency of liberal ideals, reforms, and education to solve Mexico's social problems, a position that would become more widespread as the century progressed.

Fernando Orozco y Berra (1822–51) was the younger brother of the renowned historian Manuel Orozco y Berra and his obituary in *El Siglo XIX* described him as an "esteemed young man, well known in both Pueblo and Mexico City for his writings."[68] In addition to his major fictional work, which is mentioned with some admiration in Juan Díaz Covarrubias's novel *La clase media* (The middle class; 1859), Orozco y Berra contributed articles to such periodicals as *La Ilustración Mexicana* and *El Museo Mexicano*, which sought to reform the vices of society through satirical and costumbrista sketches.[69]

The central character in *La guerra de treinta años*, Gabriel, narrates his life story through a series of failed love affairs, which are initially frustrated by his unrealistic expectations and impractical attitude regarding love and subsequently stem from his ongoing obsession with the unattainable Serafina, whose parents want to marry her off to someone considerably wealthier than Gabriel. Threaded into the narrative of Gabriel's romantic ups and downs is a sustained symbolism of drunkenness, as the young lothario repeatedly describes the experience of being in love as akin to the state of drunkenness, while he repeatedly falls into patterns of heavy drinking and indulgence in other vices during times of heartache. This dual aspect of drunkenness in the novel, linked to both Gabriel's lofty romantic idealism and his destructive pattern of seeking comfort for his soul's pain in bodily vices, foregrounds a concern with both the morally corrupt social customs of the Mexican people and the possible ineffectiveness of liberal ideals and reforms to change them.

The novel's action is overtly set in Spain but it is clear throughout that it addresses the social and political issues current in Mexico, and the author admits as much in the conclusion:

> It will be well-known that I say Burgos and Granada in vain, when the society I depict is not that of Spain . . . therefore there are some distasteful scenes . . . that serve to highlight the contrast with other scenes, which although they might be the same in essence, appear adorned with the trappings of refinement or education. The latter two things are somewhat lacking amongst Mexicans; consequently, any national writer should suffer from a certain rudeness or impropriety that our customs and manners still have.
>
> The European lifestyle is reflected amongst the highest sectors of society in the capital. When they are my object, I will make sure that the poison is drunk from a golden cup and that the aromas of the rose and the lily envelop the corruption.[70]

This disclaimer (not an unusual feature in nineteenth-century novels) as to any defects in the prose, or to any offense caused by some of the material under discussion, is actually made in quite a pointed manner. The statement suggests a larger critical agenda within the novel, namely, to highlight the misguided nature of attempts to impose abstract liberal ideals and institutions on a Mexican high society that had only adopted European upper class and bourgeois customs at a superficial level, and on a Mexican low society that was impoverished, uneducated, and uncivilized. The story of Gabriel's rollercoaster love life pursues the agenda revealed in the conclusion in a more symbolic fashion and, in doing so, reveals a changing mode of conceptualizing drunkenness in Mexican literary discourse.

Gabriel, the first-person narrator, frequently uses a metaphor of drunkenness in passages with lyrical, romantic flourishes to describe his idealized experience of love. In general, Gabriel supposes that women "intoxicate [men] with a single flirtation," and the night before his separation from his first girlfriend, Luisa, he describes their embrace thus: "Delicious ecstasies came back to me, assuring me that I still held her in my arms: I opened my eyes to give her the most tender look, and we fell back into our intoxication." He later compares the elusive Serafina to a sweet-smelling flower that "enchants, intoxicates" and imagines that the beautiful Rosa "would spend the night dreaming about me, caressing me, studying the new and most exquisite pleasures with which to intoxicate me." The evening Gabriel spends kissing Julia is also characterized by "a kind of magnetic intoxication."[71]

Despite his romantic language and high expectations, none of Gabriel's relationships with these women amount to more than fleeting courtships. The exception is Serafina, who becomes increasingly cold and hostile toward him as his obsession with her grows. Meanwhile, Gabriel's close friend Angela falls in love with him and, as a consequence of his increasing detachment from her as he chases an endless string of women, Angela's health deteriorates drastically.

The doctor treating her "advanced hysteria" realizes that her unrequited love for Gabriel is the cause of her condition and sends multiple letters begging him to visit her. By the time Gabriel gets round to visiting more than a year later, she is already dying. Reflecting back over his unfortunate romantic record, he comes to a significant realization: "When will Serafina love me? . . . When it is possible to revive Angela, killed by my indifference!"[72]

Further emphasizing the futile and illusive nature of Gabriel's pursuit of his idealized vision of love, and thus symbolically denoting the inapplicability of abstract liberal ideals to Mexican society, Gabriel resorts to bodily vices—drunkenness in particular—as solace for his heartache. This suggests a certain skepticism regarding the efficacy of liberal education and reform to conquer vices and to rationalize and civilize Mexican society. Gabriel's drunken episodes throw into sharp relief a contrast between his romantic idealism, talking about love as a heavenly intoxication, and his baser actions, indulging in "orgies," "Bacchanals," and "devilish nights" to hide from his emotional pain.[73] Both patterns of behavior—that is, both Gabriel's emotional preoccupation with the intoxication of love and his bodily indulgence in sordid drunkenness—are portrayed as irrational, uncivilized, and destructive. The implication of this representation is that abstract liberal ideals, symbolized through Gabriel's idealized image of romantic love, and the bodily vices of society, exemplified through Gabriel's recurrent drunkenness, were equally damaging to Mexico's progress as a nation.

While the metaphorical malleability of drunkenness as intoxication clearly contributes to the way that drunkenness is singled out from other vices in this novel to a greater extent than in earlier fictional works, this representational strategy might also be taken as evidence of a growing focus on alcohol consumption as the central social problem affecting Mexico's population within nation-building discourse. This idea seems to be reinforced by the novel's figurative associations between Gabriel's recourse to drunken dissipation and the misery of the lower classes. Early in the narrative, Gabriel falls in love with Mariquita, a girl from a family of low social station and questionable morality (it is intimated that the father sexually abuses the children), but his own family forbids him to continue the relationship. After a few months spent clandestinely exchanging letters with Mariquita, Gabriel becomes disillusioned with the girl and severs all ties. He then embarks, for the first time, on an extended drinking spree to try to escape from his troubles. He quickly feels the bodily effects of such excess and overindulgence, and his physical discomfort is described in some detail, alongside some moral qualms he feels with regard to his treatment of Mariquita: "I felt that listlessness, that discontent that exhausts one's energy and confuses the senses after a day of excess. The forehead is fatigued, the eyes sunken and blurry, but the imagination is clear and the past flashes through one's mind with all the clarity and vividness of a mirror: the heart beats lethargically and regrets consume one's time." Gabriel then explains that "in the midst of my dissipation," over a period of roughly six months, he gradually forgets about Mariquita, but the narrative quickly reminds him, and the reader, of her fate as a disgraced and abandoned woman.[74]

One day Gabriel picks up a prostitute and proceeds to her home with his friends, where they all take their turns using her body, until they are disturbed by her returning husband. Gabriel flees across the street to the house opposite, where he makes a shocking discovery:

> In the corner on the left, upon a fetid, black bed, lay an emaciated, yellowish woman, with grey, spiky hair and sunken, heavy eyelids. She was a corpse more than a woman, not so

much lying in bed as thrown among a heap of filthy rags, and at her head there was a boy of ten or twelve years old, almost naked, sitting on a broken chair, resting his head on the pillow of the sick woman. In front, there was a young woman sitting on the ground, with crossed arms and her forehead buried in her knees. . . . Not a wardrobe, nor a bench; not a single piece of furniture. . . . It was poverty laid bare in all its deformity.[75]

Mariquita is the girl seated on the floor while her mother wastes away from starvation and, when Gabriel offers her a peso before leaving remorsefully, she accepts his meager offering bitterly, saying, "At last, you have taken pity on me."[76] In this revealing passage two evocative and detailed descriptions of different bodies and bodily states associate Gabriel's selfish excess—his indulgence in the vices of drunkenness and promiscuity—with the poverty caused by social customs and prejudice. Having abandoned Mariquita to a miserable fate in a squalid neighborhood rife with prostitution, as a result of the pressure Gabriel feels regarding the social convention of marrying well, Gabriel himself is shown to be taking bodily pleasure from the unfortunate situation of women like Mariquita, who herself eventually turns to prostitution in order to survive.

Like Lizardi's fictional works, *La guerra de treinta años* morally condemns extremes of social inequality and the bodily inclination toward vice in which these extremes are manifested. However, while Lizardi's work focused on the expansion of liberal education and reform as the means of increasing the population's rational and moral control over bodily vices, the emphasis in Orozco y Berra's novel is much less clear and confident. Instead, *La guerra de treinta años* highlights an incongruity between idealistic liberal propositions and the realities of Mexican society by exposing the fallacies of Gabriel's idealized vision of romantic love. The figurative intoxication through which Gabriel experiences love is juxtaposed with images of the physical distress, moral corruption, and social decay that are created by his indulgence in the bodily vice of drunkenness.

In this more pessimistic outlook regarding the possibility of improving social behaviors and in the focused descriptions of the physical effects of drunkenness and other vices, Orozco y Berra's novel foreshadowed later fictional works that contained graphic depictions of the bodily consequences of drinking and reflected a more deterministic interpretive framework that characterized many social problems as the inevitable consequences of advancing modernity in Mexico. In many ways, therefore, Orozco y Berra's work can be considered as transitional, between the earlier paradigm that suggested that the immoral and bodily inclination toward vices (of which drunkenness was one among many) could be overcome through the application of reason and the later framework of understanding that transformed the specific vice of excessive drinking into a social disease and understood this disease, paradoxically, to be produced by social progress. Moreover, the grotesque language of the earlier period, creating images of dangerous, open bodies by focusing on body parts, fluids, and functions, became amalgamated within the more medicalized language that characterized fictional descriptions of alcoholism in the late nineteenth century.

Of course, these chronological breaks were not definitive; in 1861 *El monedero* outlined a radical liberal program for Mexican society in the utopian community of Nueva Filadelfia, and in 1887 Manuel Payno added grotesque imagery representing national enemies to a new edition of *El fistol del Diablo*. However, the work of José Tomás de Cuéllar also reflects a gradual transitional trend away from these paradigms. *Las jamonas* (Fashionable ladies; 1872), for instance, exhibits both the moralistic condemnation of irrational vices like drunkenness and the grotesque description of national enemies of the earlier model, alongside a more medicalized understanding of alcohol abuse and its effects. *Las jamonas* is essentially a novel about political and moral corruption preventing the political stability and cultural modernity of Mexico. As in de Cuéllar's other work, the features of French high society—the fashion, cuisine, music, and manners—have been adopted by Mexico's nouveau riche, though, since they lack any genuine cultural sophistication and moral depth, this becomes little more than a vulgar charade instead of a measure of Mexico's modernity.

One of the main protagonists, Sánchez, has become a wealthy and corrupt government official after rising through the ranks in a manipulative fashion during the Reform Wars, and enjoys an opulent lifestyle, indulging regularly in both sexual promiscuity and drunkenness. The narrator tells us that "when he [Sánchez] was good and poor, he did not drink" but, when he started to move in important social and political circles, he became reliant on drinking cognac to dispel his fear of public speaking and to overcome feelings of inferiority and shyness.[77] Before a less than sympathetic audience of aristocratic conservatives, Sánchez prattles on endlessly about the liberals' rise through the Reform Wars and drinks excessively to create a feeling of self-assurance in the absence of any validation from his hosts. On returning home at a late hour to find his girlfriend, Amalia, accompanied by her suspected lover, Ricardo, Sánchez argues with her and eventually rapes her, after de Cuéllar describes the transformative effects that the alcohol has had over him: "Here the tendency of the drunkard to act valiantly is born, because when the alcoholic gases are exciting certain organs, the cowardly drunkard feels a novel pleasure in finding himself to be brave . . . with his nervous system overexcited, Sánchez had put himself in the moral position of the madman. He was pale, his eyes shone in a strange manner, and his gaze, far from being opaque and wavering as it was initially, had a febrile fixedness that could not contemplate anything with indifference . . . he no longer had the faculty of good judgment."[78]

This description contains both the idea that drunkenness caused a loss of reasoning ability and consequently led to immoral behavior and the increasingly medicalized language that characterized late nineteenth-century descriptions of alcoholic bodies. Allusions to the specific effects of alcohol on "certain organs" and the "nervous system," and a previous reference to "aldehyde" as a chemical component of alcoholic vapor, show a gradual incorporation of medicalized language into the more moralistic outlook that condemned indulgence in the vice of drunkenness as irrational and dangerous.

Las jamonas also singles out drunkenness for criticism, in contrast to earlier fictional works that commonly represented excessive drinking as one among a number of immoral vices, perhaps reflecting the shift toward the emergence of the concept of drunkenness as some sort of medical condition that might have had biological and physical causes and effects, rather than simply being an issue of irrationality and immorality. The fourteenth chapter of *Las jamonas*, entitled "La embriaguez" (Drunkenness), begins with a philosophical exposition on the reasons behind habitual drinking and its typical outcome, which demonstrates a transitional outlook between the moral and medical understandings of alcohol use.

Chapter 14 of de Cuéllar's novel shares with the work of Lizardi, Pizarro Suárez, and Orozco y Berra the assumption that man's recourse to drunkenness usually stems from "an imperfect education, ignorance, and his natural submission to all that his conscience would admonish him to avoid," leading him "to descend from the pedestal of the free-thinking man" and to become "the madman and the pervert, the fool and the brute." However, the "symptoms of alcoholic poisoning" are also described in detail in *Las jamonas* as they are not in the other novelists' work: "the excitation of certain nerve branches" and "the inflammation of certain tissues" are stipulated as the physical cause of the drunkard's loss of modesty, propriety, morality, and reason.[79]

These descriptions of internal bodily processes and symptoms, together with the moralistic condemnation of the suppression of reason through vice and the depiction of Sánchez as a deceptive, drunken rapist, combine to create a transitional position with regard to understandings of drunkenness and alcoholism within Mexican fiction. De Cuéllar's psychological and medical language develops the grotesque bodily imagery of earlier nineteenth-century novels, focusing both on internal bodily processes and internal social problems within Mexico. Sánchez is portrayed both as a threat to the nation, since he perverts the political system for his own benefit and betrays the project of liberalism, and as a dangerous drinker, thus foreshadowing the much more explicit focus on alcoholism as a symptom and cause of national decay within later fictional works, while also preserving elements of the earlier discourse concerning drunkenness, morality, and rationality.

Novelists of the late nineteenth century were surrounded by a wealth of medical and psychiatric studies and debates concerning alcoholism as a medical concept, but there were precedents, which might have provided impetus to the gradual transition in fictional representations of drunkenness from the middle of the century. In 1847, the politician and poet Francisco Ortega (1793–1849) published a treatise that delineated the physical and moral effects of drinking and discussed the various possible courses of action that could be taken to combat the population's enthusiasm for alcohol. He demonstrates many of the same priorities as those of earlier nineteenth-century novels in that he posited that drunkenness primarily caused a heightened vulnerability to bodily passions and reduced a person's reasoning capacity, transforming the drinker into a slave devoted to "a tyrannical vice." Ortega also described his campaign as "patriotic and beneficial" and advocated the establishment of temperance societies, after the example set by North America, England, and France, which would spread knowledge about the harmful effects of drinking and would also foster the practice of and tendency toward association, a key attribute of a democratic society.[80] These two aspects of Ortega's treatise reveal that he, like early nineteenth-century novelists, considered drunkenness to be a considerable obstacle to the process of molding Mexico's population into moral and productive citizens and of making the Mexican nation more civilized. Education through temperance societies, prison reform, and the expansion of correctional programs were the main policies he offered as solutions to the problem, although, unlike many liberal journalists and novelists of the era, he also emphasized the need for trading restrictions, especially on distilled liquors.

Key elements of the medicalized language that would come to dominate Mexican discussions regarding alcoholism in the late nineteenth century, however, were also present in this 1847 treatise. In addition to the moral perils of regular drunkenness, Ortega emphasized the physical and mental ailments that "drunkenness fed by alcohol" could induce.[81] Drawing on (rather dubious) statistical information from North America, England, Switzerland, and Mexico, Ortega demonstrated that excessive drinking caused delirium tremens, dementia, sterility, impotence, liver diseases, and digestive disorders, all of which had been observed in the patients and residents in Mexico City's hospitals and charitable institutions. The treatise marks the beginnings in Mexico of a more medicalized understanding regarding the effects of alcohol consumption, which developed in the mid-nineteenth century alongside the predominantly moral understanding that characterized drunkenness as a failure of reason over bodily passions, itself the result of insufficient education and underdeveloped commitment to citizenship. This medicalized framework of understanding became an increasingly common presence in late nineteenth-century fiction that addressed Mexico's social problems in an era widely perceived as the onset of Mexican modernity.

Elements of this medicalized paradigm developed out of the earlier grotesque trope of Lizardi, Díaz Covarrubias, Pizarro Suárez, and Payno, who utilized detailed, graphic descriptions of bodily orifices, fluids, and functions to create images of dangerous, open, vile bodies that imperiled the Mexican nation. Through the transitional work of Orozco y Berra and de Cuéllar, we can see the continuation of detailed and graphic descriptions of bodies, but these became more focused on dangerous bodies *within* the Mexican nation and, certainly in the case of de Cuéllar's fiction, on internal bodily processes and features. With the gradual increase in medical studies on the effects of drinking, the series of midcentury wars that ultimately produced a compromised liberalism in the Porfirian era, and a rising awareness of the potential problems accompanying the benefits of modernity, there was a distinct shift in literary discourse away from early nineteenth-century optimism regarding the efficacy of liberal reform and education to cultivate reason among, and eliminate vice from, the Mexican population.

FOUR

Medicine, Madness, and Modernity in Porfirian Mexico

Alcoholism as the National Disease

> The Enemy has triumphed. . . . And the results are savage, primitive, identical to those of all invasions: rape, murder, degradation, annihilation of the weak, the disavowal of mercy, the destruction of beauty, the ridicule of all that is good . . . the red flag waves, it is the backward step, to the stone age, the uselessness of strength and the sterility of intentions; there is less a man and more an alcoholic.
>
> —FEDERICO GAMBOA

Federico Gamboa's 1903 comparison of alcohol's action on the human body to an enemy army invading the nation exemplifies the late nineteenth-century literary approach to alcoholism. Alcoholism is depicted both as a potent threat to national development and as an elaborate metaphor for national decay in the context of Porfirian modernity. This literary examination of alcoholism was intimately related to contemporary medical, legal, and political discourses surrounding alcohol consumption and society, as Mexico's government in the 1890s and early 1900s, dominated by positivist intellectuals known as *científicos*, sought to analyze and control social phenomena through pseudoscientific methods. This chapter draws on late nineteenth-century medical texts, newspapers, and fictional works to establish how these pseudoscientific and literary discourses about alcoholism intersected and how various intellectuals interpreted Mexico's experience of modernity and nationhood during its first prolonged period of relative political and economic stability under the leadership of Porfirio Díaz between 1876 and 1910.

In contrast to many writers of the early and mid-nineteenth century who had much faith in the transformative power of education, late nineteenth-century writers such as Federico Gamboa, Ángel de Campo, Pedro Castera, and Amado Nervo put forth a much more pessimistic prognosis regarding the ability of the Mexican population to reform its harmful drinking practices. Their fiction mobilized an increasingly medicalized language, detailing the physical and mental effects of alcohol consumption on the individual drinker, enabling them to describe the newly conceived category of the alcoholic, which they in turn associated with criminality, mental illness, and racial degeneration. This medicalized analysis reflected serious concerns about the effects of Porfirian modernization projects on society.

The first section of the chapter reviews the development of a medicalized concept of alcoholism in Europe and Mexico, identifying an increased focus on the physiological, neurological, and psychological disorders that alcohol consumption could produce. While doctors and other analysts in late nineteenth-century Mexico used the term alcoholism in a variety of ill-defined ways, their discussions of alcohol consumption shared several features that clearly distinguished them from earlier texts on the subject of drinking. For example, descriptions of the effects of alcohol consumption increasingly focused on physiological processes, involving tissues, organs, and chemical components, and alcoholism was intimately linked in these discussions to various kinds of mental illness and, often as a direct consequence, to criminal behavior. In addition, while many Mexican doctors and lawyers routinely cited statistics and studies on alcoholism by European specialists to support their arguments and conclusions, several took issue with European conclusions about the relative harmfulness of distilled and fermented alcoholic drinks as a result of domestic observations they made about pulque, a fermented drink unique to Mexico.

The second section of the chapter examines how politicians, journalists, and other social commentators utilized medical and legal opinions regarding alcohol during the Porfiriato. The establishment of theoretical connections between alcoholism, criminality, insanity, and racial degeneration, within the context of a government seeking to practice "scientific politics," helped to shape aspects of public policy, especially regarding the penal system and education. The group of technocratic politicians known as científicos, as well as other public officials and social commentators, viewed as essential for national progress the discovery of solutions to the problems they diagnosed with regard to Mexico's population. The hyperbolic and deeply pessimistic language through which they discussed alcohol and degeneration reveals the existence of deep-rooted anxieties about the future of Mexican nationhood.

Finally, representations of alcoholics and alcoholism are examined in the literary works of Ángel de Campo, Federico Gamboa, Pedro Castera, and Amado Nervo. These writers mobilized medical language and knowledge to portray alcoholism, and the criminality, mental illness, and degeneration that alcoholism was thought to produce, as problems created by Mexico's nascent modernity. Rather than representing the Porfirian government's "order and progress" as the forward path for Mexican nationhood, these literary works foreground fears that Mexico's social problems may be insurmountable, which were expressed more latently in nonfictional discourse. Because novels of the 1890s and early 1900s routinely associated alcoholism with conspicuously modern drinks, modernity itself came to act as a protagonist in these fictional works, compounding existing problems of alcohol abuse, crime, and mental illness, and leading to the projected degeneration of the nation.

The Medicalization of Drunkenness
and the Emergence of Alcoholism

Mexican research into alcoholism emerged in the context of the development of scientific medicine over the course of the nineteenth century, owing in part to the growing body of evidence proffered by European and North American investigations into alcoholism and a long history of Mexican interest and concern about drunkenness among its population. With the foundation of the Establishment of Medical Sciences in 1833 by Vice President Valentín Gómez Farías, formerly a doctor himself, and drawing on anatomy and physiology texts from France, England, Germany, and Italy, new models of understanding disease began to take shape in Mexican medical thought and practice. In this developing diagnostic framework, the inflammation of bodily tissues was understood as a primary indicator of specific, definable illnesses. The availability from the 1850s of new equipment, as well as knowledge of the emerging field of bacterial studies and vaccination, also helped to prepare the ground for a comprehensive overhaul in the treatment of physical and mental disease.[1]

Although the professionalization of medicine was, and continued to be, a contested process, the formation of institutions and the investment of public money gathered apace during the Porfiriato, especially during its later decades. To the Superior Council for Sanitation, the National School of Medicine, and the National Academy of Medicine, already founded in 1841, 1842, and 1864, respectively, the Porfirian era added the National Medical Institute in 1888 and the National Institute of Pathology in 1896, as well as some fifteen learned medical societies. While the *Gaceta Médica de México* had been an important forum for medical discussion since 1864, these new medical bodies established a plethora of additional regular publications for a medical audience. The National Medical Institute began publishing a weekly periodical, *El Estudio*, in January 1890; *La Farmacía* was published on a bimonthly basis from 1890 by the Mexican Pharmaceutical Society; a consortium of hospitals produced *Crónica Médica Mexicana*, a magazine dedicated to medicine, surgery, and therapeutics, from 1897; and the National Institute of Pathology also produced a monthly bulletin from September 1901.[2] Publications and institutions such as these afforded an expanded environment in which medical issues could be discussed and debated. Alcoholism, and its connections to mental illness and various social problems, was a central issue debated by a medical profession that drew on and challenged existing European studies as part of an ongoing international dialogue about the effects of alcohol consumption.

It should be noted here that the term *alcoholism* is, and has been since its inception, used to denote a wide variety of physical and mental conditions associated with alcohol consumption. One of the most influential works in alcohol studies during the twentieth century, E. M. Jellinek's *The Disease Concept of Alcoholism* (1960), defined alcoholism very broadly as "any form of alcohol consumption which causes harm to the individual, to society, or both," before outlining several different kinds of alcoholism with either some degree of psychological or physical dependence on alcohol, or with observable physical and psychological damage, in the absence of dependence.[3] Within alcohol studies there has been much debate as to whether alcoholism should be defined as a disease with identifiable *biological* causes.[4] Even Jellinek classified only two of his five types of alcoholism as actual diseases, since they were characterized as having biological origins, including the "adaptation of cell metabolism, and acquired increased tissue tolerance . . . which bring about 'craving' and loss of control and ability to abstain."[5] Some molecular studies have found evidence that different genetic levels of certain chemicals involved in the metabolism of alcohol might biologically predispose a person to the development of drinking problems, but theories about possible genetic origins of alcoholism also remain in dispute.[6]

In most nineteenth-century texts, however, *alcoholism* as a term is used rather vaguely, sometimes merely as a synonym for habitual drunkenness or inebriety, sometimes referring to the physical or mental ailments caused by prolonged alcohol abuse, sometimes referring to a biologically determined disease, and sometimes all three simultaneously. Since the in-depth debate as to whether alcoholism should be understood as a biologically determined disease did not emerge until the twentieth century, this analysis of nineteenth-century thought regarding alcohol consumption focuses on the emergence of a *medicalized* concept of alcoholism—as opposed to a more narrowly defined disease concept—among nineteenth-century Mexican intellectuals. This medicalized concept consisted of detailed examinations of the effect of alcohol on internal organs, tissues, and bodily processes; the establishment of pseudoscientific connections between alcohol consumption, disorders of the nervous system, and criminality; and the expression of concern that alcoholism and all its associated physical and mental problems could be transmitted hereditarily. In developing these medicalized ideas about alcohol consumption, Mexican physicians, public officials, and legal experts routinely cited statistics and opinions from European studies that had been conducted over the course of the nineteenth century and that constituted an internationally accepted corpus of knowledge on the physiological, mental, and generational effects of alcohol.

European doctors had gradually developed medical concepts of alcoholism as they investigated the causes and effects of heavy drinking among the increasing working-class populations of industrializing cities, wherein poverty, crime, and ill health appeared to contradict contemporary ideals of progress and modernity. Regular, heavy drinking was observed to cause both mental and physical illness in the individual drinker, as well as social disorder and even stagnation in the productive capacity of the nation. In addition, excessive drinking was increasingly deemed a "state of sickness" in itself and referred to by the name of alcoholism, which, once properly identified and diagnosed, could be treated through medical and psychiatric means, in addition to the moral condemnation and penal sanctions that had previously sought to reform habitual drinkers.[7]

Early nineteenth-century English doctors published treatises on the physical effects of alcohol abuse, which would later become defining symptoms of the condition known as alcoholism. Thomas Trotter (1761–1832), for instance, stated that "drunkenness is an illness of unknown cause which upsets the healthy equilibrium of the body," also leading to dropsy, gout, apoplexy, and epilepsy. Other doctors noted the appearance of liver abnormalities in the bodies of deceased drinkers, and although the physical and mental agitation that accompanies alcohol withdrawal had been documented by earlier physicians, it took on the name of delirium tremens only in the early decades of the nineteenth century.[8] The Swedish doctor Magnus Huss pulled together the fragmentary knowledge about the effects of alcohol on the human body, systematized their study, and called the condition "chronic alcoholism" in his influential 1849 book *Alcoholismus Chronicus, or Chronic Alcoholic Illness: A Contribution to the Study of Dyscrasias Based on my Personal Experience and the Experience of Others.* Like many other medical investigators, Huss focused on the harmful effects of distilled drinks, as opposed to fermented drinks, which were considered relatively benign, and considered alcoholism to be a form of poisoning. Huss defined alcoholism to be an identifiable medical problem but he also attributed its development to a lack of personal morality and responsibility, since individuals could make the decision whether to start drinking heavily or not, thus initiating the onset of the problem through a free, personal choice. Among the possible actions to be taken in the fight against alcoholism, Huss proposed antialcohol propaganda and the reform of the alcohol trade, and he also established special treatment clinics, separate from asylums, for patients deemed alcoholic.[9]

Huss's translated work and concept of alcoholism as a primarily medical condition, rather than as a moral and social crime, spread among medical specialists in Germany, North America, and France, the latter being particularly influential on Mexican doctors later in the century. The word *alcoholism* and the condition it represented became the subject of much medical interest in France from the early 1850s, reaching a peak during the last decade of the nineteenth century. Following Huss's model, the view that only distilled spirits caused alcoholism was widespread until the 1920s, with absinthe being singled out as a particularly harmful drink, due to a toxic flavoring (thuja or thujone, from the wormwood tree) thought to provoke nervous disorders. Absinthe was accordingly banned in France, Belgium, Switzerland, Italy, and Morocco by 1915. Among the defining features of alcoholism, which was understood to develop slowly and progressively with prolonged alcohol use, but which could manifest itself differently in different patients, doctors across Europe identified organ damage, delirium tremens, suicidal tendencies, dementia, violent or unstable behavior, severe disorientation, and seizures.[10]

The European conception of alcoholism as a primarily medical condition thus focused on the range of physiological, neurological, and psychological disorders that alcohol consumption could cause. European specialists also concluded that distilled high-percentage drinks inflicted the most severe damage on drinkers and identified links between alcoholism and a range of social problems. In many respects, Mexican physicians of the late nineteenth century followed this European model, producing "much more detailed descriptions of alcohol's effects, with these usually portrayed as developing in stages and eventually leading to some type of madness."[11] Mexican researchers also sought to find causal links between the incidence of alcoholism and social problems such as poverty, crime, and prostitution that were observed to be on the increase in Mexico City, as it underwent a process of modernization during the Porfirian period. Mexican investigators, however, put forth a range of arguments regarding the relative harmfulness of distilled and fermented drinks that differed substantially from their European counterparts. Since the widespread consumption of pulque was considered the main observable difference between European and Mexican drinking practices, many Mexican specialists argued that pulque was the key factor in explaining any unique manifestations of alcoholism and its associated problems in Mexico.

Jesús Barrera's 1870 medical thesis *Del alcoholismo y algunas de sus formas* introduced a model of understanding drunkenness as progressing through three distinct stages, which appeared in numerous Porfirian texts on alcoholism and was recurrently replicated in the Porfirian press.[12] The first stage was characterized by the excitation of the drinker's pulse, cognitive functions, and sexual sensations; the second was more variable from person to person but could include violent or idiotic behavior and physical weakening; and the third was "grave intoxication," featuring apoplexy, a dangerously low pulse, and very labored breathing. Barrera described delirium tremens as a further form of alcoholic disease that arose either among those not used to drinking at all suddenly having a binge, or among more hardened, habitual drinkers experiencing withdrawal. Sufferers of delirium tremens, he noted, generally experienced trembling, sadness, and uneasiness, followed by angry outbursts, terrifying hallucinations, and even permanent insanity in some cases.[13] The intellectual and politician Francisco Bulnes presented a similar appraisal of the three stages of drunkenness in 1909, as did the Mexican doctor Roque Macouzet, in 1901, and Trinidad Sánchez Santos, a notable Catholic spokesperson, in 1900.[14]

Legal expert Francisco Serralde presented a more detailed breakdown of the three stages of drunkenness, describing changes in behavior and social comportment, as well as detailing the numerous physiological changes caused by drinking. During the initial stage of excitation, he explained, the drunk maintained a regular heartbeat, frequent pulse, and good circulation but also displayed a certain rosiness of the cheek, a marked lack of inhibitions, a smiling, happy countenance, impropriety, boisterousness, some incoherence, and frustration or anger. During the second, more perverse, phase, Serralde noted a greater disturbance of the body, mind, and social behavior. Heightened circulation and facial redness accompanied a loss of willpower, a total lack of judgment, fear and shame, increased irritability, paranoia and volatility, and the (male) drinker took on a somewhat brutalized, animalized quality: "the individual becomes a tiger in his instincts and a man in appearance only." The third and final phase is described in greater technical medical detail, pointing to "frontal cephalalgia" (headache), nausea, pyrosis (heartburn), the loss of muscle function, and unconsciousness. At this stage of extreme drunkenness, the drinker would have pallid skin and a weakened pulse and could suffer involuntary defecation, or even death, as a consequence of choking on vomit or experiencing a cerebral or pulmonary embolism. Serralde then enumerated more long-term diseases caused by regular and heavy drinking: hepatitis, cirrhosis, dipsomania, alcohol-induced diarrhea, weakening of the blood vessels, epilepsy, paralysis, premature death, and "chronic alcoholism in its maniacal, melancholic, or insensible forms." Unfortunately, Serralde, a lawyer, did not elaborate on what these different forms of "chronic alcoholism" entailed, but it is clear that he conceived of alcoholism as a medical condition distinct from drunkenness; regular drunkenness caused a range of medical problems, of which alcoholism, characterized by some form of compulsion or subconscious behavior, was one.[15]

Trinidad Sánchez Santos, a leading figure in the Catholic opposition to the Porfirian regime, was more precise in expressing his understanding of alcoholism, which he defined as "the poisoning of, or pathological state in, the organism that results from the ingestion of alcoholic substances." He further clarified that the alcoholic was not just a drunkard but also "any person who customarily takes whatever dose of alcohol" if it resulted in physiological damage, such as liver dysfunction, circulation problems, digestive irregularities, memory loss, slurred speech, loss of mobility, trembling, decline in mental acuity, gastritis, tuberculosis, or dementia.[16] In his more extended 1896 study, Sánchez Santos quoted the influential French psychiatrist Valentin Magnan in an attempt to clarify the confusion between alcoholism and drunkenness: "The true alcoholic is he who does not get drunk," indicating that persistent consumption of alcohol increased an alcoholic's tolerance to the behavior-altering effects of drunkenness but caused a physical deterioration in bodily health.[17]

Other commentators, however, further muddied the waters in their distinctions between alcoholism and drunkenness. Nicolás Ramírez de Arellano, a distinguished member of Mexico's National Academy of Medicine, listed "drunkenness or acute alcoholic delirium" among "the illnesses produced by alcohol abuse," alongside dyspepsia, gastritis, gastroenteritis, liver cirrhosis, bronchitis, heart failure, aggravation of the nervous system, and madness.[18] Moreover, he insisted that all levels of intoxication were harmful to the individual and society, arguing that anyone "in a state of simple drunkenness, of pathological drunkenness, or of chronic alcoholism"—without giving any details as to what distinguished these three categorizations—should be committed into special treatment facilities until a medical specialist judged that they would no longer relinquish sobriety.[19]

Newspaper coverage of debates about alcoholism, its causes, and potential remedies also used a wide range of ill-defined terminology. A three-part article published in 1883 by *El Tiempo*, a leading Catholic daily newspaper, equated "drunkenness" with "acute alcoholism," which itself was defined as a form of narcotic poisoning. "Chronic alcoholism," meanwhile was a slow form of poisoning caused by "habitual drunkenness," which would eventually cause "dipsomania," a kind of madness characterized by an uncontrollable urge to drink heavily.[20] While the element of compulsion or lack of control in the desire to drink was a consistent feature of the nineteenth-century definition of dipsomania, the precise relationship between this compulsive mania and alcoholism was less well defined. Some, like the commentator in *El Tiempo* and Ramírez de Arellano, identified alcoholism as the cause of dipsomania, but others, like the doctors referenced by Hidalgo y Carpio in an 1899 article in *El Imparcial*, one of the Porfiriato's most widely circulated newspapers, classified dipsomania as an advanced stage of alcoholism.[21] The latter view, therefore, characterized alcoholism itself as a disease with several different, progressive stages, but the former view classified dipsomania as a disease and alcoholism as a pattern of drinking behavior that could cause mental and physical disease.[22]

At best there was a rather confused consensus among Mexican physicians and social commentators regarding the nature of alcoholism. Whether they classified alcoholism as a disease itself, a mental condition, or merely a physically harmful behavior, late nineteenth-century studies of alcoholism consistently featured a marked attention to the physiological consequences of alcohol consumption and described those physiological consequences in increasingly technical medical language. Moreover, medical texts frequently drew on international research into alcoholism to support their conclusions about alcoholism in Mexico and to identify areas where alcoholism and drinking practices in Mexico were different or unique. We have already seen that Sánchez Santos quoted the French psychiatric expert Valentin Magnan in his definition of alcoholism, and Ramírez de Arellano also cited an important French psychiatrist, Benedict A. Morel, while discussing the adverse consequences of alcoholism for reproduction.[23] Jesús Barrera's influential work introducing the theory of drunkenness advancing in three stages was itself heavily influenced by the work of German philosopher and psychiatrist Johann Christoph Hoffbauer. In his 1885 thesis, medical student Ernesto Espinosa cited physiological works by the French doctors Mathías Duval and M. Jaccoud to support his analysis of alcohol's effect on human brain functions, and he also assessed the strengths and weaknesses of French, English, Spanish, and Belgian laws regarding the issue of whether drunkenness or alcoholism should be considered grounds for diminished criminal responsibility.[24]

Porfirian newspapers similarly gave detailed attention to international dimensions of the alcohol problem, discussing findings from international conferences on alcoholism, comparing rates of consumption and alcohol-related problems across different countries, and evaluating the antialcohol strategies employed by various nations. In 1908 *El Imparcial* claimed that Mexico "had scarcely begun the fight against alcohol" in comparison to other countries, like England, Scotland, the

United States, France, and Argentina, where licensed venues had been drastically reduced and temperance movements taken much greater hold.[25] The temperance movement did remain limited in Mexico until the postrevolutionary period, although there had been some relatively isolated calls for the establishment of temperance organizations in the mid-nineteenth century.[26] The first antialcohol organizations were formed in the late Porfiriato: the Mexican Temperance Society was founded in 1903 by Addie Fields, a leading member of the World Women's Christian Temperance Union, who had lectured at Mexico City's National School (Escuela Nacional) the year before. The society's first board of directors was comprised of several prominent Mexican scholars, including Roque Macouzet, Ezequiel Rosas, Enrique Paniagua, and Angel Medina.[27] Although there was not universal approval of the appearance in Mexico of temperance groups, there was an increasing level of enthusiasm among intellectuals and social commentators for the potential role such organizations could play in Mexico's multipronged fight against alcoholism.[28] Favorable comment, or at least bewildered admiration, was even conferred on Carrie Nation, who started vandalizing the saloons of Kansas in 1900. While such newspaper coverage typically expressed caution about following the radical temperance and prohibition strategies witnessed in the United States, they also seemed to admire Nation, whose direct, dramatic action contrasted sharply with what they perceived as inaction on the part of the Mexican state toward the alcohol issue.[29]

While the United States provided intriguing evidence for Mexican intellectuals and physicians considering the merits of temperance organizations, when it came to debating the relationship between alcohol abuse and mental illness, Mexican analysts most often turned to France as an international referent.[30] Toward the end of the nineteenth century French physicians focused particularly on the psychiatric elements

FIG. 6. Illustration of Carrie Nation, an American antisaloon activist famous for destroying saloons with a hatchet, featured in a story about her campaign in *El Imparcial* ("Liga Feminina contra las cantinas," *El Imparcial*, February 17, 1901). Courtesy of Paper of Record. http://paper ofrecord.hypernet.ca.

of alcoholism, although not all alcoholic patients were considered appropriate candidates for psychiatric treatment. Chronic and "morally weak" patients, that is, those who continued to relapse into heavy drinking patterns, were often turned away since they were deemed incurable. In the Sainte-Anne Asylum in Paris, "alcoholic delirium," usually comprising hallucinations and aggressive behavior, became the most common criteria for admission. Other alcohol-related conditions treated by French psychiatrists included dipsomania, characterized by "paroxysms of drinking," and *absinthisme*, characterized by epileptic attacks, vertigo, delirium, and memory loss thought to result from drinking the popular aperitif absinthe.[31]

In Porfirian Mexico, medical, psychiatric, and legal investigations into alcoholism also identified strong links between excessive drinking habits and the development of mental illnesses; indeed, the engagement in certain excessive drinking habits was often considered to be a form of mental illness in its own right. Cristina Rivera-Garza notes that by the late Porfirian period, alcoholism had become the most commonly diagnosed mental illness in both San Hipólito and Divino Salvador, the men's and women's hospitals in Mexico City. Alcohol-induced insanity was understood at the time to be prevalent, with *El Imparcial* running an eye-catching headline in 1908 that read, "Seventy-five percent of the lunatics in our country are alcoholics."[32] In the 1880s Francisco Serralde had already claimed that more than 70 percent of those admitted as mental patients to Mexico City's hospitals had histories of excessive drinking, and he defined five different patterns of dysfunctional alcohol use as types of madness in themselves: "Alcoholism, delirium tremens, dipsomania, drunkenness, [and] alcoholic melancholia are the diverse forms of madness of which a multitude of people have been made spontaneous victims."[33] Although citing a lower figure of alcohol-related admissions to mental hospitals than Serralde, at 53 percent of male and 38 percent of female patients, Trinidad Sánchez Santos enumerated a remarkable array of alcohol-induced mental problems in 1896, including acute mania, intermittent mania, remitting mania, chronic mania, epilepsy, lypemania, delusions of grandeur, religious delusions, extreme paranoia, paralytic madness, partial madness, circular madness, dementia, alcoholic mania, acute alcoholism, and chronic alcoholism.[34] Official records of the General Insane Asylum, meanwhile, reveal that in its inaugural year of 1910, 15 percent of its patients were diagnosed as alcoholics, while drinking was also included as a contributing factor in many other psychiatric conditions under examination.[35]

In debating the causes of alcoholism, Mexican physicians and intellectuals commonly questioned European conclusions about the relative harmfulness of distilled and fermented drinks. European doctors overwhelmingly concluded that distilled spirits were more harmful and likely to cause alcoholism, since the higher concentration of alcohol they contained meant that even small quantities of a distilled drink could cause significant damage, whereas much larger quantities of a fermented drink would have to be consumed to cause comparable harm. Some temperance organizations in France even recommended the consumption of port wine as a remedy for alcoholism.[36] Many Mexican specialists, however, concluded that pulque, a fermented drink unique to Mexico, was among the most harmful drinks that could be consumed, refuting much European thought on the potency of distilled and fermented drinks.

Roque Macouzet, a pioneer of Mexican pediatrics, criminology, and temperance, argued that pulque produced a different reaction in the human nervous system than that caused by other drinks. This different reaction basically amounted to a unique state of irritability in which "a look, a smile, and even, on many occasions, real visual and audio hallucinations"

FIG. 7. *El alcohol y la locura* (Alcohol and madness). Illustration accompanying an article about "pathological drunkenness," in which state drinkers could be expected to "destroy everything in their path" and become a serious threat to others' lives (Stach, "Platicas del doctor," *El Imparcial*, July 15, 1909). Courtesy of Paper of Record. http://paperof record.hypernet.ca.

could easily provoke the drinker into aggression, often escalating into serious violent incidents. Other Mexican physicians also specifically blamed pulque for inducing catatonic mental states in hardened drinkers and producing abscesses in the stomach and liver.[37] The special harmfulness of pulque was also likened, on occasion, to the most feared liquor in Europe, absinthe, which French doctors thought could cause a unique type of madness and which was banned throughout much of Europe by the early twentieth century. Manuel Alfaro, director of the San Hipólito Asylum, declared in 1908 that pulque, "the favorite drink of our people . . . devastates the human organism and causes problems just as horrible as absinthe."[38]

Trinidad Sánchez Santos elaborated this attack on pulque in order to explicitly locate the nation's problems in the diseased, alcoholic bodies of Mexico's lower classes: "None of the drinks commonly consumed in the country merit greater attention than pulque, the great poison of our popular classes, whose effects produce the most principal part of our national pathology." Drawing on José Ramos's study about the medical effects of pulque consumption on the liver, Sánchez Santos claimed that the "fatty degeneration of the liver" observed in pulque drinkers was unique and substantively different from "the cirrhosis described by European authors." Whereas classic cirrhosis was characterized by hardening of the liver tissue, the livers of pulque drinkers, according to Ramos, became extremely soft, losing their shape, and sometimes even falling apart on examination. Sánchez Santos then extrapolated this physiological difference to speculate that pulque drinking must also have been responsible for Mexico's higher incidence of mortality, madness, and crime as compared to other nations, since a high level of pulque consumption was the only significant difference that he acknowledged between drinking patterns in Mexico and countries like France, England, and Germany.[39]

Similarly, Esteban Maqueo Castellanos, a leading Porfirian judge from a wealthy landowning family in Oaxaca, and later a novelist of the Mexican Revolution, argued in 1910 that pulque consumption was primarily responsible for the high crime rates and lack of work ethic in Central Mexico, the only region of Mexico where pulque could be manufactured and distributed. He compared various European statistics to demonstrate that France had significantly higher rates of alcoholism and crime than England and Italy and, despite citing no actual figures for the Mexican case, asserted that in Mexico "alcoholism surpassed the figures cited for France: at least in the Federal District, where pulque reigns."[40]

Although acknowledging that all alcoholic beverages contributed to individual and social problems, Francisco Serralde also singled out pulque for particular criticism, stating that its consumption was having "disastrous penal consequences," being a "vice that is damaging the poor classes, deteriorating their health, and perverting their moral standards." He argued that 80 percent of crimes were caused by drunkenness and that most cases of drunkenness derived from the excessive consumption of pulque by the lower classes, primarily on Sundays and Mondays.[41] With a similar logic, the Mexican Temperance Society, in one of its earliest campaigns, petitioned Mexico City's *ayuntamiento* in 1907 to introduce much more stringent restrictions against pulquerías, due to pulque's uniquely harmful effects on the lower-class population. Following the opinion of Roque Macouzet, the society's former president, they argued that pulque "predisposes drinkers toward violence and gives them the nerve to carry out crimes," and even to do things completely out of character, like committing suicide or homicide. Aguardiente, by contrast, "simply puts people to sleep."[42] By focusing attention on a fermented beverage, and explicitly stating that distilled drinks like aguardiente caused fewer problems, the Mexican

Temperance Society revealed a very different set of priorities to most European and North American temperance activists.

Several notable intellectuals of the Porfirian era, however, took the opposing position. The most comprehensive defense of pulque was launched by Francisco Bulnes, an important científico (positivist) intellectual, journalist, engineer, historian, and politician of the Porfirian era, who served variously as federal deputy, senator, and minister for foreign affairs.[43] Bulnes cited a range of French and other European scientists— including Dieulafoy, Jaccout, Gallard, Huss, Carpenter, and Peters—to refute the Mexican doctor José Ramos's demonization of pulque as particularly harmful to the livers of its drinkers. He referred to Ramos's work as "alarmist" and argued that the fatty degeneration of liver tissue, which Ramos identified as the unique consequence of drinking pulque, had in fact been observed by many doctors in Europe as well, where pulque was unavailable. Not only could all alcoholic drinks, and not just pulque, he argued, have this physiological effect, but fatty degeneration could also be caused by poor diet, syphilis, pneumonia, and tuberculosis. Bulnes went on to refute the work of another Mexican physician, Manuel Flores, who claimed that pulque caused a range of digestive problems, including slow digestive transit, diarrhea, and nausea. Bulnes argued that recent physiological studies had conclusively demonstrated that brewer's yeast, which could be found in all fermented drinks and not just pulque, was responsible for these problems, but that it, like pulque, could also help to remedy certain afflictions, such as psoriasis, flu, pneumonia, diabetes, typhoid fever, and tuberculosis.[44]

Bulnes was undoubtedly so thorough and passionate in his defense of pulque as a result of his membership in the Association of Pulque Retailers, a trust which sought to establish monopolistic control over the distribution and sale of pulque in Mexico City. Indeed, the association, formed in 1909, commissioned Bulnes's study of pulque in which this defense was put forward.[45] Pedro and Ignacio Blasquez, also pulque hacienda owners, made a similarly self-interested defense of pulque in 1897, claiming that "the drunkenness that pulque induces is happy and argumentative," whereas drinkers of aguardiente and *chinguirito* experienced more serious consequences, such as delirium tremens.[46] Nevertheless, Bulnes's work reveals that there was a significant debate among Mexican intellectuals regarding the relationship of pulque consumption to the development and prevalence of alcoholism among the Mexican population.

The physician Silvino Riquelme insisted that pulque was much less harmful than distilled spirits, since a much greater quantity of pulque would have to be ingested to produce the same ill effects as drinks with a higher alcohol content, following the same line of argument as European doctors in the debate over distilled and fermented drinks.[47] Other doctors went further, bolstering more traditional claims that pulque consumption could actually have health benefits. In 1879, for instance, Ladislao de la Pascua recommended small doses of pulque to combat diarrhea and to stimulate lactation in nursing mothers. Porfirio Parra, a professor of hygiene and pathological anatomy at the National School of Medicine, argued that small amounts of pulque provided nutritional support for the undernourished poor.[48] Moreover, in 1884, José Labato, a leading figure in Mexican hygienics, recommended the use of pulque in treating anemia, nausea, frail constitutions, and stomach aches. Francisco Martínez Baca, a pioneer of Mexican criminology and craniometrical analysis, documented his use of pulque to combat a scurvy epidemic in a Puebla prison in 1896, further highlighting its nutritional value, especially among the malnourished poor.[49]

Bulnes, Riquelme, and others drew on and cited European studies of alcoholism to bolster their defense of pulque and to replicate the widespread European conclusion that distilled drinks were more physically and mentally damaging than fermented drinks. However, many other intellectuals concluded that pulque consumption was the unique aspect of drinking practices in Mexico and thus explained the apparently higher rates of alcoholism, mental illness, and crime in Mexico as compared to other countries. This debate regarding the relative harmfulness of pulque is particularly noteworthy because of its apparent *absence* from late nineteenth-century literary explorations of alcoholism, an absence that will be discussed in the final part of this chapter. As chapter 1 illustrated, several novelists depicted pulquerías and pulque consumption in a negative light, while others portrayed pulque as an emblem of cultural authenticity. However, pulque barely featured at all in late nineteenth-century fiction that specifically dealt with alcoholism and alcoholics. Instead, the increasingly medicalized knowledge and language that characterized depictions of alcoholism in Mexican fiction consistently associated alcoholism with distilled drinks, particularly modern and fashionable distilled drinks such as tequila and *fósforo*, a trendy drink combining aguardiente and coffee.

These literary portraits, associating alcoholism with modern drinks, and ultimately with modernity itself, were related to the ways in which medical knowledge regarding alcoholism was situated within wider theories about racial degeneration and applied in various aspects of public policy during the late nineteenth century. The connections established in the non-literary sphere between alcoholism, modernity, degeneration, and social decay helped to shape the literary discourse that postulated similar connections. Medical practitioners, attorneys, and other intellectuals codified alcoholism as a medical condition that produced not only a wide array of physiological problems but also led to numerous mental disorders and an increased incidence of crime. In addition, the observed correlation between these three phenomena—alcoholism, mental illness, and crime—was construed as evidence that the process of racial and social degeneration was well under way in late nineteenth-century Mexico. This degeneration was understood to have potentially catastrophic consequences for the future of the Mexican nation. While many commentators held very pessimistic views about the possibility of rectifying this situation, late Porfirian administrators mobilized medical knowledge to inform public policies and aspects of public discourse in their attempts to combat alcoholism and degeneration.

Alcoholism, Degeneration, and Public Policy in the Porfiriato

From the 1890s, a small circle of positivist intellectuals known as científicos came to dominate the Porfirian administration and had a leading role in the formulation of public policy. Alcoholism loomed large among their concerns, primarily due to the potential threat that alcoholism was thought to pose for social, racial, and national degeneration. As with the range of positions put forth to define alcoholism, Mexican intellectuals, even among the relatively small circle of científicos, held different ideas about degeneration, its primary causes, its potential consequences, and its possible antidotes. Positivism was an undeniable influence on both intellectual and political culture during the Porfiriato, but it cannot really be described as a dominant ideology even among the científicos, who were as much defined by their close political and personal ties to Porfirio Díaz as they were by a common ideological outlook. Moreover, just as Mexican liberalism had embodied radical, moderate, socialist, utopian, and other forms throughout the nineteenth century, Mexican positivism was similarly eclectic, and it is also important to note that positivist ideas did not supplant liberalism within Mexican political and intellectual culture.

As Charles Hale has shown, the ideas of Auguste Comte, Herbert Spencer, Edouard Laboulaye, and Jean-Baptiste Lamarck helped to shape different intellectual positions in Mexico regarding, respectively, the evolutionary development of the human mind through education and scientific politics; the evolutionary development of human societies from simple to complex stages; the organic connection of law to the development of human societies; and the inheritance of acquired characteristics from generation to generation within human societies. In addition to these intellectual ideas—by turns treated as complementary and contradictory by different Mexican thinkers—contemporary political events helped to shape Mexican intellectual culture during the Porfiriato. The key proponents of "scientific politics," writing in *La Libertad* in the late 1870s and 1880s—Justo Sierra, Telesforo García, and Francisco Cosmes—pointed to the turn toward conservative republicanism in France and Spain as examples to follow. They argued for the need to overhaul Mexico's constitutional provisions, laid out in 1857, which they regarded as incompatible with Mexican society's current stage of development, and to implement stronger government to create the basis for political order and economic progress in Mexico.[50]

Domestically, rural unrest in southern Mexico and military campaigns against indigenous groups in the north of Mexico also helped to focus intellectual attention on the so-called Indian problem. For many intellectuals and politicians of the late Porfirian period, pseudoscientific ideas about degeneration seemed to offer a range of ways to understand and tackle this problem. Of course, elite concerns about the ability of the indigenous population to integrate with, and contribute to, society were by no means new to the Porfirian, or even the postindependence, period. Whereas indigenous rebelliousness and lack of social advancement had often been understood in the colonial period as a result of cultural inferiority, or the pernicious influence of the devil in indigenous religions, the later colonial period and the postindependence period were characterized by an increased focus on state failures to provide opportunities for education, employment, and moral role models. The latter perspectives, particularly regarding education, continued to be important in the late nineteenth century, but the Porfiriato was also marked by a proliferation of positivist-influenced thinking about the indigenous population and Mexico's lower classes in general, which was focused on the malleable concept of degeneration.[51]

Broadly speaking, degeneration theorists across Europe, North America, and Latin America argued that the physical and moral unhealthiness of one generation led to physical, intellectual, and social decay in subsequent generations. This process was used to explain the widespread poverty, crime, prostitution, disease, and general malaise that appeared as the dark side of industrial modernity and progress, especially among the lower orders of society. With regard to the condition of alcoholism, degeneration theorists held that the children of alcoholics would themselves be prone to alcoholism, would suffer attacks of neurosis, depression, and suicidal tendencies, and would be more likely to become prostitutes, thieves, liars, vagrants, and murderers. Subsequent generations, meanwhile, would evidence infertility, sterility, general physical weakening, and ugliness.[52]

Michael Aronna highlights the fundamental role of degeneration theory in processes of medicalization and nation-building in nineteenth-century Latin America, demonstrating that intellectuals and officials at the top of the social scale drew on ideas about degeneration to explain, rationalize, and justify social inequalities in experiencing the material benefits of modernity:

The medicalization of the subaltern was a fundamental task of modernity. The drive to isolate and classify the organically and socially ill was part of a greater project to rationalize, modernize, and industrialize the nation. . . . Fulfilling this need, the function of the discourse of degeneration was to determine which groups and practices constituted biological and cultural obstacles to modernity, to diagnose the illnesses afflicting these groups and to develop treatments or solutions. . . . The Latin American oligarchy generally was caught between the desire to acquire for itself the material benefits and cultural rhetoric of modernity and the unwillingness or inability to square this material and cultural "progress" with political democracy and cultural recognition for the ethnically heterogeneous Latin American masses.[53]

Through a close analysis of highly influential essays in social criticism, including Uruguayan Enrique Rodó's *Ariel* (1900) and Bolivian Alcides Arguedas's *Pueblo enfermo* (1909), Aronna demonstrates that Latin American intellectuals from both positivist and *modernista* schools utilized medical, psychological, ethnological, and criminological discourses of degeneration to explain and rationalize the contradiction in development within their nations. Both women and nonwhite men were deemed incapable of differentiating between sensual and mental experiences and were, thus, susceptible to mental instability, sexual deviance, alcoholism, and criminality. While liberal reformers of the early nineteenth century were similarly concerned with the limited capacity of women, indigenous, and lower-class groups to exercise reason and rationality, they largely attributed this limited capacity to their inadequate access to proper education and suitable moral example, rather than to inherent biological and inherited characteristics. In the late nineteenth century, many Mexican intellectuals would, like Arguedas, begin to "find the source of the nation's social and economic problems in the medically constructed figures of the alcoholic, the criminal, the prostitute, the syphilitic degenerate and the unhygienic worker."[54]

Alcoholism and degeneration were prominent themes in late nineteenth-century Mexican criminology, which effectively "naturalized and legitimized" social stratifications by transforming criminality into a generalized feature of lower-class urban culture. Francisco Martínez Baca and Manuel Vergara—who worked variously as military and penitentiary doctors, pathologists, teachers, and anthropologists—together wrote *Estudios de antropología criminal* (Studies in criminal anthropology; 1892). They argued that the environmental and social milieu could contribute to creating criminals, as could pathological character traits and improperly developed craniums. Martínez and Vergara noted a frequent occurrence of alcoholism among the criminals they studied and speculated that their inclination to both alcohol abuse and criminality stemmed from the same source, namely, their need for "stimulation to compensate for an inherited physiological deficiency."[55]

Not only criminality but also mental illnesses, among them various forms of alcoholism, were portrayed as hereditary, degenerative conditions. Trinidad Sánchez Santos classified dipsomania as "a morbid predisposition . . . that Magnan [the French psychiatrist and degeneration theorist] observes among degenerates," thus attributing at least one form of alcoholism to hereditary factors. Medical student Mariano Martínez emphasized the hereditary nature of insanity, either produced by or manifested in alcohol abuse: "Degenerated beings produce other degenerates, and this inheritance cannot be applied with more certainty than in the field of the drinkers. The multitudes of madmen that fill the insane asylums testify to this, where it is hardly possible to find even one case where alcohol has not taken a more or less active part in either the condition of the patient or in that of their ancestors."[56]

Medical experts, psychiatrists, and public intellectuals consistently framed their concerns about alcoholism and degeneration in terms of the negative impact on the population as a whole and, thus, national development. A journalist writing for *El Tiempo* in the 1880s, for instance, complained that "the pulquería and the cantina . . . pour out torrents of the venomous liquid each day, converting our men into idiots and sapping the strength of our people," while Nicolás Ramírez de Arellano warned that "the alcoholic not only conspires against himself, but also against those who succeed him." Ernesto Espinosa argued that alcoholism impeded a healthy rate of population increase, due to fertility and sterility problems, while also increasing the number of defective births, among whom he included idiots, the insane, epileptics, criminals, and future alcoholics, and he claimed that the ultimate consequence of such reproductive problems was the erosion of patriotic fervor.[57] Similarly, Francisco Serralde painted a bleak picture of the consequences of alcohol abuse for Mexico's population:

> The degeneration of the race by alcoholism is an established fact . . . the children of a drunkard are sickly, scrawny, beset by ailments and illnesses in their first years, sometimes stupid, mentally slow, depraved, and inclined toward vice; drunkenness appears at the fore of the predisposed causes of intellectual underdevelopment in its three degrees—simple-minded, imbecilic, and idiotic—ending their short lives with madness, hysteria, and epilepsy.[58]

Whereas an observer of the early nineteenth century would also have pointed out the intellectual and moral dangers of excessive drinking, these commentators clearly emphasize the hereditary, biological nature of the physical, mental, and moral consequences of alcohol consumption, using technical language to characterize alcoholism as a medical problem that would affect current and subsequent generations of Mexicans in a number of negative and unavoidable ways.

Breaking down the rather vague forecasts about the generational consequences of alcoholism, Sánchez Santos and Ramírez de Arellano drew on the work of French degeneration theorists Bénédict Augustin Morel and Valentin Magnan to detail the step-by-step effects of alcohol abuse in future Mexican generations. Ramírez de Arellano claimed that the first generation of children begot from alcoholic parents would be morally depraved and suffer "alcoholic excesses"; the second generation would partake in habitual drinking binges, suffer manias, and exhibit cerebral softening; the third generation would suffer from hypochondria, melancholia, and an inclination to commit suicide or homicide; the fourth generation would suffer from imbecility, idiocy, and sterility; and, therefore, there would be no fifth generation.[59] Morel's model of generational decline was also spread through the Porfirian press, as *El Imparcial* reproduced his four stages in an 1899 article describing the "hereditary transmission of alcohol," giving rise to disorders not only in the sons of alcoholics, but also in the second, third, and doomed fourth generations.[60]

To this model of degenerational decline, Sánchez Santos added a further possible range of unproductive and harmful characteristics that the offspring of alcoholics would bring to the Mexican population. An alcoholic's child could be a "suficientista," a generally hateful person exhibiting a cerebral disturbance that "consists of a great sense of self-importance." Or the offspring could be an "antiviviseccionista," suffering from another kind of cerebral disturbance that "reveals itself in an exaggerated love for animals," by which the author meant (I hasten to add) a proclivity for animal-rights campaigning. The most likely outcome of an alcoholic's reproduction, however, according to Sánchez Santos, was an "alcoholizable": a generally weak-willed person who would be easily induced to start drinking by others and thereafter would drink more than a sensible amount, continuing to drink periodically to assuage feelings of illness or inadequacy. Such a description might suggest, to today's reader, a fairly average social drinker, occasionally having too much to drink under the influence of friends. But for Sánchez Santos in 1896, this represented a serious defect that threatened the very future of the Mexican nation, since the chain of inheritance would produce a "race that will not know how to defend its major interests, nor to display perseverance and enthusiasm in work and study against the invasion of foreigners; a miserable race that will only serve to keep filling the prisons, asylums, and liquor stores of the slave."[61]

By the late nineteenth century, then, commentators routinely used this kind of hyperbolic language to convey a pervasive image of alcoholism and its degenerative effects in society. Mariano Martínez was surely exaggerating in his claim that the pathology of every single mental patient, among the "multitude" in Mexico, could be traced to alcohol use in their history or that of their ancestors. Francisco Serralde also wrote in grand terms, blaming alcoholism for the degeneration of the entire race and creating a particularly sad image of the diseased, imbecilic, and insane children that any, and presumably every, drunkard would beget. Sánchez Santos's forecast was even more hysterical, as his bizarre list of degenerative afflictions caused by alcoholism could theoretically account for a huge proportion of the population. In his 1896 treatise, Sánchez Santos presented the alarming calculation that, on average, one alcoholic who had four or five children would be responsible for the production of 880 degenerates over five generations. Even if a quarter of these were to die at an early age, he noted, there would still develop some 640 useless people draining society's resources as the result of just one alcoholic's legacy.[62]

A broad cross-section of the Porfirian press also dissemi-
nated ideas about the degenerational consequences of alcoholism, indicating that these concerns extended beyond the realm
of medical and legal research. Early editions of the left-wing
oppositionist *El Socialista* periodical, established by Juan de
Mata Rivera in 1871, followed the earlier nineteenth-century
pattern of blaming inadequate moral education for lower-class
drinking patterns that were harmful to family life, fostered
disorderly behavior in public, and led to impoverishment.
Although these elements of criticism did not disappear, by
the 1880s a new emphasis on the physical, mental, and generational deterioration caused by excessive alcohol use was
notable. Journalists dwelt on the suicidal tendencies, reproductive problems, and overall deterioration in health that alcoholism could cause:

> Encourage the worker to understand the dangers drunkenness
> exposes him to and the scorn that will result from frequenting
> the tavern. Paint to him, in all its true colors, the progressive
> march of alcoholism and its horrible effects. Let him know
> about the brutalization that drinking produces, including
> thoughts of suicide, misanthropy, and family ruin. Let him
> know too that drunkenness makes reproduction impossible,
> as the drunkard, as well as killing himself slowly, cannot leave
> sons behind because he cannot conceive them, or because
> those he does have will be sickly or imbecilic.[63]

An 1881 *Gazeta del Lunes* article summarizing a homicide
case displayed a yet more comprehensive absorption of the
kind of medicalized thought connecting alcoholism, criminality, and degeneration, including a detailed description of the
malignant physiognomy and character of the accused that had
either been formed by, or was manifested in, his heavy alcohol consumption. Pedro Cuenca, who, according to the newspaper report, eventually died in prison after being convicted

of murder, had "such a distended abdomen that it seemed it was destined to keep in it an extraordinary number of kilos of pulque," as well as "an organic malignity," which indicated that "he was malevolent by constitution."[64] Through the use of words such as abdomen, constitution, and organic—which lent the description a more objective, scientific character than neutral words, such as stomach, nature, or moral, might have done—Cuenca's drinking habits are associated with his abnormal physical appearance. In turn, these abnormalities are depicted as determining the aggressive, violent nature of his character that led him to commit a serious crime.

Journalists' examinations of alcoholism also echoed medical, psychiatric, and criminological investigations by mobilizing hyperbolic language and metaphors of contagion. *El Imparcial* lamented in 1897 that all the efforts of legislators and antialcohol propagandists had been in vain in the face of the "relentless, overwhelming, sinister alcoholic wave" that was filling Mexico's prisons and hospitals by spreading "an active poison . . . through society's arteries."[65] Although the same paper sometimes published more measured, restrained articles that insisted Mexico's alcohol problem was nowhere near as serious as it was in other countries, in 1899 its writers were describing alcoholics and their diseased offspring as "an immense group, a shambolic army, a tragic phalanx, an advancing troop that is painfully unfit to engage in the battle for life."[66] Other journalists agreed that alcoholism was spreading "with incredible speed" and needed an "urgent" resolution, having infected the population with the "gangrene" of criminality.[67] According to some writers, alcoholism had reached the proportions of a "contemporary plague," a poison that "degenerates and consumes entire generations," or even a "cancer" that could bring about the "extinction of the race."[68]

Consequently, for medical professionals and government officials, this disturbing diagnosis called for greater action in public policy toward drinking and its degenerative consequences, which certainly represented, in their eyes, a considerable mountain to climb. Firstly, there was a concerted crackdown on public drunkenness from the 1880s onward. Partially reflecting the heightened capacity of the Porfirian police force following major reforms in 1878–79, and partially reflecting increasing levels of concern about the implications of alcoholism for national development, there was a sharp increase in the arrest rate for "scandalous drunkenness" (*embriaguez escándalo* or *ebrio escándalo*) offences: the equivalent of modern-day drunk and disorderly charges. Between 1877 and 1891, the number of people referred to the courts or the governor by the police for being drunk and disorderly rose from 13.7 to 93.2 per 1,000 of the population. In the final decade of the Porfiriato, the number of people arrested for this offence fluctuated between 170.4 and 318 per 1,000 of the population. It is clear that this increase was due to more intense police persecution of public drunkenness, not an increase in the population's rowdy behavior. As Laurence Rohlfes's statistical analysis has shown, the arrest rate for more serious offenses, such as robbery and assault, did not show significant changes during this time period, and so the increase in arrests for drunk and disorderly charges is more plausibly explained as the result of Porfirian police broadening "their definition of scandalous drunkenness . . . to include all public intoxication."[69]

Moreover, the theory of three stages of drunkenness common to many studies of alcoholism in the late nineteenth century had a significant bearing on police and judicial practices, since the issue of criminal responsibility was often a major focus of enquiries. Police doctors worked to classify the different types of drunkenness among arrested suspects, based on observable bodily effects, from "'alcoholic breath' but otherwise normal behavior" to "'incomplete drunkenness' characterized by faster heartbeat, red cheeks and nervous behavior," and finally "'complete drunkenness' defined by ataxia, 'lack of will,' and 'loss of consciousness.'"[70]

The distinction between the latter two states of intoxication, incomplete and complete, was particularly important because article 34 of the 1871 penal code stated that criminal responsibility was removed in the case of complete drunkenness, which caused an inability to reason the difference between right and wrong, provided that the accused was not a habitual drunkard and had not previously committed a criminal offence while drunk. Perhaps the regular discussion of the three stages of drunkenness in the Porfirian press had been popularized throughout society, however, as in 1907, police doctors and their assistants were still being instructed to focus on whether suspects were in a state of "complete or incomplete drunkenness" and to ignore the three-stage model of classification.[71]

Article 41 of the penal code, which provided for the diminished responsibility of those committing crimes while accidentally or "involuntarily" drunk, was also subject to debate. In his 1885 medical thesis, Ernesto Espinosa supported article 41 and particularly emphasized that dipsomaniacs should be included in the category of "involuntary" drunkards and completely exempted from criminal responsibility, since they suffered from "a disease . . . which presents with the symptoms of a mental illness, generally of an acute mania, and which is caused by excessive drinking of alcoholic beverages. This disease is notable for its periodic nature, which makes it seem like habitual drunkenness, and for the fact that the sufferer drinks involuntarily, according to the needs of his organism that can never be overcome." Espinosa did recognize, however, that telling the difference between a genuine dipsomaniac and a garden variety habitual drinker (who made a conscious and voluntary decision to get drunk and, thus, should take responsibility for his subsequent actions) could be very difficult, which meant that his policy might result in many guilty habitual drinkers escaping prosecution.[72] Commentators at *El Tiempo* strongly disagreed, arguing that even dipsomaniacs had once had the ability to choose whether or not to drink: they were therefore responsible for inducing their own illness and should be held liable for any crimes committed while drunk, voluntarily or involuntarily, completely or incompletely.[73]

In addition to featuring prominently within intellectual debates and government policies toward crime, medical knowledge regarding alcoholism was incorporated into educational programs sponsored by the Porfirian administration, a measure that was unanimously recommended by numerous journalists, intellectuals, and traveling lecturers.[74] Manuel Villaseñor, a leading figure in Mexican education, published a series of instruction manuals that encouraged teachers to follow a demonstrative, interactive, and practical method in the classroom. In his model lesson on pulque, after a thorough description of the agricultural and manufacturing processes involved in its production, the teacher is advised to issue a severe warning against excessive consumption, which is reiterated forcefully in the summary to be made at the lesson's conclusion and is further emphasized in the text through bold highlighting of key information that the teacher should ensure the pupils remember. Villaseñor highlights the links between drunkenness, aggression, and violence that medical professionals particularly dwelt upon, and twice refers to the potential of heavy drinking to cause degeneration:

> [Pulque is] a drink that contains alcohol and abusing it leads to drunkenness.
>
> The man who consumes it in abundance becomes aggressive and quarrelsome. It is disgraceful, repulsive, and dangerous!

Drunkenness is a horrifying vice, that has a degenerative effect on man and converts him into an imbecile without dignity and will.

Oh children, it is not enough to be temperate yourself, but it is also necessary to make sure others are as well!

SUMMARY

Pulque is a foamy, milky-looking drink, with its own taste and smell, viscous, and heavier than water. It is made from aguamiel, a sugary liquid, which is extracted from the domesticated maguey plant. It is a drink that contains nutritious substances and alcohol. It is not available in the whole country. **Drunkenness is a vice that has a degenerative effect on man.**[75]

A subsequent lesson on alcohol more generally advises, again highlighted in bold and again emphasizing the central message of contemporary medical opinion, that "The use of strong liquor is highly damaging to your health."[76]

Figure 8 shows an example of the educational literature designed to spread awareness of alcohol's destructive power and to highlight the diverse physiological, mental, degenerational, and societal problems that alcoholism could induce. Commissioned in 1899 by Eduardo Liceaga, then president of the Superior Council for Sanitation, these pamphlets were to be displayed in schools, hospitals, police stations, train stations, public offices, and even public spaces of sociability. The striking visual content, including the ravaged facial features of a gentleman and various scenes indicating social humiliation, were intended to communicate with the nonliterate as well as the literate classes.[77]

The medicalized lexicon regarding alcoholism, and its relationship to criminality, mental illness, and degeneration, would also penetrate literary discourse in the late nineteenth century. Mexican doctors, legal experts, and politicians drew on and cited European medical research to make their own

FIG. 8. *Los estragos del alcoholismo* (The ravages of alcoholism). Illustration of pamphlets commissioned for public display by the Superior Council for Sanitation in 1899 ("Cuadros anti-alcohólicos," *El Imparcial*, October 29, 1899). Courtesy of Paper of Record. http://paperofrecord .hypernet.ca.

observations about the physiological, mental, and generational consequences of alcohol consumption among the Mexican population. They usually concurred with the findings of their European counterparts but occasionally diverged from the latter's conclusions to establish unique aspects of Mexican cases of alcoholism, particularly regarding the relative harmfulness of pulque. Científicos and other political figures also brought some of this knowledge to bear in their public policy, especially in the penal, judicial, and educational spheres, in their attempts to further the ideals of order and progress in the Porfirian pursuit of modernity. Due to the connections they established between alcoholism and national degeneration, however, the sheer size of the perceived problem cast considerable doubt upon the ability of preventative measures such as education to reform the harmful drinking practices of the Mexican population, and a sense of alarm and despair pervades much of their writing.

Although it is more difficult to trace the connections between these medical, legal, and political writings and late nineteenth-century fictional texts, since fictional authors generally did not cite medical or scientific authorities in their works, intertextual links can be established through the linguistic and thematic features they display. Fictional descriptions of alcoholics and alcoholism featured increasingly technical medicalized language and displayed a similarly pervading sense of alarm and despair regarding the magnitude of the problem of alcoholism and its degenerational consequences. These similarities between the nonliterary and literary discourses regarding alcoholism also make the main difference all the more significant; in contrast to the prominence of the "scientific" debate surrounding the relative harmfulness of pulque, fictional writers would focus exclusively on modern, fashionable, distilled drinks in their portraits of alcoholism, indicating that their exploration of this medicalized understanding of alcohol consumption reflected critically on Mexico's experience of modernity.

Medicalizing Literature: Alcoholism and Modernity

From the 1880s, elements of the medicalized discourse about alcoholism began to feature in literary works that moved toward developing literary modes of realism, naturalism, and *modernismo*, which dwelt on Mexico's modern experience in a variety of ways. Realism typically mobilized blunt and explicit prose to draw portraits of the hardships of modern life for the urban poor, focusing on the mundane subjects of everyday life. Naturalism—most often associated with the French writer Émile Zola—was particularly aligned with contemporary discourse on alcoholism, since it effectively combined the stylistic features of realism with an interpretive framework that established hereditary and environmental forces as the determining influence over a character's actions. *Modernista* writers also frequently employed a pseudoscientific, psychological, generational framework of understanding human behavior, but tended to replace the gritty prose of realist works with a more esoteric, ethereal, poetic style.[78] It is important to note that Mexican writers often blended realist, naturalist, *modernista*, and even romantic styles. Consequently, many fictional works of this period defy simple categorization according to these terms, which—with the exception of *modernismo*, a distinctly Spanish American literary movement different from European and North American "modernisms"—ultimately derive from European literary models.

Alcoholism is a recurrent theme in both realist-naturalist and *modernista* fiction of late nineteenth-century Mexico. In defending the graphic level of description in his realist prose in an 1891 newspaper article, Ángel de Campo highlighted both the influence of recent French literature and the theme of alcoholism as important features of this new literary direction, which sought to understand the naked reality of the nation's problems, in order to better deal with them:

> A thousand times over I prefer the feeling of disgust to the poison itself: I will grimace before the drunken spree of Coupeau, but I would not want to be a traitor, adulterer or coward like the sickly sweet, sentimental seducer that minces about in Lamartine's *Rafael*. This evil of romanticism is more fearsome than the nakedness of realism; no-one would go out and get drunk after reading *L'Assommoir*, because that novel depicts an alcoholic, yet there are those who have put a bullet in their heads after crying the tears of Werther.[79]

By exploring the theme of alcoholism, producing intensely visceral descriptions of its effects, and considering its psychological, environmental, and hereditary causes, Mexican novelists were not simply trying to discourage readers from drinking. Numerous authors used alcoholism to make a metaphoric comment on the state of the nation and its relationship with modernity. Late nineteenth-century novels explore concerns about wide disparities in material prosperity among different social and racial groups; the concomitant correlation between lower social sectors and ill health, crime, and immorality; and the implications of all this for national development in the light of emerging degeneration theories. The theme of alcoholism allowed Mexican writers to explore all these issues simultaneously, at the same time as developing a larger, metaphorical representation of the fate of Mexican nationhood.

Detailed descriptions of the alcoholic body are a prominent feature in de Campo's vignettes. In "Idilio y elegia" (Romance and elegy; 1890), the narrator recounts the decline and death of his doorman, Severiano, after a beautiful Indian chambermaid rejects his love for her:

Severiano Pérez died from liver disease after two years of alcoholism, and I saw him in the amphitheatre by chance. It provoked an indefinable horror in me: he had become a poor old man; naked, his mouth agape, his head and hands hanging over the edge, his legs askew. On his shaven head, one could see old scars and wounds, and the scratches from the razor blade; his eyes were open wide as if in shock; his sharp nose and open mouth were faking a yawn or a guffaw, whether ironic or desperate, I don't know. How dreadful it was to see the flies hovering about his body![80]

Although this description features the same focus on open orifices and bodily protuberances as did earlier nineteenth-century depictions of drunken bodies as dangerous and immoral, de Campo's image is more sharply drawn: the grotesque features of Severiano's corpse are directly attributed to a known medical condition caused by alcoholism. Severiano's body has succumbed to liver disease after two years of heavy drinking and this cause of death is crucial to the graphic depiction. Severiano is shortly afterward described, in a particularly revealing phrase, as the "embodiment of the masses."[81] An incarnation of the urban masses, the nature, lifestyle, and fate of the latter are inscribed on Severiano's dead body; alcohol abuse has caused this physical deterioration and undignified end in the individual and, by implication, the social group of which he is a part.

Although there are certainly parallels between the language used in de Campo's work and that of earlier nineteenth-century writers, de Campo's incorporation of medicalized knowledge about alcoholism and the inevitability with which Severiano's fate unfolds, reveal a much more pessimistic outlook regarding the potential for reforming alcoholism among Mexico's lower classes. Severiano's almost inevitable descent into alcoholism encapsulates the inescapable misery in which

Mexico City's urban lower classes were thought to live, as a result of the unequal distribution of wealth brought about by Mexico's uneven economic development during the late nineteenth century. The association between the urban lower classes and the physical decay brought on by alcoholism is foreshadowed more metaphorically in an earlier vignette, "El Pinto" (1890), about an abandoned dog in Mexico City. Wandering the streets and extremely hungry, El Pinto "felt drunk with pleasure on breathing in the tepid aroma of that pulp, and it was fresh! And he ate it gluttonously," when a stranger throws him some scraps of food. Unfortunately for El Pinto, the food had been poisoned and, after he convulsed and "staggered like a drunk," the dog dies. The vignette concludes with an exclamation: "How many among the masses are like El Pinto!"[82]

The allegorical relationship established between the dog of the tale and Mexico City's impoverished population suggests that the metaphorical drunkenness El Pinto experiences represents a larger concern for the detrimental effects of alcohol abuse among the urban poor. While drinking offers a temporary comfort from hardship, as a source of pleasure it can be illusory, ephemeral, and ultimately damaging, as the dog's paroxysmal death calls to mind the risk of suffering from muscle spasms, seizures, and delirium tremens. Together these two vignettes portray alcoholism as a medical condition commonly experienced by the urban poor as a result of the poverty and hardships experienced in everyday life. The exclamations regarding the typicality of El Pinto and Severiano as members of the "masses" simultaneously evoke pity for their plight and the fatalistic outlook of contemporary degeneration theory: these problems were already so widespread among the lower-class population that little could be done to remedy the situation.

Similar ideas about alcoholism are worked out in more

detail in de Campo's novella *La Rumba* (1890–91), which is about the attempts of a lower-class Mexico City girl to escape her monotonous life. *La Rumba* is particularly notable for its exploration of contemporary criminological and medical techniques. In the trial of the central character, Remedios, de Campo includes a detailed forensics report, complete with diagram of the crime scene, and an autopsy report of the victim. Corroborating Remedios's claim that her husband had been extremely drunk and abusive both at the time of the confrontation that resulted in his accidental shooting and throughout their relationship, the medical report stated that Cornichón died two days after the shooting and "after suffering alcoholic fits and febrile delirium."[83] That Cornichón had suffered from seizures and delirium, both recognized symptoms of serious alcohol abuse, added credence to the defendant's testimony and increased the jury's sympathy toward her. It also suggested that the victim's body might have been able to recover from the gunshot had it not been so weakened by alcoholism, thus lessening Remedios's culpability for his death. However, the sterile, technical language used in this passage regarding Cornichón's alcoholism, during the methodical proceedings of a criminal trial, contrasts sharply with the more detailed, verbose, and emotive description, just a few pages previously, of another alcoholic in the novel, Remedios's father Cosme Vena.

Already described as a typical lower-class "habitual drunkard" at the beginning of the narrative, Cosme undergoes a descent into alcoholism, as he seeks comfort in drinking from the shame inflicted by his daughter's elopement with Cornichón and her criminal prosecution.[84] The detailed description of the physiological and mental effects of alcoholism on Cosme bears striking similarity to medical studies on the relationship between alcoholism and degeneration:

It was not the arrogant, robust Cosme, with his frank stare, clear speech, and moderate comportment, no; the blacksmith had changed. *A yellowish pallor lent his gaunt face an air of sickness*; his vacant and stupid pupils were lost in the *jaundiced color of the conjunctiva* . . . giving him *the air of a hardened criminal*. Messy, bristly, and forming a helmet, his long greasy hair fell through the sweat on his forehead; *stultification* painted itself on his face; his mouth opened in *an idiotic gesture; his muscles shook with nervous trembling*; and *his lazy, incoherent, hoarse speech* spilled with difficulty from his lips. His clothes were dirty and dissolute: *he was the image of an incurable alcoholic.*[85]

Driven to seek "the artificial madness of alcohol" as a consequence of his daughter's failed attempt to reach beyond the social environment into which she was born, Cosme's deterioration is depicted with a sense of inevitability and, once embarked upon, he cannot turn back.[86] Formerly a respectable, articulate, and robust blacksmith, Cosme's alcohol abuse attacks his body and mind, leaving him a sickly, bloated, weakened, stupid, and degenerate criminal, harboring thoughts of killing Remedios to avenge the shame she has brought to him. The language of decay is suggestive of degeneration theory in its concern with the effects of excessive alcohol consumption not just in the diseased body of the individual, or their immediate impact on society, but also in the long term effects on the Mexican population and nation.

It is significant that, like Severiano in "Idilio y elegia," Cosme is the character whose body and mental capacity becomes subject to such descriptive scrutiny. The upper-class Cornichón also suffered from symptoms of alcoholism, but this is only revealed after his death. Although his explosive anger and false bravado are depicted as consequences of drinking, there is no equivalent graphic description of his alcohol-ravaged body to that of Cosme's. That *La Rumba* explores the effects of alcohol abuse in greatest detail, and in the language of degeneration, with regard to a once-respectable and hard-working artisan, rather than the aristocratic Cornichón, suggests a preoccupation with lower-class drinking. Moreover, the artisans with whom Cosme drinks consume tequila, the production of which began in the late nineteenth century as a result of industrialization and diversification of the economy, pointing to an association between the condition of alcoholism and Mexico's experience of modernization.[87]

Indeed, the opening description of the neighborhood in which Cosme and Remedios live, and from which Remedios is desperate to escape, features several references to the city's modern features. Michael Johns notes that the neighborhood called La Rumba, where the novel is set, is a representation of the barrio of San Sebastian, which developed in the 1880s on the fringes of older neighborhoods, as Mexico City underwent considerable expansion, with its population increasing from 230,000 in 1867 to 470,000 in 1910, mostly as the result of migration.[88] In de Campo's portrait, a municipal school is located on the main square of La Rumba, alluding to the expansion of state education in the Porfiriato, a network of trams and trains traverse the neighborhood and connect it to more outlying districts, and telephone poles have been erected. The city center, however, with its impressive buildings, electric street lightning, fashionable shops, and bustling atmosphere, stands in stark contrast to the gloomy, dirty suburb.[89]

In this opening passage, Remedios dreams of swapping her dreary life in the depressing suburb for a more refined and glamorous life in the center:

> A hidden anger, a suppressed rebellion roared inside her against her fate; she dreamed of castles in the air, the castles that only an ignorant young girl can imagine. She lost heart,

but the memory of the crowded streets returned to spur her on; she hated the elegant women, the society ladies dressed in silk; she felt an immense rage that she was a *nobody* . . . she stood up, looked into the distance, floated over the dark and sleeping city, the reflection of electric light like a luminous mist, and she murmured I don't know what phrases, as if she were dreaming, saying in a high voice, "I have to become like the *rotas* [society ladies]."[90]

This burning dissatisfaction at being left out of the elegant, exciting, prestigious lifestyles that she imagined character-ized life in downtown Mexico City is the main impetus behind Remedios's decision to elope with Cornichón, which in turn leads to her father's alcoholism, her trial for murder, and her complete isolation at the novella's close. Moreover, Remedios's attempt to move beyond her prescribed social boundaries, as part of the lower class, is doomed from the start. Cornichón, as a well-to-do, handsome, well-dressed assistant in an upmar-ket fashion store, is the embodiment of everything Remedios hoped to find in the elegant, modern city center. Her hopes turn out to be nothing but "castles in the air," since Cornichón is exposed as a violent drunkard and, therefore, no different to what Remedios would have expected to find in a husband from La Rumba.

However, Cornichón's behavior and the effects of his drink-ing are given considerably less attention than Cosme's alco-holic body. Cornichón is simply the means through which Remedios's dreams of participating in the more illustrious side of modernity in the city center are shattered. Remedios and Cosme are the characters explored in most depth; more-over, the narrative tone in describing both characters is con-sistently sympathetic, lamenting the demise of a once strong man and the sufferings of a misguided young woman. In de Campo's portrait, the frustrated lower-class woman and the alcoholic worker are the detritus of modernity, unable to participate in its benefits, partly because of the degenerative effects of sustained alcohol use and living among the urban poor, and partly because that was the way modern society worked. Established medical, criminological, and psychological knowledge regarding alcohol abuse is mobilized to diagnose the problems afflicting Mexico's lower orders, including alcoholism itself, as well as crime, promiscuity, and ill health, as part and parcel of life in the modern nation.

The determinism displayed in de Campo's body of work is even more prominent in that of Federico Gamboa, Mexico's most notable Zola-inspired naturalist writer, as his characters are powerless to overcome the social forces that govern their lives. Gamboa (1864–1939) came from a Catholic, conservative family; his father had fought against Benito Juárez during the French Intervention and Gamboa himself strongly supported Porfirio Díaz's government, despite bearing witness to the social inequalities it helped to sustain. As well as enjoying a successful literary career, Gamboa had several diplomatic and ministerial posts, including as the minister for foreign affairs within the reactionary administration of Victoriano Huerta. Despite his attraction to the pessimistic philosophies of Zola, Nietzsche, and Schopenhauer, Gamboa underwent a profound reawakening of his Catholic faith in 1901 after years of disengagement with religion, and the tensions between his newfound, unshakeable faith and the naturalist appropriation of pseudoscientific theories to explain social phenomena are evident in several of his novels.[91]

Santa (1903) explores concerns about the effects of modernity on Mexican society, and particularly on women, by charting the descent of an innocent, beautiful young woman into prostitution, alcoholism, and disease after a man seduces, disgraces, and abandons her. The attention devoted to the legal, medical, and institutional aspects of prostitution and alcoholism in the novel point to a clear concern with modernization processes affecting both state and society and an engagement with highly topical changes affecting the urban center of the nation.[92] The central character may have been modeled on a real-life Mexico City prostitute, "La Malagueña," who was shot to death by her rival, "La Chiquita." The murder was reported widely in the Porfirian press and Gamboa records in his diaries that he visited the morgue to see the dead prostitute's body.[93]

Santa's fate is foretold in the opening section of the novel with a striking contrast between Santa's physical perfection and the alcohol-ravaged body of a woman working in the Mexico City brothel where the unfortunate girl seeks refuge after her rural relatives disown her. In contrast to Santa's "splendid and semi-virginal body," the "grotesque figure" of Pepa is described thus: "Her decayed flesh, overabundant in the areas that men love and squeeze . . . her enormous stomach was that of an old drunkard, her enormous sagging breasts were those of a Galician peasant, oscillating distastefully, with something bestial about the way they moved." Santa rejects Pepa's offer of aguardiente as she is not accustomed to drinking, but Pepa insists that the youngster will soon come to rely on alcohol to lessen the feelings of sadness and self-loathing that the prostitute's life engenders. Lest the reader miss the significance of this description of Pepa's motives for drinking and the physical consequences on her body, she explicitly tells Santa she wants to display her body as a warning against the path Santa has no other choice but to take if she wants to survive as an independent woman, shunned by respectable society: "And Santa looked, in effect, at her sinewy, almost straight, calves; at some deformed and withered muscles and at a sagging, discolored stomach, with deep wrinkles that went across its entire width."[94] These descriptions are reminiscent of, although more graphic than, earlier nineteenth-century portraits of dangerous and immoral drunken bodies, with their emphasis on bodily defects, orifices, and processes. Given Gamboa's Catholic morals, it is unsurprising that he conjures images so similar to the grotesque mode employed by earlier nineteenth-century writers in depicting the ravages of drunkenness and prostitution on a fallen woman's body. Nevertheless, the placement of this episode at the beginning of the narrative creates the impression that Santa's progressive demise following her scandalous relationship is both inevitable and inexorable, revealing the naturalist schema of the novel. Gamboa's work is less concerned with cultivating rationality in order to overcome the body's vice-inclined passions and more concerned with the unavoidable effects of the modern urban environment on both the body and mind of individuals and the social collective.

Descriptions of the neighborhood surrounding the brothel provide a glimpse of the modernizing urban environment that will corrupt Santa. A range of "small industries" and businesses operating in the district are introduced, including two Italian copper workshops, a French drycleaners, a coal outlet, and a large "modern-style meat shop," creating a cosmopolitan image of a built-up district in a city that was experiencing economic development and immigration. This passage also mentions a municipal school, a network of trams and trains, and electric street lighting, as had de Campo's portrait of La Rumba. These modern aspects of the urban environment are juxtaposed with Santa's first frightened, disgusted, and distraught visit to the brothel where she goes on to work as a prostitute. That night she is confronted with a scene of drunken debauchery in the brothel that contains allusions to both immorality and degeneration: "The champagne flowed and people became animated beyond all moderation. The party degenerated into a vulgar orgy of vile words and obscene gestures, intemperate laughter, and bestial propositions. The withdrawals to the upstairs began, barefaced, without care for appearances."[95]

On the same evening, the experience of sleeping next to a completely inebriated customer, who falls into a "deep alcoholic sleep," leads Santa to reminisce about her former life in a rural community, described in nostalgic, romantic terms that contrast sharply with the detached description of the modern urban neighborhood and the lurid scene of debauchery in the brothel. Santa remembers the fresh air, tall trees, clean rivers, her family, her daily routine of domestic chores, and attending Mass. At this juncture, the narrator also establishes the patriotic, nation-helping credentials of this rural community, noting that it had been a significant stronghold of the independence insurgents and of the resistance against both the North American and the French invasions.[96] This signifies the crucial difference between the decent, rural community in which Santa was raised and the corrupt, seedy, modern underworld into which she has fallen: the former is the good side of the Mexican nation and the latter is the bad.

The nostalgic tone and past tense in which the description of the rural childhood is written, as well as the positive reference points of patriotism all being situated before the Porfirian era, suggest that this might also be the lost part of Mexico. That Santa, coming out of the idyllic past into contact with the dark side of modernity, is also lost in the course of the novel produces a bleak image of the modern Mexican nation. Debra Castillo has connected this rural-urban contrast to an extended metaphorical association of Santa's body with the meat that is butchered and packaged by workers in the meat shop near the brothel, which together signify the "progressive dehumanization" inflicted by industrial urban life.[97] Indeed, Santa's own spiral of dehumanization from innocent virgin to functional prostitute begins when she is impregnated and abandoned by a municipal gendarme, whose presence in her village represents the expansion of Mexico City and the modernization of its police force. In the corrupt urban environment, Santa increasingly turns to drinking to find solace from her situation as a prostitute, as Pepa had predicted she would, and eventually becomes so accustomed to the sexual licentiousness of life in the brothel that she rejects two opportunities to escape it through consensual relationships.

Before Santa's own rapid decline into alcoholism occurs in the narrative, Gamboa provides a richly detailed, scientifically oriented account of the physical and mental effects of alcohol abuse, in describing a drunken customer, Rodolfo. Gamboa's model, in which alcohol is "the Enemy of the species, which brings us to the edge of the precipice and to infamy," closely follows the three stages of drunkenness outlined by many late nineteenth-century medical professionals. First moving from the stomach, through the circulation system to the brain, the alcohol thus produces a heightened color, jovial attitude, and reduced inhibitions in the initial, deceptive stage that seems completely harmless and even beneficial. In the second stage, the "enemy" advances further to reduce self-control and the ability to tell right from wrong, thereby increasing the drinker's inclination toward crime, sexual deviancy, and irresponsible behavior. Finally, in the third stage, Rodolfo is an "alcoholic," no longer a man, completely bereft of reason, reduced to the state of a savage animal, capable of killing, raping, and harming anyone with impunity.[98]

This passage is worth quoting in full, since the progressive, inexorable march of alcohol throughout the body and mind mirrors the novel's structure as a whole, wherein Santa's demise is an unstoppable consequence of the society in which she lives. This is emphasized through the repetitive refrain "the Enemy advances" and "the invasion continues" and the metaphorical image of alcoholism as a relentless war machine, atavistically transforming the drinker from a man to a beastly animal:

The alcohol, meanwhile, continued its silent work, inexorable and destructive; it cascaded into the stomachs that dilated or contracted to accommodate it; like a river of fire, it ran through the veins, increasing the rhythmic circulation of the blood; it evaporated and, moving through the organisms, sneakily and unstoppably, it rose toward the brains, wrapping them with the thin, sinister membrane of a poisonous animal, and a similar, though heavier, denser membrane in the stomachs where more alcohol fell. Featuring at the beginning of the excitation are pinkness of color, ecstatic outbursts without motivation, joyfulness at being alive, the need to love; the heart is that of a merry gravedigger, burying troubles and pains; the thoughts, those of a prudent midwife, developing, plump, and seemingly destined to forever encourage the secret longings, which, if true logic applied would never be born at all; ideals impossible to realize easily by reaching with the hand that begins to shake. Life smiles on us, women wait for us impatiently, men love us. The alcohol is not the Enemy, it is the Tonic, we bless it, we ask for more.

The invasion continues, the Enemy advances. It does away with the niceties that even the crudest and most uncouth carries with him; shame and self-respect vanish; the notion of good and evil is not lost—this is everlasting!—but they become confused, dislocated, a fateful "What does it matter to me?" overpowers them, absolving us of whatever reprobate thing we want to do before the act; dignity is shaken, yet it struggles on because the enemy does not yet flee, it defends the individual in hand-to-hand combat . . .

The Enemy advances, the invasion continues, the defeat is almost complete. Dignity staggers, you play your last cards, you are going to succumb. . . . The invader opens the prisons to swell its forces and the armed convicts leave the garrisons and the guarding will is left battered and wounded, without energy, unable to resist . . . out come the perverse instincts, the catalysts of crime, the ancestral legacies and inheritances of the cavemen, of our delinquent ancestors; out come all the things chained within, which make up half of our being and would make us akin to beasts, the galley slaves that we keep chained within the dungeons of our conscience with the frail irons of morality and duty . . .

The Enemy has triumphed. The brain is obscured, the will lies immobilized, judgment is absent. And the results are savage, primitive, identical to those of all invasions: rape, murder, degradation, annihilation of the weak, the disavowal of mercy, the destruction of beauty, the ridicule of all that is good, the annihilation of the Lares gods, the prisons spitting out their filth, the violation of virgins, the slaughter of children . . . the red flag waves, it is the backward step, to the stone age, the uselessness of strength and the sterility of intentions; there is less a man and more an alcoholic. It is the triumph of the Enemy![99]

The alcohol's progress in this excerpt and Santa's fall in the novel as a whole indicate the extent to which the positivistic, scientific outlook that shaped Porfirian politics had also penetrated literary discussions of the nation. The metonymic association of alcohol with Santa's fall is symbolic of the late nineteenth-century disillusion with, yet acceptance of, the project of modernity, complete with its dark side that produced and excluded certain undesirable social groups.[100]

Reinforcing this pessimistic conclusion, Gamboa's narration of Santa's illness, alcoholism, and death is quick, detached, and full of particular medical details. She first suffers a fever, seizures, and delirium, and subsequently develops regular hemorrhages, abdominal pains, and aching limbs. Turning to alcohol to alleviate her sufferings, Santa "was gradually increasing the dose, across the range, from the finest cognac to the kind of aguardiente that burns and corrodes. She contracted alcoholism, or rather, threw herself into it, like the only Lethe that was adequate for the extent of her disgrace." Unable to gain readmission to the brothel due to her condition as a dipsomaniac, Santa falls deeper into drunken oblivion, suffering blackouts and memory loss, and relying on *fósforo* as "the only breakfast that the girl's perverted stomach could tolerate." Santa allows her devoted, blind friend Hipólito to help her, but she is too sick to make love to him as she wants to, now that her once perfect body is "converted into ruins, debris, tatters."[101] Santa's death, from cancer of the womb, follows shortly after, in the middle of a hysterectomy, paid for by the unhappy Hipólito.

Recalling to the reader's mind her previous miscarriage following her first ill-fated love affair, this death highlights a key concern produced by Mexican modernity: Mexican women were central to the future well-being of the nation, as producers of future generations, yet their fate could still be decided by irresponsible men and the condemnation of a society holding on to traditional gender values. Santa is portrayed as powerless to change the path her life takes after her family throws her out, and she is forcibly removed from a church while seeking comfort after hearing about the death of her mother, in a passage where Gamboa departs from his often dispassionate prose to evoke the reader's sympathy for his protagonist.[102] This passage is particularly provocative given the author's recent rediscovery of his own Catholic faith, as he clearly admonishes the church and the family, two institutions he was especially concerned to preserve, for their abandonment of fallen women. In order for religious and family values to keep their integrity in dangerous modern times, Gamboa's novel seems to suggest, they would have to prove themselves as the guardians of the very people that the modern urban environment put most at risk. Gamboa's naturalism depicts a bleak picture of Mexican modernity—with a hidden social sector being left behind in a dangerous urban environment of alcoholism, crime, and sexual profligacy—but the subtle advocation of change regarding the social position of women, particularly in the eyes of the church and traditional family values, does offer a ray of hope in an otherwise dark portrait.

Gamboa's exploration of female alcoholism, as a product of the conflict between the developing modern urban environment in Mexico and traditional domestic values, was unusual material among nineteenth-century novelists, who generally focused on men in matters pertaining to alcohol. While no other nineteenth-century writer focused on an alcoholic female character in such depth, several did include representations of alcoholism, linked to both insanity and degeneration, as a means of exploring what modernity would mean for Mexico's women and for the roles they were traditionally expected to fulfill in the nation-building process. Since the woman's primary role according to nation-building discourse was the reproduction of healthy, productive citizens, alcoholism and insanity emerged as great threats to her ability to do so successfully and, therefore, as serious threats to the nation's future. In literary explorations of this theme, alcoholism, insanity, and degeneration together represented fears about persistently problematic social divisions, the implications of racial miscegenation, and the prospect of modernity leading not to order and progress but, rather, to national disintegration.

Pedro Castera's most famous novel, *Carmen* (1882), is usually classified as the epitome of Mexico's romantic sentimentalist genre. While the prose is highly esoteric and a typically tortured love affair structures the plot, Castera's other works reveal the more scientific outlook he developed from his role in modernizing Mexico's mining industry. Positivist, even naturalist, ideas about degeneration are latent in *Carmen* as well, especially in its approach to the relationship between alcohol use and mental illness. After fighting in the Liberal army against the French Intervention, Castera (1838–1906) became a prose writer, poet, journalist, and politician, serving as deputy of congress in the 1880s. He also suffered a mental breakdown in 1883, was admitted to San Hipólito for an extended period, and subsequently suffered periodic episodes of illness. Perhaps intuitively aware of his deteriorating condition when writing *Carmen*, we may also speculate that the novel has autobiographical elements as it is written in the first-person narrative voice, with a rather confessional tone, and the male narrator-protagonist remains nameless throughout.[103]

The narrative begins with the twenty-year-old narrator in an extremely drunken state, his "veins truly injected with alcohol," his body trembling, his mind hallucinating, as he babbles incoherently to his own shadow. While this description bears greater resemblance to the symptoms of delirium tremens in alcohol withdrawal than to any of the three stages of drunkenness commonly outlined by nineteenth-century medical professionals, it does depict the adverse physical and mental effects of prolonged, excessive alcohol consumption, as the narrator admits to having (mis)spent a bohemian youth in drinking, womanizing, and gambling. In his inebriated state, the narrator stumbles across an abandoned baby and following the instructions of his mother, he takes the child into his household to raise as part of the family. This newfound responsibility transforms the young man into an upright citizen, but the drunken, delirious episode in which he found Carmen foreshadows the mental instability that will plague her health, as well as the profound ambiguity that will characterize their relationship.[104]

A metaphorical association between drunkenness and madness recurs repeatedly throughout the novel in the narrator's descriptions of his feelings of love for Carmen, being "maddened and drunk with love," and of her intense jealousy regarding any contact the narrator has with other women.[105] In spite of the great age difference and initial father-daughter relationship between the narrator and Carmen, they fall in love, but the need for secrecy exacerbates her already volatile character and causes Carmen to suffer from heart palpitations, melancholy, and anxiety. These are the classic symptoms of hysteria, as suffered by many a female heroine in nineteenth-century literature as a consequence of angst-ridden love affairs, but Castera introduces another element to Carmen's condition through the extended intoxication and madness metaphor, which the narrator uses to characterize their love.[106] Midway through the novel, on declaring their intentions to marry, the narrator's mother informs him that Carmen is actually his biological daughter; however, a subsequent twist in the story reveals that she is not. In the interim period, the narrator is forced to abandon Carmen and, since she does not know the reason why, her mysterious illness worsens, and she dies shortly after the two are eventually reconciled.[107]

For a significant section of the novel, then, the reader is led to believe that Carmen and the narrator are biologically related and the key points of their relationship—their meeting, betrothal, discovery of her "real" identity, and reconciliation— are marked by either literal or metaphorical states of drunkenness and madness, indicating Castera's engagement with medical and psychiatric knowledge about the effects of alcohol consumption and hereditary mental problems. Other, more unambiguously romantic, nineteenth-century novels use intoxication metaphorically, to represent love, anger, irrationality, and other extreme emotions, without Castera's latent exploration of degeneration. The difference worth emphasizing between *Carmen* and these other works is that the drunkenness-madness metaphor is built from a highly significant plot episode and contributes to the novel's overall structure, rather than simply acting as suitably romantic, hyperbolic prose.[108] Although it turns out that the narrator is not Carmen's biological father, the structural parallels between his drunkenness, whether metaphorical or real, and her hysterical episodes, in combination with the fatalistic inevitability of her death, point to a sustained interest in the links between alcoholism and hereditary mental illness. The novel, however, ultimately concludes that the cause of the relationship's and Carmen's demise is not any biological condition but the gendered inequalities and associated social etiquette that gave rise to the web of deception surrounding Carmen's identity: Lola, a discarded former lover of the narrator, did bear him a child, but left an unrelated orphan (Carmen) to his care, so that she could keep custody of the real child herself as a lone mother.

In a much more oblique manner than Castera's other fiction that deals with the hardships experienced by mine workers, *Carmen* suggests that scientific theories and methods of investigation ought not to be used dispassionately to simply explain away Mexico's social problems but to facilitate the compassionate understanding of social injustices in need of reform. Notwithstanding *Carmen*'s unique combination of romantic sentimentalism and naturalist determinism, and its less conservative outlook, Castera's novel demonstrates some similarities with Gamboa's *Santa* in its conclusions. Both novels identified social hypocrisy toward unfortunate or fallen women as a key problem within Mexico's emerging modernity. In both *Carmen* and *Santa* central female characters fall foul of traditional social values regarding women who became pregnant out of wedlock, but Lola is left in this position by a bohemian, dandy-type character (the young narrator) and *Santa* is given no alternative but to immerse herself in the seedy underbelly of modern Mexico City. Both cases seem to suggest, using medicalized language and knowledge to bolster their positions, that certain aspects of modernity were at fault in the corruption of these two women, and in certain consequences of their corruption, including Carmen's madness and Santa's alcoholism: the juncture of modern society with traditional social values left women, especially women of the lower social classes, physically, mentally, and morally vulnerable.

Modernista writers of the late nineteenth and early twentieth century also—as the name of their movement suggests—critiqued and rejected certain aspects of modernity, while embracing others. *Modernismo* emerged across Spanish America during the 1880s, drawing on influences from European literary figures such as Baudelaire, Schopenhauer, Hugo, and Verlaine to introduce a new aesthetic vision of literature and art that rejected realism-naturalism's focus on the gritty, everyday, and mundane but often shared its pseudoscientific understanding of human psychology. A kind of cosmopolitanism, seeking atemporal and universal values, as opposed to a straightforward rejection of all things native to Latin America, a heightened sensualism, and a critique of contemporary society's obsession with material progress were the central, common features of this varied literary trend at the turn of the twentieth century. Although poetry was the dominant medium for *modernistas*, some prose writers also embraced the tenets of *modernismo*—most notably in Mexico, Amado Nervo (1870–1919), who was also a poet, journalist, and diplomat.[109] Nervo frequently examines abnormal psychology in his protagonists and *Pascual Aguilera* (1892), in particular, incorporates a medicalized framework of alcoholism and degeneration in order to explore the spiritual and moral condition of the modern nation.

Nervo's protagonist, Pascual Aguilera, is the illegitimate son of an alcoholic mother and a womanizing hacienda owner. Due to his mother's death, he is raised by the hacendado, who now suffers from sexual dysfunction and cannot conceive a legitimate child with his new wife. From an early age Pascual is extremely emotional, deceptive, jealous, melancholy, irritable, volatile, and "dominated by a savage eroticism." The protagonist has clearly inherited this defective, hypersensitive character from his dissolute parents and this inheritance will also be his downfall: "The wretched offspring of a has-been and an alcoholic, with who knows what dim-witted inheritances: Redemption, for him, would be futile."[110]

After an adolescence spent seducing female hacienda workers, as his father had done before him, and having inherited the hacienda itself upon his father's death, Pascual becomes obsessed with Refugio, a beautiful, nubile household servant betrothed to the rustic peasant Santiago. Refugio and Santiago get married following several abortive attempts on the part of Pascual to seduce Refugio or force her into having sex with him. Tortured with jealous, emasculated thoughts of another man—his social inferior—possessing Refugio, Pascual turns to tequila in an attempt to blot out his emotions and physical sensations. In accordance with medical models describing the effects of alcohol on the body and mind, the alcohol heightens Pascual's lust and anger: "He wanted to get drunk because he could no longer bear the internal tumult; but as usually happens when the moral upset is powerful, alcohol, rather than anaesthetizing him, excited his spirit and increased his anger."[111] In this state of heightened passion, he fantasizes about beating Santiago and raping Refugio, and when his stepmother encounters Pascual in fits of hysterical laughter, he rapes her instead. Shortly afterward, the intense period of delirium, desire, and rage he has been experiencing induces a fatal cerebral hemorrhage.

As the child of an alcoholic, Pascual exhibits a range of characteristics outlined by degeneration theorists, including depravity in his sexual behavior, melancholia, mania, and cerebral softening, which ultimately kills him. While the Morel model of degeneration stipulated that these symptoms would be distributed across several generations, Nervo's novel concentrates them all in the single character of Pascual Aguilera, thus increasing the potency of the novel's metaphorical critique of Mexican modernity. Set into sharp relief against an idyllic, traditional, rural landscape, the adverse consequences of Pascual's parentage of an anonymous alcoholic mother and a sexually rapacious father, ironically unable to subsequently father a legitimate child, are described using degeneration theory and medicalized language. *Pascual Aguilera* thus combines the typical early nineteenth-century condemnation of parents who gave a bad moral example to their children, with the late nineteenth-century paradigm connecting alcoholism, reproductive problems, and generational defects. Both biological parents are described with authorial contempt and condemnation in stark contrast to the eulogized, saintly, hardworking, and chaste stepmother, Doña Francisca, who is loved by the local peasants and whose robust healthiness and virtue are repeatedly emphasized. Pascual himself, as the child of the morally and medically reprehensible parents, represents the infiltration of corruption, disease, and degeneration into traditional Mexican values. Firstly, traditional Mexico is represented by the hacienda, which Pascual inherits despite being illegitimate; then by Refugio, who masturbates after one of Pascual's desperate attempts to seduce her forcibly; and finally by Francisca, who shockingly "enjoys" being raped by Pascual in what is her first sexual experience. Not only does Pascual's own presence and behavior sully the land, the innocent maiden, and the virtuous widow, but his moral depravity actually *passes on* to them through their contact with him. The possibility that Pascual has impregnated Francisca remains as an ominous legacy that could continue the cycle of degeneration among the hacienda's population.

Conclusions: The Pulque Debate

As Moises González Navarro has claimed, "Alcoholism was the national calamity that most held the attention of the Porfirian elite," and literary figures like Nervo, among this elite, were no exception in their concerns.[112] In dialogue with contemporary medical and psychological discourse and degeneration theory, Amado Nervo, Pedro Castera, Federico Gamboa, and Ángel de Campo, four of Mexico's most prominent writers at the end of the nineteenth century, traversing the literary spectrum from *modernismo* and romanticism to naturalism and realism, represented alcoholism as a threat to the nation due to its alleged role in producing disease, crime, mental illness, and degenerate offspring. There was a heated debate in nonliterary discourse regarding the relative harmfulness of pulque as compared to other drinks but, although late nineteenth-century writers mobilized the technical language and pessimistic forecasts regarding alcoholism's effects on society that characterized medical, legal, psychiatric, and criminological texts, they did not seem to either accuse or defend pulque in the same way. Throughout the nineteenth century, Mexican novelists did indeed criticize pulque drinking and pulquerías as major causes of social disorder and poverty among the lower classes, and so it is even more striking that pulque does not feature in late nineteenth-century fictional portraits of *alcoholism* and its associated medical, psychiatric, criminological, and degenerational problems.

The novels of Gamboa, de Campo, and Nervo all depict the compulsive consumption of distilled spirits in their explorations of alcoholic characters, even among those hailing from the lower classes. De Campo's Severiano drinks himself to death with "strong, refined liquor with bitters," and the artisans with whom Cosme drinks in his descent into alcoholism drink tequila, aguardiente, and other cheap spirits with mix-

ers to sweeten the taste. Nervo's Pascual Aguilera tries to blot
out his sexual frustration with tequila, while Gamboa's Santa
becomes an alcoholic through her consumption of cognac,
aguardiente, and *fósforo*. In José Tomás de Cuéllar's *Las jamonas* Sánchez habitually drinks cognac for Dutch courage and
later drowns his sorrows with *fósforo*, in notable contrast to
the pulque and beer drunk by the peasant voters he attempts
to swindle. Heriberto Frías also portrayed his alcoholic character, Miguel Mercado, as a regular tequila drinker.[113]

The recurrent appearance of *fósforo* and tequila, in particular, in these fictional explorations of alcoholism is particularly significant, since they were particularly modern drinks.
Clementina Díaz y de Ovando has documented the prominence of *fósforo* as a characteristic feature of modern, polite
café society in nineteenth-century Mexico City, and the latter decades of the nineteenth century witnessed considerable
expansion in the tequila industry and commerce as a result
of technological and transport improvements.[114] The conspicuous absence of pulque and the conspicuous presence of *fósforo* and tequila in late nineteenth-century medicalized fictions
points to a representation of alcoholism as a uniquely modern
phenomenon. Beer, although a potential symbol of Mexican
modernity given that this industry was enjoying expansion
similar to the tequila industry, is also conspicuously absent
from late nineteenth-century depictions of alcoholism. Perhaps this was because beer was not yet considered sufficiently
"Mexican" to operate as a symbol of Mexican modernity in fictional discourse in the same way that tequila could. Indeed,
novels across the nineteenth century contain only a few brief
references to beer drinking that carry little symbolic investment, or are typically associated with foreign characters, not
Mexicans.[115] Moreover, in this time period perhaps beer was
not considered sufficiently alcoholic to function as a symbolic source of alcoholism. In 1912, for instance, the Superior

Council for Sanitation was investigating the basis on which the governor of the Federal District had classified beer as a nonintoxicant.[116]

The figurative association of alcoholism with modern drinks helps to characterize alcoholism as a modern condition, effectively created by Mexico's problematic experience of modernity. The picture of modernity that emerges is one that simultaneously sought to define the nation's identity through an elitist cultural experience that excluded the majority of the population and sought to define the nation's problems in the alcoholic, criminal, mentally ill, or degenerate bodies of that majority. That is not to say that these literary works advocated a more egalitarian, inclusive model for Mexican national culture. Rather, they foreground the contradictions inherent in the vision of nationhood under construction during the Porfiriato. Both Gamboa's and Castera's works highlight the difficult social position of women, who were still expected to live up to traditional ideals of chastity and virtue, despite their increasing contact with the corruption of modern, urban life, represented through alcoholism, which causes the physical decay of Santa and is metaphorically associated with Carmen's mental illness. De Campo also evokes sympathy for his leading lady, Remedios, in *La Rumba*, who is trapped by her social circumstances, and the alcoholic men who surround her and who populate de Campo's other fictional landscapes: they are depicted as the detritus of modernity, left behind in the rubble as modern Mexico City builds itself atop their hard work and misfortune. The vision of Mexican modernity proffered in these novels is decidedly corrupt, and the scientific language and theories they use to create this vision lends them a sense of finality and fatalism, disavowing the need or the responsibility to offer possible solutions. These novels seek to present modern Mexico "as it really is," in all its ugliness, and leave it at that.

Rubén Campos, another *modernista* writer and journalist, conveys a heavy sense of disillusionment permeating Mexico's literary scene at the turn of the twentieth century, treating alcoholism as a product of or, perhaps more accurately, a response to modernity. Including the medicalized paradigm and an emphasis on modern drinks in a short vignette called "El alcohol," Campos depicts a once-healthy young man developing bloodshot, sclerosed eyes, seizures, and a fatal illness after falling into a routine of tequila consumption. He explores the psychological motives for drinking more thoroughly in *El bar: La vida literaria de México en 1900* (The bar: Literary life in Mexico in 1900; 1935).[117] Several of Campos's literary friends died from alcohol-related problems in the first years of the twentieth century, including Bernardo Couto Castillo, Julio Ruelas, Alberto Leduc, and Jesús Valenzuela, and Campos portrays their heavy indulgence in alcohol as a necessary part of their vocation as artists during the Porfiriato.[118] In describing Valenzuela's incessant recourse to drinking, Campos's memoir suggests that important things were missing in modern Mexico: "He drank, he always drank, he drank more and more, without ever quenching his thirst, condemned by destiny to the torture of being his own tragic Danaid. . . . Around him there was a trill of laughter, an eternal chorus of happiness at being alive, a fascination with finishing off the drink from Dionysus's vessel, as if from it he could drink life itself, as if from it he could drink oblivion, as if from it he could drink love."[119] Valenzuela's compulsive drinking amounts to a desperate search for something more meaningful and inspirational than his contemporary environment had to offer.

The implication is that art and alcohol were, for bohemians and *modernistas* at any rate, the primary means of escape from and elevation above the dirty realities of daily struggle in Porfirian Mexico, in the absence of having any real hope of improving them. Although usually merely observing, rather than experiencing, the inequalities and hardships affecting the Mexican nation, authors like Valenzuela, Campos, Gamboa, Castera, de Cuéllar, Nervo, and de Campo feared the consequences of urbanization and modernization on the spiritual, intellectual, political, economic, and cultural development of Mexico. Perhaps unable to critique the entire notion of "order and progress" and an elite social culture heavily based on contemporary European practices, since they themselves comprised a significant part of it, the paradoxes and frustrations intuited by these writers became manifest through the discourse surrounding alcoholism that pervaded contemporary thought about medicine, psychiatry, degeneration, criminology, urban planning, and national development.

Locating the origins of alcoholism in modernity itself, through their use of exclusively modern drinks to depict alcoholics and through their contrasts of modern fictional landscapes with more wholesome, traditional aspects of Mexican culture, realists, naturalists, and *modernistas* alike largely came to similar conclusions as policymakers who sought to control the problems created by modernity with "scientific" politics. Although they were perhaps more uneasy about these conclusions, literary figures drew on pseudoscientific methods and terminology to explain the social inequalities that seemed to be an inevitable consequence of progress in late nineteenth-century Mexico.

Drunkenness, Death, and Mexican Melancholia

I like to take my sorrow into the shadow of old monasteries, my guilt . . . into the misericords of unimaginable cantinas where sad-faced potters and legless beggars drink at dawn, whose cold jonquil beauty one rediscovers in death. . . . I sometimes think of myself as a great explorer who has discovered some extraordinary land from which he can never return to give his knowledge to the world: but the name of this land is hell.

—MALCOLM LOWRY

The liquor was pure fire, but, as he had been told that drinking it quickly would make him drunk faster, he swallowed gulp after gulp, fanning his mouth with his shirttails. . . . Abundio carried on, stumbling, head hanging and, at times, crawling on all fours. He felt like the earth was twisting, turning him round, and then throwing him off. He hurried to take hold of it but just when he had it in his hands, it would start spinning again, until he found himself face to face with a man sitting outside a door.

—JUAN RULFO

Both Lowry's *Under the Volcano* (1947) and Rulfo's *Pedro Páramo* (1955), two paradigmatic twentieth-century novels concerning Mexico, engage their central characters in a dialectic process of self-discovery and self-destruction as they walk through an infernal landscape saturated with drunkenness and death. In Lowry's novel, the hell in which Geoffrey Fermin finds himself is at once his disintegrating relationship with his wife, his devastating alcoholism, and Mexico itself. Set largely during the Day of the Dead celebrations and seen largely through Geoffrey's addled eyes, the Mexico portrayed in this novel is both a lost paradise, an unfulfilled Eden, and a seething reservoir of violence waiting to explode, always under the silhouette of the Valley of Mexico's brooding volcanoes, Popocatepetl and Iztaccihuatl.

Rulfo's masterpiece, meanwhile, follows Juan Preciado through a ghost town, filled with the dead offspring of his father, Pedro Páramo, whose own death is narrated in the novel's final pages. Abundio, who Juan had met on his initial descent into the town, drinks himself into a stupor "to ease the pain" after his wife's death and murders Pedro Páramo in a haze of confusion as a result of his refusal to help with the financial burden of the funeral.[1] At the point of these revelations, Juan Preciado has long since dissolved into the mysteries of the narrative, as the first-person voice that had been his at the beginning gradually changes to the perspective of Susana, one of Páramo's dead wives, as she writhes in torment over the memory of her dead first husband.

By the middle of the twentieth century, then, drunkenness had become a central metaphor in fictional representations of Mexico, intertwined with the imagery of death that many intellectuals within and outside Mexico observed to be a major cornerstone of Mexican identity in the aftermath of the 1910 Revolution. Claudio Lomnitz's encyclopedic history of death in Mexico demonstrates both that "a densely layered repertoire of death rituals and death vocabularies" developed in Mexico over the centuries, and that post-revolutionary nation-building discourse portrayed "the playful intimacy with death as a peculiarly Mexican sign."[2] The revolution was indeed an important turning point in the ways in which the Mexican nation was imagined and narrated, but elements of the nineteenth-century discourse surrounding alcohol continued to feature significantly in postrevolutionary nation-building discourses, while others were altered or left behind altogether.

Popular drinking places and spaces appeared in literary explorations of what was culturally specific and unique to Mexico. Pulque drinkers and pulquerías were particularly prominent in such representations, and both Manuel Payno and Guillermo Prieto associated pulquerías with preconquest symbols as a means of defining the "authenticity"' of these drinking places as uniquely Mexican cultural spaces. Perhaps the nineteenth-century literary concentration on pulque in representations of authenticity was also partly the result of the need to assert Mexico City's preeminence as the political and cultural center of the nation by a group of intellectuals overwhelmingly based in the capital. Pulque was produced and consumed mostly in central Mexico and on a lesser scale in more southern regions such as Oaxaca; as a result of its rapid fermentation and decomposition, pulque could not be transported over long distances without spoiling.[3] Consequently, its fundamental association with central Mexico and the pulquerías of Mexico City made pulque a potent symbol that could contribute to elite representations of Mexico City as the heart of the nation.

In the wake of the 1910 Revolution, in which northern landowners, businessmen, and politicians asserted their economic and political importance in the nation's future, tequila, which is produced in the western state of Jalisco and widely exported, began to occupy a central place in nation-building discourse as an authentically Mexican drink. Tim Mitchell claims that revolutionary soldiers typically drank *toritos* (literally, little bulls), made from tequila and sweet soda, as part of a self-conscious effort to portray themselves as virile fighters. Meanwhile, Steffan Igor Ayora-Díaz argues that in twentieth-century Yucatán, drinking tequila was overwhelmingly associated with a macho Mexican stereotype popularized in Mexican and American cinema, against which Yucatec men commonly defined themselves by drinking beer.[4] Demetrio Macías, the indigenous protagonist of Mariano Azuela's famous novel about the Mexican Revolution, *Los de abajo* (The underdogs; 1915), prefers as his drink of choice "the flat, clear tequila of Jalisco," in a scene where he listens disinterestedly to the exaggerated boasts of murder made by other men drinking champagne, suggesting that Demetrio's consumption of tequila signified that there was something more genuine, more authentic in his character.[5]

As the contrast between the taciturn, morose, tequila-drinking Demetrio and the boisterous, swaggering champagne drinkers also suggests, alcohol continued to feature in literary explorations of Mexican masculinities, as it had done in the nineteenth century. Romantic fictions of the mid- to late nineteenth century built a heroic ideal of Mexican masculinity around the values of fraternity, courage, and patriotic duty, and drinking patterns helped to differentiate heroic and antiheroic male characters. Payno incorporated a pattern of fraternal drinking into the characterization of his heroic figure Juan Robreño and associated a violent, destructive, macho-style pattern of drinking with his main villain Evaristo. Altamirano, meanwhile, dissociated his heroic figures from alcohol consumption altogether and contrasted them sharply with drunken, unpatriotic villains. Heriberto Frías, in his realist exposé of the Tomóchic military campaign, created an alcoholic protagonist to destabilize the boundaries between heroes and villains that had been sharply drawn in other fiction, and he used this protagonist to question the ideals of fraternity, patriotic duty, and heroism that had been central to nation-building fictions in the nineteenth century.

Drinking also played a significant role in the performance of masculinities in society, in the consolidation of identities among particular groups of men, in the competition for status within those groups, and in the negotiation of relationships between men and women. Perhaps the powerful gender dynamics of alcohol consumption within broader social relations made alcohol such a potent means of exploring gendered ideals in fiction, with drinking soldiers and artisans being at the center of both literary explorations of masculinity and broader social discourse about male drinking, revealing the importance of these male groups to the imagination of Mexican nationhood. While we therefore have a reasonably clear idea of both male drinking practices and how they were interpreted through nation-building discourses, further research is needed into the issue of female drinking practices and attitudes toward women's alcohol consumption in nineteenth-century Mexico.

The early decades of the twentieth century saw the consolidation of the image of the violent, volatile, heavy-drinking, macho Mexican stereotype in literature and film that has more in common with nineteenth-century villains than with its masculine heroes. Anne Doremus has examined two novels of the revolution by Martín Luis Guzmán and Rafael Muñoz, which directly correlate machismo with a representation of the revolution as barbaric, irrational, and brutally violent. Hollywood films of the 1920s also popularized stock images of Mexican characters in folk costumes and sombreros with heavy drinking, sexual aggressiveness, and violence against women. Doremus also notes, however, that in Mexican films of the 1930s and 1940s, a more positive definition of machismo was constructed, portraying revolutionaries like Pancho Villa as charismatic, courageous leaders and Porfirian hacendados as paternalistic, fair, and generous, echoing the ways in which masculine codes were contested in the nineteenth century.[6]

Octavio Paz's famous collection of essays on Mexican identity, *The Labyrinth of Solitude* (1950), also presented machismo as one of the defining characteristics of Mexican culture. In his schematic psychoanalytical examination of "the Mexican," Paz argued that Mexican men strove to be aggressive and to assert their domination over others as a defensive mechanism against a repressed inferiority complex that ultimately derived from a collective, sublimated sense of the betrayal and violation implicated in Mexico's origins. Mexicans, according to Paz, are the "Sons of La Malinche," the indigenous woman who became translator and lover to Cortés in his conquest over the Aztecs. As such, they are in a constant state of denial about their identity, which is manifested in their aggression, volatility, and obsession with virility.[7]

Although examinations of La Malinche's role in the origins of Mexican nationhood were incorporated into several nineteenth-century literary works, as Sandra Messinger-Cypess has shown, Paz's postulation of a connection between the originary La Malinche and a particular type of Mexican masculinity was a new feature of mid-twentieth-century discourse.[8] Other elements of his argument, however, reveal the ongoing influence of nineteenth-century nation-building literary discourses on Mexican intellectuals in the twentieth century. Paz's definition of machismo ultimately relies on a categorization of open versus closed bodies, a categorization which permeated Mexican public discourse from the eighteenth century to the middle of the nineteenth century, as was demonstrated in chapter 3. Many Enlightenment philosophers, and Mexican intellectuals and government officials who engaged with their ideas, conceived of closed bodies as the manifestation of rationality, civility, and order, whereas open bodies were variously seen as grotesque, vice-ridden, and dangerous. The drunken bodies of foreign enemies, untutored Indians, misguided women, and profligate aristocrats featured prominently in early and mid-nineteenth-century fictional works that sought to expose threats to the nation, to criticize aristocratic and conservative values of excess that were deemed irrational, and to recommend an expansive program of education and liberal reform to increase the reasoning capacity of social groups such as women, the indigenous, and the urban poor, so that they might better control their bodily passions.

Paz reformulates the open/closed dichotomy: while open bodies of the Enlightenment era were grotesque, irrational, passionate, and prone to vices, Paz's open bodies are passive, vulnerable, sexualized, and feminine; where Enlightenment closed bodies were rational, controlled, civilized, and moral, the closed bodies in *The Labyrinth of Solitude* are active and aggressive, yet reserved and defensive, and, above all, male. While the conceptualization and categorization of open and closed bodies are therefore quite different, underlying continuities reveal that a similar distinction is at work. In the late eighteenth and early nineteenth century, female bodies were certainly seen as more open than male bodies, and the vulnerability with which Paz characterizes open bodies can be symptomatic of indulgence in vices, such as promiscuous sex or drunkenness. Indeed, Paz reiterates on several occasions that the closed bodies of macho men and of stoic Indians are most often transformed into open, vulnerable bodies through drinking: "We get drunk in order to confess"; "We open out during fiestas . . . or when we are drunk or exchanging confidences"; "Our intimacy never flowers in a natural way, only when incited by fiestas, alcohol, or death." In Paz's conception, then, as in the nation-building fictions of Lizardi, Pizarro Suárez, Díaz Covarrubias, and Payno, drunken bodies are open, vulnerable, threatening, and threatened, for it is in these moments of vulnerability that the normally closed and reserved Mexican "macho" remembers his connection to La Malinche and becomes violent.[9]

Elements of the grotesque mode, used in the nineteenth century to depict drunken bodies as open and dangerous, also continued to feature in twentieth-century novels, particularly those dealing with indigenous subjects. Two *indigenista* novelists, Mauricio Magdaleno and Gregorio López y Fuentes, portrayed their indigenous characters in an animalized fashion, emphasizing their habitual drunkenness, their immersion in poverty and squalor, and their proximity to death and the dying. Descriptive passages focus on bodily orifices and bodily functions in an even more graphic manner than their nineteenth-century predecessors often did, as realist authors of the late nineteenth century had already broken through the remaining barriers of literary "decency" that frequently restrained previous writers from making such lurid depictions. Furthermore, continuing the nineteenth-century trend, these authors mobilized such animalized descriptions of the indigenous population to demonstrate that Indians remained isolated from the larger national community as a result of their long history of exploitation and that the state needed to intervene to provide the indigenous population with greater access to economic and educational opportunities if this dire situation was to improve.[10]

The film industry also formulated a new mode in which to use grotesque depictions in the twentieth century. The extremely popular Cantinflas films, from the late 1930s to the 1960s, resurrected the carnivalesque spirit of the grotesque, using it to amuse rather than to warn or condemn, as literary texts had done in the nineteenth and twentieth century. Cantinflas, the pseudonym of comic actor Mario Moreno, regularly played a stereotypical *"pelado"* (poor urban migrant), who demonstrated remarkable resourcefulness and wit in extricating himself from an array of compromising situations. He was commonly half-drunk and unkempt, with "prominent facial features such as a distinctly wide nose, thick lips, widespread eyes, exaggeratedly dark and arched eyebrows . . . and acted like the clowns and fools of the carnival."[11] His characters were meant to be caricatures and to inspire laughter rather than any serious social criticism regarding the injustices of everyday life for the urban poor. In contrast to the sinister grotesque depictions of drunken bodies—whether Indian, female, poor, or foreign—in nineteenth and twentieth-century literature, the carnivalesque Cantinflas was not a call to arms or a campaign for education or reform.

The advocation of widening access to, and increasing the comprehensiveness of, education, in tandem with a range of other liberal reforms, had been a central feature of much nineteenth-century literature. In chapters 1 and 3 we traced a gradual decline over the course of the century in the levels of intellectuals' faith in the efficacy of education and liberal reform to effect change in society, particularly with regard to the erosion of popular patterns of drunkenness, social disorder, poverty, prostitution, crime, and immorality. Although support for education clearly did not disappear, late nineteenth-century nation-building discourse was markedly more pessimistic regarding the ability of indigenous and lower-class groups to reform their drunken, disorderly ways, and to become productive citizens of the nation.

This was partially the result of positivist influences in the 1890s, which sought to apply a pseudoscientific approach to governing Mexican society. A central feature of this "scientific" politics was the medicalization of thought regarding alcohol consumption and its effects upon individuals and society in general. Mexican doctors and psychiatrists developed a medical concept of alcoholism that enumerated a range of detrimental physiological and psychological afflictions caused by alcohol abuse and conceived of alcoholism, defined broadly as any pattern of alcohol consumption with harmful consequences, as a medical condition. This conception of alcoholism infiltrated public policy and discourse, which envisaged causal connections between the medical condition of alcoholism and a range of other problems, including crime, mental illness, and even racial degeneration, which, together, threatened the future of the Mexican nation. The medicalized lexicon surrounding alcoholism, and the associations between alcoholism, insanity, criminality, and degeneration, also featured prominently in late nineteenth-and early twentieth-century literature, written mostly in the new modes of realism, naturalism, and *modernismo*, or in some mixture of the three. Moreover, with their concerted emphasis on the modernizing features of Mexico City in their corrupted fictional landscapes, and in their exclusive association of alcoholism and alcoholics with more modern drinks like tequila and *fósforo* (as opposed to the traditional pulque), writers such as de Campo, Gamboa, Castera, and Nervo seemed to portray alcoholism, the medical condition, as a particularly modern phenomena. Progress came hand in hand with its dark side.

Gretchen Pierce's 2008 doctoral thesis, "Sobering the Revolution," demonstrates that alcoholism continued to occupy a prominent position in the nation-building concerns of postrevolutionary politicians and intellectuals. In this era, it seems that both early and late nineteenth-century understandings of the corrosive effects of alcohol were mobilized, as government officials, journalists, and public figures expressed concerns about the physical and moral consequences of alcohol abuse on individuals, as well as the ramifications for families and society in general. Educational campaigns, warning children and workers in particular, about the dangers of drinking were central to the postrevolutionary antialcohol movement, although they became more widespread and well-coordinated than they had been during the Porfiriato.

Temperance organizations also took on much greater importance in the fight against alcohol, following their beginnings in the final years of the Porfiriato. In the postrevolutionary period, as Pierce explains, temperance organizations were established at a national level by the state (for instance, the National Committee of the Fight against Alcoholism, formed in 1929), and at the popular level by groups of women, teachers, workers, and churchgoers. Although the idea of a national prohibition was rejected at the Constitutional Convention (1916–17) after comprehensive discussions, mainly due to the potential loss of revenue it would cause and to the impracticalities of implementation, some states within the republic imposed their own bans. Sonora, for instance, enforced a prohibition on all alcohol production and commerce from 1915, before giving in to the lucrative trading opportunities presented when the United States went dry in 1919, while Yucatán also experimented with prohibition from 1915 to 1917.[12]

Alcoholism, then, and alcohol use in general, continued to be a cause for concern among politicians, intellectuals, and, increasingly, ordinary Mexicans in the early decades of the twentieth century, as drinking and drunkenness had been throughout the nineteenth century and the colonial period. Bourbon reformers, nineteenth-century nation-builders, and postrevolutionary cultural nationalists, although informed by different philosophical and political ideas and mobilizing different strategies, sought to curtail what they understood to be the more damaging effects of the Mexican population's drinking practices. Through an analysis of medical, legal, juridical, and journalistic texts alongside the various genres and styles of nineteenth-century fiction, this study has argued that drinking places, drinking behaviors, and changing conceptions of the nature of drunkenness and alcoholism as bodily conditions, fulfilled important roles in the imagination of the Mexican nation. During the nineteenth century, novels that were engaged in nation-building discourses reiterated the wider discursive warnings about alcohol's threat to the nation, as they portrayed the worshippers at San Lunes, drunken Indians, profligate toffs, fallen women, and diseased alcoholic degenerates.

Importantly, although less commonly, literary works also recognized the culturally constitutive and socially cohesive role that certain types of drinking could play in the formation of identities and communities. The cultural authenticity sometimes ascribed to pulque and to certain pulque drinkers, and the fraternal camaraderie performed by Juan Robreño in his shared, stoic drink before the firing squad, represented an attempt to include aspects of popular culture within the idealized vision of nationhood being imagined by elite intellectuals. At times, we can also see alcohol being used to cast into doubt the prevailing values regarding the nation and what the nation should be, as in the case of Miguel Mercado's drunken ambivalence in the face of patriotic, heroic ideals of masculinity, and in the pessimistic portraits of alcoholism in the supposedly illustrious climate of Porfirian modernity. While many nineteenth-century authors therefore found many different ways to answer Mercado's question "What's wrong with a little drinking?" they also found drinking a useful means of exploring in their fiction what was "wrong" with Mexico.

NOTES

All translations from the Spanish are mine unless otherwise stated.

Abbreviations

AG	Archivo de Guerra
AGN	Archivo General de la Nación
AHDF	Archivo Histórico del Distrito Federal
CNCA	Consejo Nacional para la Cultura y las Artes
FA	Fondo Ayuntamiento
FAGDF	Fondo Ayuntamiento Gobierno del Distrito Federal
FJ	Fondo Justicia
FM	Fondo Municipalidades
FRA	Fondo Real Audencia
FRPI	Fondo Regio Patronato Indiano
SCJN	Suprema Corte de Justicia de la Nación

Introduction

Guillermo Prieto, "Cuadro de costumbres" (1845) cited in Forment, *Democracy in Latin America*, 115.

Sánchez Santos, *El alcoholismo en la República Mexicana*, 6.

1. The novel in question is *Tomóchic* by Heriberto Frías, which is discussed in chapter 2.

2. Anderson, *Imagined Communities*.

3. Sommer, *Foundational Fictions*.

4. Anderson, *Imagined Communities*, 24–26, 62–65.

5. Timothy Brennan, "National Longing for Form," 48.

6. For both a critique of Anderson's interpretation of Spanish American nationalisms and recognition of his theoretical insights see the essays

in Castro-Klein and Chasteen, *Beyond Imagined Communities*, especially Guerra, "Forms of Communication," 3–32 and Unzueta, "Scenes of Reading," 115–60. See also Lomnitz, *Deep Mexico, Silent Mexico*, 3–14, 27–33; Gerassi-Navarro, *Pirate Novels*, 70–79; French, "Imagining and the Cultural History of Nineteenth-Century Mexico," 250–53; and Ochoa, *Uses of Failure in Mexican Literature and Identity*, 4–10.

7. Sommer, *Foundational Fictions*, 7, 49–50. See also Algaba, "Por los umbrales de la novela histórica," 1:287–92; Rappaport, "Fictive Foundations," 120–22.

8. Gerassi-Navarro, *Pirate Novels*, 9.

9. Wright, "Subscribing Identities," 325.

10. On the multiple public roles fulfilled by nineteenth-century Spanish American writers, see Camarillo, "Los periodistas en el siglo XIX," 1:153, 156; Segre, *Intersected Identities*, 5–6; Brushwood, *Mexico in Its Novel*, 82, 94; Kirkendall, "Student Culture and Nation-State Formation," 85–86; Escalante Gonzalbo, *Ciudadanos imaginarios*, 259–60, 276–77.

11. Cited in Read, *Mexican Historical Novel*, 247.

12. Díaz Covarrubias, *Gil Gómez el Insurgente*, vi–viii; Agustín R. González, "La literatura mexicana," *El Siglo XIX*, July 8, 1872.

13. Cited in Franco, *Introduction to Spanish-American Literature*, 72.

14. Bhabha, introduction to *Nation and Narration*, 3–4; Timothy Brennan, "National Longing for Form," 46–47; During, "Literature—Nationalism's Other?," 138–39. See also Unzueta, "Scenes of Reading," 119–22.

15. Chanady, "Introduction: Latin American Imagined Communities and the Postmodern Challenge," x.

16. Carey, *Distilling the Influence of Alcohol*; Thomas M. Wilson, *Drinking Cultures*; Kadel, "Pub and the Irish Nation"; Holt, *Alcohol*; Pierce, "Parades, Epistles, and Prohibitive Legislation"; Heath, *Drinking Occasions*; Anya Taylor, *Bacchus in Romantic England*; Earnshaw, *Pub in Literature*; Guy, *When Champagne Became French*.

17. William B. Taylor, *Drinking, Homicide, and Rebellion*, 28–34; Anawalt, "Flopsy, Mopsy, and Tipsy," 24; Anawalt, "Rabbits, *Pulque*, and Drunkenness," 33–36; Toxqui, "Taverns and Their Influence," 245–46; Dodds Pennock, *Bonds of Blood*, 163–66; Bruman, *Alcohol in Ancient Mexico*, 63–64; Henderson, "Blood, Water, Vomit, and Wine," 60–68; Nicholson, "Octli Cult," 172–77; Gonçalves de Lima, *El maguey y el pulque*, 119–21, 207.

18. In addition to alcohol, tobacco, chocolate, blood, and hallucinogenic plants also produced altered states of being that bridged human and divine worlds in preconquest Mexico. See Norton, *Sacred Gifts*, 20–43.

19. William B. Taylor, *Drinking, Homicide and Rebellion*, 28–34; Mitchell, *Intoxicated Identities*, 13–20; Bruman, *Alcohol in Ancient Mexico*, 33, 91–92; Nicholson, "Octli Cult," 178–79; Clendinnen, *Aztecs*, 48–49.

20. Paredes, "Social Control of Drinking," 1141–51; Smith, Wharton, and Olson, "Aztec Feasts, Rituals, and Markets," 254–56; Dodds Pennock, *Bonds of Blood*, 25; Pohl, "Themes of Drunkenness, Violence, and Factionalism," 194–202; Clendinnen, *Aztecs*, 49–51, 245–46.

21. Corcuera, "Pulque y evangelización," 264–82; Earle, "Algunos pensamientos," 19–20.

22. Earle, "Algunos pensamientos," 20–21; Cervantes, *Idea of the Devil*, 5–6; Gruzinski, *Conquest of Mexico*, 185; Burkhart, *Slippery Earth*, 140, 167.

23. De Acosta, *Natural and Moral History of the Indies*, 1:160; Ruíz de Alarcón, *Treatise on the Heathen Superstitions*, 39.

24. William B. Taylor, *Drinking, Homicide, and Rebellion*, 60–62, 156; Horn, *Postconquest Coyoacan*, 23; Lockhart, *Nahuas After the Conquest*, 456–59; Mitchell, *Intoxicated Identities*, 21–22, 42.

25. Stern, *Secret History of Gender*, 173; Viqueira Albán, *Propriety and Permissiveness*, 98–115; Nemser, "'To Avoid this Mixture,'" 105–9; Earle, "Algunos pensamientos," 21–22.

26. Stern, *Secret History of Gender*, 171–74, 267.

1. Everything in Its Right Place?

Payno, *Los bandidos*, 466.

1. Payno, *Los bandidos*, 466. Xóchitl is a figure from Aztec history and mythology, reputedly involved in the discovery of pulque, whose legend was revived in nineteenth-century Mexican art and literature. See Toner, "Xóchitl's Bar."

2. Payno, *Los bandidos*, 465.

3. Throughout the colonial period, Indians frequented the central areas of the city as traders in the Plaza Mayor, to work as domestic servants in the employ of wealthy Spaniards and to find work of other kinds after migrating to Mexico City as a means of avoiding the tax obligations that were imposed on indigenous villages in the countryside.

4. The numbers cited here should be taken as estimates that reflect a definite demographic trend. The exact figures are contested, but historians agree that the later decades of the eighteenth century witnessed a sharp increase in the city's population, caused by migration from surrounding rural communities. See Florescano, *Precios del maíz*, 95; Garza Merodio,

"Technological Innovation," 117; Lear, "Mexico City," 464; Warren, *Vagrants and Citizens*, 9–10.

5. Burkhart, *Slippery Earth*, 161–64; Vargas and Casillas, "El encuentro de dos cocinas," 162–63; Lozano Armendares, "Mezcales, pulques y chinguiritos," 424; Paredes, "Social Control of Drinking," 1143–44; William B. Taylor, *Drinking, Homicide, and Rebellion*, 35–37; Smith, Wharton, and Olson, "Aztec Feasts, Ritual, and Markets," 244–46.

6. William B. Taylor, *Drinking, Homicide and Rebellion*, 36–38; Corcuera de Mancera, *Del amor al temor*, 213–16; Toxqui, "Taverns and Their Influence," 246.

7. McCaa, "Calidad, Clase and Marriage in Colonial Mexico," 477–78; François, "Cloth and Silver," 345–56; Earle, *Food, Race and the Colonial Experience*, 6–10.

8. For more detailed information about social divisions and hierarchies in Mexican society, see Corcuera de Mancera, *Del amor al temor*, 210–17; Deans-Smith, "Working Poor and the Eighteenth Century Colonial State," 48–51; Guedea, "México en 1812," 28–33; Suárez y Farías, "Ámbitos y sabores virreinales," 45–46; di Tella, "Dangerous Classes," 81, 95–98; Warren, *Vagrants and Citizens*, 7–10; Viqueira Albán, *Propriety and Permissiveness*, 98–99, 145; Gruzinski, *Conquest of Mexico*, 277–79; Stern, *Secret History of Gender*, 173, 267.

9. Viqueira Albán, *Propriety and Permissiveness*, 101, 143; Guedea, "México en 1812," 32; Scardaville, "Alcohol Abuse and Tavern Reform," 648; Corcuera de Mancera, *Del amor al temor*, 215; Staples, "Policia y Buen Gobierno," 119–21; Kicza, "Pulque Trade," 197.

10. Cope, *Limits of Racial Domination*, 143.

11. For an excellent discussion of the perceived dangers of interethnic plebeian sociability, see Nemser, "'To Avoid this Mixture,'" 106–10. See also Cope, *Limits of Racial Domination*, 155–56; Curcio-Nagy, "Giants and Gypsies," 19–20; Guedea, "México en 1812," 24–26.

12. Sigüenza y Góngora, "Alboroto y Motín de México," 137–39.

13. Pulque was typically mixed with various flavorings and preservatives, including herbs, roots, fruits, and seeds, which Spanish officials often feared made the drink more alcoholically potent and unhealthy. As Nemser has argued, pure pulque was normally seen as nutritious and medicinal by Spanish authorities, and it was the mixing of pulque with various unknown substances—much like the suspicious plebeian social mixing happening in pulquerías—that caused them such concern. Nemser, "'To Avoid this Mixture,'" 100–109.

14. Cited in Guedea, "México en 1812," 28–29.

15. Toxqui, "Taverns and Their Influence," 249. See also Warren, *Vagrants and Citizens*, 13; Morales, "Espacio, propiedad y órganos de poder," 156; Rohlfes, "Police and Penal Correction in Mexico City," 9–13.

16. Scardaville, "Alcohol Abuse and Tavern Reform," 657–60; Guedea, "México en 1812," 29, 37–40; Kicza, "Pulque Trade," 195–96.

17. AGN, FRA, Civil: vol. 2126, exp. 1, fs. 1–24: "Sobre corrección de la embriaguez," 1805–22.

18. Scardaville, "Alcohol Abuse and Tavern Reform," 645–46.

19. Viqueira Albán, *Propriety and Permissiveness*, 157, 162.

20. AHDF, FAGDF, Pulquerías: vol. 3719, exp. 52, fl. 26: "Pulquerías: Incidentes acerca de éstas. Los alcaldes constitucionales del excelentísimo Ayuntamiento de México á su fidelísimo vecindario," June 29, 1821.

21. AGN, FJ, Justicia: vol. 49, exp. 30, fl. 241: "La sentencia que ha pronunciado a favor de Don Manuel Alfaro," November 1824. A similar decree had been promulgated in 1816. See di Tella, "Dangerous Classes," 96.

22. AHDF, FAGDF, Pulquerías: vol. 3719, exp. 53, fl. 23: "Cuaderno principal de providencias acerca de pulquerías," March 22, 1831.

23. Pulquerías: vol. 3719, exp. 53, fs. 15–19: "Cuaderno principal de providencias acerca de pulquerías," December 1829–March 1830.

24. Pulquerías: vol. 3719, exp. 53, fl. 61: "Cuaderno principal de providencias acerca de pulquerías," December 8, 1833.

25. Pulquerías: vol. 3719, exp. 53, fl. 61: "Cuaderno principal de providencias acerca de pulquerías," December 8, 1833.

26. AGN, FRA, Criminal: vol. 485, exp. 4, fs. 56–57: "Contra Don José Antonio Merino, Soldado de Militias Urbanas del Comercio de esta Corte, por excesos cometidos con la Ronda del Teniente de Alguacil mayor Don Pedro 64 Castillo," January 1802; AGN, FRA, Criminal: vol. 467, exp. 6, fs. 140–49: "Desórdenes en la Pulquería de la Alamedita que es el cargo de Felipe Galan," June 1804; AGN, FRA, Criminal: vol. 363, exp. 2, fs. 149–58: "Contra José Manuel Bonilla por malos tratamientos a su mujer, ebrios y haver blasfemado," April 1803; AGN, FRA, Criminal: vol. 86, exp. 12, fs. 312–15: "Causa número 62 contra José Guillermo García por Omicida," July 1811; AGN, SCJN, Asuntos económicos: exp. 6489, 1845; AHDF, FAGDF, Pulquerías: vol. 3719, exp. 52, fs. 18–19: "Pulquerías: Incidentes acerca de éstas," May 1821.

27. AGN, AG: vol. 310, exp. 3070, fs. 523–49: "Sumaria instruida e averiguación de las escándalos cometidas el día 15 de marzo del presente año por el soldado José María Rivera," March 1858.

28. Criminal: vol. 467, exp. 6, fs.146–47: "Desórdenes en la Pulquería de la Alamedita."

29. Susie Porter has identified a similar strategy employed by female food vendors in late nineteenth-century Mexico City, who were under threat from legislative changes designed to remove them from central and "posh" parts of the city. See Porter, "'And That It Is Custom Makes It Law,'" 134–35.

30. AHDF, FAGDF, Pulquerías: vol. 3719, exp. 52, fs. 1–22: "D. Pedro José del Valle, dueño de varios puestos de pulque, sobre que se le permita abrir puestas al Sur, y al Norte, aumentando el arrendamiento," September 1813–May 1814.

31. AHDF, FAGDF, Pulquerías: vol. 52, exp. 52, fs. 94–124: "Pulquerías: Incidentes acerca de éstas. Ocurso de D. Manuel Alfaro sobre que no se comprenda en el Articulo 1° del bando de 3 de Septiembre de presente año, un puesto que tiene en la Plazuela de la Paja," September 1825.

32. AGN, FA, Policías y empedrados: vol. 32, exp. 12, fs. 264–76: "Don Manuel Cerrano, vecino de esta ciudad, sobre que no se le prive de la pulquería de Chapultepec," August 1806.

33. For a similar case further outside the city, see AGN, FA, Policías y empedrados: vol. 32, exp. 6, fl. 163: "Don Manuel Doroteo Gutiérrez del Pueblo de Xocotitlan sobre que se le permita una pulquería," February 1800.

34. *El Siglo XIX*, June 16, 1842.

35. Garza, *Imagined Underworld*, 3; Lear, "Mexico City," 463, 475–77; Porter, "'And That It Is Custom Makes It Law,'" 130–31; Garza Merodio, "Technological Innovation," 111–12; Johns, *City of Mexico*, 13–15; Wakild, "Naturalizing Modernity," 116–18.

36. AHDF, FAGDF, Pulquerías: vol. 3719, exp. 63, fs. 1–24: "Sobre que una comision especial de encargue de formar un reglamento para todas las casillas de licores embriagantes," 1845.

37. Pulquerías: vol. 3719, exp. 63, fs. 1–24: "Sobre que una comision especial de encargue de formar un reglamento para todas las casillas de licores embriagantes," 1845.

38. AHDF, FAGDF, Pulquerías: vol. 3719, exp. 66, fs. 1–2: "Policia: Sobre los perjuicios que reciente el publico por las multitud de casillas de pulque situadas en la calle del Refugio," January 21, 1845.

39. "Machaca," *El Siglo XIX*, April 19, 1845. See also: "Policia," *El Monitor Republicano*, March 25, 1849; AHDF, FAGDF, Pulquerías: vol. 3723, exp. 418, fs. 1–7: "Proposiciones de la Sociedad de Mejores Materiales, para conducir de un modo decente a los ebrios de ambos sexos," 1854.

40. AHDF, FAGDF, Pulquerías: vol. 3723, exp. 421, fs. 1–13: "Se somete a la aprobación suprema el proyecto para extinguir del centro de la ciudad las casillas de dicho piso y que se trasladen a los suburbios," July 1854.

41. Toxqui Garay, "Mexico City's Pulquerías," 130–31. The maps have since been published in Toxqui, "Taverns and Their Influence," 251, 254, 270.

42. AHDF, FAGDF, Pulquerías: vol. 3723, exp. 527, fs. 1–9: "Proyecto para reglamentarlas y sobre que cese el cuadro que esta prohibido abrir esos establecimientos," April 1861. See also AHDF, FAGDF, Pulquerías: vol. 3724, exp. 623, fs. 1–8: "Pedrosa Antonio pide licencia para trasladar la pulquería que tiene en la calle de Jesús junto al número 12 a la calle del León junto al número 3," 1863.

43. Pulquerías: vol. 3723, exp. 527, fl. 22: "Proyecto para reglamentarlas y sobre que cese el cuadro que esta prohibido abrir esos establecimientos," August 1862.

44. Toxqui, "Taverns and Their Influence," 255.

45. Toxqui Garay, "Mexico City's Pulquerías," 141–47.

46. *El Siglo XIX*, February 17, 1872.

47. Díaz y de Ovando, *Los cafés en México*; Schivelbusch, *Tastes of Paradise*, 37–52; Roche, *People of Paris*, 254. Thomas Brennan and W. Scott Haine offer an important corrective to this in the case of French cafés, arguing that the elite, sober, intellectual café was in the minority in eighteenth- and nineteenth-century France, and that, in fact, the majority of Parisian cafés catered for a wide range of social classes and served a range of alcoholic drinks, including wine, beer, and brandy. Thomas Brennan, "Taverns and the Public Sphere," 109–10; Haine, *World of the Paris Café*, 88–117.

48. Díaz y de Ovando, *Los cafés en México*, 13–25, 41, 57–61. See also Garza, *Imagined Underworld*, 77; Stoopen, "Convulsiones y revoluciones culinarias," 54–56; Pilcher, *¡Que vivan los tamales!*, 64–65; Lear, "Mexico City," 469–71.

49. *El Monitor Republicano*, March 11, 1849, and March 20, 1849. *El Siglo XIX* published similar praise for the Café del Bazar after some renovations in 1851, noting that it boasted excellent standards of cooking, service, and cleanliness, as well as a lively atmosphere and a top selection of wines. See *El Siglo XIX*, December 21, 1851. See also *El Siglo XIX*, September 16, 1851, and September 26, 1851.

50. *El Siglo XIX*, March 25, 1872. Subsequent issues in March and April 1872 also featured prominent advertisements for *La Gran Sociedad*.

51. *El Siglo XIX*, February 29, 1872; *El Siglo XIX*, February 19, 1872; *El Siglo XIX*, February 21, 1872.

52. "Confraternidad," *El Monitor Republicano*, April 18, 1849; *El Siglo XIX*, January 2, 1872; *El Siglo XIX*, August 1, 1872 and August 9, 1872.

53. "Riña escandalosa," *El Monitor Republicano*, April 10, 1850.

54. For a similar case, see *El Siglo XIX*, June 16, 1842.

55. AHDF, FAGDF, Gobierno del Distrito, Bebidas Embriagantes: vol. 1331, exp. 52, fs. 1–4: "No se concede a Salomé Bermúdez permiso para expender ponches y alcohol mexicano al café, en su café 'La Aurora,' 1a. de San Juan 4," 1902; AHDF, FAGDF, Gobierno del Distrito, Infracciones: vol. 1649, exp. 149, fs. 3, 24: "El Inspector General de Policia participa las diversas infracciones sorprendidas por la policia de la Capital durante el presente mes, a varios establecimientos," 1912; AHDF, FAGDF, Gobierno del Distrito, Infracciones: vol. 1650, exp. 195, fs. 1–6: "Café 'La Casualidad' de J. Salomé Bernudez, Avenida de la Paz," 1912; AHDF, FAGDF, Gobierno del Distrito, Infracciones: vol. 1650, exp. 300, fl. 1: "Restaurant 'El Cosmopolita' de Pedro Martínez, Avenida del 16 de Septiembre número 44," 1912; AHDF, FAGDF, Gobierno del Distrito, Infracciones: vol. 1651, exp. 306, fs. 1–21: "Café 'La Luz del Día' de Alberto Sánchez, Avenida de la Paz," 1912–13; AHDF, FAGDF, Gobierno del Distrito, Infracciones: vol. 1651, exp. 410, fs. 1–3: "Restaurante 'México Nuevo' de Fernando Pando, 5a de Bolivar," 1912–13.

56. Gobierno del Distrito, Infracciones: vol. 1649, exp. 149, fl. 34: "El Inspector General de Policia participa las diversas infracciones sorprendidas por la policia de la Capital durante el presente mes, a varios establecimientos," 1912.

57. AHDF, FAGDF, Gobierno del Distrito, Infracciones: vol. 1651, exp. 307, fs. 1–24: "Café de Filiberto Peleaz de la Avenida de la Paz," 1912–13.

58. Lear, "Mexico City," 456, 469. See also Garza, *Imagined Underworld*, 15–16, 22–23; Tenorio Trillo, "1910 Mexico City," 83–87; Tenenbaum, "Streetwise History," 128–30; Piccato, *City of Suspects*, 17–20; Johns, *City of Mexico*, 14–15; Garza Merodio, "Technological Innovation," 114–16; Wakild, "Naturalizing Modernity," 111–13.

59. Garza, *Imagined Underworld*, 24, 27; Piccato, *City of Suspects*, 29–30; Lear, "Mexico City," 480; Toxqui Garay, "Mexico City's Pulquerías," 153–55; Porter, "'And That It Is Custom Makes It Law,'" 120; Rohlfes, "Police and Penal Correction in Mexico City," 35–48, 82–88, 134–39.

60. AHDF, FAGDF, Gobierno del Distrito, Pulquerías: vol. 1769, exp. 85, fs. 1–5: "Proyecto del nuevo reglamento de ramo, elevado a Gobernación," December 1901; AHDF, FAGDF, Gobierno del Distrito, Pulquerías: vol. 1770, exp. 137, fs. 1–5: "Se recomienda la policia que cuide de la exacta observancia del Reglamento de Pulquerías vigentes," January 1902.

61. AHDF, FAGDF, Gobierno del Distrito, Pulquerías: vol. 1769, exp. 44, fs. 1–4: "El Inspector de la 5a demarcación avisa que se hallan en mal estado los mingitorios de las pulquerías situadas en el Portillo de San Diego titulada

'Pulquería' una; y la otra, en San Juan de Dios, 'El Apoteosis,'" May 1901; AHDF, FAGDF, Gobierno del Distrito, Pulquerías: vol. 1771, exp. 325, fs. 1–14: "Se ordena la clausura de las pulquerías que en seguida se expresan, por falta de los requisitos a que se refieren las disposiciones de 25 de febrero de 1903—La Reyna, Tejedores y Manuel Doblado, El Paseo de Morelos, Florida y Doaz de León," 1904; AHDF, FAGDF, Gobierno del Distrito, Pulquerías: vol. 1772, exp. 432, fs. 1–6: "Reforma del mingitorio en las casillas del ramo," 1905; AHDF, FAGDF, Gobierno del Distrito, Pulquerías: vol. 1772, exp. 457, fs. 1–10: "Varios dueños de establecimiento del ramo piden se les autorice para usar el asfalto en los mingitorios, en lugar de los materiales impermeables que está ordenado," 1906.

62. AHDF, FAGDF, Gobierno del Distrito, Pulquerías: vol. 1773, exp. 525, fs. 1–6: "Proyecto de reforma del Artículo 12 del Reglamento de Pulquerías de 18 de diciembre de 1901," 1907.

63. See map 11.4 in Toxqui, "Taverns and Their Influence," 270.

64. AHDF, FAGDF, Gobierno del Distrito, Pulquerías: vol. 1769, exp. 85, fs. 1–5: "Proyecto del nuevo reglamento de ramo, elevado a Gobernación," December 1901; AHDF, FAGDF, Gobierno del Distrito, Pulquerías: vol. 1770, exp. 137, fs. 1–5: "Se recomienda la policia que cuide de la exacta observancia del Reglamento de Pulquerías vigentes," January 1902.

65. On this aspect of *costumbrismo*, see Benítez-Rojo, "Nacionalismo y nacionalización en la novela hispanoamericana," 189; Brushwood, *Genteel Barbarism*, 5; Juana Martínez, "El cuento hispanoamericano," 231; Segre, *Intersected Identities*, 7, 11.

66. Lomnitz, *Exits from the Labyrinth*, 9; Szuchman, *Middle Period in Latin America*, 7–13. A similar dilemma was experienced by intellectual elites in other Latin American countries in the nineteenth century. See, for example, Chambers, *From Subjects to Citizens*, 120–25; Bauer, *Goods, Power, History*, 150–64.

67. Madrigal, "José Joaquín Fernández de Lizardi," 136–39; Álvarez de Testa, *Ilustración, educación e independencia*, 79–83, 132–49, 159–65; Rea Spell, "Intellectual Background of Lizardi," 414–32; Vogeley, *Lizardi*, 21–25, 40–44; Palazón Mayoral, "José Joaquín Fernández de Lizardi," 3:37–43; Shumway, "Don Catrín de la Fachenda," 364.

68. Fernández de Lizardi, *El Pensador Mexicano*, 131–32, 141–42.

69. Fernández de Lizardi, *El Periquillo Sarniento*, 1:176–77.

70. Fernández de Lizardi, *El Periquillo Sarniento*, 2:265.

71. Fernández de Lizardi, *El Periquillo Sarniento*, 1:308–9.

72. Fernández de Lizardi, *El Periquillo Sarniento*, 1:305–6.

73. For a more nuanced discussion of the liberal-conservative power struggles, the multiple factions involved within these broad groupings, and the ways in which the interested parties often represented their power struggles as the result of liberal policies toward the church without this necessarily being the case, see Fowler, "Dreams of Stability," 287–312.

74. Arguedas, "Ignacio Manuel Altamirano," 193–95; Campuzano, *Semblanza de Altamirano*, 2–7; Giron, "Altamirano, Diplomático," 162–63; Giron, "Ignacio Manuel Altamirano," 3:373–76; Nacci, *Ignacio Manuel Altamirano*, 21–33, 39–50.

75. Wright-Rios, "Indian Saints and Nation-States," 56.

76. On radical liberal policies toward the church during the reform period, see Hamnett, *Concise History of Mexico*, 160–64; Powell, "Priests and Peasants in Central Mexico," 296–313.

77. Altamirano, *Clemencia y La Navidad en las montañas*, 264.

78. Altamirano, *Clemencia y La Navidad en las montañas*, 269.

79. The narrator reiterates that the mob was made up of "drunks" (*ebrios*) but does not elaborate upon what specific drink had been consumed. Altamirano, *Clemencia y La Navidad en las montañas*, 269.

80. Márquez, "Hacia una definición del realismo," 1:246–47; Brushwood, *Mexico in Its Novel*, 118, 146; Benítez-Rojo, "Nacionalismo y nacionalización en la novela hispanoamericana," 191; Brushwood, *Genteel Barbarism*, 8–10; Varela Jácome, "Evolución de la novela hispanoamericana," 106–7.

81. On scientific politics, positivism, and the pessimistic outlook for social reform in the Porfirian era, see chapter 4.

82. The title *La Rumba* (literally, the party or the fiesta) refers to the name of a Mexico City neighborhood.

83. Brushwood, *Mexico in Its Novel*, 124–25; Juana Martínez, "El cuento hispanoamericano," 240–41.

84. Wasserman, *Everyday Life and Politics*, 203–4; Garza, *Imagined Underworld*, 16.

85. De Campo, *Ocios y apuntes y La Rumba*, 186.

86. De Campo, *Ocios y apuntes y La Rumba*, 51–58.

87. See Messinger Cypess, *La Malinche in Mexican Literature*; Pratt, "Women, Literature, and National Brotherhood," 59–60; Bartra, *Cage of Melancholy*, 155–58.

88. De Campo, *Ocios y apuntes y La Rumba*, 57.

89. De Campo, *Ocios y apuntes y La Rumba*, 210–11.

90. De Campo, *Ocios y apuntes y La Rumba*, 233, 328–29.

91. See chapter 3 for an analysis of Lizardi's treatment of women's education.

92. Margo Glantz, prologue to de Cuéllar, *Las jamonas*, 13; Brushwood, *Mexico in Its Novel*,105–7; Brushwood, *Genteel Barbarism*, 12–13; Zavala Díaz, "Los motivos de Facundo," 3:319–23; Rea Spell, *Bridging the Gap*, 312–14.

93. De Cuéllar, *La linterna mágica*, 2:vii, ix–x. Internet Archive http://www.archive.org/details/3680924_2.

94. For newspaper advertisements and articles reporting the finery of elite balls and dances, see "Confraternidad," *El Monitor Republicano*, April 18, 1849; *Periódico Oficial del Imperio Mexicano*, June 28, 1864; *El Siglo XIX*, January 2, 1872; February 25, 1872; February 29, 1872.

95. De Cuéllar, "Baile y cochino," 11.

96. On common dietary practices of the Mexican population and the construction of specific dishes as a traditional part of a national Mexican cuisine, see Pilcher, *¡Que vivan los tamales!*, 45–70; Stoopen, "Convulsiones y revoluciones culinarias," 54–57.

97. De Cuéllar, "Baile y cochino," 141.

98. De Cuéllar, "Baile y cochino," 141–42.

99. Although de Cuéllar also mentions the influence of foreign music, dances, and dress styles in corrupting the Mexican middle and lower classes, it is his treatment of drinking that ultimately produces the farcical denouement to the story.

100. De Cuéllar, "Baile y cochino," 30. Ninon de Lenclos was a salon hostess of an elite literary group in seventeenth-century France.

101. De Cuéllar, "Baile y cochino," 88–90, 145.

102. Although *El fistol del Diablo* was first published serially in the *Revista Científica y Literaria* between 1845 and 1846, all quotations here are from the significantly altered definitive edition published in Barcelona in 1887 (I use the third edition from Editorial Porrúa, which reproduces the 1887 edition). Among the key changes that this edition included are: a subtitle (*A Novel of Mexican Customs*), additional costumbrista sketches, a greater use of vernacular language, and the interpretation of historical events in a more pessimistic manner. It also emphasizes the chaotic nature of mid-century politics—culminating with the North American occupation of Mexico City in 1847—from the vantage point of relative stability in the Porfirian era. See Chaves Pacheco, "Payno criptofantástico," 66–67.

103. Read, *Mexican Historical Novel*, 125–27; Brushwood, *Mexico in Its Novel*, 73; Calderón, "La novela costumbrista Mexicana," 1:318–24; Suárez de la Torre, "La producción de libros, revistas, periódicos y folletos," 2:14; Giron, "Payno o las incertidumbres del liberalismo," 135–40, 150–51; Pérez Gay, "Avanzaba el siglo por su vida Manuel Payno," 177–83; Knapp, "Some Historical Values," 132–33.

104. José Lameiras analyzes a range of other popular sociocultural spaces depicted in *Los bandidos*. See Lameiras, "Tres relatos, tres interpretaciones y un asunto," 95–97, 118–20.

105. Payno, *Los bandidos*, 12-13. In *Angelina* (1893), Rafael Delgado also offers a positive depiction of a typical Mexican provincial town enjoying community festivals with common foods, including tamales, beans, and turkey mole, along with aguardiente or tepache as the typical alcoholic drink consumed by the popular classes. Delgado, *Angelina*, 149–51.

106. Payno, *Los bandidos*, 287–88.

107. Payno, *El fistol del Diablo*, 532.

108. *Sangre de conejo* (literally, rabbit's blood) is pulque mixed with juice from the tuna fruit, which gives the drink a dramatic blood-red color. The drink's name also alludes to Aztec mythology in which the god of pulque was called Ometochtli, or Two-Rabbit, and his four hundred rabbit sons, the centzontotochtin, were thought to represent the many different states of drunkenness that pulque could induce. See Toor, *Treasury of Mexican Folkways*, 15; Bruman, *Alcohol in Ancient Mexico*, 63–64; Mitchell, *Intoxicated Identities*, 13–14; Gonçalves de Lima, *El maguey y el pulque*, 32, 112; Anawalt, "Rabbits, *Pulque*, and Drunkenness," 19–22.

109. Payno, *El fistol del Diablo*, 338–48.

110. Payno, *El fistol del Diablo*, 349.

111. See chapter 2 for details of a brutal murder carried out by a villain drunk on *sangre de conejo* in Payno's *Los bandidos*.

112. For details of the historic basis for these events see Rosado, "Tres novelas mexicanas," 44–52; Rosado, "El pensamiento social," 48–49; Frazer, *Bandit Nation*, 35–37.

113. Payno, *Los bandidos*, 652.

114. Payno, *Los bandidos*, 778. Gambrinus was a twelfth-century Flemish king accredited with the development of brewing equipment. Payno makes reference to Holland elsewhere in the description, so perhaps Gambrinus was a contemporary brand of Belgian or Dutch beer, or perhaps merely Payno's imaginative moniker for such a brand.

115. Sandoval, "Madres, viudas y vírgenes."

116. Payno, *Los bandidos*, 113. See chapter 2 for analysis of this murder.

117. Payno, *El fistol del Diablo*, 355.

118. Payno, *El fistol del Diablo*, 360.

119. In an earlier description of Acordada Prison, Payno also comments in passing that it has a special room "where they put the bloody and deformed bodies of those who are killed in the fights that frequently go on in the neighborhood taverns." Payno, *El fistol del Diablo*, 113.

120. Payno, *El fistol del Diablo*, 589.

121. Payno, *El fistol del Diablo*, 774, 783.

122. Payno's fictionalized portrait of this National Guard dispute is in broad agreement with modern historical analyses. The moderate *polko* faction engaged in a month-long uprising in Mexico City, beginning on 27 February 1847, with the support of high clerical officials, against the radical *puro* faction under President Vicente Gómez Farías following a decree permitting the sale of church property to finance the war against the United States. The *polko* battalions were generally comprised of urban professionals, merchants, landowners, and public officials, whereas the *puro* membership was made up of laborers and servants. Payno himself was a major in the "Bravos" battalion, part of the *polko* faction, during the North American invasion, helping to establish a secret courier service between Mexico City and Veracruz. See Santoni, "'Where Did the Other Heroes Go?,'" 810, 818.

2. Patriotic Heroes and Consummate Drunks

Payno, *Los bandidos*, 497.

1. See, for instance, Tamar Diana Wilson, "Forms of Male Domination and Female Subordination," 218–19; Mirandé, *Hombres y Machos*, 45–57; Gilmore, *Manhood in the Making*, 4–5, 16.

2. Melhuus and Stølen, introduction to *Machos, Mistresses, Madonnas*, 14–15; Gutmann, *Meanings of Macho*, 26–27.

3. Gutmann, *Meanings of Macho*, 222–31.

4. Lastovicka et al., "Lifestyle Typology," 258–59; Duguid, "Addiction of Masculinity," 26; Lemle and Mishkind, "Alcohol and Masculinity," 214–15; Powers, "Lore of the Brotherhood, 150–51; Mosher and Tomkins, "Scripting the Macho Man," 60–84.

5. Driessen, "Drinking on Masculinity," 77.

6. Gayol, "Ebrios y divertidos," 65; Powers, "Lore of the Brotherhood," 150–51; Fumerton, "Not Home," 495, 506–9; Hailwood, "John Jarret and Roaring Dick of Dover," 116–19; Hailwood, "Sociability, Work and Labouring Identity," 13–17; Conroy, "In the Public Sphere," 52–57; Thomas Brennan, "Taverns and the Public Sphere," 115–16; Heron, *Booze*, 35–40, 112–27; Heron, "Boys and Their Booze," 411–52; Frantz Parsons, "Risky Business," 283–307; Krasnick Warsh, "'Oh, Lord, pour a cordial in her wounded heart,'" 72–76.

7. Gefou-Madianou, "Introduction," 8–9; Heath, *Drinking Occasions*, 73–76; Powers, "Women and Public Drinking," 46–52.

8. Bunzel, "Rôle of Alcoholism," 365–67, 372–73. For similar cases where access to and distribution of alcohol privileged mature men and men in

positions of authority, see Kennedy, "Tesgüino Complex," 623; Weismantel, "Maize Beer and Andean Social Transformations" 872–73; Butler, *Holy Intoxication*, 96–109; Heath, *Drinking Occasions*, 68–78.

9. William B. Taylor, *Drinking, Homicide, and Rebellion*, 62–64, 71, 155–56. Many anthropological investigations into drinking practices suggest that drunkenness can be *performed* without the drinker experiencing any physiological intoxication. In certain situations drinkers are expected to become drunk as a symbol of, for instance, accepting another's hospitality, displaying the wealth and abundance possessed by a community, or celebrating a rite of passage by throwing caution to the wind. In these cases, some drinkers might *perform* drunkenness, perhaps by exaggerating their heightened mood, slurring their words, saying normally inappropriate things, or behaving recklessly, although the hallmarks of drunkenness will vary in different social and historical contexts. See Butler, *Holy Intoxication*, 12, 96; Heath, "Decade of Development in the Anthropological Study of Alcohol Use," 46; Eber, *Women and Alcohol*, 54.

10. Stern, *Secret History of Gender*, 161, 170–73.

11. *El Monitor Republicano*, October 23, 1849.

12. *Periódico Oficial del Imperio Mexicano*, December 24, 1864.

13. *Breve refutación*, 7–8.

14. AGN, FRA, Criminal: vol. 467, exp. 6, fs. 140–49: "Desórdenes en la Pulquería de la Alamedita que es del cargo de Felipe Galan," June 16, 1804.

15. AHDF, FAGDF, Gobierno del Distrito, Infracciones: vol. 1642, exp. 97, fs. 1–3: "Se comunica al prefecto de Tacuba que una pulquería situada en la esquina de Juarez y Pablo Kruger en Popotla hay música en el interior casi diariamente," November 1908. See also AHDF, FAGDF, Gobierno del Distrito, Infracciones: vol. 1649, exp. 149, fl. 16: "El Inspector General de Policía participa las diversas infracciones sorprendidas por la policía de la Capital durante el presente mes, á varios establecimientos," August 1912.

16. *El Monitor Republicano*, January 4, 1849; February 4, 1849; March 4, 1849; May 5, 1849; June 4, 1849; July 4, 1849; August 3, 1849; September 4, 1849; November 4, 1849; January 3, 1850.

17. "Policia," *El Monitor Republicano*, May 12, 1849.

18. AGN, FRPI, Bienes nacionales: vol. 1056, exp. 17, fs. 1–11: "Información sumaria sobre procedimientos escandalosos del corista Fray Augustin González del convento de San Diego," March 29, 1848. See also AHDF, FAGDF, Gobierno del Distrito, Infracciones: vol. 1649, exp. 149, fs. 1, 14: "El Inspector General de Policía participa las diversas infracciones sorprendidas por la policía de la Capital durante el presente mes, á varios establecimientos," August 1912; AHDF, FAGDF, Gobierno del Distrito, Infracciones: vol. 1650,

exp. 240, fs. 1–2: "Pulquería 'El Asalto' de Ernesto Montiel, Cuauhtemotzin 6a," 1912.

19. See, for instance, AHDF, FAGDF, Pulquerías: vol. 3719, exp. 50, fs. 1–16: "Sobre que se cuide de que en los cafés, bodegones y casillas donde se vende pulque no haya excesos," September 1820; AHDF, FAGDF, Pulquerías: vol. 3719, exp. 66, fs. 1–2: "Policia: Sobre los perjuicios que reciente el público por las multitud de casillas de pulque situadas en la calle del Refugio," January 1845; AHDF, FAGDF, Pulquerías: vol. 3722, exp. 392, fs. 1-2: "Sobre que se prevenga a los dueños de aquellas pongan los mostradores y tinas respectivas, conforme a la dispuesto por las leyes," May 1848; AHDF, FAGDF, Gobierno del Distrito, Infracciones: vol. 1644, exp. 104, fl. 112: "Partes de Infracciones del número 601 al 700," September 1908; AHDF, FAGDF, Gobierno del Distrito, Infracciones: vol. 1649, exp. 155, fs. 1–2: "Jesús Alvarez é Ycaza se quejá de una pulquería clandestina en el Peñón de los Baños," July–August 1912.

20. AGN, SCJN, Asuntos económicos, exp. 6440: "Expediente relativo a que el Auxiliar del cuartel número 10, remite a la cárcel de la ciudad, a disposición del señor Juez de turno, a José Ygnacio Cirilo, Pedro Pablo, Julián Jacinto y Alfonso Antonio porque iban a matar a Margarito Fernández a pedradas porque no les daba un real para pulque," July 28, 1845.

21. The victim's profession may have been *herrero* (blacksmith); the script at this point is very difficult to decipher but it is clearly not *carnicero* (butcher).

22. For a similar case of male aggression toward an outsider within drinking places, see AGN, SCJN, Asuntos económicos, exp. 6489: "Expediente relativo a que el Capitán Comandante de la Segunda Compañía Auxiliar de Celaya, remite a la Cárcel Nacional, y a la disposición del señor Juez en turno, a los paisanos Guadalupe Galindo, Quirino Gutiérrez y Manuel Medina, quienes cometieron algunos excesos en la vinatería del señor don Manuel Ruiz," December 10, 1845; AHDF, FM, Tacubaya, Justicia y Juzgados: caja 17, exp. 29, fs. 1–6: "Contra José María Ortíz por ebrio y portador de armas con escandalo," August–September 1855.

23. AHDF, FAGDF, Justicia, Juzgados Diversos, Juicios Criminales: vol. 2893, exp. 75, fs. 1–3: "Contra Julian Martínez, Simón Barrera, y Saturnido Pimentel, por escandalosos," July 1852.

24. AHDF, FAGDF, Gobierno del Distrito, Infracciones: vol. 1650, exp. 195, fs. 1–6: "Café 'La Casualidad,' de J. Salomé Bernudez, Avenida de la Paz," July–August 1912; AHDF, FAGDF, Gobierno del Distrito, Infracciones: vol. 1650, exp. 218, fl. 1: "Pulquería 'Las Aguilas' de Francisco Hernandez, 14a de Bolivar," July 1912; AHDF, FAGDF, Gobierno del Distrito, Infracciones: vol.

1651, exp. 306, fs. 1–21: "Café 'La Luz del Día' de Alberto Sánchez, Avenida de la Paz," October 1912–May 1913.

25. AGN, FRA, Criminal: vol. 485, exp. 4, fs. 55–77: "Contra Don José Antonio Merino, Soldado de Milicias Urbanas del Comercio de esta Corte, por excesos cometidos," January 23, 1802; AGN, FRA, Civil: vol. 2126, exp. 1, fs. 27: "Sobre corrección de la embriaguez," April 1807; AHDF, FAGDF, Pulquerías: vol. 3719, exp. 50, fs. 1–16: "Sobre que se cuide de que en los cafés, bodegones y casillas donde se vende pulque no haya excesos," September 1820. For similar cases, see AHDF, FAGDF, Pulquerías: vol. 3719, exp. 23, fs. 1–2: "Sobre que el dueño de la Pulquería de la Agua Escondida divida los lugares comunes de hombres y mugeres," February 1805; AHDF, FAGDF, Pulquerías: vol. 3719, exp. 52, fl. 26: "Pulquerías: Incidentes acerca de éstas. Los alcaldes constitucionales del excelentísimo Ayuntamiento de México a su fidelísimo vecindario," June 29, 1821; AHDF, FAGDF, Pulquerías: vol. 3722, exp. 402, fs. 1–4: "Sobre que continué cerrada la nombrada de la Tarasquita, situada en la 2a calle de Santo Domingo," 1849; AHDF, FAGDF, Pulquerías: vol. 3723, exp. 418, fs. 1–7: "Proposiciones de la Sociedad de Mejoras Materiales, para conducir de un modo decente a los ebrios de ambos sexos," 1854–55; AHDF, FAGDF, Gobierno del Distrito, Infracciones: vol. 1650, exp. 195, fl. 4: "Café 'La Casualidad' de J. Salomé Bernudez, Avenida de la Paz," August 9, 1912; AHDF, FAGDF, Gobierno del Distrito, Infracciones: vol. 1650, exp. 198, fl. 1: "Pulquería 'Las Aguilas' de Isaac Zepeda, 1a de Albañiles," July–August 1912; AHDF, FAGDF, Gobierno del Distrito, Infracciones: vol. 1651, exp. 306, fl. 3: "Café 'La Luz del Día' de Alberto Sánchez, Avenida de la Paz," January 1913.

26. See, for instance, AGN, SCJN, Asuntos económicos, exp. 13426: "El cuartel número 22 envía al cabo que fue remitido a la cárcel de ciudad a Nicolás Días, José N. no quiso decir su nombre y María Lugo por ebrios y escandalosos," December 18, 1853; AGN, SCJN, Asuntos económicos, exp. 6584: "Toca al parte con que fueron remitidos Francisco Rodríguez y Manuela García por embriaguez," 1845; AGN, SCJN, Asuntos económicos, exp. 12814: "Documento relativo a la remisión a la cárcel de la ciudad a Justa López y a Juan García por ebrios," March 14, 1852; AGN, SCJN, Asuntos económicos, exp. 9078: "Acta con la ejecutoria correspondiente seguida contra Manuel, José Ortíz y Angela Ortíz, por riña embriaguez," June 1, 1865; AHDF, FAGDF, Justicia, Juzgados Diversos, Juicios Criminales: vol. 2892, exp. 105, fs. 1–3: "Contra Miguel Valenzuela, Isabel Calapiz y Lazara Rojas por riña y escandalo," January 1852; *El Siglo XIX*, February 6, 1851; *El Monitor Republicano*, May 26, 1849; June 5, 1849; AHDF, FAGDF, Justicia, Juzgados Diversos, Juicios

Criminales: vol. 2894, exp. 81, fs. 1–3: "Averiguacion hecha contra Ramon Vargas y Sevastiana Figueroa, acusados de riña," March 1852.

27. *El Siglo XIX*, December 27, 1851.

28. Wasserman, *Everyday Life and Politics*, 37. To contextualize this figure, in late-twentieth-century Greater London, 3.8 per cent of the population would be roughly 266,000 (based on a total population of seven million). The proportion of the population being arrested for drunkenness in this major urban center was clearly much less than 3.8 per cent, as the total number of cautions issued and prosecutions made for drunkenness in all of England and Wales in 1989 was a mere 92,800. These figures are cited in NHS: The Information Centre, "Statistics on Alcohol: England 2008," NHS: The Information Centre (May 22, 2008): 84. Accessed at http://www.ic.nhs.uk/pubs/alcohol08 (August 31, 2009).

29. "Detención arbitraria," *El Siglo XIX*, July 15, 1851.

30. Data compiled from *El Monitor Republicano*, October 7, 1849, to April 10, 1850.

31. Data compiled from *Periódico Oficial del Imperio Mexicano*, December 13 to 31, 1864, and *La Gazeta de Policia*, September 24, 1868.

32. AGN, FRA, Criminal: vol. 550, exp. 6, fs. 281–332: "En averiguación de la muerte de María Josefa, India del Pueblo de Acuitlapilco en la que resulta culprit José Joaquín su marido," August 1804. For a similar case in which the woman was deemed to have died as a result of drunkenness rather than foul play, despite the existence of several suspects, see AGN, FRA, Criminal: vol. 146, exp. 8, fs. 188–214: "Averiguación hecha sobre la muerte de Manuela Juliana, India de San Andrés Ocotlan," 1781.

33. AHDF, FM, Tacubaya, Justicia y Juzgados: caja 1, exp. 8, fs. 1–46: "Causa criminal seguida a peticion de Ambrosio de la Concepcion contra su muger María Francisca sobre embriaguez consuetudinaria de esta," 1808–11.

34. Criminal: vol. 467, exp. 6, fs. 140–41: "Desórdenes en la pulquería," June 16, 1804.

35. Criminal: vol. 467, exp. 6, fl. 143: "Desórdenes en la pulquería," June 1804; Gutmann, *Meanings of Macho*, 222–29.

36. AGN, FRA, Criminal: vol. 670, exp. 3, fs. 47–53: "Cuartel menor número 6 sujeto al mayor número 2," August 26, 1806.

37. AGN, FRA, Criminal: vol. 86, exp. 12, fs. 311–24: "Causa número 62 contra José Guillermo García por homicida," July 4, 1811.

38. AGN, SCJN, Asuntos económicos, exp. 6749: "Notificación de haber remitido el Guarda Mayor del Alumbrado, a la Cárcel de Ciudad, a disposición del señor Juez de turno, a don José Saganda por excesos, que

estando ebrio, le pego con el sable a unos cocheros del sitio de la Alameda," September 11, 1845.

39. AGN, SCJN, Asuntos económicos, exp. 6761: "Notificación de haber remitido el Auxiliar del cuartel número 15, a la Cárcel de Ciudad, a disposición del señor Juez de letras en turno, a Román Casas, por ebrio escandaloso y por haber querido estuprar a la quejosa María Luz Chávez," September 11, 1845.

40. AGN, SCJN, Asuntos económicos, exp. 6730: "Notificación de haber remitido el Ayudante del cuartel número 26, a la Cárcel de la Diputación, a disposición del señor Juez de turno, a José Antonio, el cual, haciéndose pasar por ebrio, provocó al referido Auxiliar de cuartel," September 16, 1845.

41. See, for instance, AHDF, FM, Tacubaya, Justicia y Juzgados: caja 17, exp. 29, fs. 1–6: "Contra José María Ortíz por ebrio y portador de armas con escandalo," 1855; AHDF, FAGDF, Justicia, Juzgados Verbales: vol. 2942, exp. 37, fs. 1–4: "Queda en la carcel Juan Escobar, Antonio Cardenas, y Maria Guadalupe Almazan, aprehendidos por el agente José María Estrada quien los acusa haber forzado a la muger," August 1850; AHDF, FAGDF, Justicia, Juzgados Verbales: vol. 2942, exp. 44, fs. 1–2: "Se remite a la carcel de ciudad Ignacio Manuel por haber dadole de asotes a su muger y haberse fugado de los guardas," September 1850; AHDF, FAGDF, Justicia, Juzgados Diversos, Juicios Criminales: vol. 2892, exp. 69, fs. 1–2: "Contra Navor Molina por escandaloso," May 1852; AHDF, FAGDF, Justicia, Juzgados Diversos, Juicios Criminales: vol. 2894, exp. 72, fs. 1–2: "Agustin Aguilar acontecio darle de polis a María de Jesus," November 1852; AHDF, FAGDF, Justicia, Juzgados Diversos, Juicios Criminales: vol. 2894, exp. 90, fs. 1–2: "José Guadalupe Ortega se remite a la carcel por briago y aber golpeado a su muger, que es Marina de Jesus Villa," 1852.

42. AGN, FRA, Criminal: vol. 363, exp. 2, fs. 146–95: "Contra José Manuel Bonilla por malos tratamientos a su mujer, ebrio y haber blasfemado," April 1803.

43. "De calidad Español" (literally, of Spanish quality) does not mean this man was Spanish, since he was born in Tlalnepantla. This term refers to a combination of racial and sociocultural criteria (such as clothing, education, wealth) that denoted him as white (even if not of all-white descent) and culturally Hispanic. Torres, therefore, would have held high standing in the village.

44. AGN, FRA, Criminal: vol. 226, exp. 11, fs. 464–65, 501: "Los Gobernadores pasados y demas principales de Tlalnepantla solicitando se remueva del empleo de Gobernador a Juan Francisco por los excesos que comete a causa de su embriaguez desordenada," September 18, 1810. For a similar

case see AHDF, FM, Tlalpan, Justicia: caja 157, exp. 34, fs. 1–3: "Queja sobre el Preceptor del Pueblo de San Juanico por embriaguez y otros casos," April 1866.

45. William B. Taylor, *Drinking, Homicide, and Rebellion*, 62–63, 71, 155–56.

46. The practice of San Lunes, or Holy Monday, was not unique to Mexico; nor was the widespread alarm the practice elicited among social commentators and politicians. See, for instance, Tandeter, "Forced and Free Labour," 132–33; Thompson, "Time, Work-Discipline, and Industrial Capitalism," 72–76.

47. Cited in Arrom, "Vagos y mendigos," 76.

48. *El Siglo XIX*, January 30, 1851.

49. Cited in Buffington, *Criminal and Citizen*, 28.

50. José María Vigil, "La embriaguez," *El Siglo XIX*, September 3, 1872. Vigil was one of the most prominent journalists of the mid- to late nineteenth century, establishing the first professional association for journalists in 1872. He also acted as director of the National Preparatory School during the late 1870s.

51. Cited in Morgan, "Proletarians, Politicos, and Patriarchs," 162.

52. AGN, FRA, Criminal: vol. 595, exp. 1, fs. 1–16: "Sumaria formada contra el cabo veterano del Granaderos Mariano Loranca, por reincidente en faltas al cuartel, y vicio de la embriaguez," May 1802. See also AGN, FRA, Criminal: vol. 680, exp. 7, fs. 61–75: "Sumaria formada contra Pedro Miraso Soldado de la Segunda Compañía del Cuerpo de Imbalidos de esta Capital, por el delito de reincidente en faltas cometidas, y otros excesos que dentro se expresan," March 1807.

53. AGN, FRA, Criminal: vol. 587, exp. 6, fs. 235–72: "Proceso formado al Teniente de la 4a. Compañia Don Estéban Hernández, sobre su mala conducta y desarreglo de vida," 1808.

54. AGN, FRA, Criminal: vol. 562, exp. 1, fs. 1–50: "Contra el Granadero Dionisio Jimental, acusado de incorregible en la embriaguez y venta de vestuario," August 1827.

55. AGN, FRA, Criminal: vol. 618, exp.7, fs. 142–49: "Sumaria formada en averiguación de haberse hallado tirado en un bodegon de las inmediaciones de la Plaza del mercado de esta cuidad el dia once del Julio del precente año el Capitan Don Manuel Maria Diaz, graduado de Comandante de Batallon," July 11, 1842.

56. AGN, SCJN, Asuntos económicos, exp. 12683: "Documento relativo al proceso del Sargento segundo del octavo Batallón de línea Manuel Flores por reincidente en la embriaguez," February 14, 1852; AGN, SCJN, Asun-

tos económicos, exp. 12685: "Documento relativo al proceso del soldado de octavo batallón de línea Manuel Flores," July 19, 1852. For further cases, see AHDF, FM, Tlalpan, Policía: caja 252, exp. 69, fs. 1–2: "El C. Gobernador remite al Soldado José María Tamudeo, de la fuerza de este Distrito que se encontró ébrio," March 1878.

57. See, for instance, ADHF, FAGDF, Pulquerías: vol. 1769, exp. 85, fl. 5: "Proyecto del nuevo reglamento de ramo, elevado á Gobernación," December 1901; ADHF, FAGDF, Gobierno del Distrito, Infracciones: vol. 1644, exp. 104, fs. 4–6, 123: "Partes de Infracciones del número 601 al 700," 1908; ADHF, FAGDF, Gobierno del Distrito, Infracciones: vol. 1650, exp. 258, fs. 1–2: "Pulquería 'La Gran Judia' de la Compañía Expendedora de Pulques, Callejón de la Unión y Calzada de San Antonio Abad," July 1912; AHDF, FM, Tlalpan, Policía: caja 259, exp. 41, fl. 1: "Se solicita de la Inspección General, la baja del Gendarme 169 por ebrio y abuso en el cumplimiento de sus deberes," October 1912; Rohlfes, "Police and Penal Correction in Mexico City," 109–15.

58. "Crimenes Imperdonables," El Siglo XIX, June 19, 1872.

59. AGN, AG, vol. 313, exp. 3098, fs. 1–15: "Sumaria averiguación sobre la conducta que observó la tarde del veinte y nueve de Agosto de 1844 el capitan del Regimiento Ligero de Infantería Don José Olvera y el de igual clase y cuerpo Don Antonio Jímenez," August 29, 1844.

60. AGN, AG, vol. 519, exp. 5028: "Información sumaria al cabo primero Antonio Ayala acusado del vicio de embriaguez," May 1835.

61. AGN, AG, vol. 519, exp. 5027: "Sumaria contra el cabo de la quinta compañía Antonio Ayala acusado del vicio de embriaguez y haber vertido espreciones contra los S.S. Gefes y oficiales de este cuerpo," March 1836.

62. AG, vol. 313, exp. 3098, fs. 35–39: "Sumaria averiguación sobre la conducta . . . Don José Olvera," August 29, 1844.

63. "Mal Hecho," El Siglo XIX, March 21, 1872.

64. AGN, AG, vol. 308, exp. 3033, fs. 33–46: "Sumaria instruida en averiguación de las faltas cometidas por el teniente Don Ramón Robles del Regimiento Ligero de Caballería estando de servicio en el paseo la tarde del 26 del corriente," January 1845.

65. AG, vol. 313, exp. 3098, fs. 18–21, 65–68: "Sumaria averiguación sobre la conducta . . . Don José Olvera," August 29, 1844. For further examples see AGN, FRA, Criminal: vol. 523, exp. 3, fs. 140–81: "Información sumaria sobre los excesos cometidos por el Portaguion del Regimiento Provincial de Dragones del Principe Don Joaquin Gonzalez del Villar," October 1818; AGN, AG, vol. 99, exp. 1228, fs. 182–210: "Proceso instruida contra el Sargento 1o. Macedonio Ramos acusado del reincidencia de la embriaguez," January

1832; AGN, AG, vol. 319, exp. 3205, fs. 1–7: "Foca a la causa del Capitan activo del batallon de Acayucan Don Ponciano Espinosa por mal manejo de interesas y otras faltas," October 1855.

66. AG, vol. 519, exp. 5028: "Información sumaria al cabo primero Antonio Ayala," May 1835.

67. Sommer, *Foundational Fictions*, 24.

68. Timothy Brennan, "National Longing for Form," 48–49; Unzueta, "Scenes of Reading"; Gerassi-Navarro, *Pirate Novels*; Gomaríz, "Nación, sexualidad y poder," 39–65.

69. Sommer, *Foundational Fictions*, 49–50.

70. Irwin, *Mexican Masculinities*, xiii.

71. Gómariz, "Nación, sexualidad, y poder," 54–55. Fernando Orozco y Berra's 1850 novel about the thirty-year rollercoaster love life of its central male protagonist springs to mind as a prominent example: its very title was *La guerra de treinta años (The thirty years war)*. This novel is discussed in chapter 3.

72. Irwin, *Mexican Masculinities*, 4–5. See also Macías-González, "Masculine Friendships," 418–21.

73. Lomnitz, *Deep Mexico, Silent Mexico*, 9–12.

74. Frazer, *Bandit Nation*, 49–51.

75. Altamirano, *El Zarco*, 24.

76. Altamirano, *El Zarco*, 59–60, 74–76.

77. Altamirano, *El Zarco*, 39–42.

78. On the antiracist emphasis to be found in *El Zarco*, see Wright-Rios, "Indian Saints and Nation-States," 67; Segre, *Intersected Identities*, 76; Arguedas, "Ignacio Manuel Altamirano," 198–99.

79. Altamirano, *Clemencia y La Navidad en las montañas*, 9, 14.

80. On the importance of the May 5, 1862, victory and the contribution of the National Guard to victory, see Thomson, "Bulwarks of Patriotic Liberalism," 34–37; Mallon, *Peasant and Nation*, 43–44.

81. Altamirano, *Clemencia y La Navidad en las montañas*, 12–13.

82. Campuzano, *Semblanza de Altamirano*, 5–6, 11–12.

83. Altamirano, *Clemencia y La Navidad en las montañas*, 189, 200.

84. Lander, "*Clemencia* de Ignacio Manuel Altamirano," 26–31.

85. Payno, *El fistol del Diablo*, 36–37.

86. Irwin, "*El Periquillo Sarniento* y sus cautes," 29.

87. Payno, *El fistol del Diablo*, 205.

88. Payno, *El fistol del Diablo*, 812–14.

89. The question of whether Manuel and Arturo have been injured fatally is deliberately left unanswered.

90. Payno, *Los bandidos*, 530.

91. An exception to this is Chris Frazer, who also analyzes the opposing models of masculinity established through the heroic Juan Robreño and the villainous Evaristo Lecuona in terms of their contrasting careers as outlaws. See Frazer, *Bandit Nation*, 123–30. For readings that focus on Juan junior, see Blanca Estela Treviño, "*Los bandidos de Río Frío* de Manuel Payno," 377–91; Glantz, "Huérfanos y bandidos," 221–39; Sandoval, "Madres, viudas y vírgenes," 58, 78–81; Rosado, "El pensamiento social," 46; García de la Sierra, "El cronotopo del autor," 72–75.

92. Payno, *Los bandidos*, 311, 73, 95.

93. Payno, *Los bandidos*, 99, 105.

94. As noted in chapter 1, Payno seems to reserve *sangre de conejo* to represent extremely sinister behavior. *Mistela* is a powerful sugarcane liquor flavored with orange.

95. Payno, *Los bandidos*, 120.

96. Payno, *Los bandidos*, 111.

97. Payno, *Los bandidos*, 880.

98. On late nineteenth-century concerns about male lower-class drinking and crime, see Garza, *Imagined Underworld*, 3–4, 40–70; Piccato, *City of Suspects*, 84–97; I. Campos, *Home Grown*, 107–12.

99. The work was published anonymously until Frías was finally accredited with its authorship in the 1899 edition, but Frías was consistently suspected of writing it and was imprisoned accordingly. He was released after four months when one of *El Demócrata*'s editors, Joaquín Clausell, claimed to have written the narrative without any specific information from the battle front in Tomóchic, basing it purely on the influence of Émile Zola's smash-hit war satire *La Débâcle* (1892), with which *Tomóchic* does have considerable similarities. See Brown, "Heriberto Frías," 467–68; Dabove, "*Tomóchic* de Heriberto Frías," 354–55. For an analysis of the short-lived rebellion and the government's crushing military response see Knight, "Rethinking the Tomóchic Rebellion," 373–93; Vanderwood, "Millenarianism, Miracles, and Materialism," 395–412.

100. I. Campos, *Home Grown*, 139–40. Rodríguez González, "Heriberto Frías," 3:521–30; Piccato, *City of Suspects*, 199–200; Brushwood, *Mexico in Its Novel*, 155–57.

101. Frías, *Tomóchic*, , 19–22.

102. Sotol is a strong distilled drink made from the Desert Spoon or sotol plant.

103. Frías, *Tomóchic*, 182.

104. Frías, *Tomóchic*, 40, 75.

105. Frías, *Tomóchic*, 23, 26.

106. Frías, *Tomóchic*, 221.

107. Chávez, "*Tomochic*: National Narrative," 86.

108. Frías, *Tomóchic*, 77, 221.

109. Chávez, "*Tomochic*: National Narrative," 83. Indeed, although Chávez is right to emphasize how tequila became an important symbol of Mexican nationalism in the wake of the 1910 Revolution, until then, as I suggest in chapter 4, tequila was more commonly used in Mexican literature to denote the deleterious symptoms of modernity against the health of the nation.

110. Frías, *Tomóchic*, 30. *Chínguere* is probably an alternative name for *chinguirito*, a strong, rough, distilled liquor, akin to the sotol that appears throughout the novel.

111. Altamirano, *El Zarco*, 43, 45, 63.

112. Altamirano, *El Zarco*, 44.

113. De Campo, *Cosas vistas y Cartones*, 6.

114. De Campo, *Cosas vistas y Cartones*, 256.

115. Santa's alcoholism is analyzed at length in chapter 4, and so I make only brief remarks here.

116. On the Porfirian discourse about motherhood and appropriate female roles in nation-building, see Agostini, "Discurso médico," 1–22; Schell, "Nationalizing Children," 559–63; Pratt, "Women, Literature and National Brotherhood," 51.

117. Gamboa, *Santa*, 217.

118. Frías, *Tomóchic*, 75.

3. Yankees, Toffs, and Miss Quixote

Fernández de Lizardi, "Los paseos de la verdad" (1815) in Fernández de Lizardi, *El Pensador Mexicano*, 95.

1. Grosz, *Space, Time, and Perversion*, 33; Canning, "Feminist History After the Linguistic Turn," 384–86; Baecque, *Body Politic*, 3–6; Poovey, *Making a Social Body*, 4–8; Prieto, *Body of Writing*, 3–4.

2. Canning, "The Body as Method?," 501–2; Outram, *Body and the French Revolution*, 6–20; Howson, *Embodying Gender*, 22–39, 66–67, 101–5; During, *Foucault and Literature*, 50–58, 126.

3. Burkitt, *Bodies of Thought*, 48; Bakhtin, "Grotesque Image of the Body," 92–95. Bakhtin's article was first published in 1984.

4. Burkitt, *Bodies of Thought*, 50–58; Falk, *Consuming Body*, 25–27; Elias, *Civilizing Process*; Howson, *Embodying Gender*, 17.

5. Kant, for instance, personally subjected his body to an austere diet, sexual abstinence, and regular exercise, in order to improve his levels of intellectual concentration and to preserve his health. See Benbow, "Theorizing the Kantian Body," 60.

6. Baecque, *Body Politic*, 247. See also Gatens, *Imaginary Bodies*, 22–23; Roche, *People of Paris*, 247–48; During, *Foucault and Literature*, 152–55; Outram, *Body and the French Revolution*, 16, 48–52, 158–62.

7. Voekel, "Piety and Public Space," 1–25. Viqueira Albán, *Propriety and Permissiveness*, 129–43; Lomnitz, *Death and the Idea of Mexico*, 265–68.

8. *Breve refutación*, 7; *Representación que algunos propietarios de fincas de los llanos de Apam; Representación de los dueños*.

9. AHDF, FAGDF, Pulquerías: vol. 3719, exp. 57, fs. 1–49: "Varios comerciantes en el Ramo de Pulques sobre que se reduzca a un número fijo las casillas que hay en esta Capital," 1842.

10. *El Siglo XIX*, June 16, 1842.

11. José María Vigil, "La embriaguez," *El Siglo XIX*, September 3, 1872. For similar rhetoric, see AHDF, FAGDF, Pulquerías: vol. 3719, exp. 68, fs. 1–9: "Los vecinos de la calle del Refugio piden se trasladan a otro lugar las casillas de pulque que ecsisten en dicha calle," 1845; AHDF, FAGDF, Pulquerías: vol. 3723, exp. 418, fs. 1–7: "Proposiciones de la Sociedad de Mejoras Materiales para conducir de un modo decente a los ebrios de ambos sexos," 1854–55; AHDF, FAGDF, Pulquerías: vol. 3723, exp. 421, fs. 1–13, "Se somete a la aprobación suprema el proyecto para extinguir del centro de la ciudad las casillas de dicho piso y que se trasladen a los suburbios," July 1854.

12. *Lobo* (literally meaning wolf) was the Mexican term for *zambo*, referring to a person of indigenous black mixed-race heritage.

13. Fernández de Lizardi, *El Periquillo Sarniento*, 1:392–94.

14. Fernández de Lizardi, *El Periquillo Sarniento*, 1:393–95.

15. Fernández de Lizardi, *El Periquillo Sarniento*, 2:24, 32.

16. John Brushwood mistakenly notes that Díaz Covarrubias was twenty-nine years old at the time of his death. Brushwood, "Juan Díaz Covarrubias," 301–6. For further details of Díaz Covarrubias's life and career, see also Brushwood, *Mexico in Its Novel*, 83; Wright, "Subscribing Identities," 258–61; Rea Spell, "Juan Díaz Covarrubias," 327–28.

17. Pizarro Suárez, *La coqueta*, 123–28.

18. Anna, *Forging Mexico*, 196–97, 224–39; Baker, "Antonio López de Santa Anna's Search for Personalized Nationalism," 62–68; Wasserman, *Everyday Life and Politics*, 17–19; Fowler, "El pronunciamiento mexicano," 5–34.

19. Díaz Covarrubias, *Gil Gómez el Insurgente*, 121–30.

20. Díaz Covarrubias, *Gil Gómez el Insurgente*, 246, 255. Amy Wright also notes that the depravity shown by Juan and Regina constitutes part of Díaz Covarrubias's patriotic expression of Mexican liberal virtues over Spanish aristocratic vice. Wright, "Subscribing Identities," 271–72.

21. Díaz Covarrubias, *Gil Gómez el Insurgente*, 184.

22. Díaz Covarrubias, *Gil Gómez el Insurgente*, 185.

23. Hamnett, *Concise History of Mexico*, 156; Santoni, "'Where Did the Other Heroes Go?,'" 807–16; Wasserman, *Everyday Life and Politics*, 76–83.

24. See note 102 in chapter 1 for further details.

25. Calderón, "La novela costumbrista mexicana," 316, 319–22; Read, *Mexican Historical Novel*, 113–23; Brushwood, *Mexico in Its Novel*, 73.

26. Payno, *El fistol del Diablo*, 881–87.

27. Chaves, "Payno criptofantástico," 65–66. See also Wright, "Subscribing Identities," 98–100. For a more detailed discussion of *Arielismo*, see Ramos, *Divergent Modernities*, 219–46; Reid, "Rise and Decline of the Ariel-Caliban Antithesis," 345–55.

28. Payno, *El fistol del Diablo*, 113.

29. Payno, *El fistol del Diablo*, 338–39, 355–56.

30. Brushwood, "Nicolás Pizarro's Grammar in Verse," 301–3; Brushwood, *Mexico in Its Novel*, 85–88; Illades and Sandoval, *Espacio social y representación literaria*, 15–16.

31. Carlos Illades has outlined the socialist utopian ethos operating in Nueva Filadelfia and explains that Pizarro Suárez was influenced by the ideas of European radicals such as Charles Fourier, Pierre-Joseph Proudhon, and Víctor Considerant. Illades and Sandoval, *Espacio social y representación literaria*, 17–19.

32. Pizarro Suárez, *El monedero*, 594–611.

33. Pizarro Suárez, *El monedero*, 147–48.

34. Pizarro Suárez, *El monedero*, 253–59.

35. Pizarro Suárez, *El monedero*, 274.

36. Pizarro Suárez, *El monedero*, 266–67.

37. Pizarro Suárez, *El monedero*, 275–76.

38. Arrom, "Vagos y mendigos," 76, 72.

39. Cited in Arrom, "Vagos y mendigos," 78.

40. Serrano Ortega, "Levas, Tribunal de Vagos y Ayuntamiento," 131–54.

41. Constitutional texts consulted at and cited from, Fundación Biblioteca Virtual Miguel de Cervantes, Constituciones Hispanoamericanas, "Mexico: Constituciones generales." http://bib.cervantesvirtual.com/portal/constituciones/pais.formato?pais=Mexico&indice=constituciones.

42. For general information about Mexican constitutions and aspects of citizenship, see del Refugio González, "Ilustrados, regalistas y liberales," 251–55; Warren, "Desafío y trastorno en el gobierno municipal," 117–30; Lomnitz, *Deep Mexico, Silent Mexico*, 47–48, 62–75; Negretto and Aguilar-Rivera, "Rethinking the Legacy of the Liberal State in Latin America," 375–77; Sabato, "On Political Citizenship in Nineteenth-Century Latin America"; Escalante Gonzalbo, *Ciudadanos imaginarios*, 17–18, 190–94; Dagnino, "Citizenship in Latin America."

43. *Breve refutación*, 7.

44. *Representación que algunos propietarios de fincas de los llanos de Apam*, 5–6.

45. AGN, FRA, Criminal: vol. 562, exp. 1, fs. 1–50: "Contra el Granadero Dionisio Jimental, acusado de incorregible en la embriaguez y Venta de Vestuario," August 1827.

46. Martínez Luna, "Diario de México," 2:43–49. See also Pérez-Rayón, "La prensa liberal," 2:150; González, *Journalism*, 15–17.

47. "Casas de vecindad," *El Siglo XIX*, November 14, 1841.

48. "Discurso sobre la reforma de las costumbres," *El Siglo XIX*, January 22, 1842.

49. "Discurso sobre la reforma de las costumbres," *El Siglo XIX*, January 23, 1842.

50. Fernández de Lizardi, *La Quijotita*, 51–52.

51. Fernández de Lizardi, *La Quijotita*, 115–16.

52. Fernández de Lizardi, *La Quijotita*, 116–17.

53. Fernández de Lizardi, *Don Catrín*, 20.

54. The aristocratic duel was a popular topic for criticism among nineteenth-century authors: see Pizarro Suárez, *El monedero*, 163–66; Díaz Covarrubias, *La clase media*, 83–96; Orozco y Berra, *La guerra de treinta años*, 2:48–72; Altamirano, *Clemencia*, 136–38.

55. Fernández de Lizardi, *Don Catrín*, 29.

56. Fernández de Lizardi, *Don Catrín*, 99–100.

57. Franco, *Plotting Women*, 81–86.

58. Pateman, "Fraternal Social Contract," 120–27; Lacquer, "Orgasm, Generation, and the Politics of Reproductive Biology," 19–24; Howson, *Embodying Gender*, 65–67; Schiebinger, *Nature's Body*, 149–59, 179–81.

59. Fernández de Lizardi, *La Quijotita*, 27–28.

60. Fernández de Lizardi, *La Quijotita*, 45, 1, 285.

61. Fernández de Lizardi, *La Quijotita*, 290.

62. Fernández de Lizardi, *La Quijotita*, 28.

63. Fernández de Lizardi, *La Quijotita*, 248–53, 275.

64. Pizarro Suárez, *El monedero*, 440.

65. Few nineteenth-century novels feature active indigenous protagonists, more often including Indians as passive background characters and
victims of circumstance. Another exception is Ignacio Altamirano's *El Zarco*,
featuring the heroic Indian Nicolás. See Frazer, *Bandit Nation*, 112–21.

66. Pizarro Suárez, *El monedero*, 220, 241–42.

67. Pizarro Suárez, *El monedero*, 440.

68. *El Siglo XIX*, April 13, 1851.

69. Díaz Covarrubias, *La clase media*, 74; Rea Spell, "Costumbrista Movement in Mexico," 299–300; Rea Spell, "Mexican Literary Periodicals," 279.

70. Orozco y Berra, *La guerra de treinta años*, 2:334–35.

71. Orozco y Berra, *La guerra de treinta años*, 1:50, 61, 197; 2:12, 253.

72. Orozco y Berra, *La guerra de treinta años*, 2:298, 332–33.

73. Orozco y Berra, *La guerra de treinta años*, 2:274–75.

74. Orozco y Berra, *La guerra de treinta años*, 1:126, 128.

75. Orozco y Berra, *La guerra de treinta años*, 1:129.

76. Orozco y Berra, *La guerra de treinta años*, 1:130.

77. De Cuéllar, *Las jamonas*, 99.

78. De Cuéllar, *Las jamonas*, 99–104.

79. De Cuéllar, *Las jamonas*, 97–98.

80. Ortega, *Memoria*, 3–4, 8, 36–47.

81. Ortega, *Memoria*, 9.

4. Medicine, Madness, and Modernity

Gamboa, *Santa*, 163–64.

1. Martínez Cortés, "La medicina científico"; Agostoni, "Discurso
médico," 3; Penyak, "Obstetrics and the Emergence of Women," 62.

2. Agostoni, "Discurso médico," 11; Agostoni, "Médicos científicos y
médicos ilícitos en la ciudad de México durante el Porfiriato,"13–31; Quevedo and Gutiérrez, "Scientific Medicine and Public Health," 182–83; Priego
Martínez, *Ciencia, historia y modernidad*, 86–88.

3. Cited in Sournia, *History of Alcoholism*, 150.

4. See Warner, "Before there was 'Alcoholism,'" 410; Alasuutari, *Desire
and Craving*, 2–3, 19–20; Brandes, *Staying Sober in Mexico City*, 158–65;
Douglas, "Distinctive Anthropological Perspective," 3; Fingarette, "Alcoholism," 3–22.

5. Cited in Dean, *Chaos and Intoxication*, 4.

6. Orford and Edwards, *Alcoholism*, 1–4; Dean, *Chaos and Intoxication*,
2–6, 16–18; Cortés, "Institutiones médicas," 93–94.

7. Sournia, *History of Alcoholism*, xi–xiv; Tyrell, "Drink and Intemperance in the Antebellum South," 497–98; Haine, "Drink, Sociability and Social Class," 130–35; Levine, "Discovery of Addiction," 499–507; Tracy, *Alcoholism in America*, 25–62.

8. Sournia, *History of Alcoholism*, 23. *Dropsy*, also hydropsy, is an out-of-use term for the condition now known as edema, the swelling of internal organs, due to the retention of fluid. *Apoplexy* is an out-of-use medical term, referring to either the bleeding of internal organs, to a stroke, or to a sudden loss of consciousness preceding death (of which there could be many causes). *Epilepsy*, in historical usage, could be loosely applied to anyone suffering from sudden seizures.

9. Sournia, *History of Alcoholism*, 46–49. *Dyscrasia*, as in the title of Huss's book, is an out-of-use, vague term describing symptoms and lesions with a specific cause, potentially throughout the whole body.

10. Sournia, *History of Alcoholism*, 69–76, 82–85; Haine, *World of the Paris Café*, 95–98.

11. I. Campos, *Home Grown*, 105.

12. For examples of newspaper articles referencing, explaining, or drawing on the three stages of intoxication theory, see "A. D. M." "Continúa la cuestion del alcoholismo y la criminalidad," *El Tiempo*, July 28, 1883; "Lo que bebemos," *El Imparcial*, May 14, 1897; "Las víctimas del alcohol," *El Imparcial*, May 20, 1899; "Son alcohólicos un 75 por ciento de los dementes en nuestro país," *El Imparcial*, December 10, 1908. See also I. Campos, *Home Grown*, 107–9.

13. I. Campos, *Home Grown*, 105–6.

14. Bulnes, *El pulque*; Sánchez Santos, *El alcoholismo ante la ciencia*, 6–7. For Roque Macouzet, see Speckman Guerra, "El cruce de dos ciencias," 218.

15. *Dipsomania* is an out-of-use term describing a condition in which a person experiences an irresistible compulsion to drink excessively at periodic intervals, often for days at a time. Serralde, *La embriaguez y la criminalidad*, 10–12.

16. Sánchez Santos, *El alcoholismo ante la ciencia*, 4–9.

17. Cited in Sánchez Santos, *El alcoholismo en la República Mexicana*, 10. On Valentin Magnan, the psychiatrist whose doctoral thesis "On alcoholism, the different types of alcoholic delirium and their treatment" was completed in 1874, see Sournia, *History of Alcoholism*, 81–85, 91–94; Gilman, *Disease and Representation*, 210.

18. Dyspepsia, gastritis, and gastroenteritis all refer to conditions of abdominal and intestinal distress, of varying degrees of severity.

19. Ramírez de Arellano, *El alcoholismo en México*, 4–5, 17–18.

20. A. D. M., "La criminalidad y el alcoholismo," *El Tiempo*, July 27, 1883. The three-part article begins in the July 26th edition and concludes in the July 28th edition.

21. "Las víctimas del alcohol," *El Imparcial*, May 20, 1899. See also Stach, "Platicas del doctor," *El Imparcial*, July 15, 1909.

22. Vicente Sánchez Gavito also propounded the view that dipsomania, not alcoholism, should be classified as a disease, at a conference held by the Academy of Medicine in 1900. "El concurso científico nacional: Profilaxis del alcoholismo," *El Imparcial*, December 29, 1900.

23. Sánchez Santos, *El alcoholismo en la República Mexicana*, 10; Ramírez de Arellano, *El alcoholismo en México*, 5. On Benedict A. Morel, whose *Analysis of the Physical, Intellectual and Moral Degeneration of the Human Species* was published in 1857, see Sournia, *History of Alcoholism*, 98–108; Bynum, "Alcoholism and Degeneration," 61–62; Greenslade, *Degeneration, Culture, and the Novel*, 16; Gilman, *Disease and Representation*, 41.

24. Espinosa, *Ligeras consideraciones*, 10–12, 16–17. On Barrera, see Campos, *Home Grown*, 105–6.

25. "Son alcohólicos un 75 por ciento de los dementes en nuestro país," *El Imparcial*, December 10, 1908. See also "Alcoholismo," *El Diario del Hogar*, May 5, 1891.

26. See Ortega, *Memoria*, 36–42; "Efectos de la bebida," *La Gazetilla*, October 6, 1877.

27. For details of Fields's talk at the National School see "Contra el Alcoholismo," *El Imparcial*, September 1, 1902. On the establishment of the Mexican Temperance Society see "Sociedad Mexicana de Temperancia," *La Patria*, February 26, 1903. American temperance advocates had been giving talks in Mexico City for some years—a "Mrs Stoddard" (possibly Helen Stoddard of the Texas branch of the wcTu, or Cora Stoddard, leader of the Scientific Temperance Federation) gave a talk at the Royal Hospital in 1897, recommending the inclusion of antialcohol lessons and literature in Mexico's schools and colleges. "Sobre la embriaguez," *El Imparcial*, August 4, 1897; "Conferencia sobre alcoholismo," *El Imparcial*, August 10, 1897.

28. Bulnes, *El Pulque*, 55; Ramírez de Arellano, *El alcoholismo en México*, 11–14; "A. D. M.," "Continúa la cuestion del alcoholismo y la criminalidad," *El Tiempo*, July 28, 1883; "Alcoholismo," *El Diario del Hogar*, May 5, 1891; "Haroldo," "Alcoholismo y alcohólicos," *El Diario del Hogar*, May 31, 1901; "Visita de la Secretaria de la Sociedad Mexicana de Temperancia," *El Diario del Hogar*, January 15, 1904. For less enthusiastic endorsements of the temperance movement, see "Triquitraque," "Una sociedad de temperancia en

México," *El Imparcial*, May 20, 1899; "El alcoholismo—Datos y noticias curiosas," *El Tiempo*, September 7, 1883.

29. "Liga Feminina contra las cantinas," *El Imparcial*, February 17, 1901; "Ejercito de la temperancia en los Estados Unidos," *El Diario del Hogar*, May 29, 1901.

30. The influence of French psychiatry on the development of Mexican psychiatry is well documented. See Ríos Molina, "Locos letrados frente a la psiquiatría Mexicana," 18–19; Urías Horcasitas, "Degeneracionismo e hygiene mental," 49–50; Sacristán, "Historiografía de la locura," 16.

31. Prestwich, "Drinkers, Drunkards, and Degenerates," 321–27, 331–34.

32. "Son alcohólicos un 75 por ciento de los dementes en nuestro país," *El Imparcial*, December 10, 1908.

33. Rivera-Garza, "Dangerous Minds," 44, 53; Serralde, *La embriaguez y la criminalidad*, 18.

34. *Lypemania* refers to an extreme kind of melancholy or mournfulness. *Paralytic madness* is probably the condition now known as Korsakov's syndrome: dementia observed after prolonged alcoholism, involving the loss of memory for recent events with the long-term memory remaining intact. *Circular madness* is now termed bipolar disorder, characterized by extreme mood alterations between depression and excitement. Sánchez Santos, *El alcoholismo en la República Mexicana*, 74–77.

35. Rivera-Garza, "Becoming Mad in Revolutionary Mexico," 267; Sacristán, "Entre curar y contener," 63–65.

36. Prestwich, "Female Alcoholism in Paris," 322–25; Sournia, *History of Alcoholism*, 46; Alasuutari, *Desire and Craving*, 10–12; J. F. Logan, "Age of Intoxication," 87–88; Schivelbusch, *Tastes of Paradise*, 164–66.

37. Cited in Speckman Guerra, "El cruce de dos ciencias," 218. See also Ramírez Rancaño, *Ignacio Torres Adalid*, 82–83.

38. "Son alcohólicos un 75 por ciento de los dementes en nuestro país," *El Imparcial*, December 10, 1908.

39. Sánchez Santos, *El alcoholismo en la República Mexicana*, 53–60. This specific focus, and blame, on pulque actually contradicts his other, shorter, published work on alcoholism, in which he specifically attributes epilepsy and other alcohol-induced seizures to distilled drinks such as whisky and absinthe due to their high content of "salicylic aldehyde." Sánchez Santos, *El alcoholismo ante la ciencia*, 8.

40. Maqueo Castellanos, *Algunos problemas nacionales* 120–21.

41. Serralde, *La embriaguez y la criminalidad*, v–vi, 10, 13–15.

42. ADHF, FAGDF, Gobierno del Distrito, Pulquerías: vol. 1774, exp. 565, fs. 1–10: "La Sociedad Mexicana de Temperancia pide se dicten ciertas dis-

posiciones para reprimir la embriaguez y los desórdenes en las pulquerías,"
1907.

43. Rodríguez Kuri, "Los usos de Bulnes," 3:413–28; Ramos, *Divergent Modernities*, 258–59.

44. Bulnes, *El pulque*, 33–38, 76.

45. Garza, *Imagined Underworld*, 29; Ramírez Rancaño, *Ignacio Torres Adalid*, 11–12. Moreover, Bulnes's report was used by major pulque retailers to petition the government's regulations against pulquerías. See, for instance, AHDF, FAGDF, Gobierno del Distrito, Pulquerías: vol. 1777, exp. 850, fs. 1–8: "Antonio Rojas y demas signatarios piden se reforme el Artículo 18 del Reglamento vigente de pulquerías," June 1911.

46. Blasquez and Blasquez, *Tratado del maguey*, 56.

47. Riquelme, *Breve apuntes sobre el pulque*, 309.

48. Cosío Villegas, *Historia moderna de México*, 4:75.

49. Rancaño, *Ignacio Torres Adalid*, 113–15.

50. Hale, *Transformation of Liberalism*, 20–33. See also Vázquez de Knauth, *Nacionalismo y educación en México*, 48–115; Vaughan, *State, Education, and Social Class in Mexico*, 13–23; Tenorio Trillo, "1910 Mexico City," 78–79; Speckman Guerra, "El cruce de dos ciencias," 211–13; Buffington, *Criminal and Citizen*, 32–36; González Navarro, *Sociología e historia en México*; Priego Martínez, *Ciencia, historia y modernidad*, 26–33; Esposito, *Funerals, Festivals, and Cultural Politics*, 9–25; López Beltrán, "Enfermedad heredetaria," 95–120.

51. Hale, *Transformation of Liberalism*, 220–52; Isaac Campos, "Degeneration and the Origins of Mexico's War on Drugs," 379–408; Knight, "Racism, Revolution, and *Indigenismo*," 78–80.

52. Bynum, "Alcoholism and Degeneration," 63–66; Sournia, *History of Alcoholism*, 98–108; Moore, "Fortunes of Eugenics," 266–97; Dowbiggin, *Keeping America Sane*, 73–82; Stepan, *Hour of Eugenics*, 92–95; Aronna, *Pueblos Enfermos*, 13–30; Urías Horcasitas, "Degeneracionismo e hygiene mental," 45; Garrard-Burnett, "Indians are Drunks," 341–56.

53. Aronna, *Pueblos Enfermos*, 14, 25.

54. Aronna, *Pueblos Enfermos*, 25–31, 97, 181. See also Piccato, "El discurso sobre la criminalidad y el alcoholismo" 77–78.

55. Buffington, *Criminal and Citizen*, 31–36, 47–49, 61–62; Piccato, "El discurso sobre la criminalidad y el alcoholismo," 85–86, 91.

56. Sánchez Santos, *El alcoholismo en la República Mexicana*, 14; Mariano Martínez cited in I. Campos, *Home Grown*, 107.

57. *El Tiempo* article cited in Johns, *City of Mexico*, 53; Ramírez de Arellano, *El alcoholismo en México*, 4; Espinosa, *Ligeras consideraciones*, 39–42.

58. Serralde, *La embriaguez y la criminalidad*, 12–13.

59. Ramírez de Arellano, *El alcoholismo en México*, 5. On Morel's theory of degeneration see Horcasitas, "Degeneracionismo e hygiene mental," 41–42; I. Campos, "Degeneration and the Origins of Mexico's War on Drugs," 390.

60. "Las víctimas el alcohol," *El Imparcial*, May 20, 1899. See also "Efectos del alcoholismo en el sentido moral," *El Imparcial*, May 24, 1899; "Haroldo," "Alcoholismo y alcohólicos II," *El Diario del Hogar*, May 31, 1901; "A. D. M.," "Continúa la cuestion del alcoholismo y la criminalidad," *El Tiempo*, July 28, 1883; "El alcoholismo—Datos y noticias curiosas," *El Tiempo*, September 7, 1883.

61. Sánchez Santos, *El alcoholismo ante la ciencia*, 9–10; Sánchez Santos, *El alcoholismo en la República Mexicana*, 17–20.

62. Sánchez Santos, *El alcoholismo en la República Mexicana*, 28.

63. *El Socialista*, April 6, 1883, cited in Fernández, "La miseria y la copa de aguardiente," 7.

64. Luis G. de la Sierra, "La semana judicial," *Gazeta del Lunes*, January 10, 1881.

65. "Lo que bebemos," *El Imparcial*, May 14, 1897.

66. "Las víctimas del alcohol," *El Imparcial*, May 20, 1899. For a more measured discussion of the alcohol problem, see "Todavía el alcoholismo: Lo que beben las naciones," *El Imparcial*, May 17, 1899.

67. Dr. Arcos, "Hombres y bestias," *El Diario del Hogar*, June 6, 1900; "A. D. M.," "La estadística y la criminalidad," *El Tiempo*, July 26, 1883.

68. "El Congreso International contra alcoholismo," *El Imparcial*, June 13, 1899; "Haroldo," "Alcoholismo y alcohólicos I," *El Diario del Hogar*, May 29, 1901; "Haroldo," "Alcoholismo y alcohólicos II," *El Diario del Hogar*, May 31, 1901.

69. Rohlfes, "Police and Penal Correction in Mexico City," 161–70.

70. *Ataxia* refers to balance and coordination difficulties, experienced as a symptom of some neurological disorders. Piccato, *City of Suspects*, 86; Campos-Costero, "Marijuana, Madness, and Modernity."

71. AHDF, FM, Tlalpan, Justicia: caja 188, exp. 52, fs. 1–6: "Disposiciones relativas a la clasificación de los accidentes del alcoholismo agudo, en periodo de embriaguez completa é incompleta," November 1907.

72. Espinosa, *Ligeras consideraciones*, 7, 29–31.

73. "A. D. M.," "La criminalidad y el alcoholismo," *El Tiempo*, July 27, 1883. See also "Reforma urgente al código penal," *El Imparcial*, February 16, 1903.

74. "Haroldo," "Alcoholismo y alcohólicos I," *El Diario del Hogar*, May 29, 1901; "Visita de la Secretaria de la Sociedad Mexicana de Temperancia," *El Diario del Hogar*, January 15, 1904; "El Corresponsal," "Los males del alcoholismo en nuestro pueblo," *El Diario del Hogar*, August 27, 1907; "Crimen repugnante: El Alcoholismo forzoso de la infancia," *El Imparcial*, November 25, 1905; Nueva conferencia sobre la embriaguez," *El Imparcial*, August 4, 1897; "Cuadros anti-alcohólicos," *El Imparcial*, October 29, 1899; "A. D. M.," "La criminalidad y el alcoholismo," *El Tiempo*, July 27, 1883.

75. Villaseñor, *Lecciones de Cosas: Primer año elemental*, 96–98.

76. Villaseñor, *Lecciones de Cosas: Cuarto año elemental*, 78.

77. "Cuadros anti-alcohólicos," *El Imparcial*, October 29, 1899.

78. Chaves Pacheco, "Mujeres en la prosa modernista," 1:232–33; Brushwood, *Genteel Barbarism*, 18–20.

79. Cited in Márquez, "Hacia una definición del realismo," 251. Lamartine's *Rafael* (1849) was considered the epitome of French romantic poetry, while Coupeau, a character in Émile Zola's *L'Assommoir* (1877), is a roofing engineer who suffers a quick descent into alcoholism after being injured on the job. Goethe's *The Sorrows of Young Werther* (1774), about a heartbroken young man who shoots himself in the head, not only catapulted Goethe to literary fame and inspired a plethora of other literary works, but also became renowned for its inspiration of a number of copycat suicides.

80. De Campo, *Ocios y apuntes y La Rumba*, 56.

81. De Campo, *Ocios y apuntes y La Rumba*, 58.

82. De Campo, *Ocios y apuntes y La Rumba*, 40–42.

83. De Campo, *Ocios y apuntes y La Rumba*, 310–11.

84. De Campo, *Ocios y apuntes y La Rumba*, 193.

85. De Campo, *Ocios y apuntes y La Rumba*, 289–90 [emphasis added].

86. De Campo, *Ocios y apuntes y La Rumba*, 292.

87. Mitchell, *Intoxicated Identities*, 96–98; Ramírez Rancaño, *Ignacio Torres Adalid*, 129–33.

88. Johns, *City of Mexico*, 33–36. Population figures from A. del Castillo, "Prensa, poder, y criminalidad," 20.

89. On the expansion of state education in the Porfiriato see Powell, "Mexican Intellectuals," 25–26; Schell, "Nationalizing Children" 560–61. On the installation of electric lighting in the Porfiriato see Bunker, "'Consumers of Good Taste,'" 229; Hibino, "Cervecería Cuauhtémoc," 26; Johns, *City of Mexico*, 15; Piccato, *City of Suspects*, 19–20.

90. De Campo, *Ocios y apuntes y La Rumba*, 194–95.

91. Brushwood, *Genteel Barbarism*, 158–62; Brushwood, *Mexico in Its Novel*, 149–55; Niess, "Federico Gamboa," 346–51; Woolsey, "Some of the Social Problems Considered by Federico Gamboa," 297; D. A. Castillo, *Easy Women*, 41.

92. Prostitution was legal in Porfirian Mexico City; registered prostitutes had to carry official papers (*libreta*) and submit to regular inspections by the sanitary police: Gamboa depicts both of these procedural aspects of prostitution in *Santa*. Unregistered prostitutes, whose health was unmonitored (at least officially), could be subject to arbitrary arrest. Garza, *Imagined Underworld*, 29–30; D. A. Castillo, *Easy Women*, 37.

93. Garza, *Imagined Underworld*, 33; Franco, *Plotting Women*, 96–97.

94. Gamboa, *Santa*, 12–14.

95. Gamboa, *Santa*, 8–10, 25.

96. Gamboa, *Santa*, 26–30, 35.

97. D. A. Castillo, *Easy Women*, 53–57.

98. Gamboa, *Santa*, 163.

99. The Lares gods are Roman deities commonly charged with the protection of the home and family. Gamboa, *Santa*, 163–64. Ellipses are the author's, not mine, possibly denoting the passage of time.

100. Piccato, *City of Suspects*, 58.

101. In Greek mythology, Lethe is one of the rivers of Hades, whose water induced a state of oblivion. There is also a poem entitled "Lethe," which dwells upon the need for drowning sorrows in the river bed, in Charles Baudelaire's 1857 *Flowers of Evil* collection. Gamboa, *Santa*, 189, 202–6.

102. Gamboa, *Santa*, 90–91; Negrín M., "Las voces narrativas," 41–42.

103. Díaz y de Ovando, "Pedro Castera," 203–23; García Barragán, *El naturalismo en México*, 14; Chouciño Fernández and Algaba, "Lectores y lecturas de Carmen de Pedro Castera," 88–89. Castera, *Carmen*, 8–16; Brushwood, *Mexico in Its Novel*, 112–13.

104. Castera, *Carmen*, 23–24.

105. See, for further instances, Castera, *Carmen*, 127–28, 159, 189, 259.

106. On hysteria and female insanity in European literature, see Gilbert and Gubar, *Madwoman in the Attic*; Peter Logan, *Nerves and Narratives*; Ender, *Sexing the Mind*; and Beizer, *Ventriloquized Bodies*.

107. For a detailed analysis of the incestuous ambiguity of the relationship, see Sandoval, "La *Carmen* de Pedro Castera," 6–27. See also Kristal, "Incest Motif in Narratives of the United States and Spanish America," 390–403.

108. For instances of the latter, see Ancona, *El Filibustero*, 309; Ancona, *La mestiza*, 61–62, 95, 171, 246–51; Delgado, *Angelina*, 183–86; Orozco y

Berra, *La guerra de treinta años*, 1:50, 64–65, 197 and 2:12, 83, 253; Rabasa, *El cuarto poder*, 56, 122; Sierra, *Cuentos románticos*, 40, 44.

109. Brushwood, *Mexico in Its Novel*, 142–48; Brushwood, *Genteel Barbarism*, 18–21; Franco, *Introduction to Spanish-American Literature*, 119–25; Chaves Pacheco, "Mujeres en la prosa modernista," 231–35; José María Martínez, "Fantasías irónicas," 406–7; Mejías Alonso, "Amado Nervo," 647–48.

110. Nervo, *Pascual Aguilera*, 29, 35.

111. Nervo, *Pascual Aguilera*, 62.

112. Cited in Cosío Villegas, *Historia moderna de México*, 4:72.

113. Castera makes a few scattered references to drinking wine throughout *Carmen* but does not specify what the narrator-protagonist had been drinking the night he discovered baby Carmen in the street. De Campo, *Ocios y apuntes y La Rumba*, 56; de Campo, *Ocios y apuntes y La Rumba*, 266; Nervo, *Pascual Aguilera*, 62; Gamboa, *Santa*, 189, 202; de Cuéllar, *Las jamonas*, 99, 189–91, 206–7; Frías, *Tomóchic*, 40.

114. Ovando, *Los cafés en México*, 20–21, 48; Mitchell, *Intoxicated Identities*, 96–98; Ramírez Rancaño, *Ignacio Torres Adalid*, 129–33.

115. An old American man is depicted drinking Pilsner beer in the background of a cantina scene in Ángel de Campo's "Un olvidado" (de Campo, *Cosas Vistas y Cartones*, 74). The soldiers drink beer together in Guerrero City in *Tomóchic*, perhaps signifying a relatively civilized, urbane environment in contrast to their subsequent experiences battling the rural community, in which rough, low-quality tequila and sotol are frequently drunk (Frías, *Tomóchic*, 19–22). Sánchez supplies beer and pulque to villagers as part of his political canvassing in *Las jamonas*, but he—the alcoholic—does not drink beer (de Cuéllar, *Las jamonas*, 206–7). A stagecoach driver who speaks English and has American friends drinks beer in *Los bandidos de Río Frío* and avoids typical signifiers of Mexican identity like pulque and tortillas. Also, beer is served in Relumbrón's renovated pulquería, and the establishment is operated by a German (Payno, *Los bandidos*, 331, 778). A background German character in *El fistol del Diablo* also drinks beer (Payno, *El fistol del Diablo*, 416–18).

116. ADHF, FAGDF, Policia, Salubridad: vol. 3671, exp. 224, fl. 14: "El C. Concejal Dr F. Gutiérrez de Lara, Comisionado de Higiene pide informe al Consejo de Salubridad sobre la falsificación del nixtamal, y al Gobierno del Distrito sobre los fundamentos que tuve para declarar que la cerveza no es bebida alcohólica," February 1912.

117. Rubén Campos, *Cuentos Completos*, 34–37.

118. The *modernista* poet Manuel Gutiérrez Nájera also died young from alcohol-induced liver disease, while Heriberto Frías also struggled

with drinking problems and morphine addiction. Johns, *City of Mexico*, 53; Rubén Campos, *El bar*, 23.

119. In Greek mythology, the Danaides were fifty sisters who murdered their new husbands under instructions from their father, the king of Danaos, and were sentenced to the underworld to endure an eternal penance of filling jugs with holes in them. Dionysus was the god of wine. Rubén Campos, *El bar*, 44.

Conclusion

Lowry, *Under the Volcano*, 35–36.
Rulfo, *Pedro Páramo*, 181.

1. Rulfo, *Pedro Páramo*, 180.

2. Lomnitz, *Death and the Idea of Mexico*, 24, 58. See also Esposito, "Politics of Death," 69–70; Brodman, *Mexican Cult of Death*; Bartra, *Cage of Melancholy*, 60–65; Kadir, *Questing Fictions*, 73–74; Walker, *Infernal Paradise*, 241–44.

3. Lozano Armendares, "Mezcales, pulques y chinguiritos," 423–25; William B. Taylor, *Drinking, Homicide, and Rebellion*, 30–37; Toor, *Treasury of Mexican Folkways*, 16–18.

4. Mitchell, *Intoxicated Identities*, 109–10; Ayala-Díaz and Vargas-Cetina, "Romantic Moods," 158, 162–63. See also Pierce, "Sobering the Revolution," 43.

5. Azuela, *Los de abajo*, 137.

6. Doremus, *Culture, Politics, and National Identity*, 31–54, 96–97; Serna, "Citizenship, Censorship, and the Campaign Against Derogatory Films in Mexico," 234–35.

7. Paz, *Labyrinth of Solitude*, 65, 77, 86–87.

8. Messinger-Cypess, *La Malinche in Mexican Literature*, 9–10, 40–89.

9. Paz, *Labyrinth of Solitude*, 23–31, 63–86.

10. Doremus, *Culture, Politics, and National Identity*, 56–57, 65–66.

11. Doremus, *Culture, Politics, and National Identity*, 97–98. See also Monsiváis, *Mexican Postcards*, 94–103; Stavans, "Riddle of Cantinflas," 9–35.

12. Pierce, "Sobering the Revolution," 42, 60–70, 192–223; Fallaw, "Dry Law, Wet Politics," 41–42.

BIBLIOGRAPHY

Archives and Collections

Archivo General de la Nación (AGN), Mexico City
    Archivo de Guerra (AG)
    Fondo Ayuntamiento (FA)
        Policias y empedrados
    Fondo Indiferente Virreinal (FIV)
        Pulques
    Fondo Instrucción Pública y Bellas Artes (FIPBA)
    Fondo Justicia (FJ)
        Justicia
    Fondo Real Audencia (FRA)
        Civil
        Criminal
    Fondo Regio Patronato Indiano (FRPI)
        Bienes Nacionales
    Suprema Corte de Justicia de la Nación (SCJN)
        Asuntos Económicos
Archivo Histórico del Distrito Federal (AHDF), Mexico City
    Fondo Ayuntamiento Gobierno del Distrito Federal (FAGDF)
        Gobierno del Distrito, Bebidas Embriagantes
        Gobierno del Distrito, Infracciones
        Gobierno del Distrito, Pulquerías
        Justicia, Juzgados Diversos, Juicios Criminales
        Justicia, Juzgados Verbales
        Policia en General
        Policia, Salubridad
        Pulquerías

Fondo Municipalidades (FM)
    Tacubaya, Justicia y Juzgados
    Tlalpan, Justicia
    Tlalpan, Policia
Biblioteca Nacional de México, Mexico City
    Fondo Reservado
Biblioteca Ernesto de la Torre Villar, Instituto Mora, Mexico City
    Fondo Antiguo

Published Sources

Acosta, José de. *The Natural and Moral History of the Indies.* 2 vols. Edited by Clements R. Markham. New York: Burt Franklin, 1970.

Adams, Rachel, and David Savran, eds. *The Masculinity Studies Reader.* Oxford: Blackwell, 2002.

Agostoni, Claudia. "Discurso médico, cultura higiénica y la mujer en la ciudad de México al cambio del siglo (XIX–XX)." *Estudios Mexicanos/Mexican Studies* 18, no.1 (2002): 1–22.

———. "Médicos científicos y médicos ilícitos en la ciudad de México durante el Porfiriato." *Estudios de Historia Moderna y Contemporánea de México* 19 (1999): 13–31.

Alasuutari, Perrti. *Desire and Craving: A Cultural Theory of Alcoholism.* Albany: State University of New York Press, 1992.

Algaba, Leticia. "Por los umbrales de la novela histórica." In *La república de las letras: Asomos a la cultura escrita del México decimonónico*, edited by Belem Clark de Lara and Elisa Speckman Guerra, 1:287–302. Mexico City: UNAM, 2005.

Altamirano, Ignacio Manuel. *Clemencia y La navidad en las montañas.* 6th ed. Edited by Antonio Castro Leal. Mexico City: Editorial Porrúa, 1971.

———. *El Zarco y La navidad en las montañas.* 3rd ed. Edited by María del Carmen Millán. Mexico City: Editorial Porrúa, 1968.

Álvarez de Testa, Lilian. *Ilustración, educación e independencia: Las ideas de José Joaquín Fernández de Lizardi.* Mexico City: UNAM, 1994.

Anawalt, Patricia. "Flopsy, Mopsy, and Tipsy." *Natural History* 106, no. 3 (1997): 24.

———. "Rabbits, *Pulque*, and Drunkenness: A Study of Ambivalence in Aztec Society." In *Current Topics in Aztec Studies: Essays in Honor of Dr H. B. Nicholson*, edited by Alana Cordy-Collins and Douglas Sharon, 17–38. San Diego CA: San Diego Museum of Man, 1993.

Ancona, Eligio. *El filibustero, novela histórica.* Mérida: 1864.

———. *La mestiza, novela original.* Mexico City: José V. Castillo, 1891.

Anderson, Benedict. *Imagined Communities: Reflections on the Origins and Spread of Nationalism.* 2nd ed. London: Verso, 1991.

Anna, Timothy E. *Forging Mexico, 1821–1835.* Lincoln: University of Nebraska Press, 1998.

Arechiga, Hugo, and Luis Benítez Bribiesca, eds. *Un siglo de ciencias de salud en México.* Mexico City: CNCA, 2000.

Arguedas, Leda. "Ignacio Manuel Altamirano." In *Del neoclasicismo al modernismo.* Vol. 2 of *Historia de la literatura hispanoamericana,* edited by Luis Iñigo Madrigal, 193–201. Madrid: Cátedra, 1987.

Aronna, Michael. *"Pueblos Enfermos": The Discourse of Illness in the Turn-of-the-Century Spanish and Latin American Essay.* Chapel Hill: University of North Carolina Press, 1999.

Arrom, Silvia M. "Vagos y mendigos en la legislación mexicana, 1745–1845." *Memoria del IV Congreso de Historia del Derecho Mexicano* 1 (1988): 71–87.

Ayala-Díaz, Steffan Igor, and Gabriela Vargas-Cetina. "Romantic Moods: Food, Beer, Music, and the Yucatecan Soul." In *Drinking Cultures: Alcohol and Identity,* edited by Thomas M. Wilson, 155–78. Oxford: Berg, 2005.

Azuela, Mariano. *Los de abajo.* Edited by W. A. R. Richardson. London: Harrap, 1973.

Baecque, Antoine de. *The Body Politic: Corporeal Metaphor in Revolutionary France, 1770–1800.* Translated by Charlotte Mandell. Stanford CA: Stanford University Press, 1997.

Baker, Shannon. "Antonio López de Santa Anna's Search for Personalized Nationalism." In *Heroes and Hero Cults in Latin America,* edited by Samuel Brunk and Ben Fallaw, 58–82. Austin: University of Texas Press, 2006.

Bakhtin, Mikhail. "The Grotesque Image of the Body and its Sources." In *The Body: A Reader,* edited by Mariam Fraser and Monica Greco, 92–95. London: Routledge, 2005.

Bartra, Roger. *The Cage of Melancholy: Identity and Metamorphosis in the Mexican Character.* Translated by Christopher J. Hall. New Brunswick NJ: Rutgers University Press, 1992.

Bauer, Arnold J. *Goods, Power, History: Latin America's Material Culture.* Cambridge: Cambridge University Press, 2001.

Beezley, William H., Cheryl English Martin, and William E. French, eds. *Rituals of Rule, Rituals of Resistance: Public Celebrations and Popular Culture in Mexico.* Wilmington DE: Scholarly Resources, 1994.

Beizer, Janet L. *Ventriloquized Bodies: Narratives of Hysteria in Nineteenth-Century France*. Ithaca NY: Cornell University Press, 1994.

Benbow, Heather Merle. "Ways In, Ways Out: Theorizing the Kantian Body." *Body and Society* 9, no. 1 (2003): 57–72.

Benítez-Rojo, Antonio. "Nacionalismo y nacionalización en la novela hispanoamericana del siglo XIX." *Revista de Crítica Literaria Latinoamericana* 38 (1993): 185–93.

Bergmann, Emilie, ed. *Women, Culture, and Politics in Latin America: Seminar on Feminism and Culture in Latin America*. Berkeley: University of California Press, 1990.

Bhabha, Homi K., ed. *Nation and Narration*. London: Routledge, 1990.

———. "Introduction: Narrating the Nation." In *Nation and Narration*, edited by Homi K. Bhabha, 1–7. London: Routledge, 1990.

Blasquez, Pedro, and Ignacio Blasquez. *Tratado del maguey de su cultivo y de sus productos en gran manera útil a los dueños de terrenos magueyeros escrito por los hacendados*. Puebla: Narciso Blassols, 1897.

Brandes, Stanley. *Staying Sober in Mexico City*. Austin: University of Texas Press, 2002.

Bray, Tamara L., ed. *The Archaeology and Politics of Food and Feasting in Early States and Empires*. New York: Kluwer Academic/Plenum, 2003.

Brennan, Thomas. "Taverns and the Public Sphere in the French Revolution." In *Alcohol: A Social and Cultural History*, edited by Mack P. Holt, 107–20. Oxford: Berg, 2006.

Brennan, Timothy. "The National Longing for Form." In *Nation and Narration*, edited by Homi K. Bhabha, 44–70. London: Routledge, 1990.

Breve refutación al dictamen de los señores jueces de lo criminal, sobre la solicitud que los comerciantes en el ramo de pulques, dirigeron al Sr. Gobernador del Distrito, para que no se cerrasen sus casillas el sábado de Gloria y el domingo de Pascua del presente año. Mexico City: Imprenta de Juan R. Navarro, 1852.

Brodman, Barbara L. C. *The Mexican Cult of Death in Myth and Literature*. Gainesville: University of Florida Press, 1976.

Brown, James W. "Heriberto Frías, a Mexican Zola." *Hispania* 50, no. 3 (1967): 467–71.

Bruman, Henry J. *Alcohol in Ancient Mexico*. Salt Lake City: University of Utah Press, 2000.

Brunk, Samuel, and Ben Fallaw, ed. *Heroes and Hero Cults in Latin America*. Austin: University of Texas Press, 2006.

Brunton, Deborah, ed. *Medicine Transformed: Health, Disease, and Society in Europe, 1800-1930*. Manchester: Manchester University Press, 2004.

Brushwood, John S. *Genteel Barbarism: Experiments in Analysis of Nineteenth-Century Spanish-American Novels.* Lincoln: University of Nebraska Press, 1981.

———. "Juan Díaz Covarrubias: Mexico's Martyr Novelist," *Americas* 10, no. 3 (1954): 301-6.

———. *Mexico in Its Novel: A Nation's Search for Identity.* Austin: University of Texas Press, 1966.

———. "Nicolás Pizarro's Grammar in Verse." *Hispanía* 44, no. 2 (1961): 301–3.

Buffington, Robert M. *Criminal and Citizen in Modern Mexico.* Lincoln: University of Nebraska Press, 1992.

Bulnes, Francisco. *El pulque: Estudio científico.* Mexico City: Antigua Imprenta de Murguía, 1909.

Bunker, Stephen B. "'Consumers of Good Taste': Marketing Modernity in Northern Mexico, 1890–1910." *Mexican Studies/Estudios Mexicanos* 13, no. 2 (1997): 227–69.

Bunzel, Ruth. "The Rôle of Alcoholism in Two Central American Cultures." *Psychiatry* 3 (1940): 361–87.

Burkhart, Louise M. *The Slippery Earth: Nahua-Christian Moral Dialogue in Sixteenth-Century Mexico.* Tucson: University of Arizona Press, 1989.

Burkitt, Ian. *Bodies of Thought: Embodiment, Identity and Modernity.* London: Sage, 1999.

Busfield, Joan. *Men, Women, and Madness. Understanding Gender and Mental Disorder.* London: Macmillan, 1996.

Butler, Barbara Y. *Holy Intoxication to Drunken Dissipation: Alcohol Among Quichua Speakers in Otavalo, Ecuador.* Albuquerque: University of New Mexico Press, 2006.

Bynum, W. F. "Alcoholism and Degeneration in Nineteenth-Century European Medicine and Psychiatry." *British Journal of Addiction* 79 (1984): 59–70.

Calderón, Mario. "La novela costumbrista Mexicana." In *La república de las letras: Asomos a la cultura escrita del México decimonónico,* edited by Belem Clark de Lara and Elisa Speckman Guerra, 1:315–24. Mexico City: UNAM, 2005.

Camarillo, María Teresa. "Los periodistas en el siglo XIX: Agrupaciones y vivencias." In *La república de las letras: Asomos a la cultura escrita del México decimonónico,* edited by Belem Clark de Lara and Elisa Speckman Guerra, 1:153–63. Mexico City: UNAM, 2005.

Campo, Ángel de. *Cosas vistas y Cartones.* 2nd ed. Edited by María del Carmen Millán. Mexico City: Editorial Porrúa, 1968.

———. *Ocios y apuntes y La Rumba*. 3rd ed. Edited by María del Carmen Millán. Mexico City: Editorial Porrúa, 1973.

Campos, Isaac. "Degeneration and the Origins of Mexico's War on Drugs." *Mexican Studies/Estudios Mexicanos* 26, no. 2 (2010): 379–408.

———. *Home Grown: Marijuana and the Origins of Mexico's War on Drugs*. Chapel Hill: University of North Carolina Press, 2012.

Campos, Rubén M. *Cuentos Completos, 1895–1915*. Edited by Serge I. Zaïtzeff. Mexico City: CNCA, 1998.

———. *El bar: La vida literaria de México en 1900*. Introduction by Serge I. Zaïtzeff. Mexico City: UNAM, 1996.

Campos-Costero, Isaac Peter. "Marijuana, Madness, and Modernity in Global Mexico, 1545–1920." PhD diss., Harvard University, 2006.

Campuzano, Juan R. *Semblanza de Altamirano*. Mexico City: Ateneo Altamirano, 1955.

Canning, Kathleen. "The Body as Method? Reflections on the Place of the Body in Gender History." *Gender and History* 11, no. 3 (1999): 499–513.

———. "Feminist History After the Linguistic Turn: Historicizing Discourse and Experience." *Signs* 19, no. 2 (1994): 368–404.

Carey, David, Jr., ed. *Distilling the Influence of Alcohol: Aguardiente in Guatemalan History*. Foreword by William B. Taylor. Gainesville: University Press of Florida, 2012.

Carrasco, David, ed. *To Change Place: Aztec Ceremonial Landscapes*. Niwot: University Press of Colorado, 1991.

Castera, Pedro. *Carmen: Memorias de un corazón*. 2nd ed. Introduction by Carlos González Peña. Mexico City: Editorial Porrúa, 1972.

Castillo, Alberto del. "Prensa, poder y criminalidad a finales del siglo XIX en la ciudad de México." In *Hábitos, normas, y escándalo: Prensa, criminalidad, y drogas durante el porfiriato tardío*, edited by Ricardo Pérez Montfort, Alberto del Castillo, and Pablo Piccato, 17–73. Mexico City: Plaza y Valdés, 1997.

Castillo, Debra A. *Easy Women: Sex and Gender in Modern Mexican Fiction*. Minneapolis: University of Minnesota Press, 1998.

Castro-Klein, Sara, and John Charles Chasteen, eds. *Beyond Imagined Communities. Reading and Writing the Nation in Nineteenth-Century Latin America*. Washington DC: Woodrow Wilson Center Press, 2003.

Cervantes, Fernando. *The Idea of the Devil and the Problem of the Indian: The Case of Mexico in the Sixteenth Century*. London: Institute of Latin American Studies, 1991.

Chambers, Sarah C. *From Subjects to Citizens: Honor, Gender, and Politics in Arequipa, Peru, 1780–1854.* University Park: Pennsylvania State University Press, 1999.

Chanady, Amaryll. "Introduction: Latin American Imagined Communities and the Postmodern Challenge." In *Latin American Identity and Constructions of Difference,* edited by Amaryll Chanady, ix–xlvi. Minneapolis: University of Minnesota Press, 1994.

Chaves Pacheco, José Ricardo. "'La mujer es más amarga que la muerte': Mujeres en la prosa modernista de México." In *La república de las letras: Asomos a la cultura escrita del México decimonónio,* edited by Belem Clark de Lara and Elisa Speckman Guerra, 1:321–44. Mexico City: UNAM, 2005.

———."Payno criptofantástico: Intermitencias mágicas en *El fistol del Diablo.*" *Literatura Mexicana* 14, no. 2 (2003): 63–74.

Chávez, Daniel. "*Tomochic*: National Narrative, Homogenizing Late Nineteenth-Century Discourse and Society in Mexico." *Chasqui: Revista de Literatura Latinoamericana* 35, no. 2 (2006): 72–88.

Cházaro G., Laura, ed. *Medicina, ciencia y sociedad en México siglo XIX.* Zamora: El Colegio de Michoacán, 2002.

Chouciño Fernández, Ana, and Leticia Algaba. "Lectores y lecturas de Carmen de Pedro Castera." *Literatura Mexicana* 14, no. 1 (2003): 87–111.

Christianson, Karen, ed. *Intersecting Disciplines: Approaching Medieval and Early Modern Cultures.* Chicago: Newberry Library, 2010.

Clark de Lara, Belem, and Elisa Speckman Guerra, eds. *La república de las letras: Asomos a la cultura escrita del México decimonónico.* 3 vols. Mexico City: UNAM, 2005.

Clendinnen, Inga. *Aztecs: An Interpretation.* 2nd ed. Cambridge: Cambridge University Press, 2006.

Conroy, David W. "In the Public Sphere: Efforts to Curb the Consumption of Rum in Connecticut, 1760–1820." In *Alcohol: A Social and Cultural History,* edited by Mack P. Holt, 41–60. Oxford: Berg, 2006.

Cope, R. Douglas. *The Limits of Racial Domination: Plebeian Society in Colonial Mexico, 1660–1720.* Madison: University of Wisconsin Press, 1994.

Corcuera, Sonia. "Pulque y evangelización: El caso de Fray Manuel Pérez (1713)." In *Conquista y comida: Consecuencias del encuentro de dos mundos,* edited by Janet Long, 264–82. Mexico City: UNAM, 1997.

Corcuera de Mancera, Sonia. *Del amor al temor: Borrachez, catequesis y control en la Nueva España (1551–1771).* Mexico City: Fondo de Cultura Económica, 1994.

Cortés, Beatriz. "Institutiones médicas y 'alcoholismo,' o de la inexistencia del paciente alcohólico." In *Prácticas e ideologías "científicas" y "populares" respecto del "alcoholismo" en México*, edited by Eduardo L. Menéndez, 91–136. Mexico City: CIESAS, 1992.

Cosío Villegas, Daniel, ed. *El Porfiriato, la vida social*. Vol. 4 of *Historia moderna de México*. Mexico City: El Colegio de México, 1977.

Cuéllar, José Tomás de. "Baile y cochino." In *La linterna mágica*, edited by Mauricio Magdaleno, 1–146. 5th ed. Mexico City: UNAM, 1992.

———. *La linterna mágica: Colección de novelas de costumbres mexicanas, artículos y poesías de Facundo*. 24 vols. Barcelona: Tipo-Litografía de Hermenegilo Miralles, 1890.

———. *Las jamonas*. Edited by Margo Glantz. Mexico City: CNCA, 1998.

Curcio-Nagy, Linda A. "Giants and Gypsies: Corpus Christi in Colonial Mexico City." In *Rituals of Rule, Rituals of Resistance: Public Celebrations and Popular Culture in Mexico*, edited by William H. Beezley, Cheryl English Martin, and William E. French, 1–26. Wilmington DE: Scholarly Resources, 1994.

Dabove, Juan Pablo. "*Tomóchic* de Heriberto Frías: Violencia campesina, melancholia, y genealogía fratricida." *Revista de Crítica Literaria Latinoamericana* 60 (2004): 351–73.

Dagnino, Evelina. "Citizenship in Latin America: An Introduction." *Latin American Perspectives* 30, no. 2 (2003): 3–17.

Dean, Alan. *Chaos and Intoxication: Complexity and Adaptation in the Structure of Human Nature*. London: Routledge, 1997.

Deans-Smith, Susan. "The Working Poor and the Eighteenth Century Colonial State: Gender, Public Order, and Work Discipline." In *Rituals of Rule, Rituals of Resistance: Public Celebrations and Popular Culture in Mexico*, edited by William H. Beezley, Cheryl English Martin, and William E. French, 47–75. Wilmington DE: Scholarly Resources, 1994.

Delgado, Rafael. *Angelina*. 3rd ed. Edited by Antonio Castro Leal. Mexico City: Editorial Porrúa, 1972.

Díaz Covarrubias, Juan. *Gil Gómez el Insurgente o la Hija del médico*. Mexico City: Imprenta de Vicente Segura, 1858.

———. *La clase media: Novela de costumbres mexicanas*. Mexico City: Manuel Castro, 1859.

Díaz y de Ovando, Clementina. *Los cafés en México en el siglo XIX*. Mexico City: UNAM, 2000.

———. "Pedro Castera, novelista y minero." *Mexican Studies/Estudios Mexicanos* 7, no. 2 (1991): 203–23.

Dodds Pennock, Caroline. *Bonds of Blood: Gender, Lifecycle and Sacrifice in Aztec Culture*. Basingstoke: Palgrave Macmillan, 2008.

Doremus, Anne T. *Culture, Politics, and National Identity in Mexican Literature and Film, 1929–1952*. New York: Peter Lang, 2001.

Douglas, Mary, ed. *Constructive Drinking: Perspectives on Drink from Anthropology*. Cambridge: Cambridge University Press, 1987.

——. "A Distinctive Anthropological Perspective." In *Constructive Drinking: Perspectives on Drink from Anthropology*, edited by Mary Douglas, 3–15. Cambridge: Cambridge University Press, 1987.

Dowbiggin, Ian Robert. *Keeping America Sane: Psychiatry and Eugenics in the United States and Canada, 1880–1940*. Ithaca NY: Cornell University Press, 1997.

Driessen, Henk. "Drinking on Masculinity: Alcohol and Gender in Andalusia." In *Alcohol, Gender, and Culture*, edited by Dimitra Gefou-Madianou, 71–79. London: Routledge, 1992.

Duguid, Scott. "The Addiction of Masculinity: Norman Mailer's 'Tough Guys Don't Dance' and the Cultural Politics of Reaganism." *Journal of Modern Literature* 30, no.1 (2006): 23–30.

During, Simon. *Foucault and Literature: Towards a Genealogy of Writing*. London: Routledge, 1992.

——. "Literature—Nationalism's Other? The Case for Revision." In *Nation and Narration*, edited by Homi K.Bhabha, 138–53. London: Routledge, 1990.

Earle, Rebecca. "Algunos pensamientos sobre 'El indio borracho' en el imaginario criollo." *Revista de Estudios Sociales* (Colombia) 29 (2008): 18–27.

——. *Food, Race and the Colonial Experience in Spanish America, 1492–1700*. Cambridge: Cambridge University Press, 2012.

Earnshaw, Steven. *The Pub in Literature: England's Altered State*. Manchester: Manchester University Press, 2000.

Eber, Christine. *Women and Alcohol in a Highland Maya Town: Water of Hope, Water of Sorrow*. Austin: University of Texas Press, 2000.

Elias, Norbert. *The Civilizing Process: The History of Manners*. Translated by Edmund Jephcott. Oxford: Blackwell, 1978.

Ender, Evelyn. *Sexing the Mind: Nineteenth-Century Fictions of Hysteria*. Ithaca NY: Cornell University Press, 1995.

Escalante Gonzalbo, Fernando. *Ciudadanos imaginarios: Memorial de los afanes y desventuras de la virtud y apología del vicio triunfante en la República Mexicana; Tratado de moral pública*. Mexico City: El Colegio de México, 1992.

Espinosa, Ernesto. *Ligeras consideraciones sobre los artículos del código penal del estado relativos a la embriaguez: Tésis presentada por Ernesto Espinosa, en su examen profesional de Medicina, Cirujía y Obstetricia.* Puebla: J. M. Osorio, 1885.

Esposito, Matthew D. *Funerals, Festivals, and Cultural Politics in Porfirian Mexico.* Albuquerque: University of New Mexico Press, 2010.

———. "The Politics of Death: State Funerals as Rites of Reconciliation in Porfirian Mexico, 1876–1889." *Americas* 62, no.1 (2005): 65–94.

Falk, Pasi. *The Consuming Body.* London: Sage, 1994.

Fallaw, Ben. "Dry Law, Wet Politics: Drinking and Prohibition in Post-Revolutionary Yucatan, 1915–1935." *Latin American Research Review* 37, no. 1 (2002): 37–64.

Fernández, Jorge B. "La miseria y la copa de aguardiente: La prensa obrera del siglo XIX contra el alcoholismo." *Historia Obrera* 17, no. 5 (1979): 2–13.

Fernández de Lizardi, José Joaquín. *Don Catrín de la Fachenda: Noches tristes y día alegre.* 2nd ed. Edited by Jefferson Rea Spell. Mexico City: Editorial Porrúa, 1970.

———. *El Pensador Mexicano.* 3rd ed. Edited by Agustín Yáñez. Mexico City: UNAM, 1962.

———. *El Periquillo Sarniento.* 2nd ed. 3 vols. Edited by Jefferson Rea Spell. Mexico City: Editorial Porrúa, 1966.

———. *La Quijotita y su prima.* Edited by María del Carmen Ruíz Castañeda. Mexico City: Editorial Porrúa, 1967.

Fingarette, Herbert. "Alcoholism: The Mythical Disease." *Public Interest* 91 (1988): 3–22.

Florescano, Enrique. *Precios del maíz y crisis agrícolas en México, 1708–1810.* Mexico City: Ediciones Era, 1986.

Forment, Carlos A. *Civic Selfhood and Public Life in Mexico and Peru.* Vol. 1 of *Democracy in Latin America 1760–1900.* Chicago: University of Chicago Press, 2003.

Fowler, Will. "Dreams of Stability: Mexican Political Thought During the 'Forgotten Years'? An Analysis of the Beliefs of the Creole Intelligentsia (1821–1853)." *Bulletin of Latin American Research* 14, no. 3 (1995): 287–312.

———. "El pronunciamiento mexicano del siglo XIX: Hacia una nueva tipología." *Estudios de Historia Moderna y Contemporánea de México* 38 (2009): 5–34.

Franco, Jean. *An Introduction to Spanish-American Literature.* 3rd ed. Cambridge: Cambridge University Press, 1994.

————. *Plotting Women: Gender and Representation in Mexico*. London: Verso, 1989.

François, Marie. "Cloth and Silver: Pawning and Material Life in Mexico City at the Turn of the Nineteenth Century." *Americas* 60, no. 3 (2004): 325–62.

Frantz Parsons, Elaine. "Risky Business: The Uncertain Boundaries of Manhood in the Midwestern Saloon." *Journal of Social History* 34, no. 2 (2000): 283–307.

Fraser, Mariam, and Monica Greco eds. *The Body: A Reader*. London: Routledge, 2005.

Frazer, Chris. *Bandit Nation: A History of Outlaws and Cultural Struggle in Mexico, 1810–1920*. Lincoln: University of Nebraska Press, 2006.

French, William E. "Imagining and the Cultural History of Nineteenth-Century Mexico." *Hispanic American Historical Review* 79, no. 2 (1999): 249–67.

Frías, Heriberto. *Tomóchic*. Edited by Antonio Saborit. Mexico City: CNCA, 2007.

Fumerton, Patricia. "Not Home: Alehouses, Ballads and the Vagrant Husband in Early Modern England." *Journal of Medieval and Early Modern Studies* 32, no. 3 (2002): 493–518.

Fundación Biblioteca Virtual Miguel de Cervantes. Constituciones Hispanoamericanas. "Mexico: Constituciones generales." http://bib.cervantesvirtual.com/portal/constituciones/pais.formato?pais=Mexico&indice=constituciones.

Gallagher, Catherine, and Thomas Lacquer, eds. *The Making of the Modern Body: Sexuality and Society in the Nineteenth Century*. Berkeley: University of California Press, 1987.

Gamboa, Federico. *Santa*. Ciudad Nezahualcóyotl: Leyenda, 2006.

García Barragán, María Guadalupe. *El naturalismo en México: Reseña y notas bibliográficas*. Mexico City: UNAM, 1979.

García de la Sierra, Rodrigo. "El cronotopo del autor en *Los bandidos de Río Frío*." *Literatura Mexicana* 14, no. 1 (2003): 63–86.

Garrard-Burnett, Virginia. "Indians are Drunks and Drunks are Indians: Alcohol and *Indigenismo* in Guatemala, 1890–1940." *Bulletin of Latin American Research* 19, no. 3 (2000): 341–56.

Garza, James Alex. *The Imagined Underworld: Sex, Crime, and Vice in Porfirian Mexico City*. Lincoln: University of Nebraska Press, 2007.

Garza Merodio, Gustavo G. "Technological Innovation and the Expansion of Mexico City, 1870–1920." *Journal of Latin American Geography* 5, no. 2 (2006): 109–26.

Gatens, Moira. *Imaginary Bodies: Ethics, Power, and Corporeality*. London: Routledge, 1996.

Gayol, Sandra. "Ebrios y divertidos: La estrategia del alcohol en Buenos Aires, 1860–1900." *Siglo XIX* 13 (1993): 55–80.

Gefou-Madianou, Dimitra, ed. *Alcohol, Gender, and Culture*. London: Routledge, 1992.

———. "Introduction: Alcohol Commensality, Identity Transformations and Transcendence." In *Alcohol, Gender, and Culture*, edited by Dimitra Gefou-Madianou, 1–34. London: Routledge, 1992.

Gerassi-Navarro, Nina. *Pirate Novels: Fictions of Nation Building in Spanish America*. Durham NC: Duke University Press, 1999.

Gilbert, Sandra M., and Susan Gubar. *The Madwoman in the Attic: The Woman Writer and the Nineteenth Century Literary Imagination*. 2nd ed. New Haven CT: Yale University Press, 2000.

Gilman, Sander L. *Disease and Representation: Images of Illness from Madness to AIDS*. Ithaca NY: Cornell University Press, 1988.

Gilmore, David. *Manhood in the Making: Cultural Concepts of Masculinity*. New Haven CT: Yale University Press, 1990.

Giron, Nicole. "Altamirano, Diplomático." *Estudios Mexicanos/Mexican Studies* 9, no. 2 (1993): 161–85.

———. "Ignacio Manuel Altamirano." In *La república de las letras: Asomos a la cultura escrita del México decimonónico*, edited by Belem Clark de Lara and Elisa Speckman Guerra, 3:363–77. Mexico City: UNAM, 2005.

———. "Payno o las incertidumbres del liberalismo." In *Del fistol a la linterna: Homenaje a José Tomás de Cuéllar y Manuel Payno en el centenario de su muerte, 1994*, edited by Margo Glantz, 132–52. Mexico City: UNAM, 1997.

Glantz, Margo, ed. *Del fistol a la linterna: Homenaje a José Tomás de Cuéllar y Manuel Payno en el centenario de su muerte, 1994*. Mexico City: UNAM, 1997.

———. "Huérfanos y bandidos: *Los bandidos de Río Frío*." In *Del fistol a la linterna: Homenaje a José Tomás de Cuéllar y Manuel Payno en el centenario de su muerte, 1994*, edited by Margo Glantz, 221–39. Mexico City: UNAM, 1997.

Gómariz, José. "Nación, sexualidad, y poder en *Clemencia* de Ignacio Manuel Altamirano." *Literatura Mexicana* 12, no. 2 (2001): 39–65.

Gonçalves de Lima, Oswaldo. *El maguey y el pulque en los códices mexicanos*. Mexico City: Fondo de Cultura Económica, 1956.

González, Aníbal. *Journalism and the Development of Spanish American Narrative*. Cambridge: Cambridge University Press, 1993.

González Navarro, Moises. *Sociología e historia en México.* Mexico City: El Colegio de México, 1970.

Graham, Richard, ed. *The Idea of Race in Latin America, 1870–1940.* Austin: University of Texas Press, 1990.

Greenslade, William. *Degeneration, Culture, and the Novel, 1880–1940.* Cambridge: Cambridge University Press, 1994.

Grosz, Elizabeth. *Space, Time, and Perversion: Essays on the Politics of Bodies.* London: Routledge, 1995.

Gruzinski, Serge. *The Conquest of Mexico: The Incorporation of Indian Societies into the Western World, 16th to 18th Centuries.* Translated by Eileen Corrigan. Cambridge: Polity, 1993.

Guedea, Virginia. "México en 1812: Control político y bebidas prohibidas." *Estudios de Historia Moderna y Contemporanea de México* 8 (1980): 23–66.

Guerra, François Xavier. "Forms of Communication, Political Spheres, and Cultural Identities in the Creation of Spanish American Nations." In *Beyond Imagined Communities: Reading and Writing the Nation in Nineteenth-Century Latin America,* edited by Sara Castro-Klein and John Charles Chasteen, 3–32. Washington DC: Woodrow Wilson Center Press, 2003.

Guerrero Guerrero, Raúl. *El pulque.* 2nd ed. Mexico City: Editorial Joaquín Mortiz, 1985.

Gutmann, Matthew C. *The Meanings of Macho: Being a Man in Mexico City.* Berkeley: University of California Press, 1996.

Guy, Kolleen. *When Champagne Became French: Wine and the Making of a National Identity.* Baltimore MD: Johns Hopkins University Press, 2003.

Hailwood, Mark. "John Jarret and Roaring Dick of Dover: Popular Attitudes toward Drinking in Seventeenth-Century England." In *Intersecting Disciplines: Approaching Medieval and Early Modern Cultures,* edited by Karen Christianson, 113–19. Chicago: Newberry Library, 2010.

———. "Sociability, Work and Labouring Identity in Seventeenth-Century England." *Cultural and Social History* 8, no. 1 (2011): 9–29.

Haine, W. Scott. "Drink, Sociability and Social Class in France, 1789–1945: The Emergence of a Proletarian Public Sphere." In *Alcohol: A Social and Cultural History,* edited by Mack P. Holt, 121–44. Oxford: Berg, 2006.

———. *The World of the Paris Café: Sociability among the French Working Class, 1789–1914.* Baltimore MD: Johns Hopkins University Press, 1996.

Hale, Charles. *The Transformation of Liberalism in Late Nineteenth-Century Mexico.* Princeton: Princeton University Press, 1989.

Hamnett, Brian. *A Concise History of Mexico.* Cambridge: Cambridge University Press, 1999.

Heath, Dwight B. "A Decade of Development in the Anthropological Study of Alcohol Use: 1970–1980." In *Constructive Drinking: Perspectives on Drink from Anthropology,* edited by Mary Douglas, 16–69. Cambridge: Cambridge University Press, 1987.

———. *Drinking Occasions: Comparative Perspectives on Alcohol and Culture.* Philadelphia: Brunner/Mazel, 2000.

Henderson, Lucia. "Blood, Water, Vomit, and Wine: Pulque in Maya and Aztec Belief." *Mesoamerican Voices* 3 (2008): 53–76.

Heron, Craig. *Booze: A Distilled History.* Toronto: Between the Lines, 2003.

———. "The Boys and Their Booze: Masculinities and Public Drinking in Working-Class Hamilton, 1890–1946." *Canadian Historical Review* 86, no. 3 (2005): 411–52.

Hibino, Barbara. "Cervecería Cuauhtémoc: A Case Study of Technological and Industrial Development in Mexico." *Mexican Studies/Estudios Mexicanos* 8, no. 1 (1992): 23–43.

Holt, Mack P., ed. *Alcohol: A Social and Cultural History.* Oxford: Berg, 2006.

Horn, Rebecca. *Postconquest Coyoacan: Nahua-Spanish Relations in Central Mexico, 1519–1650.* Stanford CA: Stanford University Press, 1997.

Howson, Alexandra. *Embodying Gender.* London: Sage, 2005.

Illades, Carlos, and Ariel Rodríguez, eds. *Ciudad de México: Instituciones, actores sociales y conflicto político, 1774–1931.* Zamora: El Colegio de Michoacán, 1996.

Illades, Carlos, and Adriana Sandoval. *Espacio social y representación literaria en el siglo XIX.* Mexico City: Plaza y Valdés, 2000.

Irwin, Robert McKee. *Mexican Masculinities.* Minneapolis: University of Minnesota Press, 2003.

———. "*El Periquillo Sarniento* y sus cautes: El éxtasis misterioso del ambiente homosocial en el siglo diecinueve." *Literatura Mexicana* 9, no. 1 (1998): 23–44.

Johns, Michael. *The City of Mexico in the Age of Díaz.* Austin: University of Texas Press, 1997.

Kadel, Bradley. "The Pub and the Irish Nation." *Social History of Alcohol and Drugs* 18 (2003): 65–84.

Kadir, Djelal. *Questing Fictions: Latin America's Family Romance.* Foreword by Terry Cochran. Minneapolis: University of Minnesota Press, 1986.

Kennedy, John. "Tesgüino Complex: The Role of Beer in Tarahumara Culture." *American Anthropologist* 65, no. 3 (1963): 620–40.

Kicza, John E. "The Pulque Trade of Late Colonial Mexico City." *Americas* 37, no. 2 (1980): 193–221.

Kirkendall, Andrew J. "Student Culture and Nation-State Formation." In *Beyond Imagined Communities: Reading and Writing the Nation in Nineteenth-Century Latin America*, edited by Sara Castro-Klein and John Charles Chasteen, 84–111. Washington DC: Woodrow Wilson Center Press, 2003.

Knapp, Frank A., Jr. "Some Historical Values in a Famous Mexican Novel." *Americas* 11, no. 2 (1954): 131–39.

Knight, Alan. "Racism, Revolution, and *Indigenismo*: Mexico, 1910–1940." In *The Idea of Race in Latin America, 1870–1940*, edited by Richard Graham, 71–113. Austin: University of Texas Press, 1990.

———. "Rethinking the Tomóchic Rebellion." *Mexican Studies/Estudios Mexicanos* 15, no. 2 (1999): 373–93.

Krasnick Warsh, Cheryl, ed. *Drink in Canada: Historical Essays*. Montreal: McGill-Queen's University Press, 1993.

———. "'Oh, Lord, pour a cordial in her wounded heart': The Drinking Woman in Victorian and Edwardian Canada." In *Drink in Canada: Historical Essays*, edited by Cheryl Krasnick Warsh, 70–91. Montreal: McGill-Queen's University Press, 1993.

Kristal, Efraín. "The Incest Motif in Narratives of the United States and Spanish America." In *Internationalität nationaler Literaturen*, edited by Udo Schöning, 390–403. Göttingen: Wallstein, 2000.

Lacquer, Thomas. "Orgasm, Generation, and the Politics of Reproductive Biology." In *The Making of the Modern Body: Sexuality and Society in the Nineteenth Century*, edited by Catherine Gallagher and Thomas Lacquer, 1–41. Berkeley: University of California Press, 1987.

Lameiras, José. "Tres relatos, tres interpretaciones y un asunto: La identidad popular en Payno, Altamirano y López Portillo y Rojas." In *El verbo popular: Discurso y identidad en la cultura Mexicana*, edited by José Lameiras and Andrew Roth Seneff, 91–126. Zamora: El Colegio de Michoacán, 1995.

Lameiras, José, and Andrew Roth Seneff, eds. *El verbo popular: Discurso y identidad en la cultura Mexicana*. Zamora: El Colegio de Michoacán, 1995.

Lander, María Fernanda. "*Clemencia* de Ignacio Manuel Altamirano: El manual de urbanidad y el proceso de formación del patriota moderna." *Literatura Mexicana* 12, no. 1 (2001): 11–37.

Lastovicka, John L., John P. Murry Jr., Erich A. Joachimsthaler, Gaurav Bhalla, and Jim Scheurich. "A Lifestyle Typology to Model Young Male

Drinking and Driving." *Journal of Consumer Research* 14, no. 2 (1987): 257–63.

Lear, John. "Mexico City: Space and Class in the Porfirian Capital, 1884–1910." *Journal of Urban History* 22, no. 4 (1996): 454–92.

Lemle, Russell, and Marc E. Mishkind. "Alcohol and Masculinity." *Journal of Substance Abuse Treatment* 6 (1989): 213–22.

Levine, Harry G. "The Discovery of Addiction: Changing Conceptions of Habitual Drunkenness in America." *Journal of Studies on Alcohol* 15 (1978): 493–506.

Lockhart, James. *The Nahuas After the Conquest: A Social and Cultural History of the Indians of Central Mexico, Sixteenth through Eighteenth Centuries.* Stanford CA: Stanford University Press, 1992.

Logan, John F. "The Age of Intoxication." *Intoxication and Literature: Yale French Studies* 50 (1974): 81–95.

Logan, Peter Melville. *Nerves and Narratives: A Cultural History of Hysteria in Nineteenth-Century British Prose.* Berkeley: University of California Press, 1997.

Lomnitz, Claudio. *Death and the Idea of Mexico.* New York: Zone Books, 2005.

———. *Deep Mexico, Silent Mexico: An Anthropology of Nationalism.* Minneapolis: University of Minnesota Press, 2001.

———. *Exits from the Labyrinth: Culture and Ideology in the Mexican National Space.* Berkeley: University of California Press, 1992.

Long, Janet, ed. *Conquista y comida: Consecuencias del encuentro de dos mundos.* Mexico City: UNAM, 1997.

López Beltrán, Carlos. "Enfermedad heredetaria en el siglo XIX: Discusiones francesas y mexicanas." In *Medicina, ciencia y sociedad en México siglo XIX*, edited by Laura Cházaro G., 95–120. Zamora: El Colegio de Michoacán, 2002.

Los mexicanos pintados por sí mismos: Tipos y costumbres nacionales por varios autores. Mexico City: M. Murgía, 1854.

Lowry, Malcolm. *Under the Volcano.* Introduction by Stephen Spender. London: Jonathan Cape, 1967.

Lozano Armendares, Teresa. "Mezcales, pulques y chinguiritos." In *Conquista y comida: Consecuencias del encuentro de dos mundos*, edited by Janet Long, 421–35. Mexico City: UNAM, 1997.

Macías-González, Víctor Manuel. "Masculine Friendships, Sentiment, and Homoerotics in Nineteenth-Century Mexico: The Correspondence of José María Calderón y Tapia, 1820s–1850s." *Journal of the History of Sexuality* 16, no. 3 (2007): 416–35.

Madrigal, Luis Iñigo, ed. *Del neoclasicismo al modernismo*. Vol. 2 of *Historia de la literatura hispanoamericana*, edited by Luis Iñigo Madrigal. Madrid: Cátedra, 1987.

——. "José Joaquín Fernández de Lizardi." In *Del neoclasicismo al modernismo*. Vol. 2 of *Historia de la literatura hispanoamericana*, edited by Luis Iñigo Madrigal, 135–44. Madrid: Cátedra, 1987.

Mallon, Florencia E. *Peasant and Nation: The Making of Postcolonial Mexico and Peru*. Berkeley: University of California Press, 1995.

Maqueo Castellanos, Eusebio. *Algunos problemas nacionales*. Mexico City: Eusebio Gómez de la Puente, 1910.

Márquez, Celina. "Hacia una definición del realismo en *La Rumba* de Ángel de Campo." In *La república de las letras: Asomos a la cultura escrita del México decimonónico*, edited by Belem Clark de Lara and Elisa Speckman Guerra, 1:245–58. Mexico City: UNAM, 2005.

Martínez, José María. "Fantasías irónicas e ironías fantásticas: Sobre Amado Nervo y el lenguaje modernista." *Hispanic Review* 72, no. 3 (2004): 401–21.

Martínez, Juana. "El cuento hispanoamericano del siglo XIX." In *Del neoclasicismo al modernismo*. Vol. 2 of *Historia de la literatura hispanoamericana*, edited by Luis Iñigo Madrigal, 229–43. Madrid: Cátedra, 1987.

Martínez Cortés, Fernando. "La medicina científico, su conocimiento y aplicación en México durante el siglo XIX." In *Un siglo de ciencias de salud en México*, edited by Hugo Aréchiga and Luis Benítez Bribiesca, 100–117. Mexico City: CNCA, 2000.

Martínez Luna, Esther. "Diario de México: 'Ilustrar a la plebe.'" In *La república de las letras: Asomos a la cultura escrita del México decimonónico*, edited by Belem Clark de Lara and Elisa Speckman Guerra, 2:43–55. Mexico City: UNAM, 2005.

McCaa, Robert. "Calidad, Clase and Marriage in Colonial Mexico: The Case of Parral, 1788–90." *Hispanic American Historical Review* 64, no. 3 (1984): 477–501.

Mejías Alonso, Almudena. "Amado Nervo." In *Del neoclasicismo al modernismo*. Vol. 2 of *Historia de la literatura hispanoamericana*, edited by Luis Iñigo Madrigal, 647–53. Madrid: Cátedra, 1987.

Melhuus, Marit, and Kristi Anne Stølen, eds. *Machos, Mistresses, Madonnas: Contesting the Power of Latin American Gender Imagery*. London: Verso, 1996.

Menéndez, Eduardo L., ed. *Prácticas e ideologías "científicas" y "populares" respecto del "alcoholismo" en México*. Mexico City: CIESAS, 1992.

Messinger Cypess, Sandra. *La Malinche in Mexican Literature: From History to Myth.* Austin: University of Texas Press, 1991.

Mirandé, Alfredo. *Hombres y Machos: Masculinity and Latino Culture.* Boulder CO: Westview Press, 1997.

Mitchell, Tim. *Intoxicated Identities: Alcohol's Power in Mexican History and Culture.* London: Routledge, 2004.

Monsiváis, Carlos. *Mexican Postcards.* Edited and translated by John Kraniauskas. London: Verso, 1997.

Moore, James. "The Fortunes of Eugenics." In *Medicine Transformed: Health, Disease, and Society in Europe, 1800–1930,* edited by Deborah Brunton, 266–97. Manchester: Manchester University Press, 2004.

Morales, María Dolores. "Espacio, propiedad y órganos de poder en la ciudad de México en el siglo XIX." In *Ciudad de México: Instituciones, actores sociales y conflicto político, 1774–1931,* edited by Carlos Illades and Ariel Rodríguez, 155–90. Zamora: El Colegio de Michoacán, 1996.

Morgan, Tony. "Proletarians, Politicos, and Patriarchs: The Use and Abuse of Cultural Customs in the Early Industrialization of Mexico City." In *Rituals of Rule, Rituals of Resistance: Public Celebrations and Popular Culture in Mexico,* edited by William H. Beezley, Cheryl English Martin, and William E. French, 151–71. Wilmington DE: Scholarly Resources, 1994.

Mosher, Donald L., and Silvan S. Tomkins. "Scripting the Macho Man: Hypermasculine Socialization and Enculturation." *Journal of Sex Research* 25, no.1 (1988): 60–84.

Nacci, Chris N. *Ignacio Manuel Altamirano.* New York: Twayne Publishers, 1970.

Negretto, Gabriel L., and José Antonio Aguilar-Rivera. "Rethinking the Legacy of the Liberal State in Latin America: The Cases of Argentina (1853–1916) and Mexico (1857–1910)." *Journal of Latin American Studies* 32, no. 2 (2000): 361–97.

Negrín M., María Eugenia. "Las voces narrativas en Santa de Federico Gamboa." *Literatura Mexicana* 11, no. 2 (2000): 27–51.

Nemser, Daniel. "'To Avoid this Mixture': Rethinking Pulque in Colonial Mexico City." *Food and Foodways* 19, nos. 1–2 (2011): 98–121.

Nervo, Amado. *Otras vidas, Pascual Aguilera, El bachiller, El donador de almas.* Mexico City and Barcelona: J. Ballescá y Compañía, 1909.

Nicholson, Henry B. "The Octli Cult in Late Pre-Hispanic Central Mexico." In *To Change Place: Aztec Ceremonial Landscapes,* edited by David Carrasco, 158–87. Niwot: University Press of Colorado, 1991.

Niess, Robert J. "Federico Gamboa: The Novelist as Autobiographer." *Hispanic Review* 13, no. 4 (1945): 346–61.

Norton, Marcy. *Sacred Gifts, Profane Pleasures: A History of Tobacco and Chocolate in the Atlantic World.* Ithaca NY: Cornell University Press, 2008.

Ochoa, John A. *The Uses of Failure in Mexican Literature and Identity.* Austin: University of Texas Press, 2004.

Orford, Jim, and Griffith Edwards. *Alcoholism: A Comparison of Treatment and Advice, with a Study of the Influence of Marriage.* Oxford: Oxford University Press, 1977.

Orozco y Berra, Fernando. *La guerra de treinta años.* 2 vols. Mexico City: Vicente García Torres, 1850.

Ortega, Francisco. *Memoria sobre los medios de desterrar la embriaguez por el Señor Francisco Ortega, presentada en 30 de abril de 1846, y premiada en el concurso abierto por convocatoria del Ateneo Mejicano de 16 de noviembre de 1845, y promovido por el Señor D. Francisco Fagoaga, a cuyos expensas se imprime.* Mexico City: Ignacio Cumplido, 1847.

Outram, Dorinda. *The Body and the French Revolution: Sex, Class, and Political Culture.* New Haven CT: Yale University Press, 1989.

Palazón Mayoral, María Rosa. "José Joaquín Fernández de Lizardi: Pionero e idealista." In *La república de las letras: Asomos a la cultura escrita del México decimonónico,* edited by Belem Clark de Lara and Elisa Speckman Guerra, 3:37–51. Mexico City: UNAM, 2005.

Paredes, Alfonso. "The Social Control of Drinking Among the Aztec Indians of Mesoamerica." *Journal of Studies on Alcohol* 36, no. 9 (1975): 1139–53.

Pateman, Carole. "The Fraternal Social Contract." In *The Masculinity Studies Reader,* edited by Rachel Adams and David Savran, 119–34. Oxford: Blackwell, 2002.

Payno, Manuel. *El fistol del Diablo: Novela de costumbres mexicanas.* 3rd ed. Edited by Antonio Castro Leal. Mexico City: Editorial Porrúa, 1976.

———. *Los bandidos de Río Frío.* Mexico City: Tomo, 2006.

Paz, Octavio. *The Labyrinth of Solitude and Other Writings.* Translated by Lysander Kemp, Yara Milos, and Rachel Phillips Belash. New York: Grove Press, 1985.

Penyak, Lee. "Obstetrics and the Emergence of Women in Mexico's Medical Establishment." *Americas* 60, no. 1 (2003): 59–85.

Pérez Gay, Rafael. "Avanzaba el siglo por su vida Manuel Payno." In *Del fistol a la linterna: Homenaje a José Tomás de Cuéllar y Manuel Payno en el centenario de su muerte, 1994,* edited by Margo Glantz, 177–84. Mexico City: UNAM, 1997.

Pérez Montfort, Ricardo, Alberto del Castillo, and Pablo Piccato, eds. *Hábitos, normas y escándalo: Prensa, criminalidad y drogas durante el porfiriato tardío*. Mexico City: Plaza y Valdés, 1997.

Pérez-Rayón, Nora. "La prensa liberal en la segunda mitad del siglo XIX." In *La república de las letras: Asomos a la cultura escrita del México decimonónico*, edited by Belem Clark de Lara and Elisa Speckman Guerra, 2:145–58. Mexico City: UNAM, 2005.

Piccato, Pablo. *City of Suspects: Crime in Mexico City, 1900–1931*. Durham NC: Duke University Press, 2001.

―――. "El discurso sobre la criminalidad y el alcoholismo hacia el fin del porfiriato." In *Hábitos, normas, y escándalo: Prensa, criminalidad, y drogas durante el porfiriato tardío*, edited by Ricardo Pérez Montfort, Alberto del Castillo, and Pablo Piccato, 77–142. Mexico City: Plaza y Valdés, 1997.

Pierce, Gretchen. "Parades, Epistles, and Prohibitive Legislation: Mexico's National Anti-Alcohol Campaign and the Process of State-Building, 1934–1940." *Social History of Alcohol and Drugs* 23, no. 2 (2009): 151–80.

―――. "Sobering the Revolution: Mexico's Anti-Alcohol Campaigns and the Process of State-Building, 1910–1940." PhD diss., University of Arizona, 2008.

Pilcher, Jeffrey. *¡Que vivan los tamales! Food and the Making of Mexican Identity*. Albuquerque: University of New Mexico Press, 1998.

Pizarro Suárez, Nicolás. *La coqueta*. Mexico City: Secretaría de Educación Pública, 1982.

―――. *Obras II: El monedero*. Edited by Carlos Illades and Adriana Sandoval. Mexico City: UNAM, 2005.

Pohl, John D. "Themes of Drunkenness, Violence, and Factionalism in Tlaxcalan Altar Paintings." *RES: Anthropology and Aesthetics* 33 (1998): 184–207.

Poovey, Mary. *Making a Social Body: British Cultural Formation 1830–1864*. Chicago: University of Chicago Press, 1995.

Porter, Roy, and David Wright, eds. *The Confinement of the Insane: International Perspectives, 1800–1965*. Cambridge: Cambridge University Press, 2003.

Porter, Susie S. "'And That It Is Custom Makes It Law': Class Conflict and Gender Ideology in the Public Sphere, Mexico City, 1880–1910." *Social Science History* 24, no. 1 (2000): 111–48.

Powell, T. G. "Mexican Intellectuals and the Indian Question, 1876–1911." *Hispanic American Historical Review* 48, no. 1 (1968): 19–36.

———. "Priests and Peasants in Central Mexico: Social Conflict during 'La Reforma.'" *Hispanic American Historical Review* 57, no. 2 (1977): 296–313.

Powers, Madelon. "The Lore of the Brotherhood: Continuity and Change in Urban American Saloon Culture." In *Alcohol: A Social and Cultural History*, edited by Mack P. Holt, 145–60. Oxford: Berg, 2006.

———. "Women and Public Drinking, 1890–1920." *History Today* 45, no. 2 (1995): 46–52.

Pratt, Mary Louise. "Women, Literature and National Brotherhood." In *Women, Culture, and Politics in Latin America: Seminar on Feminism and Culture in Latin America*, edited by Emilie Bergmann, 48–73. Berkeley: University of California Press, 1990.

Prestwich, Patricia E. "Drinkers, Drunkards, and Degenerates: The Alcoholic Population of a Parisian Asylum, 1867–1914." *Histoire Social/ Social History* 54 (1994): 321–35.

———. "Female Alcoholism in Paris, 1870–1920: The Response of Psychiatrists and of Families." *History of Psychiatry* 14, no. 3 (2003): 321–36.

Priego Martínez, Natalia. *Ciencia, historia y modernidad: La microbiología en México durante el Porfiriato*. Madrid: Consejo Superior de Investigaciones, 2009.

Prieto, René. *Body of Writing: Figuring Desire in Spanish American Literature*. Durham NC: Duke University Press, 2000.

Quevedo, Emilio, and Francisco Gutiérrez. "Scientific Medicine and Public Health in Nineteenth-Century Latin America." In *Science in Latin America: A History*, edited by Juan José Saldaña and translated by Bernabé Madrigal, 163–96. Austin: University of Texas Press, 2006.

Rabasa, Emilio. *El cuarto poder y Moneda falsa*. 2nd ed. Edited by Antonio Acevedo Escobedo. Mexico City: Editorial Porrúa, 1970.

Ramírez de Arellano, Nicolás. *El alcoholismo en México. Medidas que debían adoptarse para reprimirlo. Concurso científico de México. Discurso pronunciado en la sesión del día 15 de Julio de 1895*. Mexico City: Secretaría de Fomento, 1895.

Ramírez Rancaño, Mario. *Ignacio Torres Adalid y la industría pulquera*. Mexico City: Plaza y Valdés, 2000.

Ramos, Julio. *Divergent Modernities: Culture and Politics in Nineteenth-Century Latin America*. Translated by John D. Blanco. Durham NC: Duke University Press, 2001.

Rappaport, Joanne. "Fictive Foundations: National Romances and Subaltern Ethnicity in Latin America." *History Workshop Journal* 34 (1992): 119–31.

Rea Spell, Jefferson. *Bridging the Gap: Articles on Mexican Literature*. Mexico City: Editorial Libros de México, 1971.

———. "The Costumbrista Movement in Mexico." PMLA 50, no. 1 (1935): 290–315.

———. "The Intellectual Background of Lizardi as Reflected in El Periquillo Sarniento." PMLA 71 (1956): 414–32.

———. "Juan Díaz Covarrubias: A Mexican Romantic." *Hispanía* 15, no. 4 (1932): 327–44.

———."Mexican Literary Periodicals of the Nineteenth Century." PMLA 52, no. 1 (1937): 272–312.

Read, John Lloyd. *The Mexican Historical Novel, 1826–1910*. New York: Russell and Russell, 1973.

Refugio González, María del. "Ilustrados, regalistas y liberales." In *The Independence of Mexico and the Creation of the New Nation*, edited by Jaime E. Rodríguez O., 247–63. Los Angeles: UCLA Latin American Center Publications, 1989.

Reid, John T. "The Rise and Decline of the Ariel-Caliban Antithesis in Spanish America." *Americas* 34, no. 3 (1978): 345–55.

Representación de los dueños de las haciendas y ranchos del pulque: En el Estado de México y de los comerciantes del ramo ante el Congreso de la Unión. Mexico City: Tipografía de Neve, 1868.

Representación que algunos propietarios de fincas de los llanos de Apam: Elevan por sí y á nombre de los demás al Congreso de la Unión contra el proyecto del ayuntamiento de México de aumentar la alcabala del pulque en un 50 por 100, y el dictámen relativo de las comisiones del distrito y 1a. de hacienda. Mexico City: Imprenta Poliglota, 1874.

Ríos Molina, Andrés. "Locos letrados frente a la psiquiatría Mexicana a inicios del siglo XX." FRENIA: *Revista de la historia de la psiquiatría* 4, no. 2 (2004): 17–35.

Riquelme, Silvino. *Breve apuntes sobre el pulque considerado desde los puntos de vista higiénico, social y económico*. Mexico City: Secretaría de Gobernación, 1921.

Rivera-Garza, Cristina. "Becoming Mad in Revolutionary Mexico: Mentally Ill Patients at the General Insane Asylum, Mexico, 1910–1930." In *The Confinement of the Insane: International Perspectives, 1800–1965*, edited by Roy Porter and David Wright, 248–72. Cambridge: Cambridge University Press, 2003.

———. "Dangerous Minds: Changing Psychiatric Views of the Mentally Ill in Porfirian Mexico, 1876–1911." *Journal of the History of Medicine and Allied Sciences* 56 (2001): 36–67.

Roche, Daniel. *The People of Paris: An Essay in Popular Culture in the Eighteenth Century.* Translated by Marie Evans and Gwynne Lewis. Berkeley: University of California Press, 1987.

Rodríguez González, Yliana. "Heriberto Frías." In *La república de las letras: Asomos a la cultura escrita del México decimonónico,* edited by Belem Clark de Lara and Elisa Speckman Guerra, 3:521–30. Mexico City: UNAM, 2005.

Rodríguez Kuri, Ariel. "Los usos de Bulnes." In *La república de las letras: Asomos a la cultura escrita del México decimonónico,* edited by Belem Clark de Lara and Elisa Speckman Guerra, 3:413–28. Mexico City: UNAM, 2005.

Rodríguez O., Jaime E., ed. *The Independence of Mexico and the Creation of the New Nation.* Los Angeles: UCLA Latin American Center Publications, 1989.

Rohlfes, Laurence John. "Police and Penal Correction in Mexico City, 1876–1911: A Study of Order and Progress in Porfirian Mexico." PhD diss., Tulane University, 1983.

Rosado, Juan Antonio. "El pensamiento social en *Los bandidos de Río Frío,* de Manuel Payno." *Literatura Mexicana* 6, no.1 (1995): 45–55.

———. "Tres novelas mexicanas del siglo XIX, hoy: Bandidaje y corrupción." *Contribuciones desde Coatepec* 2 (2002): 44–52.

Ruíz de Alarcón, Hernando. *Treatise on the Heathen Superstitions and Customs that Today Live Among the Indians Native to this New Spain, 1629.* Translated and edited by J. Richard Andrews and Ross Hassig. Norman: University of Oklahoma Press, 1984.

Rulfo, Juan. *Pedro Páramo.* Edited by José Carlos González Boixo. Madrid: Catédra, 2000.

Sabato, Hilda. "On Political Citizenship in Nineteenth-Century Latin America." *American Historical Review* 106, no. 4 (2001): 1290–315.

Sacristán, María Cristina. "Entre curar y contener. La psiquiatría Mexicana ante el desamparo jurídico, 1870–1944." *FRENIA: Revista de la historia de la psiquiatría* 22 (2002): 61–80.

———. "Historiografía de la locura y de la psiquiatría en México: De la hagiografía a la historia posmoderna." *FRENIA: Revista de historia de la psiquiatría* 5, no. 1 (2005): 9–33.

Saldaña, Juan José, ed. *Science in Latin America.* Translated by Bernabé Madrigal. Austin: University of Texas Press, 2006.

Sánchez Santos, Trinidad. *El alcoholismo ante la ciencia, la familia, la sociedad y la patria.* Mexico City: Edición Popular, 1900.

———. *El alcoholismo en la República Mexicana: Discurso pronunciado en la sesión solemne que celebraron las sociedades Científicas y Literarias de la nación el día 5 de junio de 1896 y en el salón de sesiones de la Cámara de Diputados*. Mexico City: Sagrado Corazón de Jesus, 1896.

Sandoval, Adriana. "La Carmen de Pedro Castera." *Literatura Mexicana* 16, no. 1 (2005): 6–27.

———. "Madres, viudas, y vírgenes en *Los bandidos de Río Frío*." *Literatura Mexicana* 13, no. 1 (2002): 55–88.

Santoni, Pedro. "'Where Did the Other Heroes Go?' Exalting the Polko National Guard Battalions in Nineteenth-Century Mexico." *Journal of Latin American Studies* 34, no. 4 (2002): 807–44.

Scardaville, Michael C. "Alcohol Abuse and Tavern Reform in Late Colonial Mexico City." *Hispanic American Historical Review* 60, no. 4 (1980): 643–71.

Schell, Patience A. "Nationalizing Children through Schools and Hygiene: Porfirian and Revolutionary Mexico City." *Americas* 60, no. 4 (2004): 559–87.

Schiebinger, Londa. *Nature's Body: Sexual Politics and the Making of Modern Science*. London: Pandora, 1994.

Schivelbusch, Wolfgang. *Tastes of Paradise: A Social History of Spices, Stimulants, and Intoxicants*. Translated by David Jacobson. New York: Vintage Books, 1993.

Schöning, Udo, ed. *Internationalität nationaler Literaturen*. Göttingen: Wallstein, 2000.

Segre, Erica. *Intersected Identities: Strategies of Visualization in Nineteenth and Twentieth Century Mexican Culture*. Oxford: Berghahn Books, 2007.

Serna, Laura I. "'As a Mexican I Feel It's my Duty': Citizenship, Censorship, and the Campaign Against Derogatory Films in Mexico, 1922–1930." *Americas* 63, no. 2 (2006): 225–44.

Serralde, Francisco A. *La embriaguez y la criminalidad: Apuntes del discurso pronunciado por Francisco A. Serralde la noche del 28 de junio de 1881 en la Cátedra de Elocuencia Forense de la Escuela Nacional de Jurisprudencia*. Mexico City: Tipografía de O. R. Spíndola y Compañía, 1889.

Serrano Ortega, José Antonio. "Levas, Tribunal de Vagos y Ayuntamiento: La ciudad de México, 1825–1836." In *Ciudad de México: Instituciones, actores sociales y conflicto político, 1774–1931*, edited by Carlos Illades and Ariel Rodríguez, 131–54. Zamora: El Colegio de Michoacán, 1996.

Shumway, Nicolas. "*Don Catrín de la Fachenda* and Lizardi's Crisis of Moral Authority." *Revista de Estudios Hispánicos* 30, no. 3 (1996): 361–74.

Sierra, Justo. *Cuentos románticos*. 2nd ed. Edited by Antonio Castro Leal. Mexico City: Editorial Porrúa, 1969.

Sigüenza y Góngora, Carlos de. "Alboroto y Motín de México del 8 de Junio de 1692." In *Relaciones Históricas*, edited by Manuel Romero de Terreros, 95–174. Mexico City: UNAM, 1954.

Smith, Michael E., Jennifer B. Wharton, and Jan Marie Olson. "Aztec Feasts, Rituals, and Markets: Political Uses of Ceramic Vessels in a Commercial Economy." In *The Archaeology and Politics of Food and Feasting in Early States and Empires*, edited by Tamara L. Bray, 235–68. New York: Kluwer Academic/Plenum, 2003.

Sommer, Doris. *Foundational Fictions: The National Romances of Latin America*. Berkeley: University of California Press, 1991.

Sournia, Jean-Charles. *A History of Alcoholism*. Translated by Nick Hindley and Gareth Stanton. Introduction by Roy Porter. Oxford: Blackwell, 1990.

Speckman Guerra, Elisa. "El cruce de dos ciencias: Conocimientos médicos al servicio de la criminología (1882–1901)." In *Medicina, ciencia y sociedad en México siglo XIX*, edited by Laura Cházaro G., 211–300. Zamora: El Colegio de Michoacán, 2002.

Staples, Anne. "Policia y Buen Gobierno: Municipal Efforts to Regulate Public Behavior, 1821–1857." In *Rituals of Rule, Rituals of Resistance: Public Celebrations and Popular Culture in Mexico*, edited by William H. Beezley, Cheryl English Martin, and William E. French, 115–26. Wilmington DE: Scholarly Resources, 1994.

Stavans, Ilan. "The Riddle of Cantinflas." *Transition* 67 (1995): 22–46.

Stepan, Nancy Leys. *The Hour of Eugenics: Race, Gender, and Nation in Latin America*. Ithaca NY: Cornell University Press, 1991.

Stern, Steve J. *The Secret History of Gender: Women, Men, and Power in Late Colonial Mexico*. Chapel Hill: University of North Carolina Press, 1995.

Stoopen, María. "Convulsiones y revoluciones culinarias de los siglos XIX y XX." *Artes de México* 36 (1997): 50–66.

Suárez de la Torre, Laura. "La producción de libros, revistas, periódicos y folletos en el siglo XIX." In *La república de las letras: Asomos a la cultura escrita del México decimonónico*, edited by Belem Clark de Lara and Elisa Speckman Guerra, 2:9–25. Mexico City: UNAM, 2005.

Suárez y Farías, María Cristina. "Ámbitos y sabores virreinales." *Artes de México* 36 (1997): 30–47.

Szuchman Mark D., ed. *The Middle Period in Latin America: Values and Attitudes in the Seventeenth to Nineteenth Centuries*. Boulder CO: Lynne Reinner, 1989.

Tandeter, Enrique. "Forced and Free Labour in Late Colonial Potosí." *Past and Present* 93 (1981): 98–136.

Taylor, Anya. *Bacchus in Romantic England: Writers and Drink, 1780–1830.* Basingstoke: Macmillan, 1999.

Taylor, William B. *Drinking, Homicide, and Rebellion in Colonial Mexican Villages.* Stanford CA: Stanford University Press, 1979.

Tella, Torcuato S. di. "The Dangerous Classes in Early Nineteenth Century Mexico." *Journal of Latin American Studies* 5, no. 1 (1973): 79–105.

Tenenbaum, Barbara A. "Streetwise History: The Paseo de la Reforma and the Porfirian State, 1876–1910." In *Rituals of Rule, Rituals of Resistance: Public Celebrations and Popular Culture in Mexico*, edited by William H. Beezley, Cheryl English Martin, and William E. French, 127–50. Wilmington DE: Scholarly Resources, 1994.

Tenorio Trillo, Mauricio. "1910 Mexico City: Space and Nation in the City of the Centenario." *Journal of Latin American Studies* 28, no. 1 (1996): 75–104.

Thompson, E. P. "Time, Work-Discipline, and Industrial Capitalism." *Past and Present* 38 (1967): 56–97.

Thomson, Guy P. C. "Bulwarks of Patriotic Liberalism: The National Guard, Philharmonic Corps and Patriotic Juntas in Mexico, 1847–88." *Journal of Latin American Studies* 22, no. 1 (1990): 31–68.

Toner, Deborah. "Drinking to Fraternity: Alcohol, Masculinity, and National Identity in the Novels of Manuel Payno and Heriberto Frías." *Bulletin of Hispanic Studies* 89, no. 4 (2012): 397–412.

———. "Everything in its Right Place? Drinking Places and Social Spaces in Mexico City, c. 1780–1900." *Social History of Alcohol and Drugs* 25, nos. 1/2 (2011): 26–48.

———. "Xóchitl's Bar: Pulquerías and Mexican *costumbrismo*." *Art and Architecture of the Americas* 8 (2010): 1–16.

Toor, Frances. *A Treasury of Mexican Folkways.* New York: Crown Publishers, 1947.

Toxqui, Áurea. "Taverns and Their Influence on the Suburban Culture of Late-Nineteenth-Century Mexico City." In *The Growth of Non-Western Cities: Primary and Secondary Urban Networking, c.900–1900*, edited by Kenneth R. Hall, 241–70. Lanham MD: Lexington Books, 2011.

Toxqui Garay, María Áurea. "'El recreo de los amigos.' Mexico City's Pulquerías during the Liberal Republic (1856–1911)." PhD diss., University of Arizona, 2008.

Tracy, Sarah W. *Alcoholism in America: From Reconstruction to Prohibition.* Baltimore MD: Johns Hopkins University Press, 2007.

Treviño, Blanca Estela. "*Los bandidos de Río Frío* de Manuel Payno: Una lectura." In *La república de las letras: Asomos a la cultura escrita del México decimonónico*, edited by Belem Clark de Lara and Elisa Speckman Guerra, 2:377–91. Mexico City: UNAM, 2005.

Tyrell, Ian R. "Drink and Intemperance in the Antebellum South: An Overview and Interpretation." *Journal of Southern History* 48, no. 4 (1982): 485–510.

Unzueta, Fernando. "Scenes of Reading: Imagining Nations/Romancing History in Spanish America." In *Beyond Imagined Communities: Reading and Writing the Nation in Nineteenth-Century Latin America*, edited by Sara Castro-Klein and John Charles Chasteen, 115–60. Washington DC: Woodrow Wilson Center Press, 2003.

Urías Horcasitas, Beatriz. "Degeneracionismo e hygiene mental en el México posrevolucionario (1920–1940)." *FRENIA: Revista de la historia de la psiquiatría* 4, no. 2 (2004): 37–67.

Vanderwood, Paul J. "Millenarianism, Miracles, and Materialism." *Mexican Studies/Estudios Mexicanos* 15, no. 2 (1999): 395–412.

Varela Jácome, Benito. "Evolución de la novela hispanoamericana en el siglo XIX." In *Del neoclasicismo al modernismo*. Vol. 2 of *Historia de la literatura hispanoamericana*, edited by Luis Iñigo Madrigal, 91–133. Madrid: Cátedra, 1987.

Vargas, Luis Alberto, and Leticia E. Casillas. "El encuentro de dos cocinas: México en el siglo XVI." In *Conquista y comida: Consecuencias del encuentro de dos mundos*, edited by Janet Long, 155–68. Mexico City: UNAM, 1997.

Vaughan, Mary Kay. *The State, Education, and Social Class in Mexico, 1880–1928*. DeKalb: Northern Illinois University Press, 1981.

Vázquez de Knauth, Josefina. *Nacionalismo y educación en México*. Mexico City: El Colegio de México, 1970.

Villaseñor, Manuel E. *Lecciones de Cosas: Cuarto año elemental*. 2nd ed. Mexico City: Herrero Hnos. Sucs., 1907.

———. *Lecciones de Cosas: Primer año elemental*. 5th ed. Mexico City: Herrero Hnos. Sucs., 1912.

Viqueira Albán, Juan Pedro. *Propriety and Permissiveness in Bourbon Mexico*. Translated by Sonya Lipsett-Rivera and Sergio Rivera Ayala. Wilmington DE: Scholarly Resources, 1999.

Voekel, Pamela. "Piety and Public Space: The Cemetery Campaign in Veracruz, 1789–1810." In *Latin American Popular Culture: An Introduction*, edited by William H. Beezley and Linda A. Curcio-Nagy, 1–25. Wilmington DE: Scholarly Resources, 2000.

Vogeley, Nancy. *Lizardi and the Birth of the Novel in Spanish America.* Gainesville: University Press of Florida, 2001.

Wakild, Emily. "Naturalizing Modernity: Urban Parks, Public Gardens and Drainage Projects in Porfirian Mexico City." *Mexican Studies/Estudios Mexicanos* 23, no. 1 (2007): 101–23.

Walker, Ronald G. *Infernal Paradise: Mexico and the Modern English Novel.* Berkeley: University of California Press, 1978.

Warner, Jessica. "Before there was 'Alcoholism': Lessons from the Medieval Experience with Alcohol." *Contemporary Drug Problems* 19, no. 3 (1992): 409–30.

Warren, Richard A. *Vagrants and Citizens: Politics and the Masses in Mexico City from Colony to Republic.* Wilmington DE: Scholarly Resources, 2001.

———. "Desafío y trastorno en el gobierno municipal: El ayuntamiento de México y la dinámica política nacional, 1821–1855." In *Ciudad de México: Instituciones, actores sociales y conflicto político, 1774–1931,* edited by Carlos Illades and Ariel Rodríguez, 117–30. Zamora: El Colegio de Michoacán, 1996.

Wasserman, Mark. *Everyday Life and Politics in Nineteenth-Century Mexico: Men, Women, and War.* Albuquerque: University of New Mexico Press, 2000.

Weismantel, Mary J. "Maize Beer and Andean Social Transformations: Drunken Indians, Bread Babies, and Chosen Women." *Modern Language Notes* 106 (1991): 861–79.

Whitehead, Stephen M., ed. *Global Masculinities.* Vol. 5 of *Men and Masculinities: Critical Concepts in Sociology.* London: Routledge, 2006.

Wilson Thomas M., ed. *Drinking Cultures: Alcohol and Identity.* Oxford: Berg, 2005.

Wilson, Tamar Diana. "Forms of Male Domination and Female Subordination: Homeworkers versus Maquiladora Workers in Mexico." In *Global Masculinities.* Vol. 5 of *Men and Masculinities: Critical Concepts in Sociology,* edited by Stephen M. Whitehead, 215–35. London: Routledge, 2006.

Woolsey, A. W. "Some of the Social Problems Considered by Federico Gamboa." *Modern Language Journal* 34, no. 4 (1950): 294–97.

Wright, Amy E. "Subscribing Identities: The Serial Novel in the Development of Novel and Nation in Spain and Mexico from the 1840s to the 1860s." PhD diss., Brown University, 2006.

Wright-Rios, Edward N. "Indian Saints and Nation-States: Ignacio Manuel Altamirano's Landscapes and Legends." *Mexican Studies/Estudios Mexicanos* 20, no.1 (2004): 47–68.

Zavala Díaz, Ana Laura. "Los motivos de Facundo: Un acercamiento a la figura de José Tomás de Cuéllar." In *La república de las letras: Asomos a la cultura escrita del México decimonónico*, edited by Belem Clark de Lara and Elisa Speckman Guerra, 3:319–32. Mexico City: UNAM, 2005.

INDEX

Page numbers in italic indicate illustrations.

CPSIA information can be obtained at www.ICGtesting.com
Printed in the USA
BVOW05s0740060415

394717BV00001B/20/P